DATE DUE

DEC 2 9 2003	
MAR 1 1 2004	
APR 2 2 2004 DEC 1 6 2004	
APR 1 2 2005	
MAR 2 0 2006	

BRODART, CO.   Cat. No. 23-221-003

Voices of Hope

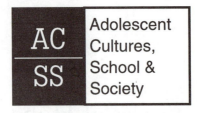

AC / SS

Adolescent Cultures, School & Society

Joseph L. DeVitis & Linda Irwin-DeVitis
General Editors

Vol. 4

PETER LANG
New York • Washington, D.C./Baltimore • Boston
Bern • Frankfurt am Main • Berlin • Vienna • Paris

Carole B. Shmurak

Voices of Hope

Adolescent Girls at Single Sex and Coeducational Schools

PETER LANG
New York • Washington, D.C./Baltimore • Boston
Bern • Frankfurt am Main • Berlin • Vienna • Paris

Library of Congress Cataloging-in-Publication Data

Shmurak, Carole B.
Voices of hope: adolescent girls at single sex
and coeducational schools / Carole B. Shmurak.
p. cm. — (Adolescent cultures, school, and society; v. 4)
Includes bibliographical references and index.
1. Single-sex schools—United States—Longitudinal studies. 2. Coeducation—
United States—Longitudinal studies. 3. Women—Education (Secondary)—
United States—Longitudinal studies. 4. Teenage girls—United States—
Attitudes—Longitudinal studies. 5. High school students—
United States—Attitudes—Longitudinal Studies. I. Title. II. Series.
LB3067.4.S56   373.1822—DC21   97-14649
ISBN 0-8204-3834-0
ISSN 1091-1464

Die Deutsche Bibliothek-CIP-Einheitsaufnahme

Shmurak, Carole B.:
Voices of hope: adolescent girls at single sex and coeducational
schools / Carole B. Shmurak. –New York; Washington, D.C./Baltimore;
Boston; Bern; Frankfurt am Main; Berlin; Vienna; Paris: Lang.
(Adolescent cultures, school, and society; Vol. 4)
ISBN 0-8204-3834-0

Cover design by Andy Ruggirello

The paper in this book meets the guidelines for permanence and durability
of the Committee on Production Guidelines for Book Longevity
of the Council of Library Resources.

© 1998 Peter Lang Publishing, Inc., New York

Printed in the United States of America.

To Steven—for thirty years of love and partnership

and Jill Susannah—for raising her parents with skill and humor

Contents

Acknowledgments

From the inception of this study through its completion, I have received help from many sources. From Central Connecticut State University, I received several research grants and a sabbatical leave that enabled me to write this book. From the four schools who must remain pseudonymous in this book, I received gracious cooperation at every turn from heads of school, academic deans, and administrative staff. It gives me pleasure to acknowledge my indebtedness to them here. The directors and staff of the National Coalition of Girls' Schools responded quickly to all my requests for information and I am grateful to them as well.

Many individuals were especially helpful: Joe Molder, who first suggested that I do the study; Dane Peters, who helped me mull over some of my findings and conclusions; Alice DeLana, who listened thoughtfully to all my many questions and responded in her own keen-minded way. I am deeply indebted to them. My special thanks go to Ann Pollina, who often challenged my ideas but never questioned my intentions or my integrity.

Three graduate students listened carefully to all the tapes and made insightful contributions to the research: Heather Wright Ryan, Kelly Conway, and Sandra Everard-Goss. I am pleased to acknowledge their valuable work.

I am also grateful to Linda Irwin-DeVitis for her enthusiastic response to the longitudinal study and for her thorough and cogent editing of the manuscript. This book profited too from the careful editorial work of Joe DeVitis.

I am also pleased to make public my heartfelt thanks for the enduring support of my husband, Steve, who patiently labored over all the drafts of this book.

My greatest indebtedness is to the students who participated in this study over its five year duration, giving generously of their time in interviews and responding enthusiastically to phone calls and E-mails. I hope that seeing their own words in print is some repayment for all they have given me.

Carole B. Shmurak

Editor's Foreword

"I don't think I will go into career that is mostly men," said Kelly, a thirteen-year-old participant in a summer discussion group. She described a pattern of sexual harassment, derision, and peer pressure at her junior high school that functioned to limit her own aspirations and those of many of her female classmates. Kelly, and many other young women Beth Benjamin and I have interviewed as part of our research on gender and curriculum, is already making choices that reflect and reinforce the gendering of aspiration and achievement in our society. Kelly's choices are shaped by a multiplicity of contexts and forces including the structure and content of her schooling. Kelly's mother and many parents, educators and educational researchers and policy-makers are considering the option of single sex classrooms or schools. Carole Shmurak's research is a timely, well-designed and fascinating glimpse into the realities of private coed and single sex preparatory schools. Shmurak introduces us to the girls who attend these schools and their visions for their futures. She examines their academic and psychological preparation for the pursuit of their dreams and she documents their achievements and setbacks through high school and the first year of college. Her research documents the lowering aspirations of many girls even in these relatively privileged schools in the 1990s.

I am frequently asked, Wasn't educational equity taken care of in the seventies? After all, Title IX has been around for a long time. Yet, the gendered reality of jobs, career goals and status documented by Inge Broverman and her colleagues in 1972 is still influencing the choices of today's high school students. The focus of research and action has moved beyond the political and legal environment to include psycho-social and developmental issues. Projects and programs designed to improve the achievement and interest of girls in math and science have proliferated. *Reviving Ophelia* by Mary Pipher, a largely anecdotal examination of the plight of young women in our society, continues to be a best-seller since its publication in 1994. Parents and educators wonder how young women can escape the silencing described by Brown and Gilligan in *Meeting at the Crossroads* (1992). How do young women marshal the strength to deconstruct the "nice girl" and find the real girl as they define personal goals? Must young women experience the loss of authenticity described by Emily Hancock in her 1989 book, *The Girl*

Within? How are girls to transcend the systemic bias and harassment described by Myra and David Sadker in *Failing at Fairness* (1994)?

A number of feminist scholars, educators, and parents seeking better options for young women are considering single sex education in the belief that it will encourage girls to explore all the options as they imagine and define their future. Girls' schools are positioning themselves as an ameliorative to the disruption and loss of voice common in female adolescence. In recent years, girls' preparatory schools have used the growing body of research on female adolescence and psychological development and the biased nature of coed classrooms and schools as part of their marketing strategy. (As Shmurak points out, it is ironic that the documentation of the crisis in female adolescent development by Lyn Mikel Brown and Carol Gilligan was based on research at an all-girls' preparatory school.) Yet, research on the impact of single sex education at the high school level is scarce.

Voices of Hope fills a void in the literature on single sex education. Carole Shmurak's longitudinal study illuminates the complex interaction of many variables in the aspirations and achievements of young women. The young women Shmurak interviews are talented, reflective, and remarkably open. They are young women we would be proud to call students, daughters, or friends. Yet many of these girls grapple with maintaining their dreams and realizing the visions that they articulated as early adolescents. Shmurak's work documents a growing sense of confusion and the shrinking aspirations of a surprising number of young women in her study. For some girls, this is apparent throughout high school, for many others it occurs in their first year of college. The dwindling vision is not unitary or universal, but it is widespread. Though Shmurak does track a number of "superstars" who appear to retain their vision and their confidence, they are a minority. There are few clear correlations between the type of secondary school (coed or single sex) and the views and achievements of these young women. Their lives and voices reflect many factors, educational, familial, and personal. Shmurak teases out the influences of family, school, curriculum, peer group, and self-image from the stories these young women share.

Shmurak's descriptive statistical analysis and interview data provide a nuanced portrait of young women in single sex and coed preparatory schools in the Northeast. Her work, like that of Deirdre Kelly on continuation high schools (*Last Chance High*, 1993) is tightly focused and suggests that there are no structural blueprints for equity. From the lower socioeconomic and marginalized girls of California's alternative high schools to the selective privilege of Northeastern prep schools, young women struggle to define themselves and their goals in a society that prizes female passivity and punishes resistance.

Parents, policy-makers, and citizens want a quick fix. Politicians and public relations experts too often respond with simplistic solutions even as solid research affirms the complexity and contextual sensitivity of educational decisions. Ideological stances and marketing schemes often dominate discussions and drive policy. *Voices of Hope* refutes simplistic solutions and universal claims about the efficacy of single sex schooling as an antidote to girls' adolescent dilemmas. Yet, advocates of single sex education will find much to celebrate in the book. Though it does not support some of the claims these schools make, it does provide insights into strengthening education for girls in single sex and coed environments. *Voices of Hope* prods educators, policy-makers, and parents to look beyond the question of coed or single sex environments. It challenges schools to recognize that a single sex environment is an opportunity, not an answer.

Linda Irwin-DeVitis
Co-editor, *Adolescent Cultures, School, and Society* series

Part One

The Educational Context:
Single Sex and Coeducational Schools

Introduction

I taught science in an all-girls high school for fifteen years.

And every year when I attended alumnae reunion, among the group of successful young professionals there were always a few from whom I heard this refrain: "I loved science so much when I was here, but that first chemistry (or biology or mathematics) course I took at Princeton (or Georgetown or Northwestern) really was a killer. I wanted to be a doctor (or chemist or biologist), but I just couldn't do it, so I changed my major, and now I'm working in an art museum (or public relations or counseling)." It was seldom a question of ability; these girls had gotten high scores on their SATs and their Advanced Placement examinations. And, although the young women seemed happy enough with their lives, I could hear the apology in their voices: they felt, despite my reassurances to the contrary, they had let me down, and I wondered if they had let themselves down too.

During my years at the school, hundreds of adolescent girls struggled with and triumphed in the biology and chemistry that I taught them. I still hear from some of them, via E-mail, class reunions and wedding invitations. I am convinced that my colleagues and I did an outstanding job of educating these young women.

Over the years, I wondered what we could do to "toughen them up" so they wouldn't be so intimidated by large impersonal classes and male professors (one of whom told my former student when she came to him, wondering where she could get some help in passing her freshman chemistry class, "You are one of the people that we're trying to weed out"). We prided ourselves on small, personalized, and supportive classes, and we weren't going to change that. I tried taking teams of girls to science competitions where they would compete with students (predominantly male) from all over the state, and we usually did well; one year our team (the only all-girls team in the competition) placed third in the state and took first or second place in two of the subjects. I don't think we ever solved the problem, and I still hear the refrain at alumnae reunions, but I did learn that this was a universal problem with women students and science, not just a problem for those from all-girls schools.

When I started teaching at the college level, I decided to take a fresh look at single sex education. An alumna of a women's college myself, I was well acquainted with the research that seemed to show that women's college graduates were overrepresented in lists of women successful in business, politics, and the sciences. Would this be true, I wondered, of girls' high schools? As I began to look at this question, I realized that both the popular press and the schools themselves were making claims for girls' schools that couldn't be supported by current research. Most were assuming that what was true for women's colleges had to be true for girls' high schools. It was obvious to me, though, that a girl of 15 and a woman of 20 are in very different developmental stages, especially with regard to career decision-making, and what was effective in one case might not be effective in another.

Thus I set out to do a study that would examine the effects of single sex education and coeducation through the high school years and the transition to college. Choosing two well-regarded girls' schools and two similar coeducational schools, I sought girls at each school who would share with me their hopes and feelings as they progressed through these years. I also obtained permission from their parents and their schools to keep records of their grades and standardized test scores so that I could do quantitative comparisons.

As I got to know the girls in my study, the original research question of whether single sex education or coeducation is more beneficial for girls began to seem too simplistic. New questions emerged: For whom is single sex education better? For the attainment of which goals? What is gained by some girls by being in classes with male peers? What is lost? And what happens to young women from single sex and coeducational schools at the critical transition from high school to college?

In light of the renewed debate over single sex education, fueled by media reports of gender bias in the schools, these questions seem worthy of further consideration. I hope this book will illuminate the important strengths of schools of both kinds and thus help reframe the terms of that debate.

Chapter One

The Single Sex vs. Coeducation Debate

The best way to educate girls has long been a source of controversy in this country. In the nineteenth century, the arguments revolved around whether girls should receive an education similar to that of boys and whether they should share their classrooms. At the end of the twentieth century, these same arguments are arising again.

Historical Overview

In the period from the American Revolution to the Civil War, advocates of education for girls saw women as the equals of men in terms of morality and responsibility, but they saw too that women's destinies were to be different from men's. Thus they argued for education that would make girls into better wives and mothers. This led to the founding of many of the private female seminaries of the early 1800s, such as Mount Holyoke Seminary (by Mary Lyon) and Troy Seminary (by Emma Willard). These proponents of girls' education sought to offer education comparable to that offered to boys at the private male academies and the public Latin grammar schools. The curricula at these seminaries stressed both intellectual achievement and development of high moral character.

When public schooling began to spread across the country, educators like Horace Mann and Henry Barnard also espoused the education of girls (to be wives and mothers) in public school classrooms. Growth of the public schools led to the need for more teachers, and soon teaching came to be seen as an extension of motherhood, and thus a respectable profession for a woman (at least until she married). Preparation for teaching became another justification for the education of girls.

Explicit arguments for and against coeducation began to appear in the mid-nineteenth century, long after coeducation had become a common practice in the rural schools of America. Coeducation in most school districts was simply taken for granted; in small communities, the creation of separate schools for boys and girls would have been prohibitively expensive. In large cities, on the other hand, the mixing of different classes and ethnic groups raised new issues about the mixing of boys and girls. Middle- and upper-class parents wanted to protect their daughters from associating with the sons of the poor. Separate sex schools became common in the cities of the Northeast, like Boston, New York, and Philadelphia, as well in cities in the South. San Francisco, on the other hand, was almost alone among Western cities in separating the sexes in school (Tyack & Hansot, 1992).

Advocates of coeducation were nonetheless in the majority, claiming that boys became better behaved and girls more self-reliant from their interactions in the classroom. The fact that girls generally did as well or better than boys in the mixed classrooms, and did not damage their femininity in the process, was further evidence that coeducation was working for girls. Despite concerns by some that giving boys and girls the same education would obliterate the differences between the sexes and would endanger women's reproductive health, by the 1890s most school administrators and teachers were firmly convinced that coeducation was best in both theory and practice. Nineteenth-century feminists, as well, were proponents of coeducation, fearing that separate schools for girls would never truly be equal. By the end of the century, only 12 cities out of 628 reported that they had single sex high schools; in most schools around the country, boys and girls studied the same subjects in the same classrooms, although they might enter the schools by separate doors (Tyack & Hansot, 1992).

By the early twentieth century, concern about the dangers of coeducation for girls gave way to concerns about the "feminization" of boys in coeducational high school classrooms being taught by women teachers. Some educators claimed that public schools were shortchanging boys, since girls did better academically than boys and tended to stay in school longer. Educational reformers tried to differentiate the curriculum to better meet the needs of young males: vocational classes and sports for boys, home economics and hygiene for girls. In some schools, experimental courses were offered in which academic subjects like English and physics were taught separately, omitting "the most difficult part for the girls" in physics (Tyack & Hansot, 1992, p. 181), and offering the boys more "manly" literature to read in English classes. But sex-segregated academic classes did not catch on, and coeducation remained the dominant practice throughout the twentieth century.

The Current Debate

Most educators from the 1930s to the 1960s did not believe there was any gender bias in the schools. But with the burgeoning women's movement in the late 1960s and early 1970s, a number of issues were raised. These included: textbooks ignoring women's accomplishments and picturing girls as passive spectators to boys' actions; counselors giving sex-stereotyped advice to girls that led to decreasing numbers of girls in mathematics and science courses; teachers interacting with students in different ways, giving the major share of their attention to the boys; funds being spent on boys' athletics that far exceeded those spent on girls' sports; administrators being predominantly male, thus leading to students' perceptions that men ran things and women took orders.

The principal tool that feminists used to fight for educational equality was Title IX of the 1972 Education Amendments, which said that no person could be discriminated against on the basis of sex in an educational program receiving Federal funding. This led to the banning of single sex public high schools and opened the door for girls to enter academically selective high schools and vocational high schools that were previously restricted to males.

It was not only the public schools that became increasingly coeducational in the 1970s and 1980s. Although not regulated by Title IX, the private sector also embraced coeducation. Women's colleges in America went from 228 colleges in the early 1970s to 94 in 1992; most became coeducational and some simply disappeared. At the secondary level, too, private schools became increasingly coeducational. Among the members of the National Association of Independent Schools, 109 schools, out of a total of 870, are currently for girls alone, whereas in 1963, 166 of the 682 members were girls' schools (Belash, 1992).

Ironically, the decrease in the number of single sex schools came about at a time when research was just beginning to demonstrate a positive effect of single sex education for women at the college level. Elizabeth Tidball (1973) showed that women's colleges were much more likely to produce women of achievement, especially in nontraditional fields like the sciences. Tidball and Kistiakowsky (1976) demonstrated that women who obtained doctorates in the biological and physical sciences were more likely to have graduated from women's colleges than from coeducational undergraduate institutions.

It should be noted that there has been some dispute over the Tidball work. Some researchers have claimed that her data were biased in that just a few of the women's colleges (the highly selective "Seven Sisters") produced most of the high achievers while the other women's colleges produced very few; thus the effect that Tidball was finding might have been the result of academic selectivity and social class, rather than the single sex environment (Oates & Williamson, 1978; Stoecker & Pascarella, 1991). Most of Tidball's studies have been well-accepted nonetheless, and research on the positive effects of women's colleges is ongoing (Riordan, 1994; Miller-Bernal, 1993).

Evidence for gender bias in the schools began to receive more attention in the popular media in the late 1980s and early 1990s with the publication of reports by the American Association of University Women (1991 and 1992) and well-promoted books (e.g., that of Myra and David Sadker, 1994). Some feminists began to look at single sex schooling in a new light: if coeducation was simply reproducing the gender stratification of society as a whole, perhaps single sex education was a better alternative. In a girls' school, female students would not have to compete with boys for the teacher's attention. They would see female administrators and girls occupying leadership posts in the school. Girls would be the focus of education, not the people on the sidelines. Some schools and communities began to discuss single sex public schools and single sex classes within coeducational schools once again (Estrich, 1994; Ravitch, 1996).

Others argued that single sex education would never address the problems of males' attitudes towards women, nor teach men and women to live together as equals (Willis & Kenway, 1986; Orenstein, 1996). Going back to single sex education would also send a message to the girls that they needed protection and special attention (Tovey, 1995). Meanwhile, research on single sex education versus coeducation began to accumulate.

Research in the United States

Because of Title IX, most of the high schools that remain single sex in the United States are either Catholic schools or independent college preparatory schools. The Catholic school population in the United States has been well studied by Cornelius Riordan at Providence

College in Rhode Island and by Valerie Lee at the University of Michigan. The independent school population has been much less studied (Trickett, Trickett, Castro, & Schaffner, 1982; Lee & Marks, 1992; Lee, Marks, & Knowles, 1994) and is the focus of my work (Shmurak, 1994a and 1994b).

Lee and Bryk (1986), using data from the longitudinal study, *High School and Beyond*, sponsored by the National Center for Education Statistics in 1980, compared girls attending coeducational Catholic schools to those at all-girls Catholic schools. They found strong effects in favor of the single sex situation. Girls at the all-girls schools were more positive about academics in general, expressed a greater interest in mathematics, showed greater achievement gains in science, and had higher educational aspirations than their peers at coeducational schools. Lee and Marks (1990) also showed that these same girls held less stereotyped views about the role of women in the workplace, and suggested that this might result in these girls' choosing nontraditional careers more frequently. Marsh (1989a, 1989b), however, has criticized these studies for not controlling for pre-existing differences, both in academic achievement and self-concept, in the students who attended these schools. He claims that the differences found by Lee and her colleagues could well be due to differences in the students who attend the schools rather than an effect produced by the schools themselves.

Riordan (1985), also using *High School and Beyond* data, found that females in single sex Catholic schools outperformed females in Catholic mixed-sex schools in vocabulary, reading, and mathematics. The single sex school graduates did not, however, turn their high school advantage into higher educational attainment. Riordan (1990) likewise determined that, even after controlling for initial ability and home background, girls in single sex schools scored higher than girls in coeducational schools on four curriculum-specific tests, most especially one in science. The girls from the girls' schools manifested significantly higher verbal and mathematical ability up to seven years after graduation. Nonetheless, there were no long-term differences in occupational achievement or attitudes regarding equal roles for men and women. Fourteen years after high school, no significant differences existed between students from single sex and coeducational high schools.

More recently, LePore and Warren (1997), using the *National Education Longitudinal Study of 1988* (*NELS:88*), which followed a cohort of 25,000 eighth graders from 1988 through 1994, studied the effects of single sex school enrollment on girls in Catholic schools.

Controlling for initial student characteristics, they found no significant differences between girls in girls' schools and girls in coeducational schools in academic achievement, educational aspirations, or self-esteem. They attribute the difference between their results and Lee's to either a recent change in the demographics of who attends Catholic schools or a lessening of sexist practices within the coeducational schools.

Thus, using the *High School & Beyond* database, both Lee and Riordan have shown positive effects of Catholic girls' schools on the achievement and attitudes of their graduates, although these findings have been challenged by others. Lee did not look at whether the higher aspirations of the girls' school graduates were translated into higher career achievements, and Riordan concluded that in fact they were not. Research in this country thus shows that Catholic girls' schools may give their students some advantages at the time of high school graduation, although LePore's work with a more recent database calls even this into question.

In a study of independent schools across the United States, Trickett et al. (1982) examined differences in classroom environments and students' experiences in 15 girls' schools and 15 coeducational schools. This study showed that students at single sex schools perceived their classes as having higher student involvement, higher academic orientation, more competition, and more order and organization than students at the coeducational schools. The two types of schools were equal in perceptions of teacher support and teacher innovation.

When Lee turned her attention to the independent school population ten years after Trickett (Lee & Marks, 1992), she examined the question of who chooses a single sex independent school and who chooses a coeducational one. After collecting data from 60 independent schools (20 girls' schools, 20 boys' schools and 20 coeducational schools), she concluded that girls' schools were chosen most often by families with a strong (Protestant) religious orientation or with a family tradition of attendance at single sex schools. Coeducational schools were favored more by families who were "first-generation" in regard to attendance at independent schools, and were more likely to be minority or non-Protestant. She also noted that the entrance examination scores in mathematics were significantly lower for the girls in girls' schools, but there were no differences in the verbal test scores.

In a later study (Lee, Marks, & Knowles, 1994), Lee and her colleagues visited 21 of these independent schools, looking for incidents of sexism or gender equity within their classrooms. She found examples of sexism in all three types of schools, although the forms of sexism were quite different. In boys' schools, sexism took the form of discussing women as sex objects, while at coeducational schools, it was manifested by differential treatment of boys and girls, particularly in chemistry classes. At girls' schools, sexism was found in classes that encouraged girls to be dependent or that taught subjects in nonrigorous, "watered-down" ways. Gender equity incidents, on the other hand, were more likely to happen at the girls' schools and at coeducational schools with strong gender equity policies.

In 1992, I did a study comparing subsequent careers established by graduates of girls' independent schools to the careers of women graduates of similar schools that are coeducational (Shmurak, 1994b). I looked at nearly 13,000 alumnae records, from the classes of 1960 through 1985, from 13 independent schools in the northeastern United States, recording the number of women in each of 10 fields. The fields were: medicine, law, engineering, dentistry, veterinary medicine, finance, computers, scientific research, architecture, and psychology.

Statistical analysis revealed that graduates of coeducational schools were more likely than girls' school graduates to have careers in four fields: law, computers, scientific research, and psychology. No significant differences were found among the other fields between girls' school and coeducational alumnae. Surprisingly, in *none* of these 10 fields did the graduates of the girls' schools have a proportionately larger number of women. My results seemed to indicate that the girls' schools conferred no advantage on their graduates in terms of establishing themselves in nontraditional careers.

Research in Great Britain, Canada, and Australia

Studies on single sex versus coeducational high schools have also come from Great Britain, Australia, and Canada, where public girls' high schools still exist. These studies have highly equivocal results.

Four of these studies have demonstrated positive effects of girls' schools. Stables (1990), working in high schools in England, showed that girls at girls' schools felt more positively about physics than girls at coeducational schools. Carpenter and Hayden (1987), working in Australian schools, both public and private, found that girls attending girls' schools received more encouragement from parents and teachers to enter college and were more likely to take science courses than girls at coeducational schools. Cairns (1990), in Northern Ireland, found that among students attending the more selective academic "grammar" schools, girls at the single sex schools had a higher academic self-concept and were more likely to attribute their successes and failures to internal, rather than external, factors than their counterparts at similar coeducational schools. Foon (1988), who studied private schools in Australia, found that girls in single sex schools were less rigidly attached to stereotyped views of English and science as feminine and masculine.

On the other hand, some workers found effects that favored coeducational schools. In England, Harvey (1985) demonstrated that girls at coeducational schools performed better on tests of science achievement than girls of similar ability at girls' schools. Stables (1990) showed that girls at coeducational schools in England appeared to be more positive about school in general than the girls at the single sex schools. Marsh, Smith, Marsh, and Owens (1988) studied a group of adolescents in grades 7–11 who were in Australian high schools that were changing from a single sex to a coeducational environment. They found an increase in positive self-concept after the transition from single sex to coeducational with no change in academic achievement for either the girls or the boys. A followup study of these schools (Smith, 1994) revealed the same findings, with the additional finding that the teachers *assumed* that coeducation would be detrimental to girls' achievement even though this was contradicted by the facts. Dyer and Tiggemann (1996), in a study of 142 girls at two private schools in Australia found greater satisfaction with body type and fewer eating disorder patterns at the coeducational school and a greater drive for thinness at the all-girls school.

Working in Canadian high schools, Schneider and Coutts (1982) found that students at coeducational high schools rated their schools as having more pleasant environments with less emphasis on control and discipline than students at either all-girls or all-boys high schools. Additionally, girls from coeducational schools ranked their schools higher in intellectual orientation than females in single sex schools. Schneider, Coutts, and Starr (1988) also found that students in coeducational schools had more positive academic self-concepts and were more positive about their school environments than students in either all-girls or all-boys schools.

By far the greatest number of studies have found no significant differences between girls at girls' schools and those at coeducational schools. In the United Kingdom, Bell (as cited in Moore, Piper &

Schaefer, 1992) found no significant differences attributable to type of school in performance on science examinations. Steedman (1985), looking at a broad range of schools in Great Britain, also found few differences in national examination results that were explained by school type, although she does note better performance in French and a small difference on one measure of general examination performance on the part of the girls' school students.

Carpenter and Hayden (1987), working in Australian private schools, found the sex composition of the school did not affect the amount of encouragement the girls received from parents and teachers to enter college or the number of science courses that girls enrolled in. A more recent Australian study (Daly, Ainley, & Robinson, 1996) found that, with regard to enrollment in biological and physical sciences, there were no significant differences between girls' schools and coeducational schools.

Peter Daly has recently looked at the effects of single sex education on girls in Northern Ireland. Unlike England, Northern Ireland has a strong partnership between church and state in the provision of separate sex schooling and thus has maintained a larger proportion of its secondary schools as single sex. Daly found no significant differences between girls at the single sex schools and girls at the coeducational schools in their scores on state examinations in mathematics or English (Daly, 1996; Daly & Shuttleworth, 1996) or in their enrollment in science courses or in their achievement in science as measured by state examinations (Daly, 1995).

Following a group of Australian adolescents from 8th grade through 10th grade, Gill (1996) found no differences in attitudes toward school and toward teachers between girls attending coeducational high schools and girls attending girls' high schools. Ninth grade girls at the girls' schools showed a significantly more positive orientation to mathematics than they had as eighth graders, but this difference disappeared by grade 10. Gill refers to "a now-you-see-it-now-you-don't effect that is both tantalising and frustrating" in all of the research on single sex schools (Gill, 1996, p. 7).

Willis and Kenway (1986) criticized many of the studies done in Great Britain and Australia on the basis that in both countries single sex schools are often private or highly selective. Thus many of the studies are confounding the variable of gender with other variables such as ability and social class. Gill (1996) argues too that success in school, self-esteem, and levels of confidence are known to be influenced by socioeconomic factors and may not be caused by gender context of the school at all.

For clarification, I have summarized all of these findings in Tables 1.1–1.3.

Table 1.1 Summary of Research Findings:
Girls' Secondary Schools More Effective

Variable studied	Country	Type of schools	Researcher	Date
Feelings about school	U.S.A.	Catholic	Lee & Bryk	1986
Interest in math	U.S.A.	Catholic	Lee & Bryk	1986
Educational aspirations	U.S.A.	Catholic	Lee & Bryk	1986
Science achievement	U.S.A.	Catholic	Lee & Bryk	1986
Nontraditional views	U.S.A.	Catholic	Lee & Marks	1990
Science achievement	U.S.A.	Catholic	Riordan	1990
Math achievement	U.S.A.	Catholic	Riordan	1985
Reading achievement	U.S.A.	Catholic	Riordan	1985
Academic orientation	U.S.A.	independent	Trickett et al.	1982
Attitude toward physics	U.K.	government	Stables	1990

Table 1.1 continued

Variable studied	Country	Type of schools	Researcher	Date
Science enrollments	Australia	government & private	Carpenter & Hayden	1987
Adult encouragement	Australia	government & private	Carpenter & Hayden	1987
Nonstereotyped views	Australia	private	Foon	1988
Academic self-concept	N. Ireland	government & private	Cairns	1990

Table 1.2 Summary of Research Findings: No Differences between Girls' Schools and Coeducational Schools

Variable studied	Country	Type of schools	Researcher	Date
Educational attainment	U.S.A.	Catholic	Riordan	1985
Occupational attainment	U.S.A.	Catholic	Riordan	1990
Academic achievement	U.S.A.	Catholic	LePore & Warren	1997
Educational aspirations	U.S.A.	Catholic	LePore & Warren	1997
Self-esteem	U.S.A.	Catholic	LePore & Warren	1997
Incidents of sexism	U.S.A.	independent	Lee et al.	1994

Table 1.2. continued

Variable studied	Country	Type of schools	Researcher	Date
Science achievement	U.K.	government	Bell	1989
Educational achievement	U.K.	government & private	Steedman	1985
Academic achievement	Australia	government	Marsh et al.	1988
Academic achievement	Australia	government	Smith	1994
Science enrollments	Australia	private	Carpenter & Hayden	1987
Science enrollments	Australia	government & private	Daly et al.	1996
Attitude toward school	Australia	government	Gill	1996
Attitude toward math	Australia	government	Gill	1996
Science enrollments	N. Ireland	government & private	Daly	1995
Science achievement	N. Ireland	government & private	Daly	1995
Math achievement	N. Ireland	government & private	Daly	1996
English achievement	N. Ireland	government & private	Daly	1996

Table 1.3 Summary of Research Findings:
Coeducational Schools More Effective

Variable studied	Country	Type of schools	Researcher	Date
Nontraditional careers	U.S.A.	independent	Shmurak	1994b
Attitude toward school	U.K.	government	Stables	1990
Science achievement	U.K.	government & private	Harvey	1985
Attitude toward school	Canada	Catholic	Schneider & Coutts	1982
Academic self-concept	Canada	Catholic	Schneider et al.	1988
Self-concept	Australia	government	Marsh et al.	1988
Self-concept	Australia	government	Smith	1994
Attitude toward body	Australia	private	Dyer & Tiggemann	1996

Unsupported Claims

While the researchers have been publishing their equivocal results in the academic journals, the popular press and some authors who write books for the general public have continued to take the early findings by Lee and Riordan as established truth. Thus it is common to see assertions like "An education at an academically demanding girls' school is the best education that a girl can get" (Mann, 1994, p. 118) stated as fact in books written by non-educators. Even educational researchers such as Myra and David Sadker fall into this, although they do acknowledge that "critics point to flaws in the research methods" (Sadker & Sadker, 1994, p. 233). The Sadkers document the positive effects of girls' schools with many studies, none newer than 1990; they include in their list the Carpenter and Hayden study in Australia mentioned above that was decidedly ambivalent in its support for girls' schools. They do, however, include a long quote from Valerie Lee, in which she indicates how equivocal the results are.

The assertions made by some girls' schools and their advocates in the popular media tend to contain several common flaws:

1) generalizing results from studies of women's colleges to girls' high schools, ignoring the difference in developmental levels of the two populations;

2) comparing the girls' high school alumnae to the general population, ignoring differences in income and social class;

3) making inaccurate or unsupported claims that cannot be verified.

The first of these flawed assumptions is probably the most common. Susan Estrich in her *New York Times* article (1994) goes from talking about math and science courses at girls' high schools in one sentence to Tidball's work on women's colleges in the next sentence, leaving the reader to assume that they are related. Judy Mann, a reporter for the *Washington Post*, makes the leap in a single sentence: "The leadership training girls get at an all-girls school was underscored in the 1992 election year when the Women's College Coalition found that 41% of the women who ran for the U.S. Senate were graduates of women's colleges" (Mann, 1994, p. 123). Diane Ravitch, writing in *Forbes* magazine about a middle school for girls in Harlem, makes an even longer jump from *middle* school to college: "NOW lamely claims that girls' schools promote gender stereotyping, but no women who ever attended a women's college would make such a silly charge" (Ravitch, 1996, p. 203). In fact, both Lee et al. (1994) and Proweller (in press) have found girls' schools reinforcing gender stereotypes.

An advertisement for a girls' school in *Harvard Magazine* (1996) takes advantage of the confusion between girls' schools and women's colleges when it states: "Graduates of girls' schools are twice as likely to earn doctorates and one-and-a-half times as likely to graduate from college with degrees in math and science. They are six times more likely to serve on the boards of Fortune 500 companies." These are, of course, research results from the women's colleges. No such results have ever been shown for girls' high schools, and, in fact, some research (Riordan, 1990; Shmurak, 1994a) contradicts these claims. Some girls' school proponents are more careful: Rachel Belash, former head of Miss Porter's School, writes, "We must show due caution in assuming that research on college achievement presents a direct analogy to high-school age girls" (Belash, 1992).

The second fallacy occurs when statistics are used to compare girls' school graduates to the general population. Again, Mann (1994) is a good example; she quotes a study done for the National Coalition of Girls' Schools in which 700 seniors at 60 girls' schools were polled about their college plans, and 48% said that they planned to pursue careers in mathematics, science, business, or engineering. This is indeed a high proportion, but then Mann states that this is twice the national average for girls (Mann, 1994, p. 119). This is the wrong reference group for comparison; if the variable of interest is the single sex environment, the girls' school seniors should be compared to girls graduating from other (coeducational) independent schools, not to those graduating from public high schools of all sizes and socioeconomic levels. Surely, small class size and income level of parents are factors in girls' aspirations and need to be controlled for in research design.

Mann does the same thing in discussing another survey done for the National Coalition of Girls' Schools, this time on personal income (Mann, 1994, p. 135). In this study, 1200 alumnae of girls' schools were found to have an average personal income of $44,000, which was $5,000 more than the mean annual income of men in 1990 and more than double the mean income for women with college degrees. Again, this is the wrong reference group; comparing women who attended private secondary schools, and thus are likely to have come from high income families, to all men (no matter what their socioeconomic group) and to all college women (most of whom attended public high schools and universities and are from lower income groups) is clearly fallacious if one is trying to prove the superiority of the all-female environment. Alumnae from girls' independent schools must be compared to alumnae of coeducational independent schools for the comparison to be meaningful. This fallacy goes unnoticed, and the popular press absorbs it as fact, so that the statement that "Graduates of all-girls high schools...as adults are more likely than other women to achieve pay equity with men" is made without a citation in a *New York Times* article (Orenstein, 1996).

The last flaw that occurs in the arguments made by some girls' school proponents is not one of faulty reasoning as the two previous fallacies were, but rather one of stating misleading information. A booklet produced by the National Coalition of Girls' Schools (1993) includes the following statement (p. 19): "Graduates of girls' schools pursue careers in math, science, and technology four times more often than their peers from other schools." A phone call to the Coalition elicited the response that this was a survey, polling 1,000 seniors at girls' schools in 1992 about what they were *planning* to pursue in college. They had no data as to what the girls had actually pursued in college, so the statement should have read "Graduates of girls' schools *aspire* to careers..." instead (Shmurak, 1994b). There is good evidence to show that at least 40% of first year college students change their minds about their major (Tobias, 1990), so there is a large disparity between what high school seniors plan to pursue and what they actually do. (Notice also that the "four times more often" is comparing these seniors to the national average again, not to seniors at coeducational independent schools, since those students were never polled.) I have been assured by the Coalition that this was an unintentional error that they have rectified.

Another unsupported claim can be found in an ad in *Harvard Magazine* (1996). It reads "Girls at girls' schools outscore their coed counterparts on both the mathematics and verbal sections of the PSAT." I checked with the National Coalition of Girls' Schools and no one there knew of a study to support such a claim. When I contacted the admissions office of the school in the ad, it turned out that there was no study. The claim was fabricated by the school's publicist by "melding together" Lee and Bryk's (1986) finding that girls at Catholic schools did better on standardized tests (not PSATs) with an in-house study that showed that their students did better on Advanced Placement examinations (not PSATs) than would have been predicted by their PSAT scores. The spokesperson at the school apologized for the ad, explaining that the public relations people want "soundbites" and don't want to have to explain complicated results.

Claims are also made for an increase in self-confidence as a result of attending an all-girls school (e.g., Belash, 1992). Self-confidence, self-concept, and self-esteem are difficult characteristics to measure, but, again, in those studies that have attempted to look at these qualities, results are at best equivocal. Some have found no differences (Riordan, 1990; LePore & Warren, 1997) or effects favoring the coeducational environment (Schneider et al., 1988; Marsh et al.,

1988), while Lee and Bryk (1986) and Cairns (1990) found positive effects of all-girls schools.

One study that is often quoted in the context of girls' loss of self-confidence during the adolescent years is that of Brown and Gilligan (1992), in which middle school girls were studied over a period of years. Almost no one makes a note of the fact that this study took place in an all-girls school. This is not to say that the results would have been different or better if the girls studied were in a coeducational school. The point is that the girls showed a striking loss of confidence and loss of voice even in the single sex environment. This aspect of the study is seldom commented on.

In order to avoid some of the problematic assumptions and design flaws of earlier research, this study (and my previous study on alumnae careers) compares girls' independent schools to coeducational independent schools so that socioeconomic level of students and class size are similar for both populations.

Chapter Two

The Longitudinal Study

The study on which this book is based is longitudinal, and the results cited here are drawn from the first five years of data on a group of young women, following them from the ninth grade through the first year of college. The purpose of the study is to trace the development of the participants' thinking about school, career, and women's roles while also tracking their grades, standardized test scores, and college admission data. This study is intended to help answer questions about the relationship between aspirations and achievement of young women in both coeducational and single sex schools, and the relative influences of high school and college on their career choices.

This study began in the fall of 1992. At that time, I obtained the cooperation of the heads of four independent college preparatory schools in Connecticut to conduct my longitudinal study at their schools. For the purposes of this book, the schools will be referred to by fictitious names: Summerford School and Watson Hill School for the single sex schools and Northington School and Egremont School for the coeducational schools.

The Schools

Summerford School

Summerford School was founded in the 1840s as a school for girls. On a 33-acre campus nestled within an affluent suburb, it enrolls just under three hundred girls in grades 9–12. Girls come principally from the Northeast (Connecticut, Massachusetts, New York, and New Jersey), as well as Florida and California, but 25 other states and 17 other countries are represented in the student body. About a third of the students are day students while the rest are boarders. Over a third of the students receive financial aid.

The faculty of Summerford is mostly female, and the head of the school and the dean of students are female; the academic dean is male.

Besides the usual academic subjects, courses are offered in marine biology, Greek, economics, and dance, with Advanced Placement courses in 14 subject areas. Thirteen different sports are offered, including equestrian activities, downhill skiing, and crew. The school prides itself on having a demanding curriculum within a collaborative environment and a supportive community. Relationships between faculty and students seem warm and informal.

Watson Hill School

Watson Hill, founded in the early 1900s, is smaller (just under 200 girls) and located in a more rural setting with a 100-acre campus. The girls come principally from the Northeast (Connecticut, Massachusetts, Vermont, New York, and New Jersey) and Florida, as well as 15 other states and 14 other countries. About a third of the students are day students. Merit scholarships as well as need-based scholarships are offered, and more than half of the students receive some financial aid.

Like Summerford, the faculty is predominantly female; the head of the school is male and the academic dean and dean of students are female. Advanced Placement courses are offered in 14 areas, and unusual course offerings include anatomy, history of mathematics, history of science, and journalism. Joint programs with a college and a school of music are also offered. Eleven sports are available including equestrian activities and canoeing. The school's purpose is to develop thinking, impart knowledge, and cultivate creativity. The atmosphere of Watson Hill is that of a close-knit community, with warm relationships between faculty and students.

Northington School

The 200-acre campus of Northington School sits on a hill above an affluent suburb. Established as a boys' school in the 1880s, it began admitting girls in 1971, and now enrolls about 200 boys and 150 girls. Day students are divided evenly between girls and boys, but the boarding boys outnumber the boarding girls by almost two to one. Twenty-six percent of the students get financial aid. Like the other schools, students come principally from the Northeast but 34 states and 14 countries are represented.

The head of the school is a male and the academic dean is a male. The faculty comprises 40 men and 26 women. Unusual courses include architecture, drafting, economics, and dance. Advanced Placement is offered in 12 subjects. Ten sports, including ice hockey and crew, are offered for both boys and girls; in addition, baseball and football are offered for the boys, and field hockey, paddle tennis, softball, and volleyball for the girls. The school stresses the importance of meeting one's obligations, making the most of one's abilities, and living cheerfully in a community. Although there is a dress code that makes the school seem more formal than the girls' schools, the atmosphere is friendly and energetic. Nonetheless, there is a definite masculine "feel" to the school.

Egremont School

Egremont School, with its 500-acre campus, is located in a rural setting off a state road. Enrollment is just under 300 students. Like Northington, there are an equal number of male and female day students, but among the boarders, boys far outnumber the girls. Established as a boys' school in the 1890s, Egremont first accepted girls in the late 1960s. The student population is drawn from Connecticut, Massachusetts, New York, New Jersey, Texas, and 25 other states and 14 other countries. Need-based scholarships are available and over a third of the students receive financial aid.

Thirty-seven men and 23 women constitute the faculty. The head of Egremont is male; the assistant head, the academic dean, and the dean of students are female. Advanced Placement courses are offered in 12 subjects, and unusual course offerings include anatomy, psychology, film, and government. Sports available to both boys and girls include wrestling, crew, and ice hockey, while baseball and football are open to boys and field hockey and softball to girls. The school emphasizes individual purpose and self-worth, as well as character, faith, and service. Like Northington, Egremont has a dress code: boys must wear jackets and ties; girls, skirts or slacks and blazers. Newly appointed female administrators make Egremont feel less overwhelmingly male than Northington.

From Table 2.1, it can be seen that the girls' schools are smaller than the coeducational schools; this is typical of girls' schools in general. Based on the median percentiles on the Secondary School Admission Test (SSAT) required for admission to all four schools, Summerford appears to take slightly weaker students, but these students do equally well or better on the SATs as their peers at the other schools. The higher proportion of students receiving financial aid at Watson Hill may mean that slightly more of their students are from lower socioeconomic backgrounds.

Table 2.1. Comparison of Schools in the Study

	Girls' Schools		Coed Schools	
	Watson Hill	Summerford	Egremont	Northington
Girls/boys	190/0	270/0	130/180	150/200
Brders/day	120/70	180/90	210/100	220/130
Tuition	$21,000	$21,000	$22,000	$21,500
% Fin. aid	60%	37%	38%	26%
Faculty (F/M)	27/9	43/9	23/37	26/40
Class size	11	11	15	11
SSAT median %	70%	63%	68%	68%
SAT verbal	550	570	520	530
math	560	570	570	580

Methodology

In the fall of 1992, all ninth grade girls in each of the four schools were administered questionnaires that included questions about college and career aspirations as well as the 15-item form of the survey known as the Attitudes Toward Women Scale or AWS (Spence & Helmreich, 1979). In some schools, one or two ninth grade girls were omitted due to absence. By administering these questionnaires early in the fall, any effects of the school itself were minimized and the attitudes thus measured should represent the girls' opinions independent of the school they attended. Results of the AWS were tabulated and appear in Table 2.2, line 1; it can be seen that there were no significant differences among the initial attitudes of girls attending the different schools. (The maximum score on the AWS is 45, representing a consistently feminist viewpoint.) Thus girls choosing coeducational or all-girls schools did not start out with different views of women's roles or careers.

Letters were sent to the parents of these girls from the administrators of the four schools, asking them to allow their daughters to participate in the study. From the total number of 114 female ninth graders at the four schools, 56 girls volunteered for the study and were given permission by their parents to participate. Since selection for the study was voluntary and not random, there may be some bias in the sample. For example, although there are a considerable number of Asian-American students attending these schools, none volunteered for the study, so this part of the independent school population is not included in the data. Additionally, one might assume that parents aware of daughters' emotional problems (such as eating disorders) might withhold their permission to participate, and so another part of the population may have been unrepresented in this study.

In May of 1993, I visited each of the four schools and conducted interviews with the girls; again, a few were missed due to absence. At this time, the subjects also chose pseudonyms and filled out the AWS questionnaire a second time. Those that missed the interview sessions returned the questionnaires by mail. The majority of the interviews were taped, with the girls' permissions, and later transcribed. A few girls requested that they not be taped, so notes were taken during those interviews. Interview questions concerning a developing sense of competence, loss or finding of voice, development of identity, and roles of parents and teachers were included. (See the Appendix A for questions asked in the five years of interviews.) In June 1993, the schools forwarded the final grades of the 56 girls and these were also tabulated.

The same interview and questionnaire procedure was followed in May of 1994, 1995, and 1996. Each June, the schools sent me information about the girls' grades and standardized test scores. Tapes were transcribed by three female graduate students, who also listened for themes at each of the schools; the graduate students and I met to discuss in detail what we were hearing in the tapes. In the process of writing this book, I have listened to all of these tapes again.

In the 1995 interviews, I was struck by the uniformity of answers I was hearing about a lack of career guidance from teachers and counselors. I wondered whether this was due to my interviewees' gender or to the upper-middle-class focus of the schools regardless of gender. Therefore, I asked if I could interview a few boys at Northington, which was the last school on my interview schedule. The headmaster was able to get three boys, who he felt were a representative sample of the boys at his school, to volunteer. This is, of course, not a true control group, but does provide some interesting contrasts nonetheless. Information from the three boys will be included as appropriate.

In the late fall of 1996, all of the young women were contacted again by mail or E-mail at their respective college campuses. All who responded to my fall 1996 queries (51 out of the original 56) were interviewed, in person or by phone, in the spring of 1997, as they completed their first year of college. These women also completed the AWS survey in the spring of 1997.

The Study Population

This original sample of girls (25 from coeducational schools, 31 from girls' schools) included members of minority groups (5 of the 56 girls were African-American and 3 were Latina). There were 30 boarders and 26 day students in the study, 5 students on full scholarship and 21 on partial scholarship. Thus the sample reflected some of the cultural and economic diversity that these schools attempt to achieve.

The AWS scores of these girls were compared across schools and again it was shown that they were not significantly different, either from each other or from the total group from which they were selected; see Table 2.2, line 2. (Only 55 AWS scores are shown because one of the participants in this study was absent on the day the AWS was administered at Northington.)

Students who apply to independent schools are asked to take the Secondary School Admission Test, or SSAT, as part of the application process; the SSATs, like the SATs, have a verbal and a mathematics section. The SSAT scores, both verbal and mathematics, of the participants were obtained (with parents' permission) from the four schools, along with data as to race/ethnicity, whether they were boarding or day students, and whether they were receiving full or partial financial aid. As Table 2.3 indicates, the average SSAT scores were consistent across the four schools; the range was about 270–330 in each school. (Nationally, SSAT scores run from 230 to 350; a score of 300 is equivalent to the 50th percentile of students taking the SSAT exam, for both the verbal and quantitative tests.) If the SSAT scores are a valid measure of academic ability, this group of girls is well matched across schools.

Table 2.2 Average AWS Scores of Female Students

	Girls' Schools		Coed Schools	
	Watson Hill	Summerford	Egremont	Northington
Fall 1992	38.72	38.61	38.10	37.89
(All 9th gr.)	(30)	(41)	(20)	(23)
Fall 1992	38.60	38.94	37.76	38.00
(Study grp)	(15)	(16)	(17)	(7)

Table 2.3 Average SSAT Scores of Students in the Study

	Girls' Schools		Coed Schools	
	Watson Hill	Summerford	Egremont	Northington
Verbal	304.1	305.8	305.8	307.8
	(15)	(16)	(14)	(8)
Math	298.2	296.4	298.2	308.9
	(15)	(16)	(14)	(8)

Students in the study come mainly from Connecticut (30 out of 56), but ten other states are represented: New York (8), New Jersey (4), Pennsylvania (2), Vermont (2), California (2), and one each from Massachusetts, Maine, Rhode Island, North Carolina, Virginia, Michigan, Louisiana, and Texas. This sample has very few girls whose parents attended prep schools themselves: three girls at Summerford had both parents who had been to prep schools, and two at Summerford and one at Watson Hill had a father who had attended such a school; at Northington one father and at Egremont one mother were prep school graduates. Lee and Marks (1992) also found a greater proportion of students with a history of private schooling at the single sex schools. Students also come from a wide range of socioeconomic levels, as can be deduced from the following tables showing the occupations of their mothers and fathers. These are not all the daughters of wealthy executives and doctors, as many people stereotypically imagine independent school students to be.

Table 2.4   Occupations of Mothers of Students in Study

Girls's Schools		Coed Schools	
Watson Hill	Summerford	Egremont	Northington
teacher's aide	retail store	nurse's aide	homemaker
driving school	lawyer	nurse	homemaker
homemaker	librarian	teacher	real estate
calligrapher	exec. assistant	teacher	bus. consultant
nurse	seamstress	doctor	computers
business	homemaker	volunteer	comptroller
social worker	bus. consultant	teacher	librarian
teacher	accountant	alumni develmt	nurse
cafeteria wrker	volunteer	health aide	teacher
business	homemaker	teacher	
homemaker	volunteer	homemaker	
teacher	tutor	advertising	
law clerk	artist	teacher	
store owner	tutor	bank supervisor	
(deceased)	lab technician	inter. designer	
	business	nurse	
		real estate	

Table 2.5   Occupations of Fathers of Students in Study

Girls' Schools		Coed Schools	
Watson Hill	Summerford	Egremont	Northington
sales mgr.	security guard	deliveryman	lawyer
technician	teacher	police dispatchr	business
kennel owner	computers	policeman	alumni office
state worker	steel trader	policeman	computers
postman	machinist	doctor	computers
doctor	accountant	doctor	(deceased)
minister	lawyer	florist	teacher
bus driver	policeman	bond salesman	personnel dir.
accountant	museum dir.	business	teacher
computers	business	state worker	
business	business	business	
accountant	advertising	stockbroker	
lawyer	doctor	in jail	
CEO	contractor	business	
doctor	doctor	investment	
	prison guard	lawyer	
		lawyer	

Scores on standardized tests and surveys and lists of parents' occupations help to establish a background of for the subjects of a study; however, during the five years I have been working on this study, I have come to know these young women as vibrant, interesting people. Their stories have sometimes made me laugh and sometimes moved me to tears. In the chapters that follow, I hope to convey to my readers a sense of who these young women really are—in their own words.

Part Two

Following the Girls:
Case Studies

Chapter Three

Scholastic Superstars

At each of the four schools, there are students that shine academically. These are the students that take the most challenging courses, get the highest grades, score in the 700s on their SATs, and get accepted into Ivy League or other highly competitive colleges. How do these students view their lives? Their schools? How does the educational environment, whether single sex or coeducational, aid or hinder their development as students and as women?

Charlie

At Northington

The girl who calls herself "Charlie" is a "faculty kid" at the coeducational Northington School. There are several such children at most independent schools, since offspring of faculty are usually awarded full scholarships to attend; not all of them, however, are as successful as she.

From her ninth grade year, she speaks without hesitation, confidently and expressively. During our first interview, she seems to quantify everything. When asked if any of her teachers have been encouraging to her, she answers, "Oh yes, three out of six have been very encouraging!" Asked what she's learned about herself, she replies: " I tested my limits and learned what they are. Earlier in the fall, I was doing two sports and six courses and it was getting near exams and I wasn't getting enough sleep and I got sick and couldn't play in five out of our last seven games. I had a temperature of 102, so that was one of my limits. I haven't done anything like that again!"

Charlie had thought of going to a different school, as a boarder, but decided that the transition from a public junior high to a private school would be enough of a challenge and that going away from home would be too big a step at that time. She didn't like the "cliqueyness" of her junior high, and is much happier at Northington where she can be "friends with everyone." She's been warned about senior boys who take advantage of the naivete of ninth grade girls ("they only have one thing on their mind," she's been told), but going on her own instincts, she's found that it's not true, and her two best relationships have been with senior boys, one whom she's dating, one who is a good friend. "But it's hard in a community where they think if you're with a guy you're going out. And I don't really like that, so I'm pushing the limits as much as I can there too."

She's close to her parents: she doesn't want to be known as her father's daughter, but she lists him among the three most encouraging teachers that year. "I was talking to my friend—my friend? No, I mean my mother!—last night, and about how she's, she just likes the way that I have male friends and there's no romantic or sexual connotations to the relationship." Yet, she's not sure what her mother does: "She works for this foundation, and does something with their newsletter, but I don't know exactly what she does for them." Two years later, she tells me that her mother, now working in the Northington school library, is "busy every minute. Brownies. Counseling. She's found a lot of things that are really important to her," she adds with pride in her voice. Charlie has a younger sister who will attend Northington in a few years.

As a sophomore, she tells me that she's learned "I've got limits of what I can do." When I point out to her that that's exactly what she said she learned the previous year, she sighs and says, "I have a real inability to say no. I can't fit it all in. I take on too much." Nonetheless, she has continued with track, has started voice lessons, and also works with a community group outside of the school that helps seventh and eighth graders make sensible life choices. That day, Charlie has called about starting a class in emergency medical technology, because she heard an older male student talking about being an EMT!

She loves her chemistry course and has wanted to be a doctor for a long time. Asked why she wants to be a doctor, she replies: "I don't know why. It started out as one of those childhood things, but I found that I enjoy it a lot." Both parents are supportive of her desire to be a doctor and her decisions in general: "They're really helpful, especially when I run into obstacles. They say if you want to do it—do it!"

As a junior, Charlie talks about taking on more responsibilities and how that has made her more self-confident. She's more involved with her community group, has joined the youth board of the community summer theatre, and volunteered at the emergency room of one of the local hospitals. "I finally got a calendar," she tells me. "I like to have my life in order. The day goes a lot more smooth when I write it all down." She's applied to another hospital for a program "six weeks, twenty hours a week in the trauma department" for the coming summer. She hasn't received much career guidance from either her teachers or her parents; she heard about the hospital program from an older girl at the school. She is the only junior in the Advanced Placement biology course, a result of encouragement by her advisor, an English teacher.

She's started looking at colleges and has already visited Wellesley and MIT. She liked the campus at Wellesley and she loved the science labs at MIT. Her father liked MIT and her mother liked Wellesley ("she really doesn't want me living in a city!"), but Charlie doesn't think she'll apply to either. "I'll integrate my parents' views into my decision," she says. "They know me well enough that I trust their ideas of what's good for me. But I'll make my own decision." Her B+ average at Northington and her SAT scores (730 Verbal, 720 Math) make her a strong candidate at most colleges.

When I see Charlie again, she's been accepted early decision into Cornell University. "It's senior spring, I got into college. I don't know how life could be much better!" she tells me. She chose Cornell because "it was sort of in a city, but not too big a city, and had really nice country, miles away from nowhere!" The summer program at the hospital was "great, all the doctors were very supportive of us" (two girls and a boy in the program). She is one of the few in my study who is still planning the major (sciences) and the career (medicine) that she aspired to at the beginning of ninth grade, but she says of medicine, "It's not the be-all and end-all." If she decides not to be a doctor, she's got no idea what she'll do, but probably something with science: "There's lots of opportunity out there."

Asked what she thinks her strengths are, she replies "the sciences" and then talks about Advanced Placement calculus. She has no doubt about her ability to grasp it, but it doesn't come easily. "I think I'll take it again next year rather than place out of it. I can get it eventually but it takes a while!" Charlie wins the prize for excellence in chemistry at graduation. She enters Cornell with AP credits in biology, chemistry, calculus, and English.

In college

At Cornell, Charlie enrolled in chemistry, calculus, Spanish, and freshman writing seminar for her first semester courses. She got Bs in calculus and chemistry and "liked them okay, but the science courses here are so big and so impersonal." Although she had a "great female TA in chemistry who really cared about her students" and she thinks repeating calculus was a good idea, Charlie no longer sees herself as a science major. Enrolled in a genetics course second semester, she withdraws from the class in early April. "It was five credits, way too much work."

Charlie is "getting interested in other things. I've been too focused for a long time." Having had a good experience in her relatively small writing seminar and greatly enjoying her music theory class, she is planning on taking mostly English and humanities courses next year. "It's disconcerting not to know what I'm going to do. I've always had a direction and now I'm playing it by ear."

Charlie finds that "the more I talk to doctors, the less I want to do medicine. Doctors don't feel in control of their patients any more and I couldn't handle that." She has been "thinking about academia and teaching. I could see myself being anything from a kindergarten teacher to a tenured professor at Cornell." Having had relatively few female teachers at Northington, she finds role models in both her chemistry TA and the female faculty-in-residence in her dormitory. "It's refreshing to see women who got here on their own. At Northington, all the women are there because their husbands are involved with the school."

And how has her science teacher father reacted to her change of heart about science and medicine? "The fact that I'm not going to take any course that ends in '-ology' startles him a little bit," she says.

Kerry

At Egremont

Kerry, like Charlie, speaks with little hesitation from the moment that I meet her at Egremont; she also speaks with incredible speed and emotional expressiveness. But she is much less focused. "Every day I want to be something different!" she tells me at our first interview. It's true that she does seem to be good at everything. In her junior year, she tells me: "I keep waiting for it to come to me in a dream— what I'll spend the rest of my life doing." But by senior year, she is still undecided and there is a desperate feeling in her voice: "I don't know how we're supposed to choose what we want to do—if we have no idea what it entails!"

At the end of ninth grade, Kerry is very "into religion," both in and out of school. She meets with a woman's Bible study group on Friday nights. In tenth grade, however, she takes a world religion class that enables her to take an objective look at religion, "from the outside looking in," and she decides that "I don't feel religious any more at all." Instead, she says "I just want to have a happy life. I really want to get married and I really want to have kids so much!" I ask her if anything in her life has influenced this decision and she replies that a 21-year-old aunt has just had twins, but she doesn't think that's a big influence.

Kerry came to Egremont from public school and is on partial scholarship. Her local high school is "almost an inner city school" and she wants more challenging courses than she would get there. She didn't look at any other private schools. She loves that Egremont pushes her to get involved both in athletics and the arts, and she is finding herself good at athletics (track) and drama, as well as the academics that she has always been good at. "I'm pretty smart in all my classes," she says at the end of 10th grade.

Kerry says that she participates in all her classes, except honors biology, where the teacher is very old and intimidating. He was at Egremont before the girls came and several of the girls confide to me that they feel that he doesn't think they should be there. There are 12 boys and only 4 girls in the honors class, and even some of the boys are intimidated by him. "He makes you feel stupid for asking a question! I don't think he should be a teacher," Kerry concludes. She relates an incident with her history teacher, also an older male, who in a discussion of women's suffrage makes disparaging remarks about "all the things women want today." Kerry really wanted to argue with him but didn't, because "you don't want people to hate you and think that you're annoying!" Her scores on the AWS are lower than most of her classmates, usually in the mid to high 30s; she is one of the few who think that boys are naturally better at math than girls (although she has consistently gotten A– in all her math courses at Egremont) and that women should do more of the child care.

Each year, she tells me that she is stressed and working very hard, but in her junior year, she has an insight about where a lot of her time is going: "I'm like a real people-pleaser—I always feel like I have to please everybody but I can't always do that because it takes up too much time, you know, like being there every time something's wrong with a friend." She mentions stress again during senior year; this time because she is taking so many AP courses and "really feeling burned out."

While considering colleges, Kerry visited 14 schools (she names most of the Ivy League and some small liberal arts colleges that are also among the most selective in the nation) because "I wanted to make the perfect decision!" She finally chose Brown University, applied early action and was admitted with a generous scholarship. "I felt it was more about learning than grades there—I couldn't do four more years of stressing out about grades at Harvard or Yale!"

With regard to Brown, she muses, "They have a really good premed program so sometimes I'm leaning toward that, but I *really* don't know. Sometimes I think I'll go into English or journalism. You only have to take 10 courses to be premed, so I'll start taking one and keep my foot in the door." Her college counselor has advised her to go into math or science because there's more money in those fields and more opportunities for jobs, but "my true love is probably English or literature."

Her grades have dropped during her senior year, and she complains that "I don't know what I'm good at anymore. There's so many people better and there's no subject that I'm at the top in anymore." Calculus has been especially difficult. "I'm getting a B but I feel like such a failure because I'll have to take it again next year. I don't understand it enough to move on in mathematics. A lot of people take it twice but I feel like a failure." (Contrast this with Charlie's statement: "I think I'll take it again next year rather than place out of it. I can get it eventually but it takes a while!")

Kerry is very close to her mother and lists as one of her reasons for choosing a college in New England the ability to "come home on weekends when I want to." Her mother teaches computers at a local high school but is working on her Ph.D. in education. Kerry can even quote me the present title of her mother's dissertation and knows that her mother's first proposal for a dissertation was turned down. She takes a lot of pride in her mother's work, and speaks fondly of her stepfather, who used to "be in computers but now owns a toy store." She sees her biological father, who works for the state, infrequently.

She says of her mother and stepfather: "They're not very strict and think I need to find things on my own. It's like, make your own decisions. But I say, help me a little bit! Sometimes I wish they would tell me what to do!" Kerry says that her parents are very young; her mother was twenty when Kerry was born, and married her stepfather when Kerry was seven. They tell her to do what she wants, including feeling free to take a year off before going to college, but "that is totally not me! I would never do that."

As she finishes her four years at Egremont, Kerry speaks enthusiastically about the teachers, especially those she has had in English and her (female) advisor/track coach. Although she has felt occasionally that some of the students are cliquey rich kids, "as a senior, you know everyone and you can just be yourself." Would she come to Egremont again? "Oh my god, yes! I've just grown so so so much and had so many opportunities!"

In college

At Brown, Kerry does retake calculus her first semester; she does well and is glad she took it "because now I know I am capable of understanding calculus." But it will most likely be the only math course that she takes in college, since "I really don't enjoy math and it does not come easily to me." She also abandons any thought of becoming a doctor because "the time, pressure, and work load is something you can only do if you really love it. I don't love math or sciences and I could not study them for eight years."

She is now thinking of being an English major and going into journalism: "I'm doing night editing for the *Brown Daily Herald* and looking into newspaper internships for the summer." Since journalism is a difficult field, she is also considering teaching at either the high school or college level. "I've been teaching English as a Second Language and enjoying that, so I think I'll get my teaching certificate."

As for marriage and children, "I think about it all the time! I would like to be married in my mid to late 20s and honestly, I'd like to be financially supported. I mean, I will always work, that's definitely important to me. I don't think I'll ever take off more than a year or two when I have children, but I would like to not have to worry about my salary as such. My mom always supported the family financially and it is just a stress I would prefer not to have." In exchange for being supported, she "would be willing to make a lot of sacrifices. I would travel with him wherever his job was. I'd be willing to wait to get my master's. I definitely would get my master's though, and I want somewhat of a career before I have children."

Jane

At Summerford

Whereas Charlie seems to find guidance and opportunities outside of her school and Kerry flounders from lack of guidance, Jane seems to have everything going for her; both school and family provide the experiences that she needs to crystallize her goals.

When I first meet Jane at Summerford, she is reluctant to have her voice taped, but for the next three years, her voice is loud and clear as she tells of her experiences. She wasn't sure at first that she wanted to go to an all-girls school, but chose Summerford for its relaxed atmosphere. Each year, she tells me how great things are— academics, friends, family. As a senior, she describes herself as someone with "lots of energy and very optimistic" and that description rings true from all that I have seen and heard of her.

Jane plays the flute and piccolo, she's on the varsity tennis team, and she does A/A– work in all her subjects. "I work at it and it comes" is how she explains her success. As an incoming ninth grader, she is thinking of being a doctor, and at the end of 10th grade, her father, an eye surgeon, arranges a summer position for her in a hospital laboratory, where she learns a lot but decides that lab work is not a career for her. She is also involved with ecological research, during the school year as well as the summer, as a result of a program in Summerford's science department. "It was just amazing. We were in a submersible at the bottom of the ocean, studying sea scallops!"

She describes her junior year as "really busy, crazy but good." As a Junior Advisor, she is responsible for advising younger students and says it is "a good feeling to have people count on you." During the winter of that year, she also did a four-week internship (arranged by the school) in surgery at a local hospital, during which she went on rounds, was in the operating room three times a week and "I actually held a human heart in my hands!" The internship made her want a career in medicine even more, she says, "but it also made me curious to try something else completely different to see if I enjoy it the same amount."

Good at everything, Jane says she is still open to English or history as a college major, because "I'd like to broaden myself before I narrow myself down in medical school." Her teachers do not give her any career guidance, but "they smile and nod their heads when you talk about being a doctor." Her mother, a sculptor, "is curious what career I'll end up choosing." Her father, unhappy with changes in the health care system in this country, advises her "to take a step back and examine it before I go into it." He also advises her that perhaps she should think about administrative positions within medicine; he gives the same advice to male friends of hers, so she is certain that he is not saying this because she is female. An older sister, out of college and living in Boston, has little influence on Jane because "we're very different, we have different motivations and different things that are important in life."

Jane is sure that she wants a coeducational college, although she loved Wellesley when she visited. "Wellesley would have been my first choice had it been coed. I really wanted a coed environment, mainly to prepare me for the coed world I guess." She is rejected by Harvard and decides to attend her second-choice school, the University of Chicago, because she thinks it has "incredible science, a beautiful campus, friendly people, and I like the city of Chicago a lot." She thinks she will do the premed program but major in philosophy or English because she really enjoys "having broad philosophical discussions with my English teacher." But biology is still a love. "My AP Bio course showed me how intricate and how simple everything is in life." She wins a prize for achievement in science at graduation.

Looking back on her four years at Summerford, Jane thinks there has been great freedom in not having boys around. "People feel more at ease, not afraid to act silly." She would certainly go there again, and has loved the student-teacher relationships, the encouragement and support; now she's ready for the coed world.

In college

At the University of Chicago, Jane finds that "roughly 85% of my friends are guys here. I have maybe four very close girlfriends and many more guy friends, as big-brotherly types, as friends to get into intellectual discussions with. I love having a broad spectrum of relationships with guys." Jane doesn't think there is much difference in having men in her class, except that they provide "a different perspective and I flirt a lot more." She is working very hard, but "having so much fun, both in classes and socializing."

She takes courses in biology, calculus, and chemistry during her first year of college, getting As in the first two and Bs and Cs in chemistry. She is not too upset about the chemistry grades because she has "spoken to lots of doctors that got Cs in chemistry" and they have told her not to worry. She has also greatly enjoyed a philosophy course, and is thinking of a combined major in history and philosophy of science, while still taking the prerequisite premed courses.

Once again, Jane will work in a laboratory over the summer, which she calls "ironic" since she knows that she is not cut out for a career in the laboratory, "but the subject is very interesting and the head of the program, conveniently a colleague and friend of my Dad, is an intelligent, instructive type of guy." She says that the desire to "go to medical school is still very strong, but I might go to law school or maybe both!"

Edith

At Watson Hill

Edith speaks so quietly that I have to strain to hear her voice, at least for the first three years that I interview her. There is a great deal of hesitation, with many sentences beginning "I don't know, um..." although by senior year at Watson Hill, she speaks with certainty and confidence in her ideas.

As a ninth grader, she doesn't want the tape recorder on as we speak. She tells me that she didn't want to attend a girls' school but her mother convinced her to come. A partial scholarship helps her family pay to send her to Watson Hill. She thinks that the lack of distractions is a good point of the school, but then tells me that the lack of boys is a bad point. Though the rules are too strict, Edith thinks she is getting a good education. She's learned that she's good at computer science and can do more than she thought she could; she thinks she has more confidence as a result of her first year at Watson Hill.

At the end of 10th grade, she tells me that her advisor at the school and her mother both tell her not to work so hard. I ask her: "Do *you* think you work too hard?" and she replies: "Maybe I do work too hard sometimes. Lately I try not to worry so much." Asked what she has learned about herself this year, she replies "I don't know, um, I'm more confident than I thought I was. I've got more self-esteem."

Edith has strong feelings that the administration of the school handles discipline issues inconsistently and in a "really degrading way" but she never voices these opinions to any of the adults for fear of repercussions. She is talking about several incidents that have occurred to her friends, not to herself, since she is the "model student." She seldom speaks in school meetings because "I'm kind of quiet" and if another person does something hurtful to her, "I usually talk to my Dad about it." She sometimes talks to friends about being upset but seldom deals directly with the person who hurt her.

As a junior, Edith still responds to questions hesitantly. Asked in what ways it has been a good year, she says "I don't know, um, I made more friends, I got good grades." As to her future, she entered Watson Hill with no idea of what she wanted to be and continues to be undecided. "Possibly marine biology or chiropracting or a doctor or something like that. I'm leaning toward math and science because I really like biology." Her biology teacher had wanted her to go into a summer program, but she has to earn money in the summers, usually working as a camp counselor or in her stepfather's business.

As 11th grade draws to an end, Edith has not started looking at colleges yet, but is certain she should go to a liberal arts college "because I'm not really sure what I want to do" and it should be "not too big because I'm coming from such a small school." She reports that her mother "is getting all excited about college and looking up all this stuff on the Internet," but Edith herself isn't enthusiastic.

Her mother, a nurse administrator in Vermont, tells her to do whatever makes her happy, but Edith can tell she's "excited about how I said I wanted to be like a doctor." Her father, a postman, also just wants her to be happy; "Mom also wants me to take a year off because she thinks I work too hard, but Dad doesn't want me to." Her parents are divorced, but Edith talks to both of them frequently. When she is in Vermont, she lives in a blended family consisting of her mother and stepfather, an older stepbrother, a stepsister almost her own age, a half sister, and a half brother.

By the end of her four years at Watson Hill, Edith's increased confidence is apparent. She speaks rapidly, with few of the hesitations that marked her earlier interviews with me. "It's been a good year," she tells me, "difficult but good. I learned a lot about myself and like myself a lot better. I took four AP classes and still did okay." Okay to Edith is an A– average.

When we meet in the spring, she is deciding between Vassar College and Wesleyan University. "It looks like Vassar, because they gave me a lot more money, but I like Wesleyan better." Edith was put on the waiting list at Brown University, her first choice school, and doesn't have much hope of going there. "I'm going to feel guilty if I go to Wesleyan, because my Mom will have to pay so much more, and I'd have to get more loans and stuff," she says wistfully. Several days after this interview, Edith writes me that her mother has worked things out with Wesleyan and she is going there.

At the end of senior year, Edith is still thinking of a career in biology, "but I'm keeping everything open. Of what I've studied here, it's what I've been interested in most, but there's many things I haven't studied yet." The chiropractor idea was "sort of a whim, I guess" and as for medicine, "I'm sort of saying that so I have something to say." She does know that "I can't see myself in a suit working in a firm. I would like something more casual, like working in the sea as a marine biologist." No teacher has given her any guidance or special encouragement about going into science, but she doesn't seem as upset by her lack of a specific goal as Kerry does.

As she leaves Watson Hill, Edith describes herself as open-minded and a good listener. One of her strengths, she says, is that "I work hard and I know what I have to do and I don't get confused about what I have to accomplish." She praises the warmth and friendliness of the school community, the helpfulness of the faculty and the challenging academics. She is still indignant about "the injustices I see here," again referring to the disciplinary actions some of her friends have experienced. Nonetheless, she would still choose to go to Watson Hill again.

In college

Edith finds that adjusting to Wesleyan "has not been too difficult. But it is simply very different from Watson Hill. It's much more free and there are many more distractions. No one holds your hand or reminds you to do things, which is I guess how it should be, however unaccustomed I am to it." She says she is "taking it a little easier this year, but my grades are still okay. I've grown a lot emotionally this year and know myself a lot better too."

Having men in her class "makes me more insecure about what I say," but she is continuing to pursue the sciences and still enjoying biology. Thinking about a career "kind of scares me. I have to declare my major next year. Biology is interesting but I want something to grab me. I'm afraid if I choose the wrong major, it will be a big problem and I won't be happy later in life, like my father." She has never wanted to be a doctor "because I don't want the pressure of having to save someone's life," but could see herself as a marine biologist. "The one thing I know for sure is that I want to go into the Peace Corps after college."

Reflections

All four of these girls were at the top of the class. All of them took four years of math, through calculus, and at least four years of science (Charlie took five) including physics. They each took many advanced placement courses. All four have gone to colleges that are among the most selective in the country (Barrons, 1995). Thus they are representative of the most successful students at each of their schools.

Only one, Jane, is from an affluent family; Edith and Kerry have partial scholarships, and Charlie is on full scholarship, a perquisite that many independent schools give to their faculty to compensate them for salaries lower than they would receive if they taught in the public schools. Kerry, Charlie and Edith are "first generation" independent school students, with parents who graduated from public schools themselves but see the independent schools as opportunities for their daughters to be more challenged than they would be if they had attended local public schools.

Charlie and Jane seem very focused in high school and have built up considerable experience in the medical world; Charlie has made her own opportunities and Jane has taken advantage of everything her school and her physician father have offered. Kerry and Edith also have "leanings" toward medicine, but Edith acknowledges that this is just something to say, and indeed it may be that any girl who shows talent in mathematics and science thinks, or is made to feel, that she should be a doctor. Kerry seems the least focused as she leaves high school, but gifted women who have the ability to be successful in many areas often have difficulty choosing a focus for their lives (Noble, 1996).

Neither Kerry nor Edith have made or seized any opportunities to experience a career firsthand; both must work during their summers to earn money and so they do not have the opportunity to take part in summer programs as Charlie and Jane do. Medicine is perhaps the most visible "scientific" career and so it is the one the girls name; none of them have received any counseling about other careers that might be open to someone with their talents, although Edith has thought of marine biology and Jane has actually done research in this field.

Despite her initial shyness, Edith has always held strong feminist views, as have both Charlie and Jane, but Kerry has consistently scored lower on the AWS (in the mid-30s rather than in the 40s) than her peers, although at the end of her senior year it has come up to 40.

As AWS score has been shown to be related to both self-esteem in female adolescents (Holland & Andre, 1994) and importance of careers to female college students (Komarovsky, 1985), this may signal that Kerry may have more trouble launching herself on a career track than the others.

All four girls are extremely able students, and thus good at most academic subjects. Like the high school valedictorians that Arnold (1995) has studied, they are good at everything they try; they lead well-rounded, busy lives. If they follow paths similar to Arnold's valedictorians, they will continue to excel academically. But Arnold also found a dichotomy in her population of female achievers: those who began to consider careers that would accommodate marriage and family showed a lowering of academic self-concept and career aspirations by their sophomore year of college, while those that did not engage in such "contingency" planning, continued, like the male valedictorians, to aspire to the highest professional levels.

Where are these young women in terms of thinking about marriage and family? Charlie says, "I think about it sometimes, but I'm still too busy figuring out who 'me' is to worry about it. I'll fit it in somehow." Jane responds, "I'm not concerned with that. I'm still too much of a kid to think about it." Edith says that she doesn't think about it all. Kerry, on the other hand, may have already begun the contingency planning, with her concerns about being supported and her consideration of teaching as a career if journalism is too difficult.

What, if anything, are the effects of the schools on these four girls? Edith speaks of (and demonstrates) a growth in confidence over her four years at Watson Hill. Jane's and Charlie's confidence seems to remain high throughout high school but there is evidence that Kerry's self-concept as a student had begun to slip by her senior year at Egremont: "I don't know what I'm good at anymore!" At the end of the first year of college, Charlie seems to have lost some confidence in herself too, although she has not begun the contingency planning that Kerry has. The two young women from the girls' schools have kept their career plans intact, whereas the two from the coeducational schools have not.

For some very bright girls, doing well in school is a vital part of who they are. Not doing well in a particular subject is a blow to their self-esteem, and one response to that is to switch to an easier major and revise their commitment to career (Holland & Eisenhart, 1990). This seems to have happened to Kerry and may also be happening to Charlie.

Table 3.1 Career Aspirations of Scholastic Superstars in the Study

Student	School	Start of 9th grade	End of 12th grade	End,1st yr of college
Jane	Summerford	Doctor	Doctor	Doctor
Edith	Watson Hill	Undecided	Biologist?	Biologist?
Charlie	Northington	Doctor	Doctor	Undecided
Kerry	Egremont	Undecided	Undecided	Journalist or teacher

Chapter Four

Students of Color

Some may object to my grouping the girls in this chapter on the basis of race alone. After all, the girls in other chapters chose to be scientists or actresses or athletes, while no one chooses their race or ethnicity. Yet as I spoke to these girls, it became apparent that their choice to attend schools in which they were so clearly in the minority was for some of them the most salient part of their high school experience; for others, it was less important, but nonetheless a significant backdrop against which their high school years were played out.

Independent schools in Connecticut strive to enroll a minority population of at least 10 to 15 percent. My sample, with five African-American girls and three Latinas, approximates this with slightly over 14% minority students; however, two of the girls identified as Latina turned out to be the daughter of a Mexican physician and the daughter of a wealthy Colombian businessman, both better classified as foreign students. Thus this chapter will look at the experience of the six students of color in the sample.

At Watson Hill, there was one African-American student and one Latina in the class of 1996 and they did not volunteer for my study. At Summerford, there were five African-American girls in the class, and one of them, Mimi, is in my study. As this makes Mimi the sole representative of the African-American experience at an all-girls school, I have recently interviewed two of her African-American classmates, now at Yale and Wellesley, in order to be able to generalize a bit more. Nonetheless, this does place limitations on what can be said about the minority experience at girls' schools.

At Northington, there was only one African-American girl, Sage, and she is in my study. At Egremont, which prides itself on its 14% minority population, four students of color volunteered for my study. I will consider in detail the experiences of two of them (Whitney and Kasmira) in this chapter, and include some of the material from the other two girls as well.

Mimi

At Summerford

Mimi came from Philadelphia to Summerford because she wanted the single sex experience: "I've been in coed all my life, and I heard that girls learn better by themselves." She has come to Summerford, on a full scholarship, after nine years in a predominantly white coeducational Catholic school, grades K–8. She talks quietly but positively about her first year, saying, "I've learned I can do a lot more than I think I can. I need to give myself more credit." But there are issues of trust that emerge right from the start: "You have to watch everything you do here because people don't forget. You can't always trust people."

Since she was a child, Mimi has wanted to be a cardiologist: "I watched heart surgery on TV and thought it was amazing." Her grades in mathematics are low (C/C+) for all four years at Summerford. She does poorly in biology (C–) during ninth grade, and then takes a lower level chemistry course, a semester of environmental science, and then finally a year of physics in which she gets a D. When I ask her if she gets any encouragement from her teachers with regard to her becoming a doctor, she tells me, "None of them know that I want to be a doctor. I haven't told them." Her teachers do tell her that she has "potential, but I just don't do anything with it." By senior year, she has rationalized it this way: "I got average grades in biology and chemistry. Physics and I don't get along. But grades don't matter. You don't have to be a genius to be in medical school."

Mimi gets lots of encouragement from her mother, a certified public accountant. Every year, her mother finds a summer program for Mimi to attend. During the summers after ninth and tenth grade, Mimi goes for six weeks to the University of Akron, for a program "paid for by the U.S. Department of Education. They pay for everything including my airfare!" After 11th grade, she participates in the Pennsylvania Governor's School for Excellence in Health Care for five weeks at the University of Pittsburgh. There Mimi gets to tour hospitals, watch arthroscopic knee surgery, and follow an operating room nurse for a day. " I said, Oh wow! They actually do this. It was my first time ever actually seeing it in person. It's what I want to do." Her mother does not force her to go to these programs, "but she says, 'It will be in your best interest. I'll be very disappointed if you don't.' " She encourages Mimi to consider research in medicine over becoming a practicing physician, because "you can't get sued for malpractice in research."

Mimi's parents are divorced, and her younger sister goes to boarding school closer to home, because "she's more dependent on my mother." Her father, a retired police officer, lives an hour away from her home, and she calls him now and then. He takes no role in her college plans, while her mother is "a little too much into it." Mimi has used the school's computer to look at the University of Pennsylvania, Stanford, and Cornell universities, all Ivy League schools, despite her overall C average. Her mother has suggested several small liberal arts colleges, including one women's college (Bryn Mawr) and one historically black college (Spelman). Eventually, Mimi ends up choosing between Spelman and the University of Pittsburgh, and chooses "Pitt because the financial situation is better and Spelman is too far away from home." Additionally, her mother has found a private foundation to help Mimi finance her education.

At my interview with Mimi during May of her junior year, I am struck by her sullenness compared to her happier demeanor during my first two visits. She explains that she is "in trouble for being not nice to my roommate. I've been removed from my dorm and I'm on probation until next Christmas, so if I do anything wrong, I get expelled." An administrator later explains to me that Mimi has locked her roommate, a quiet Vietnamese girl, out of her room several times and "generally harassed her." As Mimi looks back on it, she says, "I was suspended for a 'lack of respect for a member of the community.' My mother even felt they gave me a raw deal and so did my friends and their parents. I guess the school figures that black girls can be found anywhere but Vietnamese girls are hard to come by."

Mimi seldom mentions her status as a minority student and, when questioned about it, says, "I've never felt different from anyone here. I just felt privileged to go to this school." She has not formed any attachments to her teachers in her years at Summerford, except for her 10th grade history teacher, a young African-American woman who is also a Summerford alumna, who Mimi says "cares more about me than my other teachers."

By the end of her senior year, Mimi is happier. I ask her if it's been a good year, and she laughs and replies, "Pretty much, yeah. I made varsity soccer and then I cracked my tibia and then I got mono and pneumonia." When I show dismay at this, she adds, "Oh no, but it was fine. I had fun. I got into college, school's good, family's good."

She says that she's made good friends and would come to Summerford again.

In college

At the end of her first year at the University of Pittsburgh, Mimi still plans to be a doctor, specializing in "either cardiology or reconstructive plastic surgery." She has taken courses in biology, chemistry, and mathematics (trigonometry). Of biology, she says, "I didn't go to class and I hardly studied and I still got a C. My friends studied all the time and got a C too." She really enjoyed the chemistry class and is considering majoring in chemistry, although her grade there was a C+; her mathematics grade was a B.

Similar to her "not living up to her potential" at Summerford, Mimi admits to not working very hard because she is somewhat burned out: "I've gone to school every summer. I want to just take this summer off and maybe a semester off too." When I ask her if she ever worries about getting grades that will make her competitive for entrance into medical school, Mimi replies, "Sometimes I do worry about my grades hindering me from getting in, but then I tell myself that this is only my first year and if I do better from here on out, then I will have no problems getting into school. If I studied harder, I could get As or Bs. That's exactly what I plan to do for the next three years."

Some of her descriptions of her social life also echo experiences she had at Summerford. "My roommate moved out. We didn't get along. I couldn't stand how subservient she was to her boyfriend." Being at Summerford helped her, she explains, "to focus on being a woman and not being subservient to men." Mimi says that she has "a few female friends, but you never know who you can trust." Unlike Summerford though, Mimi finds that the different races don't mingle well at Pitt. "People are not open to others. There are black students here that just want to be with other blacks. If that's what they wanted, why didn't they go to a black college?"

Thinking about career, Mimi says that she thinks that marriage and family "will fit nicely. I won't get married until after medical school and I won't have children until after my career is established. Financial security is top priority."

Sage

At Northington

The first thing that Sage tells me when I first meet her at Northington is that she's excited to be in a study. "I've always heard about studies but I never knew anybody that was in one!" Prior to high school, she had taken a psychology course for gifted and talented students at a local college and heard the results of studies quoted in that course. She says that she wants to be a psychologist because "I love people and want to deal with people." She speaks with enthusiasm and certainty.

At the end of ninth grade, Sage talks of the good education she is receiving and the good friends she has made. She is disturbed by the pressures to be thin and says that a lot of her friends have eating disorders. She thinks she's changed a lot over this year and "can't relate to my friends back home at all." I think to myself that perhaps she has left behind black friends to come to this predominantly white school, but I soon discover that I am totally wrong. Sage was the only African-American in her former school in New Jersey. "At my old school, all I thought about was good grades and Ivy League schools. Now I realize that's not all that's important." This year, Sage has realized that "I don't like the professions that my parents are in and I don't feel pressured to do what they do."

Her mother, a lawyer who works as a business consultant, and her father, a computer consultant, divorced when she was nine years old. Prior to that, Sage had gone to an all-black public school. Her mother then sent Sage, an only child, to a white private school to get a better education and to "avoid the wrong crowd," although her father thought this was a bad idea. Sage had wanted to attend a private high school in Manhattan, but her mother did not want her commuting into the city. Northington offered her a partial scholarship and was Sage's second choice: "When I came on the tour, I felt part of the school right away. The people seemed really interested in you. They were friendly and personal."

During her sophomore year, Sage learns "how much I can push myself and how much is too much. I'm still trying to figure out if I have any limits." This sounds very much like the academic superstars of the previous chapter, and, in fact, Sage could have been considered in that chapter, had not her struggles with racial identity been a more salient part of her Northington experience. Like the superstars, she takes several AP courses, four years of science and math, and scores in the 600s and 700s on her SATs. Her grades are mostly high Bs and As.

During her second year, Sage experiences what she calls an identity crisis about both race and class: Should she "continue to foster the elitist culture that I was brought up in and that is promoted by Northington, or should I try to help people of color not as lucky as I am?" She opts for the latter. She also stops worrying about thinness, since she comes to see this as a white standard that is being imposed upon her.

Although she is still planning to major in psychology, she is now thinking about a second major in African-American studies. "I'm learning so much about my culture this year," she tells me at the end of her junior year. She has an uncle who is a professor of African-American studies and "I've gotten really close to him and he's taught me so much. I've read lots of books and stuff. I really really really am interested in it." Although there are no courses in the subject at Northington, her history teacher is interested in her ideas and information so she shares things with him. She says of her classmates: "The majority of people aren't into academics anyway. I'm more intellectually curious than a lot of people here. It makes it hard to be here, hard to explain that I just want to know things."

With regard to career, Sage says, "Everyone's telling me I should be a teacher, but I don't want to teach. I don't have the patience." She's going to look for a college that has an African-American studies department and a strong psychology program. As a result of her high PSATs, Sage is receiving letters from many colleges, and she is writing back to them asking for information on her two areas of interest. "I've learned a lot about so many different schools this way. I took my own initiative."

Northington gives advice about college entrance but not about career development, she tells me. Her mother "wants me to go to an Ivy League school and get a solid career. My dad says do whatever you want." Sage has been to her mother's office to see what she does: "She sits behind a desk and people come to her and she tells them what to do. She has meetings but I can't figure out what she does. She makes pension plans for companies." She adds, "I still don't know what I want to do, but I know what I want to learn. Wherever that takes me, that's where I'll go."

When I see Sage at the end of her senior year, she is choosing between Brown and Yale universities. "Brown is very mellow and I'd probably have lots of fun, but I think I should go to Yale. It's more intense and I need to be in an environment where I'll work." She does ultimately choose Yale. She is also thinking of going to law school, the career she had aspired to as an incoming ninth grader. "It's between psych and law. I don't know. Law seems really exciting to me now." She lists among her strengths: "I think things through very deeply. I'm always questioning things. And I'm really quick at thinking on my feet."

Summing up her four years at Northington, Sage says: "My trials and tribulations at this school have definitely made me such a strong person, especially in who I am, especially as a student of color. It's made me such a stronger person within my cultural identity." She says that she has made many friends who will be her friends for life, but there is an ambivalence there: "This school is so homogeneous ethnically, politically, socioeconomically—everyone's the opposite of who I am. I have friends who are very different from me but I love them—we share the same values and goals."

Sage says she would come to Northington again nonetheless: "I've got a great education, but no social skills. I don't know how to deal with people within my own culture and that hurts me so much. I'm the only black girl in the senior class—it's sad." She indicates that if she were to do it over, "I'd get out a lot more. I'd take off on weekends."

During Sage's last year at Northington, her mother and stepfather (this is the first mention of him) have a child. She says, "I think it's great! I love my baby brother so much! I don't want to have kids of my own, but it's fun to have a baby brother."

In college

By the middle of her first year at Yale, Sage is training to become the university's coordinator of African-American activities, a job not usually given to first year students, "but I guess they thought I could handle it." She finds the atmosphere at Yale "much more competitive than at Northington, both academically and socially." She feels that she has focused more on her social life this year and less on academics, "because in high school all I did was study. But I'm on the way to being more motivated."

Sage is planning to major in philosophy with a minor in African-American studies. She particularly enjoyed her first semester philosophy course with a woman professor, but is bothered by the professor she has in her spring philosophy course; she thinks he favors the males in the class, and allows them to dominate the discussion. Nonetheless, she describes herself as "very vocal and aggressive." Sage also loved her course in African-American literature "because I never got to read that at Northington."

She still plans to go to law school and is now interested in the field of entertainment law. "I don't like to see artists getting gypped. Especially black artists, who get like 8% royalties when the recording companies are making all the money. I want to help protect them."

Whitney

At Egremont

Whitney's first question to me is whether she has to put her correct age on the questionnaire. "I don't want people to know how young I am," she explains. Coming from a largely black and Hispanic public school in the Bronx, Whitney started at Egremont when she was only twelve years old. I assure her that no one but me will see her questionnaire and she smiles with relief; I then tell her how my daughter coped with being the youngest girl in her class throughout high school. She continues to beam at me throughout our interview.

On partial scholarship, Whitney came to Egremont because she wanted to get away from home; her older sister also attends Egremont, which "I loved immediately when I visited. It was so close and personal." Several of her friends from home go to Deerfield Academy in Massachusetts. Her mother is a home health aide and her father, who "is not in the picture very much," owns a business. She considers herself Latina as well as black, and speaks fluent Spanish.

As a ninth grader, Whitney says, "I take everything a little too seriously, like academics and sports. In a bad way, because sports are supposed to be fun. But I cry every day after lacrosse practice because I'm so frustrated. I expected to be good at it right away. In the past everything I tried I was good at." She's grown close to her teachers, especially a Spanish teacher whom she doesn't have in class but "she's really strong and caring. Being around her really inspires me." She feels too that she's made "lasting friendships" with her classmates, and her friends have helped her so much that "now I want to do something that helps people inside. I used to want to do something in science like a doctor, but now I want to help people mentally or emotionally."

As a sophomore, Whitney laughs when I ask her what she is good at. "That's a hard question. You don't stop to think about it. Usually you just think, I wish I could be better at this." Nonetheless, she finds something to say: "I'm organizational—everything in its place." She says that she is struggling in the English honors class, because "I was always more of a math-science person," but her teacher is giving her confidence in her writing. She's become more confident about talking in class, especially in English. "Even if I'm wrong that's okay. Next time I might have the right answer."

Whitney spends the first half of her junior year at the Maine Coast Semester, a program run for a large number of independent schools. She comes away from that with a leaning towards environmental science or marine biology as a major in college. "Or maybe Spanish or English." What's happened to psychology? I ask. "Psychology is just gone! I've no idea what I want to be. There are lots of things I'm interested in, but I don't see how to incorporate them in a career." Her older sister is also good at Spanish and is majoring in international relations at Syracuse University. "But I don't want to do what she does. I don't want to keep following in her footsteps."

Besides her sister in college, Whitney has a sister seven years older who is a nurse, but they are not close. She gets no career guidance from her teachers, but her mother would like her to become a lawyer. "I don't really want to do that and she definitely respects that." As to her father, "Our relationship's not that great. He's not very approachable. I try to include him in my life, but my Mom's my Mom. He's very conservative, a strict Catholic, and I'm not like that at all!"

At the end of her junior year, Whitney's math grade plummets to a C+ where before she had always achieved As; on the other hand, her English grade, previously a B, rises to an A–, and by the end of senior year, she says, "I want to pursue English. I don't know where that will go as a career. I just love to read and I love to write. Maybe newspaper or magazine journalism." She tells me that her English teacher is very supportive and she is in love with him. Out of curiosity, I ask if she's ever had a female English teacher at Egremont and she replies, "There are very few females in the English department. That's weird! I never thought about that before."

Her math teacher, a female, is "great, but I just don't see the point of math. I know I won't use it for anything. I see it's pointless so I have trouble getting anything out of it." She's looked into the idea of going into psychology again, but since you have to take math courses for the psych major, she thinks she won't major in psych. When I ask her what she sees as her strengths, Whitney answers,

"That is the hardest question! We're so used to telling ourselves what we do wrong, but we never tell ourselves, hey I'm good at this! You're never allowed to pat yourself on the back, because people would think you're cocky." Finally she decides, "I'm very outgoing. I like to think I'm a good writer."

Whitney applied early decision to Brown University and was accepted. "I'm very excited. I like the freedom and the liberal aspect. There's no core curriculum." Three other girls and one boy have also been accepted and she thinks that's great. "I'm ready for new experiences and going to college and tying up things here." Although she thinks that seniors should be trusted with more freedom, Whitney is overwhelmingly positive about Egremont. She loves the close relationships she has had with her teachers and with other students. "We've gotten beyond cliques and bonded with our entire class." Although there are some dating couples who have been going out a long time, "it's much more like brother and sister, like I've known him since I was little!"

She calls Egremont "the most racially harmonious place in the world" and is concerned about more polarization of blacks and whites that she sees on college campuses. "When we came here, we all had our stereotypes, but we were so young that our ideas weren't formulated yet. There's so much less bigotry here or it's well hidden, but mostly people are willing to learn about other cultures." She describes a "multicultural extravaganza" weekend that she helped organize: "Nikki Giovanni came and that was so exciting and the New York Boys' Choir and Brazilian dancers and Eastern European singers. We didn't want anyone to feel left out."

In college

Whitney continues to want to be a writer: "That's my passion. That's what I'd love to do. But I know how hard it is to do and how hard a goal it is to have." Her "second alternative is to be a community activist. I've accepted that I'm not going to earn a lot of money. I'll probably work for a nonprofit organization." Her plan is to have "a dual concentration in African-American Studies and Educational Studies. When I look at the problems in the world, I keep seeing that the way to solve them is through education. I don't want to be a teacher though, but maybe do something with education."

At Brown, she has found "a sense of Third World community. There's a Third World Center, where I'm very comfortable and I study there." Although she maintains a "broad range of friends, my closest friends are students of color. We've had similar experiences and I can relate to them." Most of Whitney's friends are also students who have been to prep schools or other private schools; the students of color who attended public schools seem "really different." She says that she's become "really involved and committed. I'm going to be a minority peer counselor next year. I want to make sure that everyone who comes here feels comfortable."

About herself, Whitney says, "I've grown much stronger, more comfortable with myself. I've made a point of having my voice heard. I've also grown stronger in my beliefs and convictions and expressing them."

Kasmira

At Egremont

Kasmira brings up the question of race in the first few minutes that I interview her at the end of ninth grade. When I ask her what she sees as the good and bad points of the school, she says, "People here are very ignorant toward racial issues. Rich people come here and never knew black people before. They say ignorant things sometimes and you just have to get used to it and deal with it."

Yet Kasmira herself "grew up in a white neighborhood and when I came to Egremont there were more black people here than I've ever seen." She admits to having had her own stereotypes: "I'm poor myself and coming here drove away a lot of the stereotypes I had about rich people. I expected snobs with noses in the air, but my friends aren't like that at all."

She's learned that she's good at lots of athletic things: "Basketball! I've gone from sitting on the bench all the time in my old school to JV to varsity! It's the coaching. They give you so much individual attention and push you harder." She's also gotten good at two new sports, field hockey and lacrosse, but "my study habits are still terrible." Kasmira says she's also learned that "I let people take advantage of me a lot. I don't know how to say no. But I learned that's not being nice, it's being stupid."

All of her teachers are very supportive and try to boost her confidence, but "I've always had top grades and thought I was going to go far. Now I know I'll get somewhere but it will be harder. I'm not going to go as far as I thought. There's so much competition. But if I work hard, I'll have a good future." Despite her study habits, Kasmira, who wants to be a zoologist, achieves a B average, with an A in math and a C+ in physical science.

At the end of our first conversation, she comes back to race. "I'm mixed, half white and half black. And I've lived with my mother and she's white, and my twin sister and I grew up in a white community. We were the only black girls in the town. It's like we've always tried to fit in with a white crowd and really wish we were white, until I came here. Now I've met other black students and it's like I'm happy with who I am and I'm trying to learn more. 'Cause looking at me no one's going to ask, are you white? I mean I'm black and here I've come to realize that's what I am. When I look in a mirror I see a black girl and I should be what I am."

Her twin sister has stayed home in New Jersey at the local public high school and still lives with her mother. "My mother has her master's," she tells me proudly, "and teaches special education." About her father, she says, "He's just out there in New York somewhere. He calls me once in a while, but I don't care to know him." Two years later she tells me that she saw him over her March vacation "in a halfway house in the Bronx. Now he's in Riker's Island. I hadn't seen him in over four years and now that he's in Riker's, I don't want to keep in contact at all."

Her grades improve to all Bs her sophomore year and she continues to list zoologist as her career choice. But there is a dramatic shift by the end of her junior year, both in her grades and her manner. She tells me "I haven't been doing well at all. I can't focus on my academics. I have boyfriend problems, we've been going out for two years. But he gets in trouble and he won't be back next year." What Kasmira doesn't tell me, but I learn from the academic dean, is that her mother is dying.

About her schoolwork, she says, "I need to stop procrastinating. Not that I'm a quitter but once I know it's going to be hard to get back up, I just like to stay down and just deal with the harsh consequences instead of working as hard as I can to get out of the situation. I'm so overwhelmed, I'm just going to let this year go." And she adds, "But next year, I'm not going to let myself get into that position."

She's given up on being a zoologist because her science grade is so low (a D in chemistry). "Science doesn't like me and I don't like science. I hate chemistry. I hate all the formulas and numbers and all that nonsense. Biology I liked a lot." But she still likes animals and is thinking of animal psychology. "I'm wrestling with should I help animals or people? I can go into psychology and see which way I go."

When I ask about college, she tells me that she is looking for a big school with many different sorts of people. "Here all the black people are from New York City and all the white people are from Greenwich, Connecticut! I'd like a wider range. Maybe even a black person from New Jersey like me?" She says she hangs out with the African-American girls because they like the same music and dances, but "my serious friends are three African-American girls and five white girls." Despite her reservations about the narrowness of the school population, she ran for and won the position of president of the school for the following year.

At the end of her senior year, Kasmira talks about her ups and downs of the year. "What was good was that I got into a bunch of colleges, Brown, Tufts, Wesleyan, and I started a dance class with one of the new teachers, a class in salsa and hip-hop. My nephew was born in December." This is a baby born to her twin sister. "What was bad? My grandfather died in February and my mother died last June. My sister and I and my nephew all live with my grandmother now."

Understandably, her work continues to suffer. "I don't want to work any more. I'll be able to motivate myself in college but my mind has been in other places all year." Being president of the school was "no big deal because students don't have much power anyway. I've tried to make changes, but the teachers listen and don't do anything. I run the meetings and I like that other students know me and that they can come to talk to me."

Kasmira is choosing between Wesleyan and Brown at the time of my visit. "I'll probably choose Brown because it's bigger. They're both liberal, no core curriculum. I don't need to take more math and science to find out I don't like them." She hasn't yet visited Brown, but liked that at Wesleyan she saw "an interracial lesbian couple and nobody cares. My godfather is gay and my mother knew lots of gay people, so it's cool." She adds, "I don't like it here when people try to pretend that sex isn't going on. We need to be aware of safe sex. College equals sex. There's lots of freedom."

Kasmira has decided that she should go into law, "because I love to talk. I can see myself arguing in front of a court. I don't want to be a psychologist because I don't want to have to listen to other people all day." She tells me that her strengths are "being very vocal about my opinions but I don't try to overpower and overwhelm others. I'm very open-minded." She also reads a lot when she's interested in something: "So I know what I'm talking about, like Malcolm X or *Plessy v. Ferguson*."

About Egremont, she says, "There are so many students of color here compared to other prep schools. When we go to play other schools, our teams are so colorful! We are so much more diverse!" She is quite emphatic that she would come to Egremont again: "I love it here! I get so much attention. There are so many interracial couples and nobody questions it or looks down on it. Since I am the product of a biracial relationship, that's important."

Kasmira tells me about an older half-sister (from her father), who was also a prep school student, who went to the University of North Carolina. Although Kasmira seldom sees her, she admires her half-sister: "She is so independent and smart. She doesn't let anything hold her back. That makes me feel less restricted too." Her twin sister is now working and going to night classes to get her GED. "We used to hate each other. We practically murdered each other. That's one of the reasons my mother thought I should go away to school. But now we're the best of friends. I love my nephew. I was thinking of going to the state college so we could be together."

In college

After a few months at Brown, Kasmira goes home to her grandmother, intending to return to college in January. But then she decides not to go back to Brown. She and her sister get an apartment together, and Kasmira finds employment as a cashier in a mall; she also begins classes in bartending. She has missed the deadline for regular admission to other colleges, but plans to apply to Trenton State College and New York University for January 1998 admission.

"I loved Egremont but I hated Brown," she says. "I'd never seen it before I came there. I was sort of pushed into it because it was an Ivy and my friends were going there. I didn't like Providence and thought it was too small." But, in fact, she admits that any place might have been wrong for her at this point. "I slept through a lot of classes. I kept going home for the weekend and then staying there, not wanting to go back. I think I missed more classes than I went to." Kasmira, reacting to the losses in her life, has gone through a period of depression and without the close supportive atmosphere of Egremont, she "pretty much stopped functioning." In fact, her last two years at Egremont showed a downturn in her ability to function academically, but the social supports there were so strong that she was carried through.

Seeing what her sister and her sister's friends have gone through with pregnancy and dropping out of school, Kasmira has a new direction: she wants to be a social worker or a teacher in the inner city. Law, she says, was just a good way to make lots of money, but now she thinks that money is not as important. She wants to help people "like my sister" and wonders "where I would be if not for Egremont." She herself doesn't want to have children "because I see how hard that is. If I ever do, I'd adopt because there are already children here who need someone."

Reflections

These four girls are quite representative of the experience of students of color at northeastern independent schools. In addition to these four, I have drawn information from Stephanie and Racquel, both from New York City, who were in my sample at Egremont, and from Ada and Nina who were classmates of Mimi at Summerford. (Racquel is considered again in Chapter 10, "Those Who Left.")

Like the black students in Carol Gilligan's study at Emma Willard School, almost none of these girls grew up in predominantly black communities (Ward, 1990). Even those like Whitney, whose school was "mixed black and Latino," had many friends who went away to prep schools for high school. Thus, this was not the first time for many of them to confront racial stereotypes. Yet as these young women proceed through adolescence and develop their personal identities, they must also determine what role their race will play in what they will eventually become. According to Ward (1990), as part of the identity development process, they must proclaim " 'I am not what you believe black people to be, *and I am black*' " (p. 219). For Kasmira, this came early in ninth grade, when she found herself at Egremont among other black students for the first time. For Sage, it was finding herself as the only African-American in her class at Northington that caused her "identity crisis."

For Whitney, Mimi, and others, the discussion of race during our interviews was less dramatic, but in almost all cases, it was the girl and not I who raised the issue. As a white interviewer, I was uncertain how comfortable these students would be discussing race with me, but since they brought up the subject themselves, discussion was fairly easy. This is in accord with the findings of Zweigenhaft and Domhoff (1991), who found that black students who had gone to predominantly white schools, and thus had experienced friendships with whites, tended to be candid with white interviewers.

Most of these students were brought to their prep schools by the ABC (A Better Chance) program, started in the early 1960s by sixteen independent schools with the aid of Dartmouth College and several foundations. In a study of the outcomes of the ABC program, Zweigenhaft and Domhoff (1991) concluded: "The large majority of students...were well served and emerged not only well educated but psychologically intact" (p.7). For many of the ABC students interviewed by Zweigenhaft and Domhoff, and especially for the girls, the freedom to develop academically to their fullest potential was the central component of their academic experience at these schools, and this opportunity offset many of the negative aspects. This was echoed in the statements of most of the girls I interviewed.

Like the ABC students in the Zweigenhaft and Domhoff study, Kasmira was initially offended by the naivete of her white classmates toward racial issues, but in the end she counted whites among her closest friends. At the same time, being racially isolated led many of their ABC interviewees to think more about what it meant to be black in the United States, and as one of them said, to become "blacker." This clearly happened to Sage. Although Sage may be the most obvious example of becoming more aware of her cultural identity, none of the African-American girls appeared to adapt the strategy of "racelessness," disconnecting from their culture entirely to improve their success at school (Robinson & Ward, 1991). Indeed, Sage, and to some extent Kasmira, developed what Robinson and Ward call the "oppositional gaze," a way to observe the world critically and oppose or reject those ideas that are disempowering to self-identity. Sage's rejection of the white ideal of thinness, for example, protected her from the epidemic of eating disorders she saw around her and enabled her to accept her larger body as a powerful one.

Individual personality differences, of course, affected how these girls reacted to their schools. Mimi, who tends to rationalize her own mistakes, put some of the blame for her troubles on the racism of the administration of Summerford. Her classmates at Summerford, on the other hand, did not find the school at all racist; their issues tended to focus more on matters of class than race, according to her classmate Nina. The black students simply had less money and were sometimes keenly aware of this, especially when their classmates took expensive vacations or were given new cars as graduation presents.

Ada, also of Summerford, was not only black but a Muslim, and had come to this country from Somalia as a small child. Thus she was different from most of her classmates in "race, class, religion, and language. But I found Summerford a wonderful, comfortable environment. Maybe five percent of the time, at most, I wondered if the moneyed white people thought I really belonged there." Whitney, ever the optimist, paints the rosiest picture of Egremont's racial relations, although her view is supported fairly well by her classmates Stephanie and Racquel, and even by the more critical Kasmira.

None of these girls comes from a home of poverty. Indeed, Zweigenhaft and Domhoff (1991) found that over the years, as the ABC program has lost funding, it has tended to fall back on middle class black students more and more. The mothers of these four girls are professionals or semi-skilled professionals: a lawyer, an accountant, a teacher, and a home health aide. Similarly, Racquel's mother is a bank supervisor and Stephanie's a nurse's aide. Mimi was on a full scholarship to Summerford, but the other five received only partial scholarships. Of the students of color in this study, only one (Stephanie) comes from an intact family, and in all but one case (Sage), the girls seldom see or hear from their fathers. Their mothers work at higher status occupations than their fathers; again, Sage, whose father is a computer consultant, is the exception.

These girls thus have strong female role models in their mothers, and sometimes an older sister as well. They all entered ninth grade with high career aspirations, and they continue to hold them (see Table 4.1); it may be noteworthy that only Mimi continues to be interested in science or medicine, however. Is this because she was at an all-girls school? It may be, since I did hear complaints about sexism in the science department at Egremont. On the other hand, Mimi got no support and quite a bit of discouragement in science at Summerford, and her teachers never knew she wanted to be a doctor. She may be persisting despite poor grades in science through stronger determination, her mother's support or her tendency to attribute her difficulties to others.

Since black females perceive themselves in less gender-stereotypic ways than their white counterparts do (Hollinger, 1996), it is not surprising that the six students of color in my study consistently score near the top on the AWS questionnaire (40 or over), seeing women as clearly the equal of men. Of the three boys at Northington that I interviewed, one was African-American and he too scored a 40; he is from New York City and lives with his mother, who is a semi-skilled professional. By contrast, his two white male classmates scored in the low 30s on the AWS.

Most of the students in these case studies have made a commitment in college to helping other people of color: Kasmira by being a social worker or inner city school teacher, Whitney through

Following the Girls

community activism, and Sage through being a lawyer/advocate for black entertainers. Mimi, on the other hand, does not ever mention being concerned with this. Whereas her Summerford classmates have expressed to me feelings of solidarity with other students of color at their colleges, she expressly disavows this.

Since women of color often see racism, not sexism, as the most potent form of oppression (Evans, 1996), the variable of single sex versus coeducation does not appear to have been a significant one for these girls. In Summerford, Egremont, and Northington, the issues of race and class were more salient.

**Table 4.1 Career Aspirations of Students of Color
in the Study**

Student	School	Start of 9th grade	End of 12th grade	End,1st yr of college
Mimi	Summerford	Doctor	Doctor	Doctor
Sage	Northington	Lawyer	Lawyer	Lawyer
Whitney	Egremont	Psychologist	Journalist	Comm'ty activist
Kasmira	Egremont	Zoologist	Lawyer	Social wk or teacher
Stephanie	Egremont	Accountant	Languages	Undecided
Racquel	Egremont	Doctor	Psychologist	Lawyer

Chapter Five

The Athletes

One of the most striking differences between the girls' schools and the coeducational schools was the frequency with which the girls at the coed schools mentioned sports as a reason that the school year had been a good one. Although they had not initially chosen the schools for their sports programs, 10 of the 22 girls at the coeducational schools consistently mentioned their increasing competence in athletics as a self-affirming experience. At the girls' schools, there were three who fell into this category. The girls who appear in this chapter are those who repeatedly discussed sports in their interviews and who evinced a strong desire to make athletics an important part of their college experience.

Natasha

At Northington

Unlike most of her highly verbal classmates, Natasha is very reticent to talk about herself and fills the void with nervous laughter. Coming from the local public middle school, where she says she "didn't get much attention," Natasha has come to Northington on full scholarship since her father is director of development there. She speaks, somewhat hesitantly, about being good at track, and then warms to the subject: "Shot put and discus. I've always wanted to do those but I never competed in them before." At the end of the interview, I learn that her father is also the track coach.

Natasha can't think of anything that she's learned about herself that first year at Northington. As to career, she says, "I know what I'd like to do, but I don't think I could. I'd like to play basketball." Speaking of women's professional basketball in 1993, she adds "They don't have it here now, but they do in Europe." She also muses about other career possibilities: "Since my Dad works here, I kind of feel like I should come back here and work but I probably won't. I used to want to be a writer, but now I'm not so good at English."

At the end of tenth grade, Natasha still cannot think of anything she's learned about herself. She says she's good at track and it's been a better year than last since she's made new friends. She's also trying to decide which sport to play in college, basketball or soccer, and she has started receiving mail from colleges that want her to apply. She describes herself as "kind of quiet," especially in classes like math where things move very fast. If she has a question, she asks her girlfriend after class, rather than questioning the teacher.

In her junior year interview, Natasha finally has an answer to the "what have you learned about yourself" question: "I learned that if I work really hard, I can do well. It's the most busy I've been and my grades have been the best ever." As to career, she still wants "to do something with basketball. An athlete or a coach." She isn't getting any career guidance at Northington, and as for college, "I haven't thought about it as much as I should. Good academics and I want to play sports, so either a Division 1 or Division 3 school, so there'll be good athletics." In the summers she plays on a state basketball team that holds tournaments throughout the country; its primary goal is to get the players seen by Division 1 colleges.

Her father has helped a lot with the college selection process; "he made a list of colleges for me, and he's taken me to visit a couple: the University of Richmond, and William and Mary. He's in charge of that." When I ask about what her mother, a real estate agent, thinks about her going to college, Natasha replies, "She's open to whatever."

Natasha has two older brothers, one a junior at Williams College and the other training at Dartmouth for track while working as an assistant teacher in an Upward Bound program. "Both are into sports a lot. That's what got me into it. They help me a lot." At the end of her senior year, she tells me that one of the best things that happened that year was her brother's being drafted by an NFL team. She's considering following him to Williams but she's also been accepted at Middlebury College, which she says has the better basketball team. Eventually she chooses Williams.

Looking at her future, Natasha says, "I really don't know. I want to keep up with sports but maybe I'll have to get a job doing something else and keep sports on the side. I hope I fall in love with something in college." She used to like creative writing before she came to Northington, but she's "not good at the writing we have to do in English class." The creative writing class offered by the school "seemed too intimidating so I didn't take it." Although the nervous laughter is gone and she speaks with confidence, Natasha again tells me, "I'm kind of quiet. I'm not as personable as some of my friends."

Natasha is a fairly good student with grades generally in the B to B– range; she has taken four years of math through precalculus and four years of science including physics. Her SATs in the low to mid-500s are also average, and will probably put her somewhere in the lower part of her class at Williams, which is among the most selective colleges in the country (Barrons, 1995). The teachers she has found the most encouraging are an English teacher who was her soccer and basketball coach, and her ethics teacher, who "really makes you think." Taking ethics has made her think for the first time about "how privileged all these rich kids are and how much they complain even though they're so lucky to have things." Nonetheless, she says, Northington is much more diverse than the public high school she would have attended; she's made good friends and she'd come there again.

Although she seems less forceful to me than many of her peers, I have never seen Natasha on the playing field or the basketball court, where she may be quite aggressive. Her AWS score has been consistently high and is in fact a totally feminist 45 by the end of her senior year.

In college

At Williams, Natasha continues soccer, basketball, and track. She makes the varsity team in soccer but doesn't get to play in any games since she was a goalie and there is a senior goalie on the team; in basketball, she gets a lot of playing time on a varsity team she describes as very strong. To her own surprise, the academics go well during her first semester and she makes a 3.2 GPA. She particularly enjoys her psychology and history courses.

Her two brothers continue their interest in professional sports, one playing for a professional (NFL) football team and the other getting a graduate degree in athletic training and also trying out for an NFL team. Natasha would still like to have a career in sports herself, but she cannot figure out at this point what that would be.

Lynn

At Watson Hill

Lynn is much more verbal than Natasha; there are no awkward silences or nervous laughter. She speaks simply and directly. A day student on a partial scholarship to Watson Hill, Lynn feels that English and sports are her strengths. During ninth grade, she is closest to her soccer and softball coach, a woman who is "there when I need to talk to someone. She tells me that things don't always go right and I just have to stick at it." She has also made close friends, but thinks it's important to be "dependent on myself and not let someone else solve my problems." She likes being at a girls' school so she doesn't have to care how she looks: "everyone looks like they just woke up."

Although she entered Watson Hill wanting to be a marine biologist, Lynn decides after a year of ninth grade biology, that she wants to become a writer. "I loved watching documentaries about whales on TV, but then I took biology and I was ugh! I hate it." She takes a year of chemistry in tenth grade and then gives up on science entirely, making hers one of the weakest programs in science in my study. She gets no career guidance at Watson Hill, but "they do help me to write better." She is thinking about journalism as a career, and can see herself as an anchorwoman on television or working for a major newspaper, but she adds "College is where I'll find out."

Thinking about college at the end of junior year, Lynn explains, "The way for me to get into college is through softball, pitching. Colleges have already sent me stuff. I'm sort of ahead of everyone else. I've sent a videotape of me pitching to twenty-one colleges, and after July first, the coaches will start calling." She intends to look at Division 1, 2 and 3 colleges that have strong journalism majors, and will choose the school that offers her the most financial aid.

Her father, an accountant, "wanted a son and he had me so he's all gung-ho for sports." Her mother, who works in a school cafeteria, "wants me to stay in New England. She thinks I should continue with my writing. My father just cares about the sports." Most of the schools she is interested in are in the South. Lynn has an older sister who is studying nursing at St. Anselm College in New Hampshire, but she is not at all athletic. "I was the tomboy, I grew up with a mitt in my hand. She was the girl. My mother took care of that."

When I see her at the end of her senior year, Lynn tells me that she is going to St. Anselm. She was accepted to two more selective schools but they did not offer her any money; she was recruited by three other colleges as well, but St. Anselm's offered her the most financial aid of any of them. She's comfortable with her college choice and thinks having her sister there will be good. With SATs (mid-500s) and grades (Bs) just slightly lower than Natasha's, she is going to a considerably less selective school.

During her senior year, her closest relationship to an adult is again with her soccer and softball coach, this time a man "who is like a big brother, always there when I need him." Although she thinks she has received a fine education, she's not sure that she would come there again, or any girls' school. She's seen coeducational schools with better facilities and is concerned about how she and her classmates will relate to men in college. Unlike many of her classmates, her AWS score has declined (from a 40 in ninth grade to a 35 in twelfth grade); this is largely due to her expressing mild agreement or disagreement with statements about which she had previously indicated strong feelings.

In college

Although still planning to major in English, Lynn now plans to be a junior high school English teacher instead of a journalist; she will minor in education. She is finding her English classes enjoyable but difficult: "my grades are lower on my papers here than they were at Watson Hill, which I thought was impossible."

Lynn was recruited for the softball team as a pitcher, but dropped the team "because it was already taking up too much of my time to do school work and was leaving me very tired. I also didn't like the upperclassmen because they didn't make any effort to talk to us in the beginning of the season." She is planning to try out for the soccer team next year.

Lynn also admits that she "was intimidated by the level of play on the St. Anselm team. Everyone was so good, and Watson Hill's athletic program wasn't one of the finest. My stats at Watson Hill were awesome and everyone said I was a great pitcher, but most of the teams we played weren't that good. So St. Anselm was a huge test for me to see if I was the good pitcher that my coach, Watson Hill, and my father made me out to be. Seeing the other pitchers here made me feel like there was no point to my being here."

Since she quit softball, Lynn's relationship with her father has all but disappeared: "I barely talk to him at all." But, she says, "I am starting to throw again with my boyfriend, and maybe I will play summer softball. I miss the pitching. I don't think I could ever stop pitching or playing softball. I've done it way too long and worked too hard."

Roxanne

At Summerford

A day student on partial scholarship, Roxanne arrives at Summerford as a ranked tennis player. She has chosen Summerford because she wants a better education than she would have received at her local public high school and "this was the private school closest to my house." She didn't care about the single sex aspect of the school because "I don't particularly need an all-girls school. I was always outspoken anyway. But I'll still see guys outside of school."

Roxanne is a strong student academically and like the academic superstars, she talks of hard work and considerable pressure to achieve. The daughter of Polish immigrants, she says at the end of her first year at Summerford that she's learned "how different I am from other people, from everybody else." She began playing tennis at age eight: "I was flipping TV channels and Boris Becker was playing and I asked my dad, do you know how to play tennis? He said sure, but he had no clue. We had wooden rackets in the garage and went to the park and started hitting." By the end of ninth grade, she is ranked third in singles and first in doubles in New England.

Roxanne's father is a machinist and her mother is a seamstress. They came to this country in the late 1950s; she is not sure if either ever finished high school in Poland. Her older sister is a psychiatric nurse and "my mother says why don't you be a nurse? That's all she knows." Coming into contact with rich lawyers and doctors on the tennis circuit and seeing how they live, her father "is pushing for medicine." Her sister does serve as a role model in that "she looks forward to going in to work so much. I just really hope I can find something that I enjoy that much too." Roxanne had wanted to become a professional tennis player, but when "I went to the nationals, I saw how hard everyone worked and how good they all are, how hard it would be."

Leaning toward "sports sciences," Roxanne takes biology in ninth grade, and reports that "it's hard. My bio teacher is tough." Despite a B– in biology, she goes on to chemistry where "my chem teacher encourages us to think for ourselves more," and she achieves an A–. As a junior, she continues into physics, which "I really like and I love my teacher. I don't know what you do with physics though. Psychology also fascinates me, but my parents are pushing me into medicine." She continues onto AP Physics and calculus for her senior year. Nobody, not even her physics teacher who has her in class for two years, gives her any career guidance and she does not take advantage of Summerford's internship program. She spends her summers traveling around the country playing in national tournaments or training at her club in Boston, so there is no time for career exploration.

Roxanne and her father start looking at colleges over spring break of her junior year. As to what they are looking for, "I have to be compatible with the coach, and obviously I'm looking for a really good team. They have to offer a full scholarship. We went to Wake Forest and the coach spent five hours with me and treated me great, but I thought the school was too small." During fall of her senior year, Roxanne goes on college recruiting trips every weekend.

There are some serious problems that year: "I tore all the ligaments in my knee and had to have reconstructive knee surgery. I was busy with therapy and my dad goes and has a heart attack. He had five bypasses done, but he's doing okay now." On the other hand, these contacts with the world of medicine have increased Roxanne's interest in the field. "The knee surgery was fun, being wheeled down to the OR. And with my dad, I learned a lot. I noticed that not one resident, not one cardiologist, not one doctor that I saw was a woman."

She was accepted early at Yale University and now has "to go grovel to them for more money since my dad won't be working. The coach at Yale was wonderful. I called her about my knee and she brought me down and I met their head orthopedic and I met their head of physical trauma and they just took care of me for a whole day and walked me through what they had there." Until these recent contacts with the world of medicine, she had been less certain of what she wanted to do. "My education here wasn't steering me away from medicine but it wasn't gearing me toward it either. So the interest just leaves. AP Physics doesn't have much to do with medicine." Besides sports medicine, Roxanne is thinking about sports psychology: "I could read forever and ever on that. It really fascinates me."

She sees her strength as "dedication. If I really want to do something and do it well, I can do it perfectly." Although she has appreciated the dedication of her teachers and the close relationships she has had with them, she thinks the school "pushes the feminist stuff excessively. Personally, I don't agree with all the feminist stuff." When I ask her how her attitude fits in with her wanting to go into a field dominated by men, she muses, "I guess it *is* a little ironic."

About going to an all-girls' school, she says, "For girls who were quiet and needed to find a voice, it might have made a difference. But not for me. For those girls, college might be a shock though. Like, oh wow, men." Roxanne's AWS score, which was a 44 in ninth grade, has fallen to a 33 by the end of senior year. She is agreeing with statements like "Boys are naturally better at math than girls" and "Leadership in politics should be largely in the hands of men"— statements with which she strongly disagreed in earlier years.

In college

At Yale, Roxanne continues to play tennis. The members of the tennis team become her closest friends, "because we travel together and are together so much." She continues to be interested in psychology, but has lost her interest in medicine by the time she enters college. "I spoke to too many doctors who said that the way the health care system has changed, it isn't good to be in medicine any more." Consequently, despite her strong background in science and mathematics, astronomy is the only science or mathematics course that Roxanne takes during her first year at Yale.

Instead, she finds herself drawn to the humanities. "I'm even thinking of taking a course in Polish history. I'm getting really interested in things like that." She thinks she can help others through professions other than medicine, and is considering a career as either a lawyer or a psychologist.

Christine

At Egremont

Christine talks rapidly and with enthusiasm. At the end of ninth grade, she is pleased that she has "improved in soccer and picked up lacrosse much quicker than I thought." She is also on the varsity basketball team. She has made many good friends and likes that her teachers are so available and helpful. Her basketball coach, a male math teacher, "was so connected to us. You knew he cared about you. He cried along with us."

Christine has a twin, Andrea, who is also at Egremont (and also in the study—see chapter 6). "But I've learned that we're different. We're both good in soccer and basketball and both straight A students. But I'm more likely to express my feelings if someone hurts me, while she would just joke about it." Their mother has been a first grade teacher for thirty years and is recently divorced from their father, who has been "a jeweler, a policeman, a chicken farmer, a police dispatcher, and now he works in a factory." Neither parent is particularly athletic or interested in athletics. Christine just found sports fun in school and has kept at it, as has her sister.

She has always wanted to be a teacher, but being at Egremont "has opened my horizons. Now I'm thinking about teaching English as a foreign language and going to other countries. Maybe I'll get fluent in Spanish." As a sophomore, she tells me, "I've been thinking a lot about careers. I want to know what I want to do. I went on a whale watch, thinking maybe a naturalist. But I'm not doing as well in science and math and don't enjoy it as much as I used to. And I didn't feel that well on the boat." As a junior, she is thinking about having a double major in psychology and Spanish; as a senior, she says "Still psych and Spanish. But maybe sports psychology. Or sports medicine, although I'm not enjoying chemistry that much."

Her mother encourages her to achieve: "My mom always told me, if you're going to do anything, you go the whole nine yards. You be the leader in whatever you're going to be. If you go into business, don't be the secretary, be the president of the company." Her consistently high scores on the AWS (a 43 her senior year) reflect that she has absorbed this advice. Her father, on the other hand, "still says, 'you'd be such a good teacher.' He's still stuck on that." She has an older brother and two older sisters besides her twin. From one of her sisters, she's learned not to make the same mistake: "She had a kid in college and dropped out. Now she's gone back. I'm not going to do that!" Her brother, an architect and now a restaurant owner in Philadelphia, gives her "hope that I can really get out and adapt to new surroundings!"

Having made varsity basketball in ninth grade, she makes varsity lacrosse as a sophomore. "I'm good at defense in all my sports," she tells me. Her most encouraging teacher that year is her lacrosse coach, who is also her advisor and the wife of her basketball coach. In junior year, her basketball team wins the New England championship. "I got sick and missed the middle game, but I was there for the championship game. I went to the game sick." At the end of junior year, she is looking at Division 3 colleges where she can play lacrosse. As a senior, she is co-captain of both the basketball and lacrosse teams.

Christine was waitlisted at her first choice college and rejected by her second choice school. She decides to go to Muhlenberg College in Pennsylvania, where she can play soccer and lacrosse, and which has a good premed program, if she decides to take that route. "I want to see how it goes when I get there." She thinks her strengths are working with people, "a balance between leading and supporting them," something she thinks she's learned from being co-captain of her teams. Though a little burned out from all the work, she's loved Egremont for its diversity, for the leadership positions she's had, and for her friends, both male and female.

In college

At Muhlenberg, Christine made the soccer team, but then decided that she didn't like the coach and dropped off the team. "Time constraints were also an issue. I decided to concentrate only on lacrosse, and that's going really well."

Christine is considering physical therapy or athletic training as a career. She thought about sports medicine, but getting an M.D. would "take too much time." She is one of the few first year students in Anatomy and Physiology, which she describes as "a ridiculous amount of work and much harder than the science courses at Egremont. But the professor is awesome. He's very understanding and helpful too." Christine is finding Muhlenberg too small and not as diverse as Egremont and may look into transferring to the physical therapy program at Boston University or Pennsylvania State after sophomore year.

Reflections

Little research has been done on the high-achieving female athlete. The importance of the family in guidance and support of athletic talents has been demonstrated; families with strong sports backgrounds and a work ethic that promotes self-discipline and the satisfaction of accomplishment tend to help females develop their athletic talent (Wildenhaus, 1996). This is clearly illustrated in three of the four case studies in this chapter. With the exception of Christine, it is obvious that fathers have played a crucial role in the lives of these girls, coaching and advising them both in sports and college selection. Natasha, Lynn, and Roxanne never mention their mothers unless I ask specifically about them. When I ask Roxanne about this, she replies: "I'm definitely closer to my dad, but it wasn't totally because of tennis. I just think I'm more like my father, and tennis forced us to spend a lot of time together and get to know each other better."

Athletics can be protective for girls during adolescence in that they learn to see their bodies as functional rather than merely decorative. As Pipher (1994) has pointed out, athletic girls "have developed discipline in the pursuit of excellence. They have learned to win and lose, to cooperate, to handle stress and pressure. They are in a peer group that defines itself by athletic ability rather than popularity, drug or alcohol use, wealth, or appearance" (p. 267). Sports are a way that adolescent girls can feel competent and in control. In schools where girls' sports are seen as important as boys' sports, they can earn the respect of their classmates, male and female. Through sports, they can learn, as Christine did, how to balance teamwork and leadership. This may be an important lesson in terms of career achievement; almost all of the women listed among *Fortune 500*'s top executives reported that as girls they were active in team sports (Walker & Mehr, 1992).

Since historically playing sports has been essential to a boy's identity as a man but counter to a girl's development as a woman, girls may experience gender role conflicts with regard to sport. As early as first grade, girls perceive themselves as less athletic and less interested in sports than boys (Wildenhaus, 1996). The four girls in this chapter clearly have avoided the identification of athletics with masculinity, and do not seem to be finding a conflict between sports and being female. Indeed, Lynn spends time with her college boyfriend throwing a softball.

The greater emphasis on sports at the coeducational schools may have made it easier for Natasha and Christine to a find the "peer group" that Pipher suggests is so important. Over the four years of interviewing at the coed schools, 20 of the 22 girls (90%) named sports as one of the important things that made the year a good one, and 10 of these mentioned it consistently. At the girls' schools, 17 of the 25 girls (68%) named sports at least once, but only three did so repeatedly. Most of the girls mentioning sports at the girls' schools did so in ninth or tenth grade, so that by senior year, there were only 5 out of 25 who thought it was worthy of mention.

Roxanne and Lynn, who have attended girls' schools, seem somewhat disillusioned about the single sex experience, and are among the very few in the study whose AWS scores fell during the four years of high school. Perhaps they would have been happier at schools like Northington and Egremont where they might have found more highly athletic women like themselves. At the coeducational schools, even the girls like Charlie or Kasmira, who did not define themselves as athletes, mentioned sports often as one of the ways they had learned to feel good about themselves. Additionally, the girls at Northington and Egremont mentioned that they felt respected and supported as athletes by the *boys* at their schools, especially if their teams were having a successful season.

Is all this emphasis on athletics at coeducational schools a positive thing? Some like Riordan (1990) might argue that this accentuates the "adolescent subculture" and detracts from the intellectual nature of the school. Certainly, Sage (chapter 4) did not find many of her Northington classmates interested in intellectual matters, and my study indicates a higher academic intensity at the girls' schools. On the other hand, it does seem that the argument that at coeducational schools, "the role models are successful male athletes and scholars, homecoming queens and cheerleaders" (Riordan, 1990, p. 149) does not hold up. Girls like Natasha and Christine are respected as successful female athletes at these schools, and girls like Charlie and Andrea (chapter 6) are respected for being both athletes and scholars.

In applying to college, all four girls were confident of their athletic abilities, although Lynn and Christine found that they were not the key to getting into the colleges of their choice. Since arriving at college, both Lynn and Christine have been disappointed by either their coaches or their teammates and cut back on their participation in sports. Lynn also found that she was not the "star" athlete that she thought she was. Natasha and Roxanne, on the other hand, are still finding their sports a source of great satisfaction and friendship.

In terms of careers, all four have mentioned at least once trying to find an occupation that would make use of their athletic abilities. Yet, as Csikszentmihalyi, Rathmunde, and Whalen (1997) have pointed out, athletic talent does not translate easily into an adult occupation in the minds of middle class adolescents. Both Christine and Roxanne have thought about sports psychology and sports medicine; Christine's plans to go into physical therapy and Roxanne's ideas about psychology may still be manifestations of this. Lynn, when she was still thinking about journalism, had mentioned being a sportscaster. If she becomes a teacher, coaching may become a facet of her life, although she herself has not made this explicit. Natasha would very much like to make a career in sports, but is unsure how to do it, despite the fact that her brothers seem to be following professional sports career paths. Perhaps with the emergence of professional women's basketball in this country, she can find a way.

Table 5.1 Career Aspirations of Female Athletes in the Study

Student	School	Start of 9th grade	End of 12th grade	End,1st yr of college
Roxanne	Summerford	Undecided	Sports medicine	Psycholgst or lawyer
Lynn	Watson Hill	Biologist	Journalist	Teacher
Natasha	Northington	Writer	Athlete	Sports??
Christine	Egremont	Teacher	Sports psychologist	Physical therapist

Chapter Six

The Scientists

As mentioned in chapter 3, the career of medicine is the most visible of the careers that involve science, and thus it is not surprising that girls who are good at science name "doctor" as a career choice most often. They see it as a high status profession that earns large monetary rewards and helps people at the same time. In my original survey in the fall of 1992, 24% of the 114 ninth graders surveyed wrote in "doctor" as a career choice, especially at the girls' schools (30% at the girls' schools and 16% at the coeducational schools). This is not uncommon; Dick and Rallis (1991) found a similar proportion of young women aspiring to careers in medicine in high schools in Rhode Island.

In the study sample of 56, there were 10 girls who initially wanted to be doctors (7 at the girls' schools and 3 at the coeducational schools). By the end of 12th grade, there were nine girls who wanted to be doctors, but the distribution had changed, with five at the girls' schools and four at the coeducational schools.

The other science-related careers that girls have named are veterinarian, physical therapist, pharmacist, medical researcher, and marine biologist. Few of them seem to know about or consider scientific occupations that are not among the "helping professions."

The girls considered in this chapter fall somewhere below the scholastic superstars of chapter 3, both in academic grades and standardized test scores, although two, Anne and Andrea, come close to their superstar classmates.

Anne

At Summerford

Anne enters Summerford thinking that she might become a lawyer. In ninth grade, she describes herself as "really pushy and competitive," although in her interview with me she speaks quite softly and can find nothing to say when I ask her what she's good at.

In her previous school, a private K–9 coeducational day school, she had to "compete to get attention" but she is trying to tone down her competitiveness at Summerford. Anne says that she would have preferred a coed school, but figures that "it's for only four years" and she can get a good education. She is a strong student but takes no science in ninth grade.

As a sophomore, Anne says she's enjoying herself more and finding her classes less difficult. When I ask her what she's good at, she replies "My art has developed a long way and my science too. Biology class can be boring, but I've gotten interested in the topic." Speaking about her future, she says, "I've always been ambitious, but now I'm really interested in science research. Not being a doctor though." In eleventh grade, she changes her mind: "I'm leaning towards biology, thinking about being a doctor. That's one of the few things I could be happy doing. I could never sit at a desk all day. I don't like chemistry and physics though. I actually like biology and math." In her first three years at Summerford, Anne does not mention one teacher that she finds especially encouraging: "They're all good but there's no one special."

Anne's father is a lawyer and her mother does "something with computers. I've tried to understand it but I don't." When Anne is in ninth grade, her mother works for a local company, but by the end of 10th grade, she has become a systems manager for a company outside of Boston, a switch that requires her to commute three hours a day. By Anne's junior year, her mother is back working locally, but her parents are considering a move so her mother can get a better job. Anne explains: "If they moved, my Dad would just do something else like work for a bank. She makes more money than he does." Although she has a mother who is clearly a career woman, Anne scores consistently low on the AWS, compared to many of her classmates. Several times she agrees with the statement that "Boys are better at math than girls," and also with "It looks ridiculous for a woman to run a locomotive or a man to sew."

Anne is their only child and describes herself as "independent and introverted, although people who meet me think I'm outgoing. I'm not a people person though. I'm quiet, happy to stay home in my little hole." Her parents "think I'm like some genius. They really want me to go to Williams, but the more they push me, the more I back away from it." She says she wants a college with happy students, small classes, and a "lively social scene, or else I'll just study all the time." Her SATs are high (600s and 700s) and her grades are mostly As (in chemistry and precalculus) and Bs.

She takes four AP classes her senior year and finds the year stressful. Rejected at her first choice, Duke, Anne decides to go to Emory, because she likes the feel of the campus and the cosmopolitan atmosphere. Her plans are to major in neuroscience and behavioral biology, a new program at Emory, in which several medical school faculty teach. She still intends to go to medical school and can picture herself in a hospital or private practice. She describes herself as "very driven and overly competitive." Her AP biology teacher has been very challenging this year and that "helps me flourish." Because she omitted science in ninth grade, she graduates with three years of science, which does not include physics; she does, however, take AP calculus and AP biology and wins a biology prize at graduation.

In college

Anne heads directly into her science and math courses, taking chemistry, honors biology, and calculus her first year at Emory, and getting As in all of them. Although she enjoys the science courses, she says that "the math is horrible." Her chemistry class is a large lecture of over 200 students, but the honors biology section is both smaller and "surprisingly female, with twelve women and six men."

Anne finds Emory "more cliquey, and more segregated by class and race" than Summerford. The fraternity/sorority system "is a big deal" and she has joined a sorority. She thinks that not having boys in her class in high school "had no effect either way, good or bad" and says that having males in her classes in college is "pretty much the same" as not having them in class.

She feels that she has changed a lot this year, becoming "more open, more fun, and better able to deal with people." Her plans to go to medical school are still firmly in place.

Betsy

At Watson Hill

Betsy comes to Watson Hill because her mother, a social worker, thought she should attend an all-girls school, although she adds, "I probably would have thought of it on my own. I've been reading studies about girls' education." In both ninth and tenth grade, she can name nothing that she is good at and no teacher in particular that has encouraged her; "they all push you to do your best." Although she has said she wanted to major in science and be a doctor since the start of ninth grade, Betsy takes no science her first year at Watson Hill.

She speaks more readily at the end of junior year; a leadership position as a proctor has boosted her confidence, she says. She still wants to be a doctor and to major in psychobiology. She's not sure where the desire to go into medicine came from, "except I have a real fear of doctors. I worked in Yale Children's Hospital this past summer and I'd like to be a pediatrician." She doesn't discuss her goals with her teachers so they have no way of knowing that she wants to be a doctor. Her grades in math are Cs and her science grades are Bs and Cs, so she receives no special encouragement from her math or science teachers.

Her parents, on the other hand, "have a lot of influence. They encourage me to be a doctor but to keep other options open too." Her parents are also encouraging her to go to a women's college, "especially if I'm preparing for medical school." Betsy's father, a minister, "just loved Mount Holyoke" when they went to visit, but her mother preferred Smith. Betsy was "not too happy with the idea of a women's college at first," but has concluded that it won't be "too bad because of the five college consortium" (which includes Mount Holyoke, Smith, Amherst, and Hampshire colleges, as well as the University of Massachusetts).

Betsy applies early decision to Mount Holyoke and is accepted. "I just felt comfortable there. I really liked it, and tried not to make single sex an issue." She still wants to be a doctor but is "getting scared about it. I don't know if I want all that pressure, not just in school." She spent another summer at Yale Children's Hospital and really likes "helping people. I love little kids." She thinks that being at Watson Hill has made her more confident and clarified her interests. Her strength, she says, is "determination," and she cites her AP calculus class as an example. She graduates with three years of science (biology, chemistry, and physics) and four years of math.

In college

Betsy is the only student in my study who has gone from an all-girls school to a women's college. For her, the transition has been easy. "Maybe the hardest adjustment was being in such a similar environment but not having my old friends here with me." She is planning to take some courses at either Amherst College or the

University of Massachusetts in the next two years to "be sure I get a sense of what the coeducational world is like."

Lecture classes of fifty students seem huge to her, "but my friends at big universities just laugh when I say that." Not used to lecture classes, Betsy finds that "I'm so busy taking notes that I don't have time to think of any questions to ask. There are some people that never stop asking questions. The labs and discussion groups are much smaller so I get to ask my questions then."

She has taken biology courses both semesters and earned grades in the A–/B+ range. The first course was organized around various topics— "I can tell you everything about squid!"—and the second is a course in developmental biology. Betsy has found both courses challenging and enjoyable; she also loves her psychology course. Planning to major in neuroscience, she definitely wants "to do something in medicine." If she becomes a doctor, her field will be pediatrics, because "I love kids and want to make them less fearful of doctors and hospitals."

She is also considering "child psychology in a health care environment or being a physician's assistant." Betsy admits, "I definitely have my fears about medical school. Initially it's: can I get in? But once I'm in, then I worry about it being too much pressure and too much time. I don't want it to jeopardize getting married and having children."

Eliza

At Watson Hill

Eliza wants to be a veterinarian from the start of ninth grade, when she enters Watson Hill. She is shy and soft-spoken, and tells me that she has been homesick for much of the year. Yet she has many positive things to say about the year: she is really enjoying sports for the first time and loving both her math and biology courses. She calls her algebra and biology teachers, both females, especially encouraging.

Eliza is from Virginia and has done considerable moving around during her first fourteen years. "I was born in Texas, then we moved to North Carolina, then Minnesota, then Belgium, and South Carolina, then Georgia, and now Virginia." The moves were necessitated by her father's position with a large multinational corporation; he has recently quit and started his own small business in

Virginia. Eliza's mother, who hasn't worked until recently, is now vice president of the company and does the computer work while "my father travels and deals with customers." There are three younger siblings, two boys and a girl, back home.

At the end of tenth grade, Eliza tells me that she is more outgoing and open and has recently been elected a proctor for next year. Her chemistry teacher has been encouraging and she continues to want veterinary medicine as a career; however, she receives a C in chemistry, and in junior year, the only science course that she takes is a one trimester course in astronomy. When I question her about career, she still wants to be a veterinarian because she would like to "help animals and their families. My dog died of leukemia and I know how that feels. Also, over the summer I worked with a horse trainer and loved that." As for her teachers, she feels that "they're pointing me towards English. I can do English but I don't enjoy it. I really liked astronomy."

For college, Eliza is looking at several women's colleges near her home (Sweet Briar, Randolph-Macon, and Hollins) and wants "a small liberal arts college with a core curriculum. My dad suggested that." Her parents would like her to go to the University of Virginia so she would be closer to home; her mother now works at the university since her father closed his business. Both parents think "it's okay for me to be a vet." At the end of eleventh grade, Eliza is elected head of the school for her senior year.

When I see her at the end of twelfth grade, Eliza has decided to attend Virginia Tech. "It was a tough decision between Virginia Tech and Sweet Briar. But Sweet Briar was too small and all women, and I think I need a change, though the temptation was to go to Sweet Briar. It was such a safe, close environment. But Virginia Tech will challenge me to reach new limits." She still wants to be a veterinarian, "but if I change my mind, they have everything there. I can go into teaching or arts and sciences."

Eliza has scored low on the AWS survey throughout her years at Watson Hill, consistently agreeing with statements like, "There are many jobs in which a man should be given preference over women in being hired or promoted" and "The father should have greater authority in the household than the mother." Yet she tells me that her mother has quit her job at the University of Virginia "because of sexism. They wouldn't let her do what she was good at." Her mother is now "doing newsletters and teaching adult education courses in computer." Her father has recently opened a ballpark outside of Charlottesville.

Explaining her desire to be a veterinarian, Eliza says: "We always had animals at home. Over the summer we adopted an abused horse. It had a wound over one eye and it was wild and neglected. There's such a difference now. Working with her made me see how much I really want to do this." When I ask why she didn't take more science at Watson Hill, she replies, "I don't know. Mostly scheduling problems, I guess." She finishes the year with a B in physics, graduating with four years of math through precalculus and three and one-third years of science (biology, chemistry and physics, plus a trimester of astronomy).

In college

The transition to Virginia Tech is a difficult one for Eliza. "The first semester blew me out of the water, to say the least. I was definitely not ready for the classes of 500 or so, or the teachers that don't know your name. It was hard to realize that no one really does care if you do well or if you fail out, and no one pushes you to succeed and go that extra mile, as they did at Watson Hill."

Eliza signs up for an ambitious course load during the fall semester: mathematics for engineers, biology, biology lab, and entomology, as well as courses in religion and political science. "The smaller classes I did very well in, with an A in religion and Bs in math and biology lab. The larger classes I did not fare as well. I got Cs in biology, entomology, and political science." Exempt from English first semester, Eliza takes an English course in the spring and finds that she is "doing well and loving it."

Her desire to be a veterinarian is gone. "I have discovered I hate science. I took bio last semester and hated it and I am taking Intro to Animal and Poultry Science this semester and hate it also. I am thinking of majoring in psych and minoring in English. One thing that I learned, and learned well, at Watson Hill was how to write." She is thinking of going to business school after she graduates from college. "That way I can major in something I like here and not worry about getting a job."

When I ask her to explain her newfound hatred of science, Eliza replies, "Biology was boring, too factual. It was a huge class and there was none of the personal contact or discussion that I was used to from Watson Hill." When Eliza did go to see the (female) biology professor for help, "She didn't have much patience. She answered my questions and that was it. There were so many students waiting in line to see her that she couldn't have given me any more time, I guess."

Having men in class was "a big shock, for maybe a week, then I adjusted." She is glad that she went to Watson Hill because "of the friends I made and the teachers I had. Sometimes I wish that I had gone to a women's college, for the close-knit community and the high expectations, but I'm glad to be here at this stage in my life. Change is good, I've found, even if it's hard."

Andrea

At Egremont

Andrea is the twin sister of Christine, the athlete from Egremont discussed in the previous chapter. Like Christine, Andrea loves sports and mentions them every year; her grades and SATs are slightly higher than her twin's, and indeed she comes close to being a scholastic superstar. But Andrea is one of the girls who has been interested in the sciences throughout this study and thus is considered here.

Like several of her classmates, Andrea speaks directly, decisively and rapidly. As a ninth grader, Andrea makes the crew team as well as varsity soccer and basketball teams. She feels "inspired" by her female geometry teacher as well as by her basketball and crew coaches, both males. Her first year at Egremont, she says, has broadened her a lot "about different people, different situations and backgrounds. I was sheltered and close-minded when I came here." At the start of ninth grade, she is undecided about a career, but by the end of the year, she is thinking about a major in marine biology and a career as a biologist, aspirations that persist through her years at Egremont.

In tenth grade, she speaks, much like the academic superstars, about "learning about my limits, how far I need to push myself to do my best." Her basketball coach, now also her algebra teacher, is again her inspiration: "Everyone wants to impress him, to make him proud of you." Unfortunately, the teacher of her honors biology class, an older male, is the kind of teacher who "makes you feel dumb. When you ask a question, he gives you this look." (This is the same teacher to whom Kerry alludes in chapter 3, who doesn't like having girls at Egremont.) Thinking about career, Andrea says she is looking for "something that will challenge me every day," and continues to write marine biology as her career goal.

As a junior, Andrea's team wins the New England basketball championship and Andrea is given an award for contributing the most to the spirit of the team. She continues to speak of pushing herself harder in both academics and sports. As for marine biology, she has been on several whale watches and really likes whales. There are several teachers at Egremont that are "really into it and when they tell you about their experiences, it makes you want to do it too."

Looking ahead to college, Andrea sees herself majoring in biology or animal behavior, and playing Division 3 sports. Her father, who has had many jobs but is currently laid off, wants her to go to school close to home and to go somewhere that she can get considerable financial aid. Her mother, a first grade teacher recently divorced, tells her to "find out where you want to go, then worry about the money. They're both excited that I want to do science though. They expect I'll be happy and do well whatever."

Andrea applies and is accepted to Brown University via the early action option. She is looking forward to being on the crew team there and says that Brown has "an atmosphere that's great for learning." A strong feminist like her sister, Andrea says that her strength is "I work hard. I want to do well, and I'll work hard and get it done."

During senior year, Andrea takes a class in marine mammals, and as a result of a spring trip to Bermuda, she concludes that research "wouldn't agree with me. But I definitely like science." She's taken four and a half years, including physics, and math through calculus. "Science is funny because I have good years and bad years. It varies with the teacher a lot." She's liked her (male) chemistry teacher and her marine biology teacher, of whom she says, "She's a role model that I might follow, although I don't know if I want to teach. She's shown me all these things you can do to help out the environment or work with animals."

In college

Andrea continues her interest in science, taking calculus, biology, and oceanography during her first year at Brown. Although the classes are a lot bigger than the ones at Egremont, she finds the TAs are helpful, and she especially enjoys the oceanography class. She is planning to "major in aquatic biology, and become a marine biologist, although teaching would be a second choice." She's obtained a summer job in Wood's Hole working with horseshoe crabs in the lab of a commercial company there.

Andrea's plans include going to Australia in the fall of her junior year and taking courses at a university in Queensland. "I want to study the Great Barrier Reef. It would be good for me study-wise and to grow up, to be so far away." She also thinks it would be good to spend some time apart from her boyfriend, whom she dated at Egremont and who is also at Brown. "We're considering getting married and time apart would be good for the relationship." They have also talked about how their lives together might go: "He's in computer science so he's probably going to get a job on the West Coast after graduation. I would go to grad school there. We'd get married before or after we get jobs. I know I want my own job, my own everything, and I know I can't do much in biology with only a bachelor's degree."

Although Andrea tried keeping up her rowing at Brown, she decided that she didn't enjoy it anymore and stopped. "Then I tried water polo and I liked it a lot, and now I'm on the team. I'm not too bad, but I still have so much to learn. Water polo is really hard. I've never played a water sport before and the other girls on the team have done swimming as a sport before. Just another challenge for myself!"

Leah

At Egremont

Leah comes to Egremont from Texas; she finds the people very different from those she's known, especially in their frequent use of sarcasm. She begins ninth grade thinking of being a math major and an actuary, but by the end of the year, she is undecided about major and career. "I'm not as good in math and science as I thought. School was easier in Texas. The way they teach here is so confusing, I'm completely lost." She does have success with her flute and with choral singing and says, "I might look into the arts instead of math and science."

At the end of tenth grade, she is feeling better about herself and about Egremont. "I felt last year that it was a mistake to come, but now I've learned how to study and the future is brighter. There are more possibilities." Grades that were mostly Cs in ninth grade have risen to mostly Bs, and Leah is considering a math major once again. She describes herself as "very domineering—like in relationships and sports. But I don't use it to my advantage. It's often bad timing."

Leah's father is a cardiologist in a town two hours from Dallas; her mother, who does various volunteer activities, is president of the women's medical auxiliary one year and president of the women's symphony league another year. She also has an older brother in law school and a younger brother who will be starting prep school in Boston the following year. Her parents "would like me to go to Harvard or Princeton, but they realize now that I won't be able to get in." Her mother would like her to return to Texas to go to college, "but I'm leaning towards New England." She hopes to find a college where people are open-minded, where "they don't close people off because of race," as they did in Texas.

As a junior, Leah is considering math or science as a college major and considering research, "maybe medical research although I'm kind of iffy about the ethical questions about genetic engineering. There are too many moral questions, so maybe I'll help find a cure for disease." She gets no guidance from her teachers because they don't know of her interest. Her father thinks medical research is fine and is helping her find a summer job at the hospital near her home. (She does not find a job though.) Her mother, she says, "has no opinion."

Leah applies to ten colleges. She is rejected at Wellesley, her first choice, and chooses Smith College over Southern Methodist University. "I'm not too excited about a women's college, but I know I'll get an excellent education there." When I point out that Wellesley too was a women's college, she explains that she liked its proximity to Boston and is worried that at Smith she'll have "no social life. I'm not an outgoing person." Her AWS score, which started out low, has risen to a 44 by the end of her four years at Egremont. She thinks that the best thing about Egremont for her was "being away from my parents," but she thinks she might have gotten into more colleges if she'd stayed at home.

Leah has taken four years of science courses, including physics, and math through calculus. In addition, she has done an independent study project on the Ebola virus, which involved working with two science teachers, and a lot of work on the Internet, including the homepages of the World Health Organization and the Center for Disease Control. At the end of the year, she will give a presentation to the school and write a thirty page paper on what she has learned. The independent study was her idea: "I read a few books and got an interest in emerging virus diseases."

In college

Leah is very happy at Smith, although she does miss having males around. "I'm amazed how many people here are just like me. At Egremont, everyone said I was too anal and they would tease me about it. Here people are more anal than I am!"

She says that her "science courses make more sense to me. At Egremont, it was just memorize this. Now I'm told to understand it. Everything makes sense if I put in the time." She has taken a heavy load including biology, chemistry, and calculus. "I *love* biology more than I ever have." She is having some difficulty with calculus, "but the professor helps me every day before class." About chemistry, Leah says, "I think they are trying to weed people out, but that's motivation for me to work harder."

Although she worries about getting high enough grades to get into medical school, she is certain that she wants to do it. "I walked around with my father at work this past January and I said, this is what I want to do. I love it. It's awesome. I saw some interesting things in the operating room and I think I can face anything now." She also met a female surgeon who is a role model to her: "I'd like to be a surgeon. I can see myself cutting rather than medicating. I want to see results. This woman was a surgeon and she had two kids, was married to a neurosurgeon, and was doing fine."

Leah has decided that she definitely wants to be a doctor, not a researcher. "At Egremont, they told me I wasn't a people person, so I should do research, not practice. Now, here, I'm very much a people person and I want to go into patient care."

Elizabeth

At Northington

Elizabeth prefers that I not tape her for the first two years that I interview her. She has come to Northington because her family has been friends with Charlie's (chapter 3) family since they were both babies; "I've wanted to come here since I was little." Her father is deceased, and her mother, the comptroller of a law firm, lives in a nearby town. The rest of her family—aunts and uncles—live in Montreal. Although she's never done much with sports before, Elizabeth has found that she's "not that bad" and her volleyball coach has given her a lot of confidence, "in volleyball and in general." When she entered Northington, she was thinking about math or science as a college major, and law or architecture as a career. By the end of ninth grade, she is undecided about a major and leaning more toward law.

At the end of 10th grade, Elizabeth is getting ready to do "School Year Abroad" in France, which she attributes to the encouragement of her French teacher. She says she's grown in many ways and "I can accomplish what I set my mind to. There's nothing I can't do if I try." Elizabeth has decided to go into science, although she hasn't liked chemistry as much as biology. She is an A student in math and gets Bs in her science courses. She is able to take math in France, but not science, so she graduates from Northington with biology, chemistry, and physics and four years of math through precalculus.

Although her junior year in France was "fabulous! absolutely amazing," Elizabeth has a difficult senior year: "I tore my ACL ligament in September, but they didn't find out it was that until February and I didn't have surgery until March. My mom was diagnosed with cancer and had lung surgery too." Her injury has convinced her "never to go on a soccer field again. I'm not good at sports and I just don't care about them." She thinks that Northington is "too sports-oriented. I don't like that." She feels that the teachers "all love the jocks. The sports awards are more important than how you do academically."

Nonetheless, the year was good academically and at the time of my visit she is choosing between Brandeis and McGill universities. About Brandeis, she says "Students all seem to love it there. They have huge smiles on their faces, so how could you go wrong? You get the feeling, I belong here, I need to go here." She needs full financial aid to attend, and although she was offered "lots of financial aid, I went back and begged for more."

Although McGill has the attraction of being near her family in Montreal, Elizabeth gets the money from Brandeis and decides to go there. Family is clearly important to her, and she tells me that one of the best things about France, was that the French family with whom she stayed "became actual family. I had a real father and mother and brother and sister. That was really neat for me because at home, I only have my mom." For someone considering the sciences, Elizabeth's AWS scores have been consistently low, most often a 34. She continually agrees that the father should have more authority in the home than the mother and thinks that women should not have to share expenses with their dates.

At the end of senior year, Elizabeth is "still leaning toward medicine, but I don't have enough science credits to go directly into premed, so I might start with a major in French while getting science credits." She says she likes the idea of helping people and is really interested in the biological sciences. "Now I'm taking physics and I hate it. But no other courses interest me. I don't like English or history. Science and math are my strong points. I'm good at math without trying." Elizabeth also mentions that her father was an engineer, so "I might try out engineering." When I point out that engineering might involve a lot of physics, she replies, "Hmmm, yeah."

In college

Adjusting to Brandeis is difficult for Elizabeth. "The classes seemed huge and the teachers don't care about you." She is taking chemistry and calculus and getting Bs and Cs in them. "The work is difficult and the competition is really cutthroat. About 400 students enter wanting to be premed and only about 80 graduate as premeds so there's a lot of pressure." She has hated calculus and thought "the chem was okay."

The courses she has enjoyed have been French and a freshman seminar on detective fiction, as well as a course in emergency medical technology. "EMT is really cool. I love it. I meet a lot of great people that are interested in the same things that I am. Plus the subject is really interesting." Elizabeth is still committed to medicine: "I have a deep interest and know I want to be a doctor. I have to work hard, but I'll get there."

Reflections

While in high school, most of the girls listed in Table 6.1 said they were "really interested in biology" but expressed a dislike for physics and often for chemistry as well (the exceptions being Roxanne and Charlie, who took two years of physics and chemistry respectively). Many aspired to careers in medicine or biology because they wanted to help people or animals or the environment. Only a few talked about the "wonder" of biology; Jane's expression of "how intricate and how simple" life is (chapter 3) is one of the few examples of this. Leah's pursuit of an independent study on emerging viruses after reading a few books on her own reflects her fascination with a part of biology.

Some of these girls also pursued science activities outside of the classroom while in high school. Mimi has done summer programs at several universities; Jane, Charlie, and Betsy have worked in hospitals over the summers. Jane and Andrea have gone on special trips to study marine biology, and Eliza has worked with horses over two summer vacations. These are the girls that tend to be the "persisters" throughout high school.

As a former science teacher myself, I am dismayed at how little guidance these girls received from their science teachers. Why did no one mention engineering to Roxanne when she expressed enough interest in physics to take two years of it? Why did Eliza, who wants to be a veterinarian, feel that Watson Hill was pushing her toward English and why did "scheduling problems" stand in the way of her taking four years of science? And what were the mathematics teachers doing? Not one girl ever mentioned a mathematics-related career, not even the girls who found mathematics easy and enjoyable. Some of the girls (Anne, Eliza, and Andrea) did mention their science or mathematics teachers as being especially encouraging or challenging, and one (Andrea) saw her marine biology teacher as a role model. On the other hand, Andrea and her classmates also had to persevere in science despite a male biology teacher who made them "feel dumb."

Csikszentmihalyi et al. (1997), in their study of talented teenagers, notes that one of the problems for adolescents talented in math and science is that although they perceive the usefulness of their math and science courses in the long run, they seldom find the pure joy in doing these subjects that students talented in the arts or athletics do. Practicing mathematicians and scientists often talk ecstatically of their experiences of discovery; seldom, however, is this sense of joy and wonder communicated by teachers to their adolescent students. College courses in the sciences are perceived as especially "tough" and demanding. For those girls whose commitment to science is not that strong, who have never experienced the "wonder" and who are additionally not well prepared by their high schools for the competition of college classes, persisting in science in college is very unlikely.

Hilton and Lee (1988) found that interest in math/science is not fixed in early high school, with almost as many students moving into the pipeline as out between tenth and twelfth grade; the biggest loss in potential science majors occurred at the high school to college transition. This study corroborates their finding, with girls like Anne,

Elizabeth, Andrea, and Roxanne finding an interest in science during sophomore year or later, but with almost half of the students changing their minds during the first year of college. Defectors are not replaced, as females not originally planning to major in math or science seldom move into the pipeline (Hoffer, 1993). Certainly, none of the girls in my study who were not interested in science in high school have evinced any interest in it after a year of college.

Why do young women with strong math/science ability give up on science? Henderson and Dweck (1990) have shown that bright girls, in particular, may view ordinary difficulties in math and science as indicating that they lack ability. They begin to doubt that they can do well in these subject areas and focus their energies on subjects that allow them to apply skills they have already mastered, making it easier for them to maintain confidence in their abilities. Henderson and Dweck report an experiment showing that girls did well on a task if there was no confusion at the start, but were severely debilitated by initial confusion; the brightest girls were the most debilitated.

Persistence in science majors in college, especially among women, has been widely studied for the past decade. Women who disagreed with the assertion that men do better at math and science were more likely to complete their science courses (Boli, Allen, & Payne, 1985). Anne's agreement that "Boys are naturally better at math than girls" on both the 1994 and 1995 AWS surveys calls her persistence into question, but she appears to be having no difficulty at this point in her career with either math or science; her lack of physics in high school may be problematic as well, but perhaps she will have built up enough momentum through her successes in math/science to surmount this obstacle when she comes to it.

Civian (1996) found that the best predictors of who persisted in science were high SAT-math scores and good grades in college math/science courses. On the basis of SAT-math scores, one would have expected Charlie, Edith, and Leah to be the persisters, and perhaps Roxanne and Anne as well, but among this group, only Anne, Edith, and Leah have persisted. Persistence in a math/science major in college has also been shown to be influenced by the number of math and science courses taken in high school (Ethington & Wolfle, 1988; Ware & Lee, 1988; Maple & Stage, 1991) with interest in science as a high school sophomore being a strong predictor of a science major in college (Ethington & Wolfle, 1988; Maple & Stage, 1991). Again, the defection of Charlie runs counter to what one would predict.

Students majoring in male-dominated fields endorse less traditional sex roles attitudes (Ruble, Cohen, & Ruble, 1984; Ware &

Lee, 1988). Komarovsky (1985) also found that "career shifters," those that gave up on their intended fields early on in college, tended to have more traditional attitudes to gender roles. The low scores of Anne (37), Elizabeth (34), Roxanne (33), Eliza (35), and Lindsay (36) on the AWS survey would predict that they would not persevere in science, and indeed the last three have not.

Parental support for an occupation in the sciences is closely tied to persevering in this field; having a close relative in the chosen occupation is often helpful (Komarovsky, 1985). Leah and Jane both have fathers who are physicians and who introduce them to others in the profession, and Mimi's mother, while not a doctor, has found many opportunities for Mimi to explore the world of medicine. Betsy's parents are also strongly behind her; I am not sure if her work at Yale Children's Hospital was in some way arranged by one of them. I have not heard of such strong support from the others. It is noteworthy that while Jane, Charlie, and Roxanne all expressed concerns about the role of the physician in today's health care system, Charlie and Roxanne cited this concern as a reason for dropping out of medicine. Jane, on the other hand, also sees "how much my father loves what he does," and she perseveres.

A survey of senior women at both a small women's college (Mount Holyoke) and a large coeducational university (University of Michigan) found very little difference in the rate of persistence in science majors; the main difference was in how they attributed their persistence, with the Mount Holyoke women more likely to attribute their continuing interest to faculty, while the University of Michigan women said it was *despite* the courses (Thomas, 1994). In the present study, the two girls at the women's colleges are both persisters, although Betsy is expressing some doubts about her own ambition. The large universities have shown more attrition: Charlie's disillusionment with science is related to the large impersonal nature of her classes, as is Eliza's. Certainly, Leah's experience (at Smith College) with her math professor who gives her help every day before class is very different from Eliza's experience of her biology professor (at Virginia Tech) who barely had time or patience to answer her questions. Anne and Elizabeth are persisting despite the size and competitiveness of their university science classes.

Enjoyment of a science course during the first year of college is an important factor in deciding to major in science (Ware & Steckler, 1983), so the fact that many of the persisters (Jane, Anne, Betsy, Leah) in this study list biology as a course they enjoyed this year would seem to indicate that they will continue in this field. Women doing poorly in a first science course are more likely than men to attribute this to their own inadequacy (Ware & Steckler, 1983). I have not heard this attribution in the girls in this study; more often they have attributed their grades to a loss of interest or to the way the course was taught. The Cs that Eliza received in biology, for example, were attributed to her discovering that "I hate science" and that "Biology was boring, too factual." Nonpersistent females tend to see their values as incongruent with those of science, whereas persisters see congruence in values (Worthley, 1992). Here the switch from science to fields like psychology among some of these girls (Eliza, Roxanne, perhaps Betsy) may signal a conflict of values; Roxanne seems to say this explicitly.

Of the girls' school alumnae, four out of the original seven have persisted in their interest in science across the high school to college transition. Among the coeducational school alumnae, three out of seven have persisted. This would not appear to be a significant difference. Individual values of the girls themselves, parental support, and the nature of their first science course experiences would seem to be more relevant than the type of school from which they came.

Table 6.1 Career Aspirations of
Science-Oriented Students in the Study

Student	School	Start of 9th grade	End of 12th grade	End,1st yr of college
Jane	Summerford	Doctor	Doctor	Doctor
Mimi	Summerford	Doctor	Doctor	Doctor
Roxanne	Summerford	Undecided	Sports medicine	Psycholgst or lawyer
Anne	Summerford	Lawyer	Doctor	Doctor
Edith	Watson Hill	Undecided	Biologist?	Biologist?
Eliza	Watson Hill	Veterinarian	Veterinarian	Business
Betsy	Watson Hill	Doctor	Doctor	Doctor or psycholgst
Charlie	Northington	Doctor	Doctor	Undecided
Elizabeth	Northington	Undecided	Doctor	Doctor
Lindsay	Northington	Physical therapist	Physical therapist	Kindergtn teacher
Alexandra	Northington	Doctor	Doctor	Envir. law
Leah	Egremont	Actuary	Research	Doctor
Andrea	Egremont	Undecided	Biologist	Biologist
Jocelyn	Egremont	Undecided	Pharmacist	Undecided

Chapter Seven

Artists and Actresses

Unlike the sciences, the arts are domains in which many adolescents can find the kind of involvement that is intrinsically rewarding. Csikszentmihalyi et al. (1997) describe the arts as "flow experiences par excellence" (p. 115), where "flow" is defined as the state of "being involved in something to the point of losing track of time and of being unaware of fatigue and of everything else but the activity itself" (p. 14). On the other hand, the external rewards for dedication to the arts may be considerably less: often the arts are not seen as viable careers by parents and are treated by the school as something outside the academic curriculum. Thus in Csikszentmihalyi's terms, the arts are often seen as "low importance/high involvement (p. 230)."

The five girls discussed below are those who found the arts central to their lives in high school. Their case studies illustrate both sides of the "low importance" and "high involvement" aspects of the arts.

Lita

At Summerford

Lita has wanted to be an actress since she was a young child. "I don't think I made a decision. It just happened. It's just been there since I was five years old. It's part of who I am." As a ninth grader, she speaks with great precision, sounding almost pompous. She came to Summerford from a public school where "boys were the main priority" and where "we were encouraged to pass but not encouraged to learn." She is a bit disappointed with her classmates though: "A lot of the girls here are flaky, just not very bright. They're well meaning and nice, but I expected people here to be very smart." Lita says that she has learned that "I'm a lot more intelligent than I thought." Her test scores on the SSAT used for admission to prep schools show that she is indeed strong in verbal skills but low-average in mathematics. Nonetheless, her grades at the end of ninth grade are mostly Cs, even in English.

In 10th grade, Lita tells me that her strengths are drama and photography and that the only teacher who has been encouraging is her photography teacher. At the end of 10th grade, she says she has learned that she has "a very low level of tolerance. It's very difficult for me to tolerate people who don't think." She also complains that the school and her classmates "are only accepting of views that are the same as theirs, that are politically correct."

As a junior, Lita tells me that she's "realized a lot of my potential. I'm a better writer. I have confidence in my writing and singing." She wants a career in drama because "It's the most fulfilling thing I've done. I like being on stage because it's something I can do better than other people. It's really appreciated as something unique about me." She complains that her English teacher is sexist, a male who "doesn't relate to girls well," but her drama teacher "tells me the necessary steps I need to make it, with auditions and such."

A day student at Summerford, Lita is on partial scholarship. She lives with her mother, an attorney who practices family law; her father is an English teacher at a public high school in another part of the state. Her mother "doesn't know anything about theatre, so she lets me go where I want and think what I want. She doesn't think I know this, but I know she researches colleges for me and then she says, 'Oh I heard about this school.' " Her father, she tells me, "isn't playing any role whatever." Her two older brothers are not very academic, but "they are extremely focused in what they do."

At the end of her senior year, Lita is happy that she was accepted into the Tisch School of the Arts at New York University. "I've really wanted to go there since middle school." Lita worked all fall on a one-woman show about Zelda Fitzgerald that she performed for the whole school in January. "It was the best thing I've ever done, ever!" This year she credits both her drama teacher and her English teacher with being very encouraging, and indeed she is getting As in both subjects. She stopped taking math after three years, finishing with Algebra 2, and after being away from science for a year, she tries chemistry and gets a D; nonetheless, her other grades bring her GPA up to a high B average.

Her greatest strength, she believes, is "My ability to separate what's important and what not to sweat. I know I'll have to deal with a lot of rejection in my career and to remain focused means I will continue to go to auditions understanding what's important. I'm not being rejected for who I am, but because I'm not right for the part." She says that she doesn't know much about films or television, but would like to find out. Live theatre is her first love, playing "roles of women with intensity and strength."

Lita's disdain for her classmates continues. "I suppose all-girls is good for girls who lack self-confidence, for a few years, so they can feel stronger. But I don't like girls that much. They bother me. They play a lot of games and aren't completely honest with themselves or others. They're catty, always talking about each other. And they talk all the time, saying everything that's on their minds."

In college

Lita has completely changed her appearance while at NYU. With bleached hair, dramatic makeup, and new clothes, she is "very New York." She is finding the adjustment to NYU difficult. Her female classmates are her competitors, not her friends, and "I do not know how to act around men." She finds herself "more self-conscious in every way—in terms of my looks, my work, looking stupid in class." Her professors are mostly female, and they help "the females to hold their own," so the males do not dominate the classes.

The curriculum is very different from Summerford, with mostly acting classes, but Lita has found her few "academic" classes like writing very easy. She is going "full-steam ahead" with her career plans to be an actress. "I'm working very hard," she says, "but it's been a very difficult change."

Trudy

At Watson Hill

Trudy's voice varies from a near-whisper to a loud sing-song with a sarcastic edge to it. Unlike Lita, whose SSAT scores showed a great disparity between her verbal and math abilities, Trudy enters Watson Hill with high scores in both areas. In fact, during ninth grade, she expresses a desire to be a surgeon and names her biology teacher as her most encouraging teacher; she does, however, mention the arts program as one of the strongpoints of Watson Hill. As a ninth grader, she says she has learned to "think higher about what I can do and not to let boys scare me from answering questions and expressing opinions."

Her grades in ninth grade are mostly Cs and in 10th grade they fall to Cs and Ds. Her strengths, she says, are in the arts: sculpture, painting, and photography; she is taking no science and getting failing grades in math. A summer course at a local hospital between ninth and tenth grade convinced her that she didn't want to be a surgeon. "We dissected and dissected and dissected. Dissecting isn't my thing! My future is all scrambled up now. I haven't the slightest idea of what to do now."

By junior year, Trudy has decided that she wants to travel and photograph exotic civilizations. She says that she was interested in being a surgeon mostly for the money and "I realized that money wouldn't make me happy and now I don't care anymore!" Her mother, a former medical researcher who now teaches calligraphy, is trying to stay out of the college selection process because "she thinks she pressured me into the wrong school, which now I don't want to leave. She doesn't think this is the right school for me because my grades aren't wonderful and I'm not happy all the time." Her father, who works for the state department of mental retardation, is concerned about Trudy's ability to earn a living as an artist or photographer. "My mother has many arts friends with BFAs and MFAs and no jobs." Trudy has no brothers or sisters.

Trudy goes to the Rhode Island School of Design for the summer between 11th and 12th grade. At the end of senior year, Trudy is deciding between the Art Institute of Chicago and Rochester Institute of Technology. She thinks Chicago would give her the broader arts background: "I liked Chicago immensely. The studios are just wonderful and it seems like I would thrive there totally." On the other hand, "RIT is bland, the campus is bland, the people are bland. But it's the best photography school in the country." She eventually decides to go to RIT, largely because of "the great future job prospects."

She sees herself as strong in both drawing and photography. "I have a passion to—it's about people. My photography is of people. I swing from deep-down portraits where I'm capturing your soul to fashion photography, cute little things with dresses and such." But her mother feels that Trudy has had her confidence eroded away at Watson Hill to the point where she feels that she can only be good at photography. "My mother feels, and I guess it's sort of, in a way it's true, that this school has messed me up in a way. I came in with standardized test scores that showed I was brilliant at math but my entire career here was a bad story with math. Science was the same thing. 'We don't give As here' and by not giving As it destroys your self-confidence." (Of course, "they" do give As at Watson Hill, but not to Trudy.) Indeed Trudy, whose SSATs were so high, scores very average 400s and 500s on her SATs, although she does do well on the AP exam in Studio Art.

Trudy thinks the all-girls "viewpoint was good for me because I was always sort of—I didn't have high self-esteem and I don't now either, but I have more now." She adds, " I don't like the male race. It's not that I'm a strong feminist, but I never was very fond of them. I find them vulgar. There's a few nice ones, of course. And now I don't care, I just say what I want." In fact, her AWS score has been consistently high, showing that she is a strong feminist.

In college

Trudy's low opinion of men is confirmed by her first year at RIT, where the ratio of males to females is about four to one. "I am one of eight females on a floor of fifty guys, who are mostly computer science majors with raging hormones. And to tell the truth, I am scared to go to the bathroom at night because I have been cornered and propositioned so many times by scary drunk males. The guys here have greatly decreased *any* respect or good thoughts I had of males. The only good ones are gay, so I stick with the gay guys."

On the other hand, Trudy is finding "the photo classes, the teachers, and the facilities are great. I made the dean's list with a 3.63 GPA. I'm thinking that I'd like the School of Visual Arts in New York City much better, but I'm thinking I'll try to stick it out here for a while, basically for the school's reputation and the classes and facilities."

Maria

At Summerford

Although she lives just a few blocks away from the school, Maria is a boarding student at Summerford. Having a roommate for the first time, she tells me in her quiet but direct way, is difficult: "I prefer to be by myself. I need my personal space, rather than always being in a big crowd of people." Nonetheless, she knows that she is being more challenged than she would have been at her local public high school and has found that she is good in art, particularly jewelry-making.

By the end of her sophomore year, Maria has acquired two interests that will be with her for the rest of her years at Summerford: rowing and architecture. Rowing, she says, is "demanding but I love it." Her interest in architecture has been sparked by an art history course. "This school has let me spread out and see who I am. I've discovered myself this year." Maria declares, "I've definitely decided I want to be an architect. Next year I'm going to do an independent in architecture and take more art history. I'm also going to do an internship at an architectural firm." When I ask her about the math/science requirements of being an architect, she replies "No problem. I love math."

Maria does not follow through on either the independent or the internship; about the internship she says, "I didn't get my act together on time." She does maintain her interest in architecture though: "I like to do useful things. I want to design houses. I have some good ideas about how to make homes more efficient. I've been playing around with some designs that my sister thought were really ingenious."

Maria's older sister and brother, as well as her father, work for computer companies. Her mother is deceased, and her stepmother is a librarian. "They all think it's fine that I want to be an architect, although they might like me to be more like them and work in the computer field. I do love math but it's not my best subject."

Maria is looking for a college in the Northeast that has an architectural program and a crew team. She finds that Northeastern University in Boston has what she wants; she applies and is accepted early. At the end of her senior year, she tells me, " I really want to design homes. I went to Falling Water by Frank Lloyd Wright and I started crying because it was so beautiful." She adds, "I see myself designing houses for middle class families, modest houses that are very practical and enjoyable. I don't know if I see myself with a family of my own or not." Her AWS score, which started out as a 28, one of the lowest of any of the girls, is now a solidly feminist 40.

She cites her art history teacher as consistently the most encouraging of her teachers and lists her strengths as "definitely math and certain sciences." Of physics she says, "It is one of the few classes that I can understand and grab onto." When I check her records, I am surprised to find that she has taken only the lower level physics course, in which she received a B, and the lower level precalculus course, in which she received a B-minus. Most of her grades are low Bs and Cs. Maria explains, "I don't get the best grades. I have trouble with testing and writing." Her standardized tests are high 500s.

In college

At Northeastern, Maria joins the crew team as she had planned. Her plans for being an architect, on the other hand, are abandoned. She is now planning to major in sociology and her career plans are up in the air. "I know that I don't want to study architecture for five years. I think that I could make it, but I just did not enjoy my studio classes as much as I had hoped. I have taken Basic Drawing, Visual Studies I, Visual Studies II, and Art History here. I enjoyed them, but I decided that I don't want to study that way for five years. I had never taken any architecture classes at Summerford except Art History. That was obviously not a good enough way to judge."

Shelby

At Egremont

Shelby describes herself at the end of her first year at Egremont as "less shy, better at talking to new people;" nonetheless, she does not want to be taped. She is a day student who thought the "kids at the public high school were horrid," but finds the work at Egremont very challenging: "It used to be easy to get As. Here it's easy to get Cs." When I ask her how this year has affected her future, she replies, "I see a closing down of possibilities. I'm not good at science so I couldn't be a doctor." Undecided about her future at the start of ninth grade, she is now thinking of majoring in English and becoming a teacher.

At the end of tenth grade, Shelby speaks in a clear, expressive voice and cannot believe that she wouldn't allow me to tape her the previous year. She tells me that she has become a lot more involved in drama ("varsity drama") and is in a more select group of singers this year. There have been "some rough spots" as well, mostly to do with competing with a friend for a boyfriend.

Shelby's father is a general manager for a multinational corporation and his job has required that they live in Pennsylvania, New York, Michigan, West Virginia, and Connecticut; at the end of her sophomore year, they are moving to North Carolina, so Shelby will become a boarder at Egremont in her junior year. Her mother was a teacher who decided to stay at home when Shelby's older sister was born. "My mother stays at home and that's what she loves. Ideally that's what she would want for me. She feels there's not much need to go out and have a career."

As a junior, Shelby says, "If I had my choice, I would go and major in drama, no question. But I realize that's just ridiculous. It's too big a world out there to go make something of yourself. But that's what I really love." Her drama teacher "says I'm good. But in high school, it's too soon to know if I'm really good enough. It's just sort of a dream." She's looking for a college where she can be involved with theatre without being a drama major; "in some big schools, if you're not a major, you can't be in the shows."

As a boarder this year, Shelby says she's "become more my own person. I always leaned on my parents a lot." She also has an older sister, who is an English/communications major at Grove City College in Pennsylvania, but Shelby says of her: "Personality-wise we're so different, that she's not an influence on my life. I used to sort of follow her, but now it's almost a complete reversal."

Yet when I see Shelby at the end of senior year, she's decided to go to Grove City College and major in English. Her reasons: "My mother went there, my sister goes there, they accepted me. It's not too close to home, it's a beautiful campus, and it has a lot to offer in English." They do not have a theatre major.

Shelby says that her strength is "drama definitely. That's what I spend most of my time doing. This spring, I'm directing two shows." As to her future, "I'll always do drama as long as it makes me happy. There's always community theatre. But it's hard to say I'll do this and plan on eating." Her parents have given her the option of "transferring to a theatre school. I'm not closing all the doors, but I don't see it happening." As to a career of any kind, Shelby has "no idea. When I was younger, I definitely wanted a career and wanted that to be the most major thing in my life, but now I just don't know."

Shelby has high SAT scores (in the 600s and 700s) but her grades tend to be low Bs and Cs. She has tried to be "well rounded" and graduates with four years of both math and science. Her AWS score, which started out a low 33, is a highly feminist 43, despite her own uncertainties about a career for herself.

In college

Shelby says that she knew almost immediately that she had chosen "the wrong school. It didn't feel right. It was too small, very conservative, all white upper-middle-class Republicans. And there was no drama major." There was also a lot of pressure to date and "a lot of juniors getting married." Shelby quotes the dean of students as saying early in the semester, "Look to the left, look to the right. Your future mate may be in sight."

Although she felt comfortable with her three roommates and was doing well in her English classes, Shelby came home in November. She has been working at a movie theatre and was recently accepted to the College of Charleston, which is four hours from home and has a strong drama department. "I thought I could make an English major do, but it didn't work," she says. "I need to do drama."

Carla

At Northington

Carla says that she was nervous about the emphasis on sports when she first came to Northington. She is "more into the arts." She was able to count dance as her sport for the fall and will be able to "tech for a show" as her spring sport, but for the winter she had to take swimming. She surprised herself by winning some "first places by the championships." She says that this year taught her "If I try something hard enough, I can do it."

By tenth grade, Carla is clear that her strength is dance. The interest in dance is a longstanding one, but this year she has been accepted as a member of the school dance ensemble, which does mostly modern dance, and she also studies ballet at another private school. Although she was a bit nervous about returning to Northington as a sophomore "because I was uncomfortable here last year," she has found new friends and "adjusted to school more."

As a junior, Carla has decided that she wants a career in magazine journalism, but not just the writing. "I want the bustle of it all, the art and layout as well as the writing. I don't just want to sit at a desk and write." She says that "English has always been my strong suit." She is looking for colleges that have both a strong dance department and a communications/journalism department. An only child, Carla has the full support of her parents. About her being a magazine editor she says, "They love that. They think that's great." Carla's mother is a registered nurse at a retirement home; a former graphic artist, she also does public relations pamphlets for the home. Carla's father is a director of one of the departments of the state of Connecticut, although she is never quite sure of what he does since "he keeps getting promotions and it changes all the time."

At the end of senior year, Carla has chosen to go to nearby Trinity College. "At first I didn't want to go to school so close to home, but I looked at ten schools and none grabbed me. When I visited there, I got that special feeling I'd been looking for." She is happy that they have a good English department and a fine dance program.

She is feeling more certain about a career in journalism after a year of "concentrating more on my writing. I've always liked writing and it comes easily to me." Carla has taken courses this year in the writing of poetry, essays, and short stories. Her English grades have been mostly Bs and B pluses. Her SATs in English are high 600s, much higher than her math SATs, but she has completed four years of math and four years of science nonetheless.

Carla still dances a lot, both ballet and modern, as well as doing acting and singing. "This has been my big issue at Northington. I feel like I have had to constantly fight for my right to be a dancer and not a soccer player or lacrosse player." Nonetheless, she cannot see herself having a career on the stage. "Dance is something I enjoy and will always love, but it's not what I want to *be*."

In college

Carla continues to pursue both English and dance at Trinity College. She takes dance courses for academic credit as well as continuing ballet with the Hartford Conservatory. She does well in her English courses and especially enjoys creative writing and "Reel Fiction, a course in English and film." She still hopes to be an editor at a magazine, and can see herself happily living in New York City.

She is a little concerned that Trinity is too similar to Northington in size, location, and composition of the student body. "It's even less diverse than Northington! I know I need to spend some time in a very different atmosphere, like on the West Coast and in a large university with an urban atmosphere."

Reflections

In these five girls, there seems to be a sharp division between those at the girls' schools and those at the coeducational schools. The three at the girls schools speak about their art with passion. Lita says, "It's who I am." Maria speaks of crying at the beauty of Falling Water. Trudy speaks of "capturing your soul" and describes her interest in photography as "a passion." They seem to exemplify the high involvement "flow experience" of the arts. For the two girls at the coed schools, drama and dance are things they do for pleasure, but their descriptions are more matter-of-fact: "It's what I do but not what I want to be." Being at an all-girls school appears to give the first three more freedom to experience and express the emotions associated with their arts.

In addition, each of the three students at the girls' schools was more committed to her art as a career. These girls plunged themselves into their arts. Lita and Trudy have chosen colleges that are among the best in the country for drama and photography respectively, and Maria found a school that she thought would let her take undergraduate courses in architecture. Shelby and Carla, on the other hand, appear to see drama and dance as irrelevant to future careers— the "low importance" aspect of the arts. Do the girls in the arts at the girls' schools find more support for their career goals from their schools? Or are the girls at the coed schools being more realistic about earning a living?

None of these five girls graduated with an especially strong academic record; the time they put into their arts was time not spent studying other subjects. Much of what they did work at did not earn academic credit. Being less committed to careers in the arts, Shelby and Carla are "keeping their options open." Thus they take more well-rounded high school programs, including four years of both math and science. The three at the girls' schools are less concerned with this, and Lita and Trudy take the weakest math/science programs in my study. A striking finding is that although Shelby and Trudy enter their schools with nearly identical SSAT scores, Shelby graduates with SAT scores nearly 200 points higher in English and 100 points higher in mathematics than Trudy. In her giving up on traditional academic pursuits, Trudy lost the advantage in standardized test-taking she had as a ninth grader.

Did the girls at the girls' schools choose to go to girls' schools because they knew that they would find support for the arts there? That doesn't appear to be the case: none of them listed the arts program as among the reasons they chose the school, although all three of them mentioned it as one of the best things about the school by the end of their first year. Trudy, in fact, started out wanting to be a surgeon, and she and her mother tend to blame the school for her turning away from that goal; it is clear, however, that a summer program of dissecting was as much a deciding factor in Trudy's turning away from science as her courses at Watson Hill. Carla clearly expressed discomfort with the emphasis on sports at Northington and describing herself as "more of an arts person," found ways to get her dance and theatre to count as sports.

Csikszentmihalyi et al. (1997) report that students in the arts often do not see the future importance of the fields in which they excel. This was not true of the girls at the girls' schools. All three were planning to make the arts the centers of their future lives. Futhermore, Lita and Trudy have persisted in their ambitions despite some unhappy experiences during their first year of college. Maria, on the other hand, has become disillusioned with her career choice. Of the two from the coeducational schools, Carla continues to find pleasure in her dancing but keeps it as a hobby, while Shelby has realized how crucial drama is to her happiness and plans to major in it; however, she cannot yet commit to acting as a career.

Table 7.1 Career Aspirations of Arts-Oriented Students in the Study

Student	School	Start of 9th grade	End of 12th grade	End,1st yr of college
Lita	Summerford	Actress	Actress	Actress
Maria	Summerford	Architect	Architect	Undecided
Trudy	Watson Hill	Doctor	Photographer	Photographer
Carla	Northington	Undecided	Editor	Editor
Shelby	Egremont	Undecided	Undecided	Undecided

Chapter Eight

"Different Drummers"

At each school, I found at least one girl who appeared to me to be markedly different from the other girls I was interviewing; indeed each of them indicated that she felt different in some way from her classmates. Yet, each of them stayed at her respective school for the entire four years and concluded at the end of that time that they would make the same choice were they to do it over.

I originally intended to title this chapter "The Outsiders." But as I listened again to these girls' stories, I decided that such a title would miss an essential truth: although these are girls who do "march to different drummers" in some significant ways, each found her niche at the school and was able to develop a supportive network of friends. It is a tribute to the community atmosphere of each of these schools that these girls were *not* outsiders.

Beth

At Summerford

Beth appears to me to be painfully shy. For the first two years, her answers are mostly monosyllables, and several times over the years, she bursts into tears over questions that I think are fairly innocuous. Beth is from a small town in Pennsylvania, although she had previously lived in an urban environment in New Jersey. She is one of the very few white students on full scholarship at Summerford. Her father is a retired security guard and her mother is a housewife, who later finds employment in a store "like a Kmart."

In our first interview, which she will not let me tape, she tearfully tells me that it is very hard being away from home. Although many ninth grade girls have trouble with homesickness initially, it is quite unusual to find one this overwhelmed by such feelings at the end of the year. When I ask her what she is good at, she answers, "not much." Asked if she's learned anything about herself this year, Beth responds, "Not really." She says she came to Summerford because "they have really bad schools where I live" and she couldn't see herself turning down a full scholarship.

Beth allows me to record her voice on tape at the end of sophomore year. She appears a bit happier but her answers are still extremely brief. She is less homesick and getting better grades, she says, and she is good at photography. Her photography teacher is "a great person who will do anything for you." She is thinking of going into accounting because she likes math. An older brother will be entering Pennsylvania State University next year and he will be going into accounting too. Beth's grades are mostly Bs and Cs, but she does get an A minus in geometry.

At the end of her junior year, Beth is still thinking about accounting because "math is easy for me and I don't know anything else you can do with math." Her grade in Algebra 2 is a B-plus. She knows that she doesn't want to be a math teacher or college professor. None of her math teachers has ever mentioned math-related careers. She also likes photography but doesn't see that as a potential career. Her parents are "happy with whatever I do."

Beth went to a large public school before coming to Summerford and wants to go to a small coeducational college near her home. When I mention her brother at Penn State, she begins to cry. She explains, "I'm just very emotional about my family." Her brother had started school at Penn State, but got married and had a baby and so had to drop out of college in order to work; he now works in a Ford plant in New Jersey. Another older brother "works in some warehouse."

Beth has never once mentioned any friends at Summerford; I have assumed that she is a loner. I am surprised to hear, from the dean of students, that she was chosen as a junior advisor, someone who advises new students. Having conquered her own homesickness, she is now helping other students with theirs.

At the end of her senior year, Beth tells me for the first time that it has been a good year, and she cites winning the state championship in badminton as one of the reasons. In fact, she's played three sports and "really enjoyed that." She also mentions photography and her friends as things that have been good. Far from being the loner I had assumed she was, she is part of a close-knit group of girls, most of whom are black. "I was born and raised in Irvington, New Jersey, which is very urban, pretty much of a slum. Coming from the city and being poor made me realize I was different from other girls, but I knew that I belonged here equally, if not more, than the others because I had worked hard to get my scholarship."

She's decided to go to Moravian College, a small liberal arts college near her home. She was accepted by another college that "was really good in badminton" but didn't get enough financial aid to go there. She still thinks that "math is my strongpoint, but I'm really undecided about a career." She also says, "I'm good at listening to people. You have to be at this school, have to be open to so many different people. If you're not, you're just making it hard for yourself."

Beth still has mixed feelings about coming to Summerford. "I stayed, so obviously it's livable." She thinks that people work too hard and lose perspective about what's important. "I try not to overdo it because what am I going to remember in a few years? That one paper or enjoying myself and my friends?" Another thing that bothers her is the lack of boys: "every other word out of people's mouths is 'I wish there were boys here.' You go to the mall and you see guys and say, ah, that's what we're missing." When I mention that many of her classmates have said the absence of boys is one of the good things about Summerford, she says "You say it, but you don't mean it. But it's a better environment to learn in, I think."

In college

Beth finds Moravian "far less diverse than Summerford. It's very small and mostly everyone is from New Jersey or Pennsylvania. That bothers me a lot because I've always had friends from different backgrounds. Keeping in touch with my friends from Summerford helps so much. I started this group E-mail letter and it's great. It feels like we are sitting back at Summerford with everyone again."

Beth took calculus her first semester, but did not do well. "I had always done very well in math, but it was my worst grade this year. When we started with what the professor called a review in the beginning of the semester, it was already new material for me so I was already playing catch up. Most of the people in my class had already taken a calculus course before. I did not like the teacher at all. I always enjoyed going to math class before but I began to dread going to this class. I realized my problems during the semester but I didn't do anything to solve them." She says she found the professor unapproachable and she "didn't know enough people in the class" to get help from another student. Beth gets a C in calculus, which she says "is not a horrible grade but I didn't learn enough to continue with Calculus 2 which I had always thought I would continue with."

Although she was state champion in badminton her senior year, Beth says, "Unfortunately I'm not playing badminton or any other sport. It's all quite depressing actually. I miss my sports *so* much. I dream about practices and matches sometimes." She explains to me that time constraints are preventing her from participating in sports. "But maybe when the weather gets nicer, I can find some time to play tennis. Squash and badminton are out of the question since there aren't any courts or rackets."

As far as career goes, Beth says "I am still very confused. I took the intro economics course here, which was pretty much of a review of what I learned at Summerford, but I still enjoyed it. I'm going to take an intro accounting class and an intro management course next year and see how I like them. I'm leaning towards a business major." She also continues her love of photography: "One thing I will hopefully do is minor in art. I have taken two photography courses here which makes it my fifth year in photography and I have really enjoyed them so far."

Kelly

At Watson Hill

Kelly seems like Beth's opposite: she talks and talks. Whether it's been a good year or a horrible one, Kelly has a lot to tell me. As a ninth grader, she likes Watson Hill because it is all girls and you "don't care how you really look or what you wear." She also likes the small classes and the individual attention of the teachers. "At the beginning of the year, I was really paranoid that no one liked me, but soccer helped me get friends." She's also discovered that "I make people laugh. I guess I'm funny."

Her teacher in the basic design course has told Kelly that she has "great artistic ability and can see things. I'm happy that she can see that in me." Kelly says that "I used to have the whole future planned out. I wanted to go to Princeton and be a brain surgeon. Now I'm here I have to face reality." She's thinking of being an artist or a psychiatrist and wants to go to college out west.

But at the end of tenth grade, Kelly confides, "It's been horrible, the worst year of my life." She had to face Discipline Committee for drug use, and her parents are very angry at her. "All of my friends are having breakdowns, they're totally stressed out and messed up. They have to take medical leaves." She also feels that her classmates are breaking up into cliques whereas in ninth grade she was friends with everyone. She and her "really special friend from last year drifted apart and she's with her clique now."

Her grades have fallen from mostly Bs and Cs to low Cs and Ds. She's thinking about leaving and starting over somewhere else, but "my friends and I are like a family." On the other hand, she says that in the future, "I don't want a lot of friends. I can't handle it. When I've got two friends in the same room, I worry all the time that I'm leaving one of them out." Then she looks at me and asks, "Am I like this weirdo?"

As a junior, Kelly has a better year, although she says she has been troubled by rumors. I ask what sorts of rumors and she replies, "Lesbian rumors." She says that she's learned that "No matter what kind of front I put up, people see through it. I might as well be honest." She thinks that "the teachers here think I'm like the biggest loser in the school. I'm not really close to any of them."

Kelly is considering a career in music or art. "I play the bass and I'm going to try to get into Rhode Island School of Design for art for the summer." She would like to go to college, or perhaps art school, in Boston or New York. Her father is a technician for a large communications company and her mother, a native of Ecuador who attended college in this country, owns and operates a driving school. "They say whatever I do is okay with them, but I know they don't mean that. They want me to be like some big doctor or something. But I just want to be happy and I don't care what they think." Kelly has an older sister "who's supposed to be in college, but she doesn't do anything. She worked two years in Colorado and then came back. She's kind of the bad kid and they want me to be the good kid. She got off so easily and I'm here."

When I see Kelly at the end of her senior year, she tells me, "I'm really happy. A lot of good things have happened. I have a girlfriend and really like her a lot. We never were friends before this year and then all of sudden it happened. I'm so happy. We say we're soulmates and I was, oh wow, I've finally found her!"

Kelly is going to go to Manhattanville College. "I'm only going because they offered me financial aid." Her first choice was the University of Massachusetts at Amherst; she got in but didn't receive sufficient financial aid so "my dad said I had to go to Manhattanville. I didn't like it when I saw it. It was kind of like here but with more freedom." Kelly's girlfriend was accepted to the University of Massachusetts, but will be taking the next year off; "it's cool because she lives in New York City and I'll only be twenty minutes away."

She has "no idea at all" about what she would like to do as a career. "I can't see myself getting dressed up and going to work every day. Maybe I'll be my own boss." Kelly says her strengths are being a good writer, being empathetic, and being fun-loving. "People say they've never met anyone like me before. Some of the teachers think I'm funny too, but others just give me looks." Her art history and English teachers have had "nice things to say about my writing." Her SATs are mostly mid-500s, except for a 610 in writing, and her academic average is a C-minus for her last three years at Watson Hill.

Although she indicates on her questionnaire at the end of her senior year that she thinks she will go into a business career, on her AWS Kelly disagrees with the statement that "Women should assume their rightful place in business and all the professions along with men" and agrees with the statement that "There are many jobs in which men should be given preference over women in being hired or promoted."

As for Watson Hill, Kelly thinks that the school "cares more about its reputation than about each individual student. Every year I wanted to leave, but looking back, I'm glad I didn't. It all worked out the way it was supposed to work out."

In college

Kelly "never got my act together to go to RISD." Over the summer, Kelly broke up with her girlfriend, largely at the urging of her sister. "I told my sister and she got so concerned. She was introducing me to all these guys and she was taking me to bars." Of her former girlfriend, Kelly says, "she probably hates me now." Yet at Manhattanville, "I met someone else, and it's just easier, because girls come up to me and say, I like you. If a guy would be that honest, that would be fine."

Manhattanville was an academic disaster for Kelly. She spent her time with her roommate "doing everything we weren't supposed to do—partying, doing drugs." She took a biology course, but withdrew from it, and an introductory college math course, "which was so easy but I still didn't go to class," and an art history class in which she "tried so hard to stay in the class, but couldn't." Only her professor in her Preceptorial (freshman seminar) tried to encourage her: "he gave me a D instead of an F." Instead of waiting to be thrown out, Kelly comes home and gets an apartment with her sister.

Her parents are very upset: "They say, I sent you to this great high school and look at you now." Kelly confides in her sister, but says "I can't tell my mother stuff 'cause it would break her heart." Her mother gave up a career in psychology "to stay home and take care of us and we hear it every single day." Kelly is working at a gas station to earn money; she has enrolled in night classes at a nearby state university, but isn't attending those either, and plans to withdraw. She says she thinks she should go into the computer field, because "I can hack, I can do the Internet, I can do all that, and my parents won't let me do art."

All that she knows about her future career is that she wants to earn lots of money. "If I have enough money, then I will have a family. I have to have enough money to get married 'cause you can't depend on the guy. I was raised to think the mother should stay home, but I never really believed it." Yet, she confesses, "The attraction to women will always be there. With guys, I get the idea first, with girls, it's their idea. It's the person not the gender. I can go either way."

As Kelly looks at her future, she says, "I don't know what I expected when I left Watson Hill, but it wasn't this." Then she adds, "I'm lost right now, I'm so lost."

Taylor

At Northington

Taylor appears to have much more traditional values than any of her classmates at Northington, or indeed than any of the girls in the study. From ninth grade on, she indicates on her survey that she intends to be a wife and mother. Her AWS score is usually around 30, although at one point it falls to a 25. She is soft-spoken but not at all hesitant about speaking about her views and experiences.

She tells me that she used to be shy, but this year "has brought me out of my shell." At her former public junior high school, "most of my friends were shy too." But she has also learned that "I can't please everyone. I'm always too nice. I do people's laundry for them and bake them cookies and cakes just to be nice." Taylor had a boyfriend who was a senior and "I did everything nice for him and his friends, and so my friends were jealous. So I tried to be better friends to people in my grade and it was like I was being too nice to them. I don't know why being too nice is wrong, but I did learn I can't please everyone."

Taylor tells me that she loves "little kids so I know I want to go off and have a family pretty quick after college. I baby-sit almost every night. When you have a fight with your friends, you can go off and play with little kids and they always make you happy and make you smile." Taylor's mother is a housewife, who does volunteer work and sometimes works as a day care provider; she also works occasionally for Taylor's father who owns a distributing business.

Taylor's career plans continue to revolve around children and motherhood for the rest of her years at Northington. As a sophomore, she tells me "I want to be an English teacher and come back to teach at a private school like this right after college and then get married and have kids. Teachers make a difference in kids' lives." In eleventh grade, she says, "I'd like to teach elementary school or maybe bilingual education or maybe be a preschool teacher." She is working in a shelter in Hartford with homeless children, and this has confirmed her ideas. "I always thought everyone was good with kids, but I see my friends and I guess it is a gift, one that I have that a lot of people don't have."

She is looking for a college with a good elementary education program. Taylor is admitted to Miami University of Ohio, which she "went to visit and loved it." She plans to major in elementary education with a minor in Spanish. Taylor graduates with a solid B average, four years of math through precalculus and four years of science including physics. Her SATs are mid-500s except, surprisingly, Spanish where her scores are mid-300s.

Over the four years, Taylor has expressed to me some discontent with Northington and with her female classmates. As a sophomore, she says, "The girls here are catty. There were many times when I've wanted to leave." Her English teacher, a male who is also her basketball and soccer coach, has encouraged and helped her through some unhappy times. At the end of her senior year, she refers enthusiastically to her math and physics teacher, a young male who is also her swim coach, as "wonderful, almost a friend," and to her advisor whom she calls "a father figure." She adds, "I work a lot better with males. Most of my good friends are guys. Guys are a lot easier to get along with than girls. Girls are so catty. Guys will always be your friend. They don't care about anything, what you look like or that stuff."

During her junior year, her younger sister is expelled from Northington for stealing. About this incident she says: "She's attention deficit disorder and Northington was not the right place for her. You have to be an average happy kid to go here. They are not accepting of other kinds of people." As a senior, Taylor concludes, "This school likes people to be a certain way. They want everyone to be a Goody Twoshoes." She is also critical of Northington in that "they tend to only appreciate those who are best in the classroom or athletic field. Average people don't get recognized. I've played twelve seasons of varsity sports and been on the honor roll my whole time here and never got any recognition."

In college

Taylor discovers at freshman orientation that "it would be really hard for me to graduate in four years with my teacher's certification and a major in Spanish, which I really wanted to do." So she is no longer an elementary education major, about which she says, "I am sad that I did not do it, but it's not that big of a deal. I'm a business major with a minor in Spanish. Honestly I don't know what I want to do." She says she is looking for a job or profession that would combine all her talents: "I love children and being with them comes naturally. I love to do crafty things, listen to music, play sports. I'm good at interacting with people."

She still finds that "men make great friends but I'm finding a bunch of girls who make great friends out here. The environment that Northington provides is a very competitive one. They reward people who are what they want them to be. I resented the girls who were like that, because they were not being true to themselves, but were getting rewarded for their fakeness. I think this is what created tension between me and a lot of girls when I was there. Out here, I am not compared to anyone else. None of the girls measure my worth compared to their own success."

Taylor still believes that "marriage and family come first." As for a career, she thinks she might be good at "sales, dealing with people. Or maybe doing admissions work for a school."

Jocelyn

At Egremont

Jocelyn, unlike her peers at Egremont, decides early in high school that she doesn't want an Ivy League school, or a small liberal arts college or a glamorous career. From the start, her goals are more modest than most of her classmates in terms of college and career: the local state university and a career in an allied health field are just fine with her.

As a commuting student, Jocelyn finds it difficult her first year to adjust to the long days: "I don't get home until so late. I have dance at 3:15 and sports practice at 5:15. My public school friends are all done at 2 P.M.." Although she finds that she is a better student than she expected to be, Jocelyn says she has become "very quiet and very shy. I'm reluctant to raise my hand in class even if I know the answer. I'm too afraid to be wrong."

She repeats this again her sophomore year, saying "I don't know if I'll ever get over that really. I see other people and they're very outspoken. They seem to have no fear of being wrong." Her not speaking up in class is mirrored in her social life as well, about which she says, "I don't speak up for myself. I don't want to offend anybody." Nonetheless, she's had a good year, both by getting better grades (mostly Bs) and by making the crew team. She lists as her strengths: "I'm a good person. I'm sociable, I'm honest." As a junior, Jocelyn's relationships with her peers seem to have improved. "I know who my friends are. I'm not out to impress anybody. I can just be me."

Her mother, a second grade teacher, and her father, a florist, do not want her to go far from home for college, so she is looking at both the University of Connecticut and the University of Massachusetts as possible places to which to apply. She knows that she doesn't want a small liberal arts college like her older brother's; he "went to Bates and got an economics degree that he couldn't do anything with so he had to go to law school." Jocelyn wants something practical: "I want to get a degree in something I can do." Her mother advises her to do something like speech pathology, "and work in a clinic or hospital or school where you're the only one there and you can be your own boss. She also stresses that I should get a job that if you want a family, you're able to do both. That's the most important thing."

In her senior year, Jocelyn applies to and is accepted at the University of Connecticut. "That was the one and only school I applied to. The price is right." Although she loves science and has taken five years of it, she thinks going to medical school would be "a lot of work, a lot of time, too much." Instead, she is interested in pharmacy; "that's the closest thing to medical school without going to medical school. You can work in all sorts of places. You can work in a hospital or a CVS, and it's very good pay, and lots of flexibility." She is happy that the University of Connecticut has a very good program in pharmacy, although she would still consider nursing or speech pathology as possibilities.

Jocelyn says she has loved her time at Egremont, although she has never in her four years of interviews named a single teacher as especially encouraging. "I got to do things that I wouldn't have done at the local high school, like crew and drama and pottery." She still has reservations about the life of a day student at a boarding school like Egremont: "we're set apart, kind of a minority. You have to make more effort to be a part and you might be overlooked."

In college

After one year in college, Jocelyn says that she is "still shy. I think that is a good word for it." But she is no longer interested in pharmacy as a career. "There's too much chemistry involved and as a pharmacist, you just sit behind a counter all day. There's not the contact with people that I want." She says that she's "in limbo" about career: "I just have no idea." She's surprised that the course she most enjoyed this year was English, since she never liked the subject much at Egremont, but a very good female professor got her really involved. After being determined to major in something practical, being an English major is not what she had in mind, but may be a possibility.

Jocelyn took college math, statistics, and chemistry during her first year; she earned Bs in the first two, and "a solid C" in chemistry. She is proud of the C: "it was a weeder course, and they didn't weed me out, because I had such a great background from Egremont." So she has kept the option open to do something in the scientific field, and she is questioning the idea of building her career planning around marriage and children, as her parents have always encouraged her to do. "I'm not even sure I want to have kids," she says.

Reflections

All four of these girls feel in some way different or isolated from their classmates, whether for reasons of social class, traditional values, or sexual orientation. Three out of four call themselves "shy" and one worries about being thought "weird." Yet each was able to make friends and in some way feel a part of the school community.

Beth had the biggest adjustment in terms of social class and yet seems to have most successfully integrated herself into the school. Jocelyn, by being a day student rather than a boarder like Beth, does not fully become a part of the school community. Even as a senior, she feels she has to work to be noticed. Taylor, feeling estranged from her female classmates, found solace in the friendships of male students at Northington, many of whom shared her traditional views of women.

Kelly seems the only one at this point who is truly "lost." While she was able to function in the supportive, feminist world of Watson Hill, even there she thought people—the adults—saw her as "a weirdo" and "a loser." Kelly may indeed be bisexual as she claims she is, or she may be trying hard to deny her lesbian orientation. Many young lesbians date men in high school and college as an adaptive strategy to societal and parental norms (Raissiguier, 1997). Homophobia is so pervasive in this society that individuals may voluntarily abandon close friendships, as Kelly did with her "soulmate," rather than risk charges of homosexuality (Raymond, 1994).

Unlike members of other minority groups, gay or lesbian adolescents may be isolated from their families and struggling to establish their identities against familial pressures to conform. Kelly's sister is "concerned about her" and has warned Kelly not to tell her parents about her girlfriends. Internalized homophobia occurs when a gay or lesbian adolescent feels self-hatred in the form of denial or guilt or identity confusion (Raymond, 1994). Whereas people of color may be taught by their families the survival skills necessary for coping with a racist culture, gay and lesbian adolescents often have families that are themselves homophobic. Gay and lesbian adolescents, in order to develop a sense of affirmative identity must resist the dominant culture's messages about gender roles, sexuality, love, and romance (Raymond, 1994).

Most persons who identify as lesbian had some internal awareness of being different in early childhood; however they do not attribute this sense of differentness to being lesbian; rather they feel that they never fit in and don't know why. The approximate age of recognizing that this differentness has something to do with lesbianism is fourteen (Zemsky, 1991). Zemsky's case study of an adolescent, describing her girlfriend as special, "like coming home," the focal point of her life for a year, sounds much like Kelly and her "soulmate."

Adjusting to college has not been too difficult for either Taylor or Jocelyn, although both have given up their previous career plans as a result of events during the first year. Taylor is pleased to finally have female friends and Jocelyn is proud of her ability to survive the "weeder" course in chemistry. Beth has abandoned her plan to be a math major, and misses her Summerford friends and her badminton;

she finds her situation "depressing," but "will stick it out." Kelly has left one college and is clearly not ready to take courses at another one, so her future is the most unsettled of all.

Table 8.1 Career Aspirations of Students in the Study Who Feel Different

Student	School	Start of 9th grade	End of 12th grade	End,1st yr of college
Beth	Summerford	Undecided	Accountant	Business?
Kelly	Watson Hill	Undecided	Business	Undecided
Taylor	Northington	Physical therapist	Mother	Mother
Jocelyn	Egremont	Undecided	Pharmacist	Undecided

Chapter Nine

Those Who Left

In the previous chapter, I described the girls who were out of the mainstream, but who felt that the school was meeting enough of their needs to stay for the full four years. In this chapter, we will examine the reasons some girls found it impossible to stay at these schools. The seven girls whose case studies follow have been dutifully, and in some cases, enthusiastically, returning questionnaires and answering E-mail during the years since they left the four schools.

Lenore

At Watson Hill

From the start, Lenore expresses some dissatisfaction with Watson Hill. She is used to having freedom, she says, and doesn't "like to feel pampered or babied or sheltered." She bristles at the rule that lights have to be out at 10:30, for example. "Some people are learning to be more independent here, but me, it's teaching to be less independent." On the other hand, she is very happy with the academic focus of the school. "I like that I'm not considered weird because I want to learn," she explains. Lenore chose the school for its academic challenge and didn't especially care that it was all girls.

She thinks that Watson Hill is a good place to try new things, but says that making new friends and living with strangers is difficult for her: "It's a real shocker to find everything's harder than you thought it was." Her family lives in Vermont, where her father is a lawyer and her mother is studying for a law degree. Lenore would like to be a photographer, but hasn't yet taken the photography course at Watson Hill since there is a prerequisite basic design course that she is taking first.

When I see her again at the end of tenth grade, she has decided to take a year abroad in Germany during her junior year. After that, she thinks she will finish high school back in Vermont at the public high school in her town. When I ask her about how difficult it will be to make friends just for that one final year, she assures me that she has kept up her friendships at home through letters and summer vacations, so "I have people I can depend on there." She also wants to spend another year with her parents before going off to college, probably in Chicago, a city she finds very attractive.

Lenore has done well at Watson Hill, with As in math, science, and photography and Bs in everything else. She describes her teachers as "very helpful and encouraging. They teach insightful material and make it apparent that they enjoy their work." But "people relations" are problematic: "I never feel very comfortable with the other students. I feel very much different, as though they all have common interests and goals that I don't share. I never clicked with any one person and don't feel as though anyone here could be a true friend to me. They seem very narrow-minded in many ways. I feel attacked a lot for my beliefs." She is still concerned with losing her independence and individuality if she were to return to Watson Hill.

After Watson Hill

Lenore spends her junior year in Germany, which she "did not on the whole enjoy, but I am happier for having had the experience. I learned that people are not the same everywhere, and there are some things that just don't work out without a little more effort than normal." She spends her senior year at the local high school, where "I felt more adult and responsible, whereas at Watson Hill, I felt insecure and doubtful."

While living at home, Lenore takes an improvisation course at Middlebury College that "led me to want to explore possibilities like performance art, dance, and theatre." She is accepted into the University of Chicago. At the end of her first year there, Lenore says, "I still have photography as a future career in mind, but I'm even more interested in tying that into other art forms and performance art." She is thinking of majoring in chemistry or creating her own major. "I want to broaden myself while I'm here. I am exploring my other interests first and planning to go back to photography later."

Melissa

At Watson Hill

Melissa lives near Watson Hill and thus is a day student. Her aunt used to recruit for the school and she has always wanted to attend. She definitely wanted an all-girls school, because in her former school "boys got more attention. They always got called on." She likes not having to "always try to look the best. I can just be myself." Unlike Lenore, she praises the freedom that the school gives her and says she feels part of a family here. When she enters Watson Hill her career goal is to be a veterinarian, but by the end of ninth grade, she wants to be a psychiatrist because "I like helping people and listening to their problems."

At the end of her sophomore year, Melissa says that she still enjoys her friends, but that academics are "not so good." She is getting Cs and Ds, and she is failing English. She acknowledges that she has "not been focused on my schoolwork. I have to buckle down and study." She also thinks that "next year will be more important for getting into college."

Frustrated with how hard her daughter is working for so little reward, Melissa's mother, a teacher, withdraws her from Watson Hill.

After Watson Hill

Melissa is tested for a learning disability and is diagnosed as dyslexic. She repeats tenth grade at another independent school, a coeducational one, where she is given extra help in dealing with her dyslexia. She loves the new school and by senior year is earning "high honors in English, but math is still tough."

At the end of her senior year, Melissa is accepted into Northeastern University, where she plans to major in psychology. She still has hopes of being a psychiatrist, but does not seem to be aware that this would necessitate her going to medical school.

Corrine

At Summerford

Corrine, who is from upstate New York, was "originally deadset against an all-girls school, because lots of my good friends are males." But she kept an open mind and when she came to Summerford, "this felt like home." She thinks that "it's such a better education without guys. It's more comfortable. You don't have to look good. I'm looking for an education, not a boyfriend."

She says she's good at meeting people and has made friends quickly, but as for the academic side of school, "I definitely have to apply myself. Public school was a lot easier." She tells me that she's not good in math but her algebra teacher has been very encouraging to her. She finishes the year with Cs in algebra and French, and Bs in all of her other courses.

When I meet her again at the end of tenth grade, Corrine's views of the school and her classmates have changed considerably. "I dislike this place," she says, "I'm not coming back." She tells me that there are many things that "I don't approve of, things the teachers and faculty do and the restrictions they place on us. I've always been a very independent and responsible person and to have rules as to who I could get into a car with or whose house I could stay the weekend at seems excessive. Being at Summerford with all those restrictions took my independence away from me. I also miss my home and family a lot." She says she learned this year "how to make big decisions. What's important to me and what's not. Also how to choose my friends. Who I can trust and who I can't." She hasn't spoken to her former best friend in a month.

Corrine plans to attend her local public school where "the education is awful, but being here has taught me what I need to do and how to achieve it schoolwise. Being here has taught me a lot, but it will stay with me." Her English teacher has been supportive this year and English has been her favorite class. Her grade in English is her only B this year, the rest of her grades being Cs.

Corrine will go back to living with her mother, who owns her own collections agency. Her father, a corrections guard, lives nearby and she sees him frequently. Corrine has wanted to be a businesswoman since she started ninth grade.

After Summerford

Corrine says of her two years at public high school: "They were nothing spectacular. The quality of the education was not nearly as good as Summerford. The teachers didn't care as much and the students' drive to learn and excel was minimal." Yet she doesn't regret leaving because "I did make some lifelong friends and fell in love. I learned a great deal about myself in those last two years of high school and if I had stayed at Summerford, I don't think I would have discovered those things in myself."

Corrine continues to be interested in a business career and attends Bentley College. She plans to major in international culture and economy, and hopes to work for a large international corporation.

Ellen

At Summerford

Ellen is from California, and although she is away from home for the first time, she says of Summerford, "I love it. The girls are really nice and the dorm is like one big family." She chose to go to school in New England because "I would be more independent. At home, I depend on my parents so much." She wanted an all-girls school because "I felt if I went to a coed school, I wouldn't talk in class. I was afraid I wouldn't develop myself. Here you can dress however you want, you don't have to worry every minute how you look." Her fears were probably well-founded; she spends the next five minutes telling me about what she wore to the last dance.

Ellen's father is a foot surgeon and her mother is a medical technologist. As a ninth grader, she declares "I have my future all planned out. I'm going to graduate from here, and I'm going to go to University of California at San Diego, then I'm going to go to Stanford Med School. I'm going to become a cardiologist and live in San Diego. I'm going to have a practice and marry a guy with brown hair." Her year at Summerford has not affected the plan in any way, she assures me. What she does not mention is that she received a D– in biology during first semester and dropped down to a more basic science course for her second term.

In tenth grade, she amends the plan: "I'm going to end up being a lawyer. I still want to be a cardiologist but somehow I have the odd feeling I'll become a lawyer. I just realized that now. God, that's so scary. I wanted to be a doctor my whole life." Ellen describes her strengths as "debating and stuff. I'm good at arguing and sticking up for other people." Nonetheless, she continues to write "cardiologist" on her career survey.

Ellen feels very close to her friends and is happy that she has a boyfriend, but, as in ninth grade, she can name no teacher that she feels has encouraged her. She still talks a lot about how people dress and how they look; it comes up in her discussion of events in her dorm and in her description of her future husband: "the guy has to have beautiful eyes—you look into them and you want to cry." Despite the emphasis that she seems to place on looking good and dating, Ellen scores in the 40s on the AWS throughout high school.

She finishes sophomore year with Ds in both geometry and biology, which she is taking for the second time.

After Summerford

Ellen returns to California where she attends the local public school. She explains, "The decision to leave Summerford was mine. I wanted to be nearer to my home. Getting poor grades didn't help though." She gives up her ambition to become a cardiologist because of her consistently poor grades in science. At the end of junior year, her survey indicates that she plans to be a defense attorney, but by the end of senior year, she has changed that to psychiatrist, perhaps unaware (as so many of these girls are) that psychiatry requires a medical degree.

Ellen attends the University of Arizona, where her goals are still unclear. "Law is still an option though," she says.

Veronica

At Egremont

"Everything has gone wrong for me this year," Veronica tells me at our first interview. Although she praises Egremont for its friendly, warm atmosphere and "caring, interested teachers," she is having a difficult time. "I'm doing terrible, I'm on academic probation. I'm on regular probation and I was sent to Discipline Committee." Since she is having trouble with her math and science courses, "I have to spend time on that, so it's hard to do all the arts courses that I would like."

Still, "I'm able to push forward. I never would have thought I could keep going. I'm doing really well at writing even though I'm flunking two other courses." Veronica says that she "used to take a lot for granted about doing well in school," but she's learned that "if I want to be successful, I have to work hard and not take it for granted." She says she wants to be a journalist.

Veronica chose Egremont because when she looked at a variety of boarding schools, she "liked this the most. I felt at home." Her father, who is an investment advisor, lives in New York City, while her mother, an interior designer, lives in western Connecticut. Veronica had attended an independent day school near her mother's home through eighth grade. At Egremont, she has found that "I am more subject to peer pressure than I thought I was. I get stressed out more when living with a large group of people."

Veronica hasn't found any of the teachers at Egremont encouraging: "I haven't found any teacher that I could bond with."

She finishes ninth grade with two Cs, a D, and two Fs, and is told by Egremont not to return for tenth grade.

After Egremont

Veronica goes to summer school to make up the two failed courses and enrolls in a small girls' boarding school in Maryland for tenth grade; thus she does not lose the year of school as Melissa did. She specifically chooses the all-girls atmosphere because she (and her parents) decide that she needs "a more supportive environment." Egremont was "just not the right place for me, although I would have had a hard time anywhere. It was just a hard time in many ways." At her new school, she does considerably better, and takes Advanced Placement English her senior year, where she learns that "I hate a competitive environment."

Veronica enters Saint Lawrence University thinking she will major in environmental studies, because she loves the outdoors and is concerned about the environment. After one week in an environmental science course, "I decided no. I wasn't interested. The class drove me away." In fact, although she claims to love Saint Lawrence, Veronica has had a difficult adjustment to college. "I got too caught up in the social scene, and didn't go to classes. I ended up taking a medical withdrawal for first semester, so in the spring, I'm still a first semester freshman."

Although writing is still a strength of hers, she decides to focus on art history and fine arts, and takes several courses in art history second semester. "I hope to work in an art gallery eventually, then go to grad school, I'm not sure in which area, probably decorative arts." When I ask about her earlier plans to be a journalist, she replies, "I'm not focused enough for a career in writing."

Penny

At Egremont

Penny comes to Egremont from New Orleans. Like Veronica, she discovers in ninth grade that "I don't have much self-discipline. I'm usually in people's rooms when I should be studying." Yet she says that one of the things that she likes best about the school is that "there is a lot of time to yourself, lots of unscheduled time."

Unlike Veronica, Penny does not get into disciplinary problems; she manages to get three Cs with Bs in French and algebra. She praises her math teacher who is also her basketball and cross-country coach for being encouraging and "caring how we feel." She says that she has learned to "see things more realistically. I can work hard or not—it's up to me." Penny has her sights set on going to Davidson College; "my brother and sister didn't get in, so I'm the last one who can." She stays through tenth grade.

Her mother, a nurse, and her father, a lawyer, both attended boarding schools, as did her brother. An educational consultant in New Orleans recommended Egremont to Penny and when she came to visit, "I liked it a lot." She does have some reservations about the administration and faculty though: "Students here aren't well heard," she claims. After another year at Egremont, in which she gets all Cs, Penny leaves.

After Egremont

Penny enrolls in a coeducational independent school in New Orleans. She says that she left Egremont not because of her grades, but because "I didn't like being so far from home. But I did better at my new school anyway." She never applies to Davidson because she decides "it was way too out of my reach." She is admitted to Presbyterian College in South Carolina, where she hopes to major in biology and become a nurse like her mother. "I have always been inspired by her."

Racquel

At Egremont

Racquel, already mentioned in chapter 4, is an ABC student from Brooklyn, New York. She is happy to be at Egremont where she does not "have to take the train to school or worry about violence." As a ninth grader, she praises Egremont for its diversity and for "expanding my ideas." She has been helped and encouraged at Egremont by her Spanish teacher, a woman she describes as "strong, with a lot of perseverance. She really cares about her students."

Her mother, with whom she lives, is a bank supervisor. Her father owns a shipping business in St. Vincent in the West Indies. Racquel came to Brooklyn from St. Vincent seven years earlier. In both ninth and tenth grade, she expresses a desire to be a pediatrician because she likes science and children. Her grades both years are mostly Cs and Ds, although she does earn a B in geometry.

At the end of her junior year, Racquel talks about classes being "hectic." She says that she has "to deal with lots of things. People come to me with lots of problems." After a year of physics, she is no longer interested in science, and wants to be a child psychologist. "I want to be closer to children than just giving them medicine for a cold. I want to have more interaction and more impact." Although she's received no guidance about this career goal, Racquel has mentioned this interest to some of her teachers, who have said "that's good." Her mother says "do what you're interested in," and Racquel doesn't "really speak to my father."

She's looking for a college where she "can be more than just a number, where you can be one-on-one with the teachers." Her older brother, also an ABC student at a school in Connecticut, is "a real role model for me. He completely influences me. I call him all the time to ask advice." A year older than Racquel, he will be going to Boston University in the fall. Not surprisingly, Racquel also plans to apply to Boston University.

Racquel's grades fall to mostly Ds at the end of junior year, and although the academic dean of Egremont tries to persuade her to stay, Racquel decides to return home.

After Egremont

Racquel spends her senior year at Middle College High School in Queens, New York, which she describes as "Great! The best year I've had. I got involved in extracurricular activities that I had no time for at Egremont, like being a peer mediator and an AIDS counselor." She thinks that Egremont was "just not the right environment. I needed to ease up on the academics. There was too much pressure there."

Racquel applies and is accepted to Union College in upstate New York. She is enjoying her year there and, although undecided about a major, plans to become a lawyer.

Reflections

Students leave these schools for many reasons. For some, poor grades reflect that they are not meeting the school's expectations; parents, who are spending considerable amounts of money to send their daughters to these schools, often make the decision to take them out. In the case of Melissa, an undiagnosed learning disability made it impossible for her to do the work expected of her, and her mother, a teacher, made the decision to withdraw her. In Veronica's case, the freedom she was given at Egremont was too much for her at the time, and she needed a more structured environment in which to thrive academically. Unfortunately, she seems to be having a similar problem in the transition from her high school to Saint Lawrence University.

Other students find the rules and regulations of a boarding school too constricting and choose to go to what they know are lesser schools academically rather than live in what they feel is too structured an environment. A recent article in *Town and Country* magazine, entitled "America's Top Boarding Schools" (Biggs, 1996), acknowledges the fact that some students will find these schools too rigid, warning of one that it is "not ideal for rebels or nonconformists" (p. 96), of another that it is "not good for those who have a problem with structure" (p. 105) and of a third, "eccentric iconoclasts should steer clear (p. 106)." (None of the three schools thus described are in my study, but they are similar to them in many ways.)

Clearly, Lenore, who is one of the nonconformists and iconoclasts, found Watson Hill to be too constricting. She and Corrine talk about being highly independent and feeling that this is being taken away from them. Both Lenore and Corrine also complain about not making good friends while they were at these schools, perhaps because they are so different from the rest of the students there. Making close female friends is one of the elements that the girls at the girls' schools especially treasure, so without these bonds to hold them to the school, they make the decision to leave.

Others, who are far from home like Ellen and Penny, make the choice to leave based on a desire to be closer to family. If their academic records had been stronger, nonetheless, they might have been more likely to stay at their respective schools.

In general, then, most girls who left did so because their academic records were not strong enough to warrant the continued expense of going to these schools. For two of the girls at the girls' schools, the restrictions placed on them by boarding school life were the deciding factor, even though their academic records were respectable (and in the case of Lenore, very strong). For Veronica, on the other hand, it seems to have been the structured environment of the girls' boarding school she attended after Egremont that enabled her to succeed.

The decision to leave, whether made by the girls, their parents, or the schools, does not seem to have had a detrimental effect on any of the girls. They have few regrets and are proceeding on with their lives well-satisfied with where they are.

**Table 9.1 Career Aspirations of Students
in the Study Who Left**

Student	School	Start of 9th grade	End of 12th grade	End,1st yr of college
Corrine	Summerford	Business	Business	Business
Ellen	Summerford	Doctor	Psychiatrist	Undecided
Lenore	Watson Hill	Photogrphr	Photogrphr	Photogrphr
Melissa	Watson Hill	Veterinarian	Psychiatrist	Psychiatrist
Veronica	Egremont	Journalism	Undecided	Art gallery
Penny	Egremont	Lawyer	Nurse	Nurse
Racquel	Egremont	Doctor	Psychologst	Lawyer

Part Three

Lessons from the Girls

Chapter Ten

Results of the Study

Over the five years of the study, both quantitative and qualitative data were collected; most of these data showed no differences between the two types of schools. All quantitative data is tabulated and presented in Appendix B. In this chapter, I will highlight the most significant findings and relate, where possible, the quantitative measures to the information learned from interviews.

Attitudes Toward Women's Roles

There were no significant differences among the schools in the girls' responses to the gender attitudes survey (AWS) during the four years of high school. At both types of school, most scores increased between ninth and twelfth grade. Thus, the girls who enroll at all-girls schools do not seem to be more feminist in their attitudes than the girls who enroll at coeducational schools, either at the start or at the end of high school.

Table 10.1   Average AWS Scores of Students in the Study, 1992-1996

	Girls' Schools		Coed schools	
	Watson Hill	Summerford	Egremont	Northington
Fall 1992	38.6	38.9	37.8	38.0
	(15)	(16)	(17)	(7)
May 1996	39.5	40.6	41.2	38.8
	(10)	(14)	(13)	(9)

Average score (1992): Girls' Schools = 38.8   Coed Schools = 37.8
Average score (1996): Girls' Schools = 40.1   Coed Schools = 40.2

Since the girls' schools do have an explicitly feminist agenda, it is interesting that the girls at the coeducational schools are so similar in attitudes to their single sex peers. This similarity may reflect attitudes they have learned in their families, from the school culture, or from the larger culture.

In the few cases where there was a small decrease in a girl's score, the most common reason was a tendency to go from a strong response (strongly agree or strongly disagree) to a weaker one (mildly agree or mildly disagree) rather than switching entirely from an agree position to a disagree position or vice versa. A small drop in score may thus have indicated an understanding of the complexity of some of these issues (i.e., not seeing things as either/or issues), rather than a reversal of values.

As I have talked with these girls over the years and compared their stated goals and attitudes to what they have answered on the AWS survey, I have come to the conclusion that a high score (40 and above) on the AWS may reflect a girl's superficial assimilation of the feminist values in the school culture (or in the larger culture) or it may reflect her own strongly held beliefs, and it is often difficult to distinguish these two outcomes. On the other hand, a score considerably lower than her classmates' (35 and below) almost always represents a girl's true beliefs, often held in opposition to most of those around her.

Thus it is interesting to look at the girls in the study whose scores either fell over the five year period or remained low throughout the five years. In the case of Roxanne, the athlete from Summerford, it was a rebellion against feminist values that she felt she was being "force-fed" at Summerford that caused her score to drop from a 44 to a 33. (After a year at Yale, Roxanne's score had rebounded to 40.) Although she was not as explicit as Roxanne, Lynn, the athlete from Watson Hill, also showed a (smaller) drop in AWS score (from 40 to 36); both of these girls identified closely with their fathers, and this may have led them to take the male perspective on some of these issues. Other girls at the all-girls schools whose scores dropped included Mimi (44 to 38), who is discussed in chapter 4, and Cindy (39 to 29) at Watson Hill, who is not included in the case studies. Similar drops were recorded for some of the girls at the coeducational Egremont: Anna (42 to 37) and Robin (38 to 28). It is difficult to assess why these girls' attitudes changed in this way.

Some girls, on the other hand, entered with low AWS scores and maintained them over the five years. Notable among these are Taylor at Northington (discussed in chapter 8) whose scores ranged from 25 to 33, and who is the only girl in the study to consistently write that she wanted to be a wife and mother for a career; her stated preference for males over females as friends and her characterization of her female peers as "catty" are consistent with these traditional, even patriarchal, attitudes. Also at Northington, Elizabeth (chapter 6) and Lindsay had scores that ranged from 33 to 38. At the girls' schools, Anne at Summerford (chapter 6) and Sydney at Watson Hill had scores ranging from 30 to 38; the scores of Eliza (chapter 6) at Watson Hill were almost as low as Taylor's, ranging from 28 to 35. All of these girls entered their respective schools with more traditional attitudes than their classmates toward women's roles and the schools had little effect on dissuading them from their views.

Since AWS score has been shown to be related to both self-esteem in female adolescents (Holland & Andre, 1994) and importance of careers to female college students (Komarovsky, 1985; Betz & Fitzgerald, 1987; O'Brien & Fassinger, 1993), I thought it possible that lower AWS scores senior year in high school might be predictive of which of the girls would lower her aspirations as a result of the transition to college, but this has not seemed to be the case. While Eliza of Watson Hill (chapter 6) and Lindsay of Northington may have backed off from careers as veterinarian and physical therapist, both Anne of Summerford (chapter 6) and Elizabeth of Northington (chapter 6) have maintained their desire to be doctors despite low AWS scores.

AWS scores do not correlate with SAT scores, overall average, grades in English, grades in math, or grades in science at any of the four schools. There were occasional significant correlations between AWS score and other scores: college acceptance correlated positively with AWS at Northington, and during junior year at Watson Hill, there was a positive correlation between AWS score and English grades, as well as AWS and SAT-V.

There also does not seem to be any relationship between AWS score and mother's career, as some of the girls whose mothers have high-powered careers score quite high and others quite low. Many of the girls who score lower than their classmates on the AWS survey indicate that religion is an important part of their lives, but not all; and some of those who say religion is important to them score quite high. I did not go into depth with any of them about their religious beliefs so I can say little else about this, except to note that, unlike Lee and Marks (1992), I did not find that the girls at the girls' schools were more religious than their coeducational school counterparts.

Standardized Tests and Course Grades

There were no significant differences in SAT scores between girls' schools and coeducational schools for the girls in this study. This is similar to what Lee and Marks (1990) found in their comparison of single sex and coeducational Catholic high schools.

Table 10.2 SAT Scores of Students in the Study

	Girls' Schools		Coed Schools	
	Watson Hill	Summerford	Egremont	Northington
SAT-V	594 (11)	624 (14)	614 (13)	612 (9)
SAT-M	557 (11)	574 (14)	589 (13)	603 (9)

Average SAT-V: Girls' Schools = 610.8 Coed Schools = 613.2
Average SAT-M: Girls' Schools = 566.5 Coed Schools = 594.7

Although ETS examinations tended to correlate highly with each other (i.e., SSATs with SATs, PSATs with SATS), they did not correlate consistently with grades achieved at these schools, apparently because of the wide variety of courses from which the girls can choose. For example, a girl with low math ability (as indicated by a low SAT-M score) may take a low level math or science course and do quite well, whereas a girl with high ability (and a high SAT-M score) may take calculus or an AP science course and do less well; such cases occurred among these girls and led to low or even negative (though nonsignificant) correlation coefficients. The only significant correlation found involving the SAT-M was at Summerford, where it was positively correlated ($p<0.05$) with senior science grades.

SAT-V was positively correlated ($p<0.05$) to both senior English grade and overall academic average at Watson Hill, and to senior English grades at Summerford; no significant correlations were found with SAT-V at the coeducational schools. It is harder to explain a lack of correlation between SAT-V scores and English grades, except in terms of girls working harder to make up for lack of "ability" (as measured by SATs) or not working up to potential. Scores on the Writing Achievement (SAT-II) examination did not correlate significantly with English grades except at Summerford (and just missed significance at Watson Hill).

Advanced Placement examinations were taken by many of the girls in this study. A t-test, combining all AP scores for the girls' schools and comparing them to the combined scores for the coeducational schools, showed a highly significant result ($p=0.001$) favoring the girls' schools. The girls at the girls' schools took more AP examinations and did significantly better on them than their peers at the coeducational schools, even though their grades and SAT scores were not significantly different.

Table 10.3 Advanced Placement Exam Results of Students in the Study

	Girls' Schools		Coed Schools	
	Watson Hill	Summerford	Egremont	Northington
Number of TestsTaken	26	27	25	18
Average AP grade	3.58	3.85	3.08	3.03

Average AP grade: Girls' Schools = 3.72*   Coed Schools = 3.06

* Significantly higher, $p=0.001$.

This difference may reflect a stronger "academic intensity" (in the words of the head of Watson Hill) at the girls' schools. I found this also corroborated in the interviews, in which fourteen girls at the girls' schools but only two at the coeducational schools named their personal strength as being "hard-working and focused." Riordan (1990) has also commented on the greater academic focus of girls' schools in the Catholic school population, and Trickett et al. (1982) found this to be the case in a study of independent school classrooms. Without the social distractions of the opposite sex and with less emphasis placed on athletics, the girls at the girls' schools may see the primary purpose of school as that of academic achievement and this may be reflected in their Advanced Placement scores.

Additionally, among the girls in this study, Advanced Placement work in studio art or art history was only done in the girls' schools. Advanced Placement physics was not offered at all at Egremont; although it was offered at Northington and three girls (and six boys) were enrolled in the course in 1995–96, none were in my study. Thus in this study, Advanced Placement work in physics was found only in the girls' school students.

With regard to course grades, there were no significant differences between the girls who attended all-girls schools and those at coeducational schools on the following measures: grades in mathematics, science, and English, and overall academic average.

College Acceptances

The colleges that the girls attended in the fall of 1996 were ranked on a scale of 1 through 5, based on the rankings in the 1995 edition of *Barron's Profiles of American Colleges.* Schools rated as "most competitive" were given a 5, "highly competitive" a 4, "very competitive" a 3, "competitive" a 2, and "less competitive" a 1. (Colleges given a + in any of these categories were given an additional 0.5; for example, Vanderbilt University is listed as highly competitive, but given a + to show that its median SAT scores are higher than most of the others in that category, so it was given a 4.5 in my rankings.) Only one of the girls in the study (Anastasia at Summerford) did not apply to college during her senior year.

A t-test between the girls' school graduates and the coeducational school graduates found a significant difference between them favoring the coeducational schools ($p= 0.008$). Although their grades and SAT scores did not differ significantly, the girls at the coeducational schools got into significantly higher ranking colleges than the girls at the girls' schools; the difference was particularly marked at Watson Hill.

Table 10.4. College Acceptances of Students in the Study

	Girls' Schools		Coed Schools	
	Watson Hill	Summerford	Egremont	Northington
Average College Ranking	2.73 (11)	3.65 (13)	4.08 (13)	4.33 (9)

Average ranking: Girls' Schools = 3.23   Coed Schools = 4.18*

* Significantly higher, p=0.008.

One assumes that a girl will always go to the most selective school she can, and that the college that she attends is the most selective place to which she can gain entrance. But this is not always the case. Sometimes, girls may have preferences that lead them to accept a less competitive college; a special program (in art or business), location (near home), financial aid packages, etc., may attract a girl to a school that ranks lower than some others to which she could go. I believe this happened in several cases at Watson Hill. On the other hand, the large number of positive correlations of SAT scores and grades with college acceptance at Watson Hill (see Appendix B) does indicate that girls with high scores and grades tended to get into very competitive schools and those with lower scores and grades into less competitive schools. Girls at Watson Hill had lower grades and scores in general (though not significantly lower statistically) and thus got into less competitive colleges.

Of course, other things affect college acceptances. Athletic ability, parents who are alumni, and minority status may tip the balance for some girls; in this sample, there were more athletes and more minority students at the coeducational schools. No one except Shelby (from Egremont) mentioned going to a parent's alma mater. It is also possible that some colleges may favor students coming from a particular school; four Egremont girls were accepted at the highly selective Brown University, for example. The academic dean at Watson Hill has indicated to me that she believes that their college advising office will be doing more to make colleges aware of the quality of their program, and that may affect future college acceptances there.

Mathematics and Science Enrollments

Examining the patterns of course enrollment in mathematics and science reveals some striking differences among the schools.

Mathematics

Table 10.5 displays the data for math enrollments. Since Watson Hill offers a "fast track" to calculus which requires only three years and two trimesters to complete what takes four years at the other schools, the courses taken are more significant than the total number of years of math. For example, looking at the percentage of girls in the study who completed calculus, it becomes apparent that at each of the schools about a third of the girls in my study completed a year of calculus. The difference occurs in the percentages of the girls who take precalculus. Summerford offers a lower-level precalculus course (Fundamentals of Precalculus) and half of the girls in this sample took it; the other three schools have similar options (elementary functions, trigonometry, etc.), but very few of them took these courses.

Table 10.5 Math Courses Taken by Students in the Study

	Girls' Schools		Coed Schools	
	Watson Hill	Summerford	Egremont	Northington
Years of Math				
4 years	68%	93%	100%	100%
3–3.7 yrs	32%	7%	0 %	0 %
Highest math course				
Calculus	36%	29%	39%	33%
PreCal	55%	21%	39%	56%
Other	9%	50%	22%	11%

Because I found the differences among the schools so striking, I asked each of the schools to provide me with an additional piece of information about mathematics enrollments: the total number of girls in the graduating class of 1996 who graduated with a year of calculus. This revealed quite a different pattern: where my sample showed about one third of the girls taking calculus at all four schools, the data for the entire class of 1996 showed that Summerford outperformed the others with 44% of the class taking a year of calculus, while the figure is about 30% of the girls at the other three schools. A chi-square test performed on these calculus data showed no differences between all-girls and coeducational schools. The fact that my sample at Summerford underestimated the number of girls taking calculus there will be commented on further below.

Science

Science enrollments appear to be an area in which schools' cultures have a major influence. Table 10.6 shows the patterns of course-taking in science. Note that at the coeducational schools four years of science is the norm, whereas at the girls' schools four years of science is the exception. (All schools have a 2-year science requirement, but happily, most girls at all the schools go beyond this.) In general, the girls at the coeducational schools took more science than the girls at the girls' schools. A chi-square test was done on the science data from the girls in the study. Comparing the number of girls who took four years or more of science to those who took less than four years, a significant difference ($p=0.0008$) was obtained favoring the girls at the coeducational schools.

At some schools (e.g., Summerford and Egremont) the ninth grade science course is an environmental studies or introductory physical science course with biology delayed until 10th grade, while at other schools (e.g., Watson Hill and Northington), biology is taken in the ninth grade; thus a girl might only take three years of science and still get the basic sequence of biology, chemistry, and physics that might take four years to complete at another school. A more significant comparison might thus be comparing the number of girls who have completed the biology/chemistry/physics sequence to those that have taken less. A chi-square test was performed on those data for the girls in the study, and again the result favored the coeducational schools, although the level of significance was not as high ($p=0.068$).

As with mathematics, I asked the four schools to supply me with statistics on the entire class of 1996 with regard to science courses taken. These are shown in Table 10.7.

Table 10.6   Science Courses Taken by Students in the Study

	Girls' Schools		Coed Schools	
	Watson Hill	Summerford	Egremont	Northington
Years of Science				
4 or more	18%	29%	77%	67%
Less than 4	82%	71%	23%	33%
Science Courses				
Bio & Chem & Physics	82%	29%	69 %	89%
Weaker programs	18%	71%	31%	11%

Table 10.7 Science Enrollments for All Female Students in the Class of 1996

	Girls' Schools		Coed Schools	
	Watson Hill	Summerford	Egremont	Northington
4 or more yrs science	29%	39%	81%	69%
1 year of physics	76%	41%	77%	92%

(Number of girls in class of 1996 at each school: Watson Hill = 41, Summerford = 59, Egremont = 26, Northington = 49)

Comparing Tables 10.6 and 10.7, it can be seen that my sample did underestimate the number of girls at the girls' schools who graduate with four or more years of science. Nonetheless, the original pattern still holds: it is much more common for girls at the coeducational schools to graduate with four years of science than girls at the girls' schools (overall, 73% at coed schools vs. 34% at girls' schools). This data was tested with a chi-square test, and again a highly significant difference was obtained ($p=0.00000024$) favoring the coeducational schools.

The pattern for taking a year of (regular) physics also holds. For these schools, it is more likely that a girl at a coeducational school will take physics than her counterpart at an all-girls school; Summerford's enrollment is particularly low in this subject. Using the physics data from all the girls in the class of 1996, a chi-square test showed a highly significant difference ($p=0.0000077$) favoring the coeducational schools.

The pattern at Summerford is especially noteworthy. If one looks carefully at the data, it seems as if there is a solid core, about 40% of the class, who have taken physics, calculus, and four years of science. Only a few of this group were in my study; instead I got a large group of girls who were taking considerably weaker programs in mathematics and science. There is perhaps a greater polarization at Summerford such that the dedicated math/science students take all the math and science that the school has to offer while the rest of the girls take weaker programs, and see physics only for the "math/science types." At the other schools, many girls seem to take physics as a matter of course whether they are "math/science types" or not.

Of additional concern at Summerford is the fact that six of the fourteen girls in the study graduated with no exposure to physics at all (not even the lower level physics course). When one adds to this the fact that many of these same girls took the lower level precalculus course, and yet their SAT scores indicate that they are not inherently weaker in mathematics, it must be asked if perhaps they were just given too many ways to "opt out" of standard math and science courses. The claims of the National Coalition of Girls' Schools that girls take more mathematics and science at girls' schools is not supported by the girls in this study (but recall that the Coalition's reference group was *all* high schools, not coeducational independent schools).

The fact that girls at the coeducational schools appear to take more science than girls at the girls' schools came as a surprise. The coeducational schools were formerly boys' schools, and it appears that the norm in math and science is four years of each. Does this mean that boys are still the norm at these schools? And is that a bad thing? Yes, if it means that girls are made to feel that the boys' experience is the valid one and they must try to live up to it. No, if it means that boys and girls are expected to do equally well in math and science. If we want women to enter fields that have been traditionally male-dominated (and more importantly, if they want it for themselves), we should be careful to prepare them equally as well as we prepare the boys.

It is clear from my sample that a very bright, very determined girl will get an equally fine education in math and science whether she attends a girls' school or a coed school: the rigorous courses and the dedicated teachers exist at both types of schools. But for the less focused girl, the atmosphere of some girls' schools may allow her to opt out of math and science more easily and thus close doors for her prematurely.

I have discussed my conclusions with the Summerford math and science departments and they have offered some alternative interpretations. The mathematics department states that, by offering the Fundamentals of Precalculus course, they are helping girls develop confidence in mathematics and providing more avenues by which girls can attain the goal of studying calculus and other higher level math courses. Indeed, they provide evidence that some of those who take the course as juniors do go on to calculus as seniors; however, the girls in my sample all took the course as seniors and none has indicated that she will take calculus in college except Mimi (chapter 4) who must take it as part of her premedical program.

The science department objects to my characterization of the courses called Introduction to Physics and Introduction to Chemistry as "lower level" or "less rigorous" courses. They believe that their introductory courses are equal to the regular courses at other schools, and that their regular courses are equivalent to the honors courses at other schools. I do not know how familiar they are with what is taught in the other three schools in my study, although they did cite another school (not in my study) as the basis for this belief. An inspection of the final examinations in chemistry and physics at the four schools revealed great variety in what was taught but did not reveal a consistent pattern in levels of difficulty. At best then, they have named these courses in ways that are idiosyncratic and probably confusing to college admission offices. Even allowing Introduction to Physics to count as a "regular" physics course, there are still more girls from Summerford than at the other three schools who have graduated with no physics course at all: six girls at Summerford as opposed to one, two or three at the other schools. (See Table 4 in Appendix B.)

Arts and Athletics

Girls at coeducational schools were more interested in sports and based more of their self-satisfaction on it. Since this had been true since ninth grade, I wondered if one of the reasons these girls had chosen coeducational schools in the first place was the stronger sports programs there. Looking back at the ninth grade interviews, I noted that none had mentioned sports as a reason for choosing the school. Once there, however, most of them found the sports program one of the things they liked best about the school. For a few of the less athletically inclined girls, such as Carla (chapter 7) and Elizabeth (chapter 6), both at Northington, the emphasis on sports at the coeducational schools was problematic.

Many fewer girls at the girls' schools mentioned sports as a source of satisfaction. Among those that did were Roxanne (chapter 5), a nationally ranked tennis player, and Beth (chapter 8), a state champion in badminton, both at Summerford, and Lynn (chapter 5), the softball player at Watson Hill. None of the girls at the girls' schools talked about learning the leadership and interpersonal skills that playing on a sports team provides.

On the other hand, the girls at the girls' schools were much more likely to mention the arts programs as a source of satisfaction. Being an artist or an actress at the girls' schools was clearly more likely to be appreciated by one's classmates as well. There were girls at Egremont who also mentioned the arts program there as being particularly important to them: Shelby (chapter 7), the actress, Leah (chapter 6), one of the scientists, and Kerry (chapter 3), the academic superstar, were among these. But none of the girls at Northington mentioned the arts program there, and Carla, in particular, felt she had to "fight" to gain recognition for the dance and theatre work that she did. Dramatic productions and dance group performances also provide opportunities for teamwork similar to sports, and perhaps deserve more recognition at the coeducational schools than they currently receive.

The culture of the girls' schools appears to be more supportive of the arts in general; on the other hand, the culture of the coeducational schools appears to put more emphasis on athletics than the girls' schools do. This study confirms, to some extent, the stereotypes that many people hold of these two types of schools. More will be said about this in the following chapter.

Incidents of Sexism

With regard to the sexism found by Valerie Lee at independent schools, several of her observations were borne out in this study. Lee et al. (1994) found the science classroom the principal source of sexist incidents in coeducational independent schools. In 1994 and 1995, there was evidence at Egremont of girls' feeling intimidated by two male science teachers (although it was never clear that the teachers were making *only* the girls feel intimidated).

Leah (chapter 6) also mentioned a math teacher who, she felt, was overly sarcastic to her when she was the only girl in a class with seven boys during her first year at Egremont; at one point, he told her "to go off and bake some cookies!" This is the same math teacher that Kerry described as sexist during her sophomore year. In the few such cases in which the girls at Egremont encountered blatantly sexist attitudes in their teachers, they seem to have been able to identify them as sexist, to discuss these attitudes among themselves and to discount them. None of the girls at Northington ever mentioned a sexist teacher of any subject, even when I asked specifically about it.

The only Egremont student who thinks she was negatively affected by a gender-biased teacher is Kerry, who after a year in class with the mathematics teacher who clearly preferred males, agreed with the statement that "Boys are naturally better at math than girls." (It should be noted, however, that two girls at the all-girls schools agreed with this statement several times.) Looking back on the experience, she says, "He wrote on my final comment something like 'Despite lack of natural talent, Kerry earned one of the highest grades because of her effort and determination.' My mother, who's a feminist, was livid, and wanted to call the school. She thought he was sexist the entire year, from things I told her. He also told us that girls always cry in his class. I wonder if that was a turning point in my math career."

At the girls' schools, Lee et al. (1994) observed a different kind of sexism, which she characterized as "gender reinforcement." Lee has typified this as "wrapping Calculus in a pink ribbon" (Lee, 1997,

p. 155). The "watered-down" nature of courses that Lee observed at girls' schools was reflected in the large number of Summerford girls taking courses such as Fundamentals of PreCalculus and Introductory Chemistry or Introductory Physics.

One might ask whether taking four years of science at a coeducational school where the teachers are intimidating to the girls is better than taking less science (or watered-down science) at a school where the teachers are encouraging. The answer to this, it seems to me, is how the girl interprets her experience. If she concludes, as Kasmira did, that the problem is hers ("I just can't do chemistry"), then this could be harmful. (There was at least one girl at all four schools who came to a similar conclusion about math and science, and this may, of course, reflect natural ability more than the effect of her teachers.)

Since girls are more likely than boys to attribute failure to their own shortcomings than to external factors, it surprised me how many girls at Egremont were able to attribute the problems in their math and science classrooms to the teachers' treatment of them and not to their own lack of ability. For those girls, getting through the science course with a solid understanding of the subject matter was obviously a good thing and did not seem to be damaging to self-esteem, except perhaps for Kerry. The fact that they could identify the teacher as sexist and discuss it among themselves may even help them deal with intimidating professors in college. (I am not, however, recommending this behavior for science teachers as a way to "toughen up" the girls!)

Institutional sexism is an issue separate from the way that girls are treated in classrooms. At Northington, for example, there were many fewer female teachers than at the other schools and no female administrators. Looking back on Northington, Charlie (chapter 3) thinks her mostly male teachers were "very fair and great teachers, but the administration doesn't welcome female teachers. The young single females stay a year or two and leave. The married women are wives of teachers. They're the ones who bake cookies for dorm parties. They're where their husbands are and that defines them." She faults the school for providing very few role models for their female students. At Egremont, the headmaster has hired three female administrators in the last three years, in an attempt to counteract this sort of sexism. At the girls' schools, on the other hand, female heads and deans are prominent examples of women in positions of authority.

Career Aspirations

Many girls at all four schools aspired to "nontraditional" careers. There did not seem to be any difference in the careers to which the girls aspired based on what type of school they attended. These aspirations seemed largely unrelated to parents' careers, and unfortunately, in some cases, to the girls' abilities.

But the range of these careers was limited. Among these girls, there were none who wanted to be engineers or dentists or computer scientists, and only one or two who ever wanted to be architects or veterinarians. This is consistent with my earlier findings (Shmurak, 1994b) that independent school alumnae do not tend to enter these fields. Graber (1994) has also found very few girls who are interested in careers in science or engineering in her longitudinal study of girls attending independent schools in New York City. The fact that high socioeconomic status, though positively correlated with academic achievement, is negatively correlated with majoring in quantitative fields in college (Ethington & Wolfle, 1988; Maple & Stage, 1991; O'Hara, 1995) may mean that the economic incentives to entering fields like engineering or computer science are absent for most of these girls. Even among the scholarship students at these schools, there were no aspiring engineers or computer scientists, so the culture of the independent school may tend to discourage girls from aspiring to these fields. Girls from public high schools have entered these fields in increasing numbers over the years (Shmurak, 1994a).

Most of the girls, at both types of schools, were "clueless" as to the requirements of their "chosen" fields (as were the three boys that I interviewed at Northington in 1995). Career aspirations measured during high school are very volatile and often unrealistic (Jordaan & Heyde, 1979) and independent schools, whether coeducational or single sex, have never emphasized career planning, so this was not extremely surprising.

Over and over, the girls told me that no one ever talked to them about potential careers. Usually the topic came up for them for the first time when they went to see their college counselor at the end of junior year. At Summerford, an internship program provides some of the girls, like superstar Jane (chapter 3), with career exploration opportunities in senior year, but too many of the girls in my study said they "never got their act together" to apply for an internship, so it appears that only the most focused girls take advantage of the internship program. The other three schools do even less in career guidance.

There were relatively few exceptions to this. Language teachers at Summerford, Northington, and Egremont seemed to provide some (limited) information as to the usefulness of being bilingual in certain careers. Teachers of drama and art history provided some career information and encouragement to Lita and Maria at Summerford. Mathematics and science teachers seemed to be particularly remiss, however, in providing girls with career guidance. Roxanne at Summerford (chapter 5) showed both talent and interest in physics— she is one of the very few in the study who took two years of physics—and yet no one ever talked to her about engineering as a career. Girls who said that they liked science were unaware of career opportunities except for the most obvious ones like medicine.

This did not seem to be a result of sexist attitudes or of teachers' taking girls' careers less seriously than that of boys. Of the three Northington boys that I interviewed, none had ever discussed career aspirations with a teacher. All three aspired to science-related careers (engineering, medicine, and physical therapy) and yet had not discussed this with anyone at Northington except the college counselor. One of the three boys, on the other hand, had been taken by his father to a career counseling service because his father was concerned that he still had no career direction by eleventh grade. Not even one of the girls in the study mentioned any such concern on the part of their parents. Most said that their parents "just want me to be happy." This probably does reflect the fact that parents are still more concerned with their sons' careers than with those of their daughters.

The fact that the aspirations of the students at the girls' schools in this study did not differ from those at the coeducational schools appears at first to contradict the claims made by the National Coalition of Girls' Schools (1993). In fact, when one looks closely at the results of the National Coalition of Girls' Schools survey (personal communication, December 13, 1993), one sees that their results are quite close to my own. In their survey of 1,000 seniors at girls' schools in 1992, they found 23% who planned to major in science, mathematics, or engineering; among my sample of 25 seniors at Watson Hill and Summerford, there were six planning to major in science and one planning to major in mathematics, a total of 28%. So my smaller sample is actually in quite good agreement with the findings of the Coalition.

The Coalition then compared the 23% to the national average of 6% of high school senior girls planning to major in these fields; however, when I compare the girls at girls' schools in my sample to the girls at coeducational independent schools, a very different picture emerges. For in my sample, 6 out of 22 senior girls at Egremont and Northington planned to major in science, a total of 36%—somewhat higher than the girls' schools.

Similarly, the Coalition survey found that 17% of seniors at girls' high schools aspired to careers as physicians. In my sample, 20% of the girls at the two all-girls schools planned to be doctors at the end of their senior year, again a result close to the findings of the Coalition. At the two coeducational schools, 23% of the girls planned to be doctors—about the same as in the girls' schools. Thus, my results both support the findings of the National Coalition of Girls' Schools and illuminate the importance of using the correct group for comparison.

High School to College Transition

Most of these young women have made good adjustments to their colleges, although there are some notable exceptions. Among those who have dropped out of their colleges already, some were influenced by personal problems (Kasmira, chapter 4 and Kelly, chapter 8) and others by choosing a college that simply didn't meet their needs (Shelby, chapter 7). Of the others not mentioned in the case studies, two were from Watson Hill: Alexia, who left Saint Anselm College because she wanted to be closer to her family, and Sydney, who left Bucknell University for reasons that I have not been able to discover. Thus, three students from Watson Hill and two from Egremont had left their respective colleges midway through their first year.

A great many of these young women, not surprisingly, were dismayed by the large impersonal lecture classes they found at the universities, particularly those in the sciences. After four years in the close, caring communities provided by all four schools in my study, classes of 200 or more and professors who don't know one's name come as quite a shock. Perhaps the most unhappy stories came from two who went from a girls' school to a school of technology: Trudy (chapter 7) of Watson Hill who went to Rochester Institute of Technology and Eliza (chapter 6), also of Watson Hill, who went to Virginia Tech. For others, the adjustment has gone a bit more smoothly, but there is still much discussion of "weeder courses" (Jocelyn of Egremont, chapter 8) and "cutthroat competition" (Elizabeth of Northington, chapter 6) in the science courses. I cannot help feeling that this also played a large role in Charlie's (chapter 3) decision to abandon the sciences.

Some of the students who went to smaller colleges have complained that they found the colleges less diverse than their previous schools. Shelby (chapter 7), and Christine (chapter 5), both of Egremont, and Beth (chapter 8) of Summerford are in that group. Shelby has left her college and Christine is thinking about transferring after sophomore year to a large university; Beth, ever the survivor, will "stick it out" at her college.

Four of the students in my study went to women's colleges. Betsy (chapter 6) of Watson Hill and Leah (chapter 6) of Egremont seem to have had very little trouble adjusting to their new environments. For Betsy, the all-female environment is "very comfortable," though she worries a little about facing a coeducational world after eight years of single sex education; she plans to take courses at nearby coeducational colleges to help her with this. Leah misses having men in her life, but is so much happier than she was at Egremont that it doesn't affect her very much.

Robin, also from Egremont, did not choose Simmons College because it was a women's college, but has found it "more serious and less competitive" than Egremont, and says she barely notices the difference in not having men in her classes. Anna, likewise from Egremont, chose Wellesley College not for its single sex environment but for its academic reputation; like Leah, she sometimes misses having males around but realizes that the comfortable living style and intellectual atmosphere that she is experiencing is at least partially the result of her being in a women's college.

How have the students from the girls' schools adjusted to the coeducational colleges that they now attend? Overall, the transition has been smooth. The most common response to my question about the difference in having boys in classes has been "Not much." A few students mentioned that it made classes fun and that flirting was now an aspect of going to class. Others talked of "being intimidated at first" or being "distracted": Nina of Summerford said "It was like sixth grade all over again for the first few weeks." In general, most of the girls indicated that intimidation and distraction were temporary phenomena. As mentioned above, the two girls' school graduates that had the most severe adjustment—Eliza (chapter 6) and Trudy (chapter 7)—were at the technical schools, where both the size of the school and the high male/female ratio have made the transition very difficult.

Some students seem to have lowered their aspirations as a result of their first year of college, as Arnold (1995) and Holland and Eisenhart (1990) have reported. One difficulty with quantifying how many students to include in this category is the question of what actually constitutes a lower aspiration. For example, several students have decided to become teachers who have never mentioned this as a career before—is this a lowered aspiration? Certainly, teaching is a more traditional women's career and of lower status in American society than medicine or law. On the other hand, a woman pursuing a traditional career such as nursing or teaching could be as strongly career-oriented as a woman pursuing a nontraditional career (Betz & Fitzgerald, 1987).

The question, I think, is whether the student herself sees this as a lesser career. In the cases of Kerry of Egremont (chapter 3) and Lynn of Watson Hill (chapter 5), both seem to me to be "falling back" on teaching as something they can easily do, whereas journalism (the previous career choice for both of them) would require more ambition. The same appears to be the case of Lindsay of Northington (briefly mentioned in chapter 6) and Robin of Egremont, who are abandoning careers in physical therapy and medical ethics respectively, and going into teaching because they don't want to deal with the challenging science courses and competition required by their previous career choices. In the case of Kerry and Lynn, the importance of boyfriends in their lives at present seems to be a factor that leads them to "scaled down ambitions and notions of self" (Holland & Eisenhart, 1990, p. 186).

Some are harder to judge. Both Charlie of Northington (chapter 3) and Roxanne of Summerford (chapter 5) no longer want to study medicine. Both give as their reason changes in the medical care system. Charlie is considering teaching for the first time, but isn't sure at what level; she could equally well see herself teaching college or kindergarten. Roxanne is thinking about being a psychologist or a lawyer. These two do not seem to me to have significantly lowered their aspirations.

Betsy of Watson Hill (chapter 6) still wants to be a doctor, but is considering being a physician's assistant or a child psychologist if she decides that the competition and pressure of medical school are too much for her. Eliza of Watson Hill (chapter 6) and Maria of Summerford (chapter 7) have given up their nontraditional career aspirations of veterinarian and architect, respectively, as a result of disillusionment with their entry level courses. They have not yet made firm commitments to new careers, so it is too early to say that they have lowered their aspirations.

Tables 10.8–10.12 summarize the changes in career aspirations from ninth grade through first year of college of all the students in the study. (A question mark in the right-hand column indicates that the student has not responded to letters or E-mail this year.)

Table 10.8 Summary Career Profiles of the Girls in this Book: Summerford School

Student	Chapter	Start of 9th grade	End of 12th grade	End,1st yr of college
Jane	3	Doctor	Doctor	Doctor
Mimi	4	Doctor	Doctor	Doctor
Roxanne	5	Undecided	Sports medicine	Psychologist or lawyer
Anne	6	Lawyer	Doctor	Doctor
Lita	7	Actress	Actress	Actress
Maria	7	Architect	Architect	Undecided
Beth	8	Undecided	Undecided	Business
Dina		Undecided	Speech pathologist	Speech pathologist
Christina		Physical therapy	Undecided	Undecided
Amelia		Mother	Undecided	Undecided
Anastasia		Doctor	Marketing	*
Nichelle		Actress	Undecided	Undecided
Vivien		Undecided	Lawyer	Lawyer
Wanda		Diplomat	Counseling	*

* Did not attend college in 1996-97.

Table 10.9 Summary Career Profiles of the Girls in this Book: Watson Hill School

Student	Chapter	Start of 9th grade	End of 12th grade	End, 1st yr of college
Edith	3	Undecided	Biologist	Biologist
Lynn	5	Biologist	Journalist	Teacher
Eliza	6	Veterinarian	Veterinarian	Business
Betsy	6	Doctor	Doctor	Doctor or psychologist
Trudy	7	Doctor	Photographer	Photographer
Kelly	8	Undecided	Business	Undecided*
Cindy		Undecided	Business	Business
Sydney		Doctor	Business	? *
Alexia		Psychiatrist	Teacher	Business**
Anne		Psychiatrist	Undecided	Undecided
Marie		Undecided	Undecided	Undecided

* Did not finish first year of college
** Transferred to state university near home for second semester

Table 10.10 **Summary Career Profiles of the Girls
in this Book: Egremont School**

Student	Chapter	Start of 9th grade	End of 12th grade	End,1st yr of college
Kerry	3	Undecided	Undecided	Journalist or teacher
Whitney	4	Psychologist	Journalist	Community activist
Kasmira	4	Zoologist	Lawyer	Social wker or teacher*
Stephanie	4	Accountant	Languages	Undecided
Christine	5	Teacher	Sports psychologist	Physical therapist
Andrea	6	Undecided	Biologist	Biologist
Leah	6	Actuary	Researcher	Doctor
Shelby	7	Undecided	Undecided	Undecided*
Jocelyn	8	Undecided	Pharmacist	Undecided
Jill		Designer	Undecided	?
Britt		Stockbroker	Writer	Business
Robin		Architect	Medical ethicist	Teacher
Anna		Doctor	Undecided	Undecided

* Did not finish first year of college

Table 10.11 Summary Career Profiles of the Girls in this Book: Northington School

Student	Chapter	Start of 9th grade	End of 12th grade	End,1st yr of college
Charlie	3	Doctor	Doctor	Undecided
Sage	4	Lawyer	Lawyer	Lawyer
Natasha	5	Writer	Athlete	Sports
Lindsay	6	Physical therapy	Physical therapy	Kindergtn teacher
Elizabeth	6	Undecided	Doctor	Doctor
Alexandra	6	Doctor	Doctor	Environ. Law
Carla	7	Undecided	Magazine editor	Magazine editor
Taylor	8	Mother	Elem. teacher	Undecided
Paige		Undecided	Real estate	Physical therapy

**Table 10.12 Summary Career Profiles of the Girls
in this Book: Those Who Left**

Student	Chapter	Start of 9th grade	End of 12th grade	End, 1st yr of college
Corrine	9	Business	Business	Business
Ellen	9	Doctor	Psychiatrist	Undecided
Lenore	9	Photographer	Photographer	Photographer
Melissa	9	Veterinarian	Psychiatrist	Psychiatrist
Veronica	9	Journalist	Undecided	Art gallery
Penny	9	Lawyer	Nurse	Nurse
Racquel	9	Doctor	Psychologist	Lawyer
Anne		Lawyer	?	?
Monica		Psychologist	?	?

Limitations to the Study

One must be cautious about generalizing these findings to students and schools that are very different from those in my study. The girls studied are predominantly white and middle-class and the schools are all small and highly oriented toward academics and college admission. All four schools are located in Connecticut and most students are from the northeastern United States.

Even within the four schools, it is possible that a particular sample of students may not fairly represent the school, despite the precautions that the researcher has taken to make the groups equivalent and representative. The academic dean at Watson Hill has noted, for example, that the class of 1996 was a weaker class academically than either the class before or the class after it; the academic dean at Egremont, on the other hand, has characterized the girls in the class of 1996 as being an extremely strong group of advocates for the Egremont experience. As noted above, the Summerford sample, while representative of the school in many ways, contained a disproportionate number of girls who were not strong students in mathematics and science.

Nonetheless, this study does illuminate the experiences of a group of girls going through adolescence at two girls' schools and two coeducational schools. While it may not be possible to generalize these results to all independent schools, single sex or coeducational, the study may help us understand the factors related to career orientation and school success of a group of bright adolescent females who have many educational and economic opportunities available to them. It may also reveal some of the factors that encourage or thwart the career development of young women like them.

Impact of the Study

Although not intended, the study has had some effects on the girls and the schools in the study, as well as on the researcher herself. Many girls whom I interviewed this past year have told me that being in this study has made them think about issues that they might not have considered on their own. Students have told me that being in this study "has made me more aware of my surroundings and how they affect me." Others have said that "listening to myself talk to you helps me grasp where I am" or "it makes me look at myself and my life more objectively." Still others have said that "knowing that someone cares what I think has made me feel special."

Each year, I have summarized the interviews and quantitative data and issued a brief report to the heads and academic deans at the four schools (while being careful to preserve the anonymity of the girls). The school administrators have used these reports in various ways. At Egremont, my documentation of the sexism in the science department was used by the academic dean as part of her rationale for hiring two female science teachers, whose effect on students like Andrea was immediate. At Watson Hill, the academic dean used excerpts from all four reports to stimulate thoughtful discussion of school change at the first faculty meeting of every year. At Summerford and Northington, I was invited by the heads of the schools to speak to faculty groups about my findings, perhaps to challenge some of the teachers' own assumptions about their schools.

Doing this research has had a profound effect on me. Certainly, I have had to question many of my own beliefs about single sex education and coeducation. I have come to see more of the complexities of the issues involved in educating adolescent girls. But most of all, I have come to know and care deeply about many wonderful young women who have shared their thoughts and experiences with me.

Chapter Eleven

Reconsiderations

In 1978, feminist poet and teacher Adrienne Rich encouraged teachers of female students to "listen to the women's voices. Listen to the silences, the unasked questions, the blanks. Listen to the small, soft voices, often courageously trying to speak up, voices of women taught early that tones of confidence, challenge, anger or assertiveness are strident and unfeminine" (Rich, 1978, p. 243). I have been listening to the voices for five years—sometimes soft and small, often assertive and confident—and the following are my conclusions.

Girls' Schools vs. Coeducational Schools

There were few differences between the girls' schools and the coeducational schools. Why should this be? Lee (1997), trying to replicate her findings from the Catholic schools in the independent schools, also found that "on some outcomes, students in girls' schools did better than their coeducational counterparts, on others the reverse" (p. 147). She concluded that, due to differences in clientele between the Catholic and the independent schools, her earlier studies that showed the benefits of single sex Catholic schools were not generalizable to the independent school population.

Lee (1997) further suggests that the organizational features that enhance both school effectiveness and equity include: small school size, a curriculum that emphasizes academics, expectations for high student involvement in their own learning, teachers' willingness to take responsibility for students' learning, and a feeling of community to the social relations within the school. She concludes, "Single sex schools for girls often look this way" (p. 152). Certainly, both Summerford and Watson Hill exemplify these criteria; however, since Northington and Egremont were chosen for this study because they were so similar to the girls' schools on most measures, they also meet the criteria quite well. Thus, the gender composition of the schools had little effect on most of the outcomes.

Nonetheless, there were some differences: a higher academic orientation (at least as measured by Advanced Placement test scores) and greater support for the arts at the girls' schools, and a stronger college acceptance record and greater emphasis on athletics and science at the coeducational schools. Also, as Lee et al. (1994) found, there were different types of sexist practices found at the different types of schools: gender reinforcement at Summerford and gender discrimination at Egremont.

I commented in chapter 10 that some of the differences found seemed to corroborate stereotypes that many people hold about girls' schools and coeducational schools that were formerly boys' schools. I think there is good reason for this. As the head of one of the schools put it to me, "Schools change slowly." I think she could have added, "And New England boarding schools change more slowly than most."

There is much anecdotal evidence to support this contention; I will give some from my own experience. In 1974, when I first came to Connecticut in search of a science teaching position, I found that many newly coeducational (formerly boys') schools had all-male science departments. Twenty years later, schools such as Egremont and Northington still had all or mostly male science departments. Why had they failed to hire any women over all those years? To some extent, it is because the teachers who were there twenty years ago are still there. One of the sexist teachers at Egremont, as Kerry and Andrea described it, "was there before the girls came, and he still resents that we're here!" At Northington, as Charlie explained it, institutional policies tend to discourage single women from staying and married women from joining the faculty. I myself rejected a job offer from such a school in 1974.

On the other hand, when I did take a position at a girls' school, I was told by a teacher who had been teaching chemistry there for eighteen years that "our girls cannot understand equilibrium." Fortunately, I paid no attention to her remark and initiated the first rigorous chemistry course at that school in many years, which included many topics requiring an understanding of the concept of equilibrium and all the attendant calculations. Nonetheless, this teacher continued to teach at the school for nearly twenty more years; although she switched to teaching biology after I arrived, I am not sure what concepts in biology she assumed that "our girls" could not master.

The fact that these schools are the close community systems that make them so effective in many ways also insures that teachers stay for many years. The "family atmosphere" so treasured by the schools also makes it difficult to dismiss teachers from the faculty or confront older teachers about outmoded ideas. And so "schools change slowly." As the older teachers at both types of schools are replaced with teachers who accept females as the equals of males, the sexist practices that Lee and I have observed should disappear. The heads of these schools can try to change school cultures regarding athletics and science at girls' schools, and arts at the coeducational schools, but they will certainly meet some resistance from the established faculty. Heads of coeducational schools can also examine their administrative policies to see what conditions hinder their ability to hire and retain effective female teachers.

Having found so few differences between the two types of schools, I am left to conclude that both types are very effective learning environments. As the case studies illustrated, some girls may have been better served by one type of school, but almost all of the girls found their experience to be a positive one and almost all felt that they had grown in confidence and academic skills. To some extent, self-selection may play a role in this. Most of the girls told me that they chose the school they did "because it felt good when I visited here." Thus the feeling that the school puts forth when prospective students visit is very important and most girls tend to choose the school that fits them best.

At the start of the book, I asked a question about what is gained and what is lost in both single sex schools and coeducational schools. I asked the students in my study the same question this year. The girls from the coeducational schools told me that they enjoyed the competition and different perspective that the boys brought to their classes. Many said that being with males "helped me to be aggressive." Indeed many psychologists believe that "*already* aggressive girls don't usually fare better in all-girls schools" (deGroot, 1994, p. 61). Girls from coed schools thought the social interactions "made school fun," and helped them learn that "boys were people who could be my friends." They thought it was "good practice for college and the real world." The majority thought having boys in their class was an entirely positive experience, although two mentioned "being self-conscious" or "holding back on asking a question because I didn't want to look stupid."

Over and over again, the girls from the girls' schools told me that they were enabled, by the absence of boys, to speak out and to be themselves. As Walker and Mehr (1992) found in their study of the all-girls Hunter High School, the girls' school graduates in this study spoke of the lack of social distractions and the focus on learning.

They also confirmed Sadker and Sadker's (1994) report that girls' school alumnae feel that their school helped them develop self-confidence, assertiveness, and a strong sense of identity. Some of the girls also said that they learned that "It was okay to be smart." Most of them said that being without boys for four years had no negative effects, although a few mentioned that they "missed the high school social scene," "missed the male perspective in their classes," or found it "difficult to have men as friends now." Walker and Mehr and Sadker and Sadker also report these reactions from girls' school alumnae.

Having worked in a girls' school for many years, I can attest that there is a particular atmosphere at these schools that is very distinct. In 1992, I visited Philadelphia Girls' High School as part of my research on girls' school alumnae (Shmurak, 1994a). Although the school was an urban public high school and its population was predominantly students of color, it felt very much like Summerford and Watson Hill. The atmosphere is difficult to define: Jane of Summerford (chapter 3) talked about feeling "comfortable being silly." I think it may be a playfulness that adolescent girls have when there are no boys around to inhibit them. Additionally, when the students are all female and considerably more than half the faculty is female, "there is an unspoken validation of female norms and their consequences" (Belash, 1992). One of the consequences that I see is a willingness, on the part of both adults and students, to show affection and perhaps even passion.

Does this have any effect on their future academic achievement or their eventual careers? The results of this study (and others) do not support any such effect. Alumnae of girls' schools often attribute their successes in business and other fields to the years they spent in the single sex atmosphere (Sedgwick, 1997), but this is difficult to demonstrate empirically. Nonetheless, there is much anecdotal support for alumnae feelings that the single sex experience helped them develop self-confidence that has carried them through the challenges of adulthood. To my knowledge, no one has ever done a study of alumnae of coeducational independent schools to determine if they attribute their success to their years at those schools.

As Moore, Piper, and Schaefer (1992) have concluded, the results "are inconclusive as to whether one type of school is more effective than another in promoting higher academic achievement and psychosocial achievement" (p. 17). Single sex schooling represents one effective approach, and as such, girls' schools should not have to feel that they must prove they are *more* effective than coeducational schools in order to survive; simply being equally effective for most girls and more effective for some girls should be enough (Moore, 1992).

College Preparation

All four schools in my study are college-preparatory schools. What does it mean to prepare students for college? Does it mean to help them achieve an academic and extracurricular record that will get them into a selective college? Does it mean giving them the skills to do the academic work once they get there? Or does it mean preparing them to cope with the challenges of college life as well?

From what I have heard from the girls in this study, the schools do an excellent job in helping them get into college. The teachers also impart many academic skills that will help them succeed in college courses. But none of the schools appear to make any effort to give their students strategies for coping with some of the difficulties that arise in the transition from small supportive communities to larger, more impersonal universities. Every student that I interviewed at the end of her first year of college commented that one of the biggest differences between prep school and college was the fact that "no one cares about you here."

Particularly in the sciences, but in other subjects as well, large impersonal lecture classes and unavailable (or seemingly unapproachable) professors caused students to give up long-held interests. This was explicitly the case for Beth of Summerford (chapter 8) in mathematics and Eliza of Watson Hill (chapter 6) in veterinary medicine. Although she gave other reasons, I think this also had much to do with the decision to abandon a career in medicine on the part of Charlie of Northington (chapter 3).

A recent study (Geraghty, 1997) of students in the sciences showed that the way the sciences are traditionally taught in college has a disproportionately negative effect on female and minority students, many of whom prefer to learn in the context of a more personal teacher-student relationship. What distinguished those who stayed with their planned science majors from those who switched was the development of coping strategies. Could these coping strategies be documented and then taught to young women as part of their preparation for college? Could these schools that treasure their small supportive communities warn girls that learning will be much more impersonal in the future, and that this is a problem in the structural organization of universities, not a personal problem? Could they encourage them to find supportive peer groups for learning (Komarovsky, 1985)?

Of course, if college professors of the sciences were to take seriously the flight of so many bright women from their fields, they might attempt to change their pedagogical methods. Certainly, this has been suggested several times (Tobias, 1990; Dembner, 1993; Geraghty, 1997), but the traditions of how science is taught, with its "weeder" introductory courses, are very strong and will change slowly. Structural changes in the universities would be necessary to allow professors more time for teaching and interacting personally with undergraduates. In the meantime, I believe all the small college preparatory schools, both single sex and coeducational, could be doing more to prepare girls for these courses. I wish I had done more when I was a teacher at these schools—perhaps the stories at alumnae reunions would be less apologetic if I had.

That the problem was not just in the sciences was brought home to me by a letter I received from a former girls' school student, who had heard about the research I was doing. I have her permission to quote from this letter:

> When I set off for Yale, I didn't think twice about finding leadership positions or speaking up in class. I brashly enrolled in an American Military History course with 85 football players and three women. While I enjoyed the subject matter immensely, I found myself growing mute as the semester progressed. I was unaccustomed to the way in which comments were presented and it rattled my own confidence to speak. Most of the men contributing in our discussion section had a definite opinion. They weren't interested in bringing up the ultimately ambiguous, indeterminable issues of warfare. Rather they knew exactly what the North or South should have done in a given battle. I kept coming up with more questions, questions which did not have answers, while the men kept denying there could ever be any doubt. It is this experience which turned me toward literature... I wish I had seen my overreaction to militant military historians for what it was: simply getting used to different learning and communication styles. It didn't occur to me that I may have to change my communication style or understand that others approach things differently and that did not mean that my viewpoint was any less valuable and valid. Because we were all girls, there were certain styles and approaches and attitudes that one encounters every day in the real world that I was not accustomed to dealing with. (Amanda, letter dated 3/12/97)

Amanda's letter has provoked much thought and discussion. That male and female communication styles may be different has been written about and publicized quite widely (e.g., Tannen, 1990). The girls in my study, from both types of schools, have also told me that they hear men speaking with more certainty in their college classes "even when they don't know what they are talking about." For some of them, this has not been a problem, but for others, like Amanda, it has been intimidating.

If going to a girls' school means that one style of communication is heard almost exclusively, then the transition to coeducational classrooms may be more difficult for some girls. I wonder if the girls' schools, in preparing their students for college, could warn them that they may feel as Amanda did, and assure them that their female style of communication is different but not invalid. They might also attempt to develop flexibility in communication styles in their girls.

This doesn't mean that the coeducational schools should ignore this issue. In the coeducation schools' classes, is the male communication style always favored? Are their female students learning this style? Or are both styles equally accepted in their classrooms? Could their male students also learn to hear the female style as a valid one? It seems to me that these schools have the opportunity to teach both boys and girls to be flexible in both speaking and listening to different communication styles. The fact that the two white males at Northington who took the AWS were so much more traditional in their attitudes toward gender roles than their female classmates leads me to believe that the coeducational schools could be doing much more with getting their male students to explore gender issues and the viewpoints of their female classmates.

The above recommendations are not as farfetched as they might sound to some. I have been assured by the head of one girls' school that these things could easily be included in a program that the school already has for seniors. As she put it, "Sure we can do a better job of preparing them to take the knocks of college life. But I also want them to know that it's not right. I want them to recognize that, for now, the male model is the real model of power. And we need to work to change that."

I have also been working with a "gender study" faculty group of a nearby coeducational school that has been examining male and female styles in their classroom. Part of their goal is to make both teachers and students more flexible in the communication styles they use and value.

Career Guidance

According to Farmer (1985), motivation to pursue a career develops through three sets of interacting influences: background variables (gender, ethnicity), psychological variables (attitudes, self-concept), and environmental variables (support from parents and teachers). Having a working mother is a positive influence for a girl to pursue nontraditional careers (Betz and Fitzgerald, 1987), as is parental support in general (Farmer, 1985). Girls come to high school with many attitudes well-formed, and as this study showed with AWS scores, some of these attitudes are difficult to change. Thus, the influence that a school can have on career aspirations is limited.

Even so, the lack of career guidance provided by the four schools in this study was striking. Except for the college counselors who met with them near the end of their junior year, almost no faculty seemed to spend the time talking to these girls about possible careers. As I confirmed at Northington, this was true for the boys as well. With respect to career guidance, these schools provide what Betz and Fitzgerald (1987) characterize as a "null environment;" that is, they do nothing specifically about career guidance. Because there continues to be more cultural and parental support for young men's careers, Betz and Fitzgerald conclude that failure to counteract the null environment is discriminatory against women. Eccles (1989) agrees that equal treatment in schools is not enough to increase the probability that young women will seriously consider nontraditional educational or vocational options, since they are exposed to heavy doses of gender-role socialization outside of school.

Walker and Mehr (1992), studying 600 alumnae from the formerly all-girls Hunter High School in New York City, found that almost all of them wished they had had more help setting career goals as teenagers. Ninety-eight percent said that a missing aspect of their education was a person who could help them to prepare for the obstacles in the world outside their sheltered one at the high school. The alumnae said "they wanted to do something, but didn't know what. Sometimes they knew what, but didn't know *how*" (p. 42). With adult guidance lacking in high school, they hoped that "when I started college that something would come to me" (p. 96) and often described themselves as "tripping" into their life choices (p. 46). Walker and Mehr conclude that high school girls need guidance to help them to imagine future lives and to devise strategies to overcome the barriers that might stand in their way.

Adolescents are in the stage of career development called "crystallization of vocational preference" by Super (1963); they are just beginning to formulate ideas as to fields and levels of work that are appropriate to their self-concepts and making tentative choices that will enable them to get the education needed for a specific occupation. Teachers can help by opening their eyes to fields of which their students may be unaware. Csikszentmihalyi et al. (1997) report that teachers who take their students' abilities seriously and talk to them about their futures often provide the experience that crystallizes a career goal. Eccles (1989) recommends active career counseling on the part of teachers, providing students with a reason for studying their subjects and telling them how these subjects relate to the occupational world.

It may be that the teachers themselves are unaware of many careers associated with their respective subjects; in that case, it behooves them to make the effort to find out, and the schools to provide the resources and time for the teachers to do it. Teachers would likewise have to know the requirements for certain occupations so that they could advise a student interested in architecture, for example, that physics courses may be as important as art classes for her future. Holding "career fairs" with women and men from various less publicized careers (e.g., forensic chemistry and medical illustration) in attendance as role models would also open new horizons for some girls (and boys).

Another aspect of this study that relates to career development is the repeated difficulty that the girls at all schools had with answering the question, "What are you good at?" At first, I assumed that they were reluctant to seem immodest about their accomplishments; in the third year of the study, however, I asked many of the girls directly why the question was difficult to answer, and discovered that this was simply a question that they never posed for themselves. "I'm always concentrating on what I have to improve, not what I'm good at," was the common answer.

It seems to me that during this period of career exploration, asking this question of themselves is crucial. With the strong advisor system that these schools possess, it should be fairly simple for adults in the community to help girls (and boys) assess realistically what their strengths are. Internship programs, such as that at Summerford, should be expanded to help students better assess what their interests and abilities are. Noble, Subotnik, and Arnold (1996) also mention the need to increase the opportunities for bright young women to explore talent domains and learn of career possibilities. Lyons, Saltonstall, and

Hanmer (1990) propose internships that rotate girls through several different jobs to provide a variety of career experiences. This seems to me an excellent way for girls to test their present career ideas and to try out careers that they may not have known existed.

Hopes, Aspirations, and Courage

I named this book *Voices of Hope* for several reasons. Most obviously, I wanted the girls to speak in their own voices and tell their own stories. I used the word "hope" to emphasize that the stories would include their views of their futures; a "hope" is "a wish or desire accompanied by confident expectation of its fulfillment" (*American Heritage Dictionary of the English Language*). But there are also "false hopes" and "hopes that are crushed," and I think that this book has shown some of each. Girls who decide at an early age to be doctors or architects without the realization of what their personal strengths are, or what those professions require, are filled with false hopes. Girls who face challenging and competitive college courses without any strategies for coping with them are set up for crushed hopes.

Finally, I wanted to distinguish between a "hope" and an "aspiration." To "aspire" to something is more than to simply hope for it; it is "to strive toward an end" (*American Heritage Dictionary of the English Language*). Striving requires taking action and knowing what actions to take. In this sense, only a few girls in this study truly seemed to have career *aspirations*— Jane of Summerford in medicine, Lita of Summerford in drama, Andrea of Egremont in marine biology come to mind first. Although the rest had hopes for their future, many had vague hopes—the end for which to strive was unclear. Their parents gave them little guidance ("Do whatever makes you happy") and their teachers seldom saw beyond college acceptance. Even those girls with an end in mind seldom knew what actions to take to achieve that end. As Walker and Mehr (1992) put it, "They wanted to do something, but didn't know what. Sometimes they knew what, but didn't know *how*" (p. 42).

And yet, having put the word "hope" in my title, I feel responsible to my reader for ending on a positive note. And so I must point out that many career paths are not the straight ones that career development theory posits. For many, the path is a circuitous one, and some return later in life to a goal they had abandoned. My favorite example of this is a former student named Anita, who has given me permission to tell her story.

Anita could well have been one of those at alumnae reunions who sing the apologetic refrain of abandoned hopes for a career in science. She loved chemistry and advanced biology in high school, and went to Tulane University with the intent of being a doctor. Enjoying the social whirl of college perhaps too much, she got Ds in both chemistry and calculus her first semester of college. "Forget it! There's no way I can do this!" was what she told herself and transferred into English and studio art courses. After two years at Tulane, her interest in art took her to Rhode Island School of Design, where she majored in art and photography.

Coincidentally, Anita's first job out of college was as a medical photographer at Boston Children's Hospital, where she found herself in the operating room photographing things like kidney transplants. Her career as a photographer took her next into photojournalism at *Time* magazine. After three years at *Time,* Anita mentioned to her editor, an older woman, that she had always wanted to go to medical school. The older woman said, "I wanted to do that too. It's too late for me, but you gotta do it!"

With that encouragement, Anita enrolled in a summer program at Bryn Mawr, where she took a course in general chemistry. "It was really hard. I cried every night, but I got a B+." Then she entered a postbaccalaureate premedical program at Columbia University, where her advisor in the program told her, "You'll never make it to medical school." Anita said to herself, "I'm going to show you!" and got straight As in organic chemistry, microbiology, calculus, and physics. When she was accepted into Columbia's College of Physicians and Surgeons, she proudly waved the letter at the man who said she'd never get in anywhere.

After medical school, Anita finished a four year residency in internal medicine, and is now doing postdoctoral research in cardiology. Along the way, she married and had two children. Her plans are to stay in academic medicine and do a fellowship in cardiology. "Life is hectic but it's great!" she says. "I'm so glad I didn't give up."

Could Anita's path to a medical career have been a straighter one? And what of the others who settled for lesser careers because of discouraging experiences in their early college years? No secondary school, whether single sex or coeducational, can guarantee a student will attain her goals. But those schools that prepare their girls to find ways to cope with the negative forces they encounter will make it more likely that their alumnae achieve success.

I will close with my own personal hope: may those girls whose long-standing dreams of careers have been crushed or abandoned in this first year of college find the courage to follow Anita's example.

Appendix A. Interview Questions

Year One
1) If you had a younger sister who was thinking of coming to this school, what would you tell her were the good points and the bad points of this school?

2) Have you discovered something this year that you are good at? Or something you are better at than you thought you were?

3) Have there been any teachers in particular that have encouraged you?

4) What have you learned about yourself this year?

5) How has this year affected how you look at your future?

6) Why did you choose this school?

7) Where are you from?

8) What does your mother do? Your father?

Year Two
1) Has it been a good year? In what way?

2) Have you discovered something this year that you are good at? Or something you are better at than you thought you were?

3) Have there been any teachers in particular that have encouraged you?

4) What have you learned about yourself this year?

5) How has this year affected how you look at your future?

6) Was there a time this year when you wanted to speak out about something you really believed in or wanted to tell someone something that they didn't want to hear? How did you handle it?

7) Do you participate actively in your classes? Why or why not?

8) Any changes in home situation or mother's or father's occupation?

Year Three
1) Has it been a good year? In what way?

2) What have you learned about yourself this year?

3) In 9th grade, you wanted to be a _____ and in 10th grade, a _____. What are you thinking about now? Why? (if something different from previous years): Why the change?

4) What help or guidance with respect to thinking about careers have you received from teachers here?

5) What help or guidance with respect to thinking about careers have you received from your parents?

6) What are you thinking about with regard to choosing a college? What things are important to you?

7) Do you have brothers or sisters? How many and what ages? (if older siblings) How have they influenced you?

8) Any changes in home situation or mother's or father's occupation?

Year Four
1) Has it been a good year? In what way?

2) What have you decided about college? Why?

3) What are your present career goals? Why?

4) What do you think are your strengths? How will these help you in the pursuit of your career?

5) Have there been any teachers in particular that have encouraged you this year?

6) Looking back over your four years here, what are your feelings about this school? What are the good points and the bad points?

7) If you had it to do over again, would you choose to come here again?

8) Any changes in home situation or mother's or father's occupation?

Year Five

About former high school:
How concerned were girls with their appearance?
How important was it to have female friendships?
How important was it to have a boyfriend?
(Coed schools) Was there a lot of "pairing off" into couples?
(Coed schools) Did males dominate your classes?
(Coed schools) Did any teachers seem to prefer male students?
(Coed schools) How did having boys in your class help you? hurt you?
(Girls' schools) How did NOT having boys in your class help you? hurt you?

About present college:
Do any professors seem to prefer male students?
Are most of your professors male or female?
Do males dominate your classes?
How does college differ from prep school?
How much harder do you have to work here as opposed to high school?
How important is it to have female friendships?
How important is it to have a boyfriend?
Is there a lot of "pairing off" into couples?
Is there pressure to have a date on Saturday night?
Is there a fraternity/sorority system and how important is it?
Are there any racial issues on campus?
Did you take math/sci courses? How did you do? Did you like them?
What courses did you do especially well in? particularly enjoy?
(If from a girls' school) What is the difference in having boys in the class? Or just around?
(If interested in sci) How do sci courses differ from those in high school?
(If left college) Why? What will you do now?

Personal

Are you close to your mother? Are there ways in which you want to be like her?

Did both of your parents graduate from college? Did either go to prep school?

Is religion important in your life?

How do you think you've changed this year?

What are your present thoughts about career?

How do you see marriage and family fitting into your career? Or don't you worry about that?

Has being in this study affected you in any way?

Appendix B. Quantitative Data

Table 1. Average Scores on AWS

	Girls' Schools		Coed Schools	
	Watson Hill	Summerford	Egremont	Northington
Fall 1992	38.6 (15)	38.9 (16)	37.8 (17)	38.0 (7)
May 1993	38.8 (15)	40.5 (16)	38.1 (17)	38.4 (8)
May 1994	38.4 (14)	39.4 (16)	40.3 (15)	38.4 (9)
May 1995	39.4 (11)	41.0 (14)	39.9 (14)	39.3 (8)
May 1996	39.5 (10)	40.6 (14)	41.2 (13)	38.8 (9)
May 1997	39.9 (10)	41.2 (12)	40.1 (12)	37.2 (8)

No significant differences were found among the schools at any time.

Table 2. Average Grades, 1993–96

| | Girls' Schools | | Coed Schools | |
	Watson Hill	Summerford	Egremont	Northington
Math				
1993	8.3 (15)	6.9 (16)	7.3 (17)	7.6 (8)
1994	7.2 (14)	6.8 (16)	7.8 (16)	8.0 (9)
1995	7.2 (11)	7.1 (14)	7.4 (14)	8.1 (8)
1996	5.8 (9)	7.4 (13)	6.8 (13)	8.3 (9)
English				
1993	7.1 (15)	7.0 (16)	7.4 (17)	8.1 (8)
1994	6.6 (14)	8.1 (16)	7.0 (16)	7.8 (9)
1995	7.0 (11)	8.1 (14)	7.9 (14)	7.4 (8)
1996	7.1 (11)	8.3 (14)	8.2 (13)	8.3 (9)

Grades were computed on a 12 point scale, where 12=A+, 11=A, 10=A–, 9=B+, 8=B, 7=B–, 6=C+, 5=C etc.

No significant differences were found at any time.

Table 2. Average Grades, 1993–96 (continued)

	Girls' Schools		Coed Schools	
	Watson Hill	Summerford	Egremont	Northington
Science				
1993	7.0 (12)	6.9 (15)	6.2 (17)	8.5 (8)
1994	7.3 (12)	6.5 (16)	7.1 (16)	7.2 (9)
1995	5.5 (8)	7.6 (8)	6.6 (14)	7.9 (7)
1996	7.9 (8)	6.0 (11)	6.7 (12)	7.6 (8)
All Subjects				
1993	7.7 (15)	7.0 (16)	7.1 (17)	8.2 (8)
1994	6.8 (14)	7.8 (16)	7.5 (16)	7.8 (9)
1995	6.8 (11)	7.6 (14)	7.4 (14)	7.8 (8)
1996	7.3 (11)	7.8 (14)	7.8 (13)	8.3 (9)

Grades were computed on a 12 point scale, where 12=A+, 11=A, 10=A−, 9=B+, 8=B, 7=B−, 6=C+, 5=C etc.

No significant differences were found at any time.

Table 3. Math Courses Taken

	Girls' Schools		Coed Schools	
	Watson Hill	Summerford	Egremont	Northington
Years of Math				
4 years	7	13	13	9
3–3.7 years	4	1	0	0
Highest Math Course				
AP Calculus	4	1	0	2
Calculus	0	3	5	1
PreCalculus	6	3	5	5
Algebra 2	0	1	0	0
Other	1(Trig)	6(FPC)*	3**	1 ***

*FPC=Fundamentals of PreCal, a lower level PreCal course

** 1 in math functions after Alg 2, 1 in elem functions after Alg 2, 1 in elem functions *after* PreCal

*** Discrete math, taken *after* PreCal)

Table 4. Science Courses Taken

	Girls' Schools		Coed Schools	
	Watson Hill	Summerford	Egremont	Northington
Years of Science				
More than 4	0	0	3	3
4 years	2	4	7	3
3–3.5	7	9	3	2
2–2.5	2	1	0	1
Courses taken Beyond Biology				
Chem & Physics & more	4	3	3	6
Chem & Physics	5	1	6	2
Other strong programs		2*		
Weak programs**	2	8	4	1
No exposure to physics	2	6	3	1

* One girl took Chemistry and AP Bio, another took Chem and AP Chem.   Lack of physics may be a problem in college science courses.

** Examples: Chem & plants (Watson Hill); intro chem only (Summerford); chem & marine bio (Egremont); chem only (Northington).

Table 5. Comparison of Sample Group to Whole Class

	Girls' Schools		Coed Schools	
	Watson Hill	Summerford	Egremont	Northington
Number of Girls				
Class of '96	41	59	26	49
Sample	11	14	13	9
	(27%)	(24%)	(50%)	(18%)
4 or more yrs of science				
Class of '96	12	23	21	34
	(29%)	(39%)	(81%)	(69%)
Sample	2	4	10	6
	(18%)	(29%)	(77%)	(67%)
1 year of physics				
Class of '96	31	24	20	45
	(76%)	(41%)	(77%)	(92%)
Sample	9	5	9	8
	(81%)	(36%)	(69%)	(89%)
1 year of calculus				
Class of '96	13	26	8	15
	(27%)	(44%)	(31%)	(31%)
Sample	4	4	5	3
	(36%)	(29%)	(38%)	(33%)

Table 6. SSATs (1991) and SATs (1995)

	Girls' Schools		Coed Schools	
	Watson Hill	Summerford	Egremont	Northington
SSAT- Verbal	304 (15)	306 (16)	306 (14)	308 (8)
Highest SATV	594 (11)	624 (14)	614 (13)	612 (9)
SSAT-Math	298 (15)	296 (16)	298 (14)	309 (8)
Highest SATM	557 (11)	574 (14)	589 (13)	603 (9)

There were no significant differences found among schools.

Table 7. Achievement Test (SAT-II) Scores

	Girls' Schools		Coed Schools	
	Watson Hill	Summerford	Egremont	Northington
Writing	605 (11)	589 (13)	586 (13)	618 (9)
Math 1C	530 (5)	547 (12)	546 (9)	521 (8)
Math 2C	579 (7)	620 (3)	640 (4)	603 (4)
Spanish	410 (1)	556 (8)	670 (4)	340 (1)
French	645 (2)	690 (3)	560 (2)	685 (2)
Latin	565 (2)	570 (1)	-	-
Biology	620 (2)	523 (8)	-	593 (3)
Chemistry	555 (2)	510 (2)	-	485 (6)
Physics	610 (1)	-	-	550 (1)
U.S. History	440 (1)	570 (1)	610 (4)	520 (4)
Literature	640 (6)	-	705 (4)	690 (2)

For the Writing and Math 1C and 2C exams, no significant differences were found among schools. For the other exams, small numbers precluded meaningful statistical comparisons.

Table 8. Correlation Between Senior Grades and SATs

	Girls' Schools		Coed Schools	
	Watson Hill	Summerford	Egremont	Northington
SAT-Verbal & English	0.74*	0.57*	−0.23	0.16
SAT-Math & Math	0.43	0.13	0.13	0.29
SAT-Verbal & Overall Average	0.66*	0.50	−0.08	−0.30
SAT-Math & Overall Average	0.40	0.36	−0.20	0.34
SAT-Verbal & Science	0.15	0.35	−0.32	−0.09
SAT-Math & Science	−0.31	0.68*	−0.10	0.68

* These are statistically significant at the 0.05 level. (Due to the small numbers of girls at Northington, the correlation coefficient for SAT-M and science, which is high, just misses being statistically significant.)

Table 9. Average Scores on AP exams

	Girls' Schools		Coed Schools	
	Watson Hill	Summerford	Egremont	Northington
Art History	-	4 (2)	-	-
Biology	3.5 (2)	5 (2)	-	3.2 (3)
Calculus AB	3.5 (4)	5 (1)	3 (1)	3.5 (2)
Chemistry	-	2 (1)	-	3 (1)
Computer	3 (1)	-	-	-
English Language	3.2 (5)	-	3 (7)	-
English Lit.	5 (1)	3.6 (5)	3.6 (7)	3.5 (4)
European History	4 (3)	4 (2)	3 (1)	-
French Language	3.5 (2)	-	-	3.3 (3)
French Lit.	-	4 (2)	-	3 (1)

Table 9. Average Scores on AP exams (continued)

	Girls' Schools		Coed Schools	
	Watson Hill	Summerford	Egremont	Northington
Latin	3 (1)	3 (1)	-	2 (1)
Physics	3 (1)	3.5 (2)	-	-
Spanish Language	-	4 (1)	3.3 (3)	1 (1)
Studio Art	4 (1)	3.75 (4)	-	-
U.S. History	3.8 (5)	4 (4)	2.5 (6)	2.5 (2)

Table 10. College Acceptances & Correlates

	Girls' Schools		Coed Schools	
	Watson Hill	Summerford	Egremont	Northington
Average	2.73	3.65	4.08	4.33
Ranking	(11)	(13)	(13)	(9)
Correlation w/ college acceptances				
SAT-V	0.73*	0.48	0.48	0.40
SAT-M	0.67*	0.23	0.43	0.21
Math 2C	0.78*	0.24	0.46	0.05
English grade	0.60*	0.68*	−0.16	0.71*
Overall aver. (11th grade)	0.80*	0.76*	0.20	0.33
Overall aver. (12th grade)	0.71*	0.71*	0.13	0.29

* These are statistically significant at the 0.05 level.

(There were no significant correlations between scores on either the Writing Achievement or the Math 1C and college acceptances, nor were there any significant correlations between math or science grades and college acceptances at any school.)

References

American Association of University Women. (1991). *Shortchanging girls, shortchanging America.* Washington, DC: AAUW.

American Association of University Women. (1992). *How schools shortchange girls.* Washingon, D.C.: AAUW.

Arnold, K.D. (1995). *Lives of promise: What becomes of high school valedictorians.* San Francisco: Jossey-Bass.

Barron's Profiles of American Colleges (20th ed.). (1995).

Belash, R.P. (1992). Girls' schools: Separate means equal. In P.R. Kane (Ed.), *Independent schools, independent thinkers* (pp. 73–90). San Francisco: Jossey-Bass.

Betz, N.E. & Fitzgerald, L.F. (1987). *The career psychology of women.* Orlando, FL: Academic Press.

Biggs, M.E. (1996, August). America's top boarding schools. *Town and Country,* pp. 89–110.

Boli, J., Allen, M.L., & Payne, A. (1985). High-ability women and men in undergraduate mathematics and chemistry courses. *American Educational Research Journal, 22*(4), 605–626.

Brown, L.M., & Gilligan, C. (1992). *Meeting at the crossroads: Women's psychology and girls' development.* Cambridge, MA: Harvard University Press.

Cairns, E. (1990). The relationship between adolescent perceived self-competence and attendance at single-sex secondary school. *British Journal of Educational Psychology, 60,* 207–211.

Carpenter, P., & Hayden, M. (1987). Girls' academic achievements: Single-sex versus coeducational schools in Australia. *Sociology of Education, 60,* 156–167.

Civian, J.T. (1996, April). Pathways for women in the sciences II: Retention of women in math and science at the college level. Paper presented at the meeting of the American Educational Research Association, New York, NY.

Csikszentmihalyi, M., Rathmunde, K., & Whalen, S. (1997). *Talented teenagers: The roots of success and failure.* Cambridge: Cambridge University Press.

Daly, P. (1995). Science course participation and science achievement in single sex and co-educational schools. *Evaluation and Research in Education, 9*(2), 91–98

Daly, P. (1996). The effects of single-sex and coeducational secondary schooling on girls' achievement. *Research Papers in Education, 11*(3), 289–306.

Daly, P., Ainley, J., & Robinson, L. (1996). The influence of single-sex secondary schooling on choice of science courses. Paper presented at the meeting of American Educational Research Association, New York, NY.

Daly, P., & Shuttleworth, I. (1996). Determinants of public examination entry and attainment in mathematics: Evidence on gender and gender-type of school from the 1980s and 1990s in Northern Ireland. *Evaluation and Research in Education, 10*(1), 1–11.

deGroot, G. (1994, July). Do single-sex classes foster better learning? *APA Monitor*, pp. 60–61.

Dembner, A. (1993, December 8). Women in math, science are studied. *The Boston Globe*, p. 16.

Dick, T.P., & Rallis, S.F. (1991). Factors and influences on high school students' career choices. *Journal for Research in Mathematics Education, 22*(4), 281–292.

Dyer, G., & Tiggemann, M. (1996). The effect of school environment on body concerns in adolescent women. *Sex Roles, 34*(12), 127–138.

Eccles, J.S. (1989). Bringing young women to math and science. In M. Crawford & M. Gentry (Eds.), *Gender and thought: Psychological perspectives* (pp. 36–58). New York: Springer-Verlag.

Estrich, S. (1994, May 22). For girls' schools and women's colleges, separate is better. *New York Times Magazine*, p. 39.

Ethington, C.A., & Wolfle, L.M. (1988). Women's selection of quantitative undergraduate fields of study: Direct and indirect influences. *American Educational Research Journal, 25*(2), 157–175.

Evans, K.M. (1996). Counseling gifted women of color. In K. Arnold, K.D. Noble, & R.F. Subotnik (Eds.), *Remarkable women: Perspectives on female talent development* (pp. 367–381). Cresskill, NJ: Hampton Press.

Farmer, H.S. (1985). A model of career and achievement motivation for women and men. *Journal of Counseling Psychology, 32*, 363–390.

Foon, A.E. (1988). The relationship between school type and adolescent self-esteem, attribution styles and affiliation needs: Implications for educational outcome. *British Journal of Educational Psychology, 58*, 44–54.

Geraghty, M. (1997, January 10). Why bright students abandon plans to major in the sciences. *The Chronicle of Higher Education*, p. A50.

Gill, J. (1996, April). Different contexts: Similar outcomes. Paper presented at the meeting of American Educational Research Association, New York, NY.

Graber, J. (1994, November). The influence of educational context on life and career aspirations: A longitudinal investigation. Paper presented at Studies in Success conference, Mount Holyoke College, South Hadley, MA.

Harvard Magazine (1996, November/December). Advertisement, p. 5.

Harvey, T.J. (1985). Science in single-sex and mixed teaching groups. *Educational Research, 27*(3), 179–182.

Henderson, V.L., & Dweck, C.S. (1990). Motivation and achievement. In S.S. Feldman & G.R. Elliott (Eds.), *At the threshold: The developing adolescent* (pp. 308–329). Cambridge, MA: Harvard University Press.

Hilton, T.L., & Lee, V.E. (1988). Student interest and persistence in science: Changes in the educational pipeline in the last decade. *Journal of Higher Education, 59*(5), 510–526.

Hoffer. T.B. (1993, April). Career choice models based on the *High School and Beyond*. Paper presented at the meeting of the American Educational Research Association, Atlanta, GA.

Holland, A., & Andre, T. (1994). The relationship of self-esteem to selected personal and environmental resources of adolescents. *Adolescence, 29*(114), 345–360.

Holland, D.C., & Eisenhart, M.A. (1990). *Educated in romance: Women, achievement and college culture.* Chicago: University of Chicago Press.

Hollinger, C. (1996). An examination of the lives of gifted black women. In K. Arnold, K.D. Noble, & R.F. Subotnik (Eds.), *Remarkable women: Perspectives on female talent development* (pp. 383–398). Cresskill, NJ: Hampton Press.

Jordaan, J.P., & Heyde, M.B. (1979). *Vocational maturity during the high school years.* New York: Teachers College Press.

Komarovsky, M. (1985). *Women in college: Shaping new feminine identities.* New York: Basic Books.

Lee, V.E. (1997). Gender equity and the organization of schools. In B.J. Bank, & P.M. Hall (Eds.), *Gender, equity and schooling: Policy and practice* (pp. 135–158). New York: Garland Publishing.

Lee, V.E., & Bryk, A.S. (1986). Effects of single-sex secondary schools on student achievement and attitudes. *Journal of Educational Psychology* , *78*(5), 381–395.

Lee, V.E., & Marks, H.M. (1990). Sustained effects of the single-sex secondary school experience on attitudes, behaviors and values in college. *Journal of Educational Psychology, 82*(3), 578–592.

Lee, V.E., & Marks, H.M. (1992). Who goes where? Choice of single-sex and coeducational independent secondary schools. *Sociology of Education 65*(3), 226–253.

Lee, V.E., Marks, H.M., & Knowles, T. (1994). Sexism in single-sex and coeducational secondary school classrooms. *Sociology of Education, 67*(2), 92–120.

LePore, P.C. & Warren, J.R. (1997). A comparison of single-sex and coeducational Catholic secondary schooling: Evidence from the National Educational Longitudinal Study of 1988. *American Educational Research Journal 34*(3), 485–511.

Lyons, N.P., Saltonstall, J.F., & Hanmer, T.J. (1990). Competencies and visions: Emma Willard girls talk about being leaders. In C. Gilligan, N.P. Lyons, & T.J. Hanmer (Eds.), *Making connections: The relational worlds of girls at Emma Willard School* (pp. 183–214). Cambridge: Harvard University Press.

Mann, J.W. (1994). *The difference: Growing up female in America.* New York: Warner Books.

Maple, S.A., & Stage, F.K. (1991). Influences on the choice of math/science major by gender and ethnicity. *American Educational Research Journal, 28*(1), 37–60.

Marsh, H.W. (1989a). Effects of attending single-sex and coeducational high schools on achievement, attitudes, behaviors and sex differences. *Journal of Educational Psychology, 81*(1), 70–85.

Marsh, H.W. (1989b). Effects of single-sex and coeducational schools: A response to Lee and Bryk. *Journal of Educational Psychology, 81*(4), 651–653.

Marsh, H.W., Smith, I.D., Marsh, M., & Owens, L. (1988). The transition from single-sex to coeducational high schools: Effects on multiple dimensions of self-concept and on academic achievement. *American Educational Research Journal, 25*(2), 237–269.

Miller-Bernal, L. (1993). Single-sex versus coeducational environments: A comparison of women students' experiences at four colleges. *American Journal of Education, 102*, 23–54.

Moore, M. (1992). Single sex schooling: Perspectives from practice and research. In D. Hollinger & R. Adamson (Eds.), *Single-sex schooling: Proponents speak.* (pp. 69–76). Special report from the Office of Educational Research and Improvement, U.S. Department of Education.

Moore, M., Piper V., and Schaefer, E. (1992). Single-sex schooling and educational effectiveness: A research overview. In D. Hollinger & R. Adamson (Eds.), *Single-sex schooling: Proponents speak (*pp. 7–67). Special report from the Office of Educational Research and Improvement, U.S. Department of Education.

National Coalition of Girls' Schools. (1993). *What every girl in school needs to know.* Concord, MA: National Coalition of Girls' Schools.

Noble, K.D. (1996). Resilience, resistance and responsibility: Resolving the dilemma of the gifted woman. In K. Arnold, K.D. Noble, & R.F. Subotnik (Eds.), *Remarkable women: Perspectives on female talent development* (pp. 413–423). Cresskill, NJ: Hampton Press.

Noble, K.D., Subotnik, R.F., & Arnold, K.D. (1996). A new model for adult female talent development: A synthesis of perspectives from *Remarkable Women.* In K. Arnold, K.D. Noble, & R.F. Subotnik (Eds.), *Remarkable women: Perspectives on female talent development* (pp. 427–439). Cresskill, NJ: Hampton Press.

Oates, M.J., & Williamson, S. (1978). Women's colleges and women achievers. *Signs, 3*(4), 795–806.

O'Brien, K.M., & Fassinger, R.E. (1993). A causal model of the career orientation and career choice of adolescent women. *Journal of Counseling Psychology, 40*(4), 456–469.

O'Hara, S.K. (1995). Freshmen women in engineering: Comparison of their backgrounds, abilities, values and goals with science and humanities majors. *Journal of Women and Minorities in Science and Engineering*, 2, 33–47.

Orenstein, P. (1996, July 20). All-girl schools duck the issue. *New York Times*, p. 19.

Pipher, M. (1994). *Reviving Ophelia: Saving the selves of adolescent girls.* New York: G.P. Putnam's Sons.

Proweller, A. (in press). *Constructing female identities: Meaning making in an upper middle-class youth culture.* Albany: SUNY Press.

Raissiguier, C. (1997). Negotiating school, identity and desire: Students speak out from the Midwest. *Educational Foundations*, 27(4), 31–54.

Ravitch, D. (1996, November 18). Stereotype bashing. *Forbes*, p. 203.

Raymond, D. (1994). Homophobia, identity and the meanings of desire: Reflections on the cultural construction of gay and lesbian adolescent sexuality. In J. Irvine (Ed.), *Sexual cultures and the construction of adolescent identities* (pp. 115–150). Philadelphia: Temple University Press.

Rich, A. (1979). *On Lies, Secrets and Silence.* New York: Norton.

Riordan, C. (1985). Public and Catholic schooling: The effects of gender context policy. *American Journal of Education, 93*, 518–540.

Riordan, C. (1990). *Girls and boys in school: Together or separate?* New York: Teachers College Press.

Riordan, C. (1994). The value of attending a women's college: educational, occupational and income benefits. *Journal of Higher Education, 65*(4), 486–510.

Robinson, T., & Ward, J.V. (1991). "A belief in self far greater than anyone's disbelief": Cultivating resistance among African American female adolescents. In C. Gilligan, A. G. Rogers, & D. L.

Tolman (Eds.), *Women, girls & psychotherapy: Reframing resistance* (pp. 87–103). New York: Haworth Press.

Ruble, T.L., Cohen, R., & Ruble, D.N. (1984). Sex stereotypes: Occupational barriers for women. *American Behavioral Scientist, 27*(3), 339–356.

Sadker, M.P., & Sadker, D.M. (1994). *Failing at fairness: How America's schools cheat girls.* New York: Scribners.

Schneider, F.W., & Coutts, L.M. (1982). The high school environment: A comparison of coeducational and single-sex schools. *Journal of Educational Psychology, 74*(6), 898–906.

Schneider, F.W., Coutts, L.M., & Starr, M.W. (1988). In favor of coeducation: The educational attitudes of students from coeducational and single-sex high schools. *Canadian Journal of Education, 13*(4), 479–496.

Sedgwick, J. (1997, March). What difference does a single-sex school make to a girl later in life? *Self,* pp. 148–171.

Shmurak, C.B. (1994a). Girls' high schools—How empowering have they been? *The High School Journal, 78*(1), 1–12.

Shmurak, C.B. (1994b). What will she be when she grows up? Career paths of independent school alumnae. *Independent School, 55*(1), 36–42.

Smith, I.D. (1994). The coeducational/single-sex schooling debate. *Forum of Education, 49*(1), 15–31.

Spence, J.T., & Helmreich, R.L. (1979). *Masculinity and femininity: Their psychological dimensions, correlates and antecedents.* Austin, TX: University of Texas Press.

Stables, A. (1990). Differences between pupils from mixed and single-sex schools in their enjoyment of school subjects and in their attitudes to science and to school. *Educational Review, 42*(3), 221–230.

Steedman, J. (1985). Examination results in mixed and single-sex secondary schools. In D. Reynolds (Ed.), *Studying school effectiveness* (pp. 87–101). London: Falmer Press.

Stoecker, J.L., & Pascarella, E.T. (1991). Women's colleges and women's career attainments revisited. *Journal of Higher Education, 62*(4), 394–406.

Super, D.E. (1963). Vocational development in adolescence and early adulthood: Tasks & behaviors. In D.E. Super, R. Starishevsky, N. Matlin, & J.P. Jordaan (Eds.), *Career development: Self-concept theory* (pp. 79–95). New York: College Entrance Examination Board.

Tannen, D. (1990). *You just don't understand: Women and men in conversation.* New York: Ballantine.

Thomas, N.G. (1994, November). Persistence in science: A developmental perspective. Paper presented at Studies in Success conference, Mount Holyoke College, South Hadley, MA.

Tidball, M.E. (1973). Perspective on academic women and affirmative action. *Educational Record, 54,* 130–135.

Tidball, M.E., & Kistiakowsky, V. (1976). Baccalaureate origins of American scientists and scholars. *Science, 193,* 646–652.

Tobias, S. (1990). *They're not dumb, they're different: Stalking the second tier.* Tucson, AZ: Research Corporation.

Tovey, R. (1995, July/August). A narrowly gender-based model of learning may end up cheating all students. *Harvard Education Letter,* 3–6.

Trickett, E.J., Trickett, P.K., Castro, J.J., & Schaffner, P. (1982). The independent school experience: Aspects of normative environments of single-sex and coed secondary schools. *Journal of Educational Psychology, 74*(3), 374–381.

Tyack, D.B., & Hansot, E. (1992). *Learning together: A history of coeducation in American public schools.* New York: Russell Sage Foundation.

208 *References*

Walker, B.A., & Mehr, M. (1992). *The courage to achieve: Why America's brightest women struggle to fulfill their promise.* New York: Simon & Schuster.

Ward, J.V. (1990). Racial identity formation and transformation. In C. Gilligan, N.P. Lyons, & T.J. Hanmer (Eds.), *Making connections: The relational worlds of girls at Emma Willard School* (pp. 215–232). Cambridge: Harvard University Press.

Ware, N.C., & Lee, V.E. (1988). Sex differences in the choice of college science majors. *American Educational Research Journal, 25*(4), 593–614.

Ware, N., & Steckler, N. (1983). Choosing a science major: The experience of women and men. *Women's Studies Quarterly, 11*(2), 12–15.

Wildenhaus, K.J. (1996). The talented female athlete: Issues in the development of competitive excellence. In K. Arnold, K.D. Noble, & R.F. Subotnik (Eds.), *Remarkable women: Perspectives on female talent development* (pp. 335–348). Cresskill, NJ: Hampton Press.

Willis, S., & Kenway, J. (1986). On overcoming sexism in schooling: To marginalize or mainstream. *Australian Journal of Education, 30* (2), 132–149.

Worthley, J.S. (1992). Is science persistence a matter of values? *Psychology of Women Quarterly, 16,* 57–68.

Zemsky, B. (1991). Coming out against all odds: Resistance in the life of a young lesbian. In C. Gilligan, A. G. Rogers, & D. L. Tolman (Eds.), *Women, girls & psychotherapy: Reframing resistance* (pp. 185–200). New York: Haworth Press.

Zweigenhaft, R.L., & Domhoff, G.W. (1991). *Blacks in the white establishment: A study of race and class in America.* New Haven: Yale University Press.

Index of Study Participants

Note: page numbers in *italic* indicate references to tabular material

General Index

Note: page numbers in *italic* indicate references to tabular material

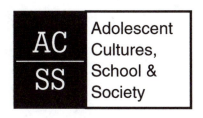

General Editors: Joseph & Linda DeVitis

As schools struggle to redefine and restructure themselves, they need to be cognizant of the new realities of adolescents. Thus, this series of monographs and textbooks is committed to depicting the variety of adolescent cultures that exist in today's post-industrial societies. It is intended to be a primarily qualitative research, practice, and policy series devoted to contextual interpretation and analysis that encompasses a broad range of interdisciplinary critique. In addition, this series will seek to provide a pragmatic, pro-active response to the current backlash of conservatism that continues to dominate political discourse, practice, and policy. This series seeks to address issues of curriculum theory and practice; multicultural education; aggression and violence; the media and arts; school dropouts; homeless and runaway youth; alienated youth; at-risk adolescent populations; family structures and parental involvement; and race, ethnicity, class, and gender studies.

Send proposals and munuscripts to the General Editors at:

Joseph & Linda DeVitis
Binghamton University
Dept. of Education & Human Development
Binghamton, NY 13902

POISONING THE IVY

POISONING THE IVY

The Seven Deadly Sins and Other Vices of Higher Education in America

MICHAEL LEWIS

M.E. Sharpe
Armonk, New York
London, England

Library of Congress Cataloging-in-Publication Data

Lewis, Michael, 1937 Oct. 2–
Poisoning the ivy :
the seven deadly sins and other vices
of higher education in America /
Michael Lewis.
p.   cm.
Includes bibliographical references (p.) and index.
ISBN 0–7656–0071–4 (alk. paper)
1. College teachers—Professional ethics—United States.
2. College teaching—Corrupt practices—United States.
I. Title.
LB1779.L45   1997
378.1'21—dc21
96–40284
CIP

The paper used in this publication meets the minimum requirements of
American National Standard for Information Sciences—
Permanence of Paper for Printed Library Materials,
ANSI Z 39.48-1984.

EB (c)   10   9   8   7   6   5   4   3   2   1

These pages are dedicated to the memory
of three remarkable teachers:

Charles R. Lawrence, who taught me that
protestations of principle can never mean more
than the acts they inspire;

Louis Schneider, who taught me that
when decency is out of fashion,
its protection becomes our paramount task;

Melvin Tumin, who, in the example of his work, taught me
it is possible to incorporate the lessons of the others into mine.

*Probability demands considerably more of pessimists
than it does of optimists.*

Contents

Preface

Since beginning this book, I have come up against a persistent concern. Many of my academic colleagues—either because they apparently view my effort as little different than treason or because they view it as an exercise in symbolic self-immolation—keep asking why: Why would I write a book the avowed purpose of which is to present an unrepentant critical attack on what they take to be the most honorable of institutions, a book that, in their eyes, will only give aid and comfort to the most implacable foes of higher learning? Why would I take on a project that will likely earn the enmity of many professors and make me the target of their vilifying slings and arrows?

During the several years it has taken me to complete the writing of this book, I have at times embraced the position that I need not explicitly address this matter. It can, after all, be justifiably maintained that the value of an argument should be established independently of the motivations driving those who advance it. I have now, however, concluded that there is indeed a compelling reason to visit the concern in question before getting on with the business of these pages.

My motives for writing this book are likely to be mischaracterized by those whose interests are offended by its contents. In what is rapidly becoming a standard ploy, critics bother less and less with efforts to defeat arguments hostile to their own positions, opting instead to attack the interests, motives, and character of those who have made them. It is a tactic having reference points in the overly reductive class-bound relativism of Karl Marx, Sigmund Freud's equally reductive emphasis upon the unconscious overdetermination of ideas, and the postmodern insistence on context as the only reality. Whether or not they seek to justify themselves in terms of this intellectual provenance, many contemporary critics seem unable to resist the intuitive allure of ad hominem attacks. What they engage in is criticism by association. The

validity of an offending argument, they seem to believe, will be undermined if its maker's motivation can somehow be rendered impure. They are thus likely to dwell on those inescapable human characteristics that do indeed move us to make particular arguments regarding particular issues. The list of characteristics that attracts pejorative critical attention is virtually inexhaustible—masculinity, femininity, heterosexuality, homosexuality, bisexuality, wealth, poverty, racial identity, ethnic identity, nationality, class position, religion, regional background, rural origins, urban origins, body type, marital status, age, profession, personal habits, appearance, political leanings—and any other trait that can conceivably have motivational relevance. In effect the critics suggest that since the proponent of an argument probably has traceable human reasons for making it, the argument cannot be valid. Since he or she has the proverbial ax to grind, truth must suffer a mortal blow.

Rather than abandon the why question to the reductive fantasies of critics who would diminish the significance of this book's argument by casting it as just another self-serving complaint (the "what would you expect from someone who . . ." criticism), I think it necessary to offer my own contemplation of its sources. While the availability of this version will not likely interdict the mischaracterizations others may make, it will at least allow readers to decide for themselves what interests are being served in these pages and whether or not that service is truth's enemy.

Disappointment and anger fuel the book you are about to read: disappointment at the way the well-meaning academic majority allows the self-serving and incompetent minority in its midst virtual free rein, anger at the refusal of that majority even to consider the possibility that it has been willfully inattentive and therefore negligent. Why I should have become particularly sensitive to these failings cannot be definitively ascertained—not by me or anyone else, for that matter. I have colleagues whose backgrounds are similar to my own but who nevertheless do not share my robust alienation from everyday academic reality. Some, it must be said, profess astonishment regarding my views. But if I cannot offer a definitive account of how I have come to my disappointment and anger, I can isolate at least two experiences that appear to have nurtured my sensibility.

Coming of age in the 1950s, I benefited from the special largess that for decades (but alas no longer) the people of New York City bestowed upon their children. In a manner that, on reflection, impresses me as heroic, New Yorkers of mostly modest means determined that the city's children would be guaranteed access to a truly dazzling array of educational opportunities. Public secondary schools not only offered standard academic fare but provided specialized courses of study as well. Aspiring young artists, actors, fashion designers, engineers, scientists, printers, chefs, navigators, machinists, and musicians all could find the training they sought, if not in their district high schools, then in one of the specialized high schools that drew students from across the city.[1] But providing such secondary school opportunities was just the half of it. Believing that a college education was essential to personal advancement and social progress, New Yorkers determined that any qualified son or daughter of the city would be offered a tuition-free baccalaureate. The city, with state assistance, funded four institutions—Brooklyn College, City College of New York, Hunter College, and Queens College[2]—that allowed access to first-quality higher education for young men and women who would otherwise have been denied it.

I was graduated from one of New York's specialized high schools (the High School of Music and Art) and received a B.A. from Brooklyn College. As an adolescent, I did not appreciate that I was on the receiving end of a great gift. School was simply school. I felt lucky to attend Music and Art because it had an important reputation and as such made me feel that maybe, just maybe, my dream of becoming the next George Gershwin might come true. I was grateful to have been accepted at Brooklyn College because attending a municipal school was my only option as regards higher education. As an adult, a parent who has seen two children through their educational experiences and a professional whose career has been in higher education, I have, however, had occasion to recollect in awe the gift given me and so many others. But it isn't so much the gift itself—impressive though it was—as it is the gift givers who fill me with awe. My benefactors were not wealthy philanthropists. They weren't Rockefellers, Guggenheims, Carnegies, Pulitzers, or others of their privileged ilk. My benefactors didn't have campus buildings named after them, and they were never invited to participate in ground-breaking or ribbon-cutting ceremonies. My benefactors, the benefactors of several New York generations,

were ordinary people, people who worked hard and took home less
than they should have, people for whom every dollar counted. They
had names like Glasser, Machanofsky, Catanzarro, Pereira, Walker,
and Chin. For six of the week's seven days, they routinely got up
before dawn, rode an hour or so on the subway, labored for eight or
more hours at jobs that regularly mocked the American dream, then,
gray with fatigue, reversed their morning's subterranean journey, returning often in darkness to apartments whose insufficient size they
were too exhausted to notice. Frequently uneducated themselves, my
benefactors were nevertheless more than willing to surrender their tax
dollars (a not insignificant portion of their limited incomes) for educational purposes.[3] These Machanofskys and Chins, these Catanzarros
and Glassers, Pereiras and Walkers worked as hard as anyone I've ever
known, and while they regularly complained about the long hours, the
bosses, and their underfilled pay envelopes, they rarely if ever complained about their hard-earned tax dollars' being expended on educational frills or the unreasonable generosity of providing tuition-free
higher education for other people's children.

Thinking about these people, about their grinding, undercom-
pensated labor; the counterpoise of their remarkable ability to envisage
a future ennobled by education; and consequently their generous support of educational programs, has, I believe, contributed significantly
to my alienation from what I take to be an academy grown unaccept-
ably self-indulgent. Their example of hard work, faith in education
(however naïve), and generosity when no one could have blamed them
for guarding pennies made so valuable by their scarcity, stands in the
sharpest contrast to the work world I have experienced for thirty plus
years. Once I recognized that I had been given the great gift of an
education by people who could ill afford it, by people who despite
their hardships signaled with this gift their faith in the future, by people
who never so much as asked for a thank-you, the spectacle of academic privilege so often unearned and so often subversive of my
benefactors' dreams became intolerable. How could I continue to justify silence when exploitation, laziness, and incompetence were being
celebrated as their opposites with hardly a second thought?

I decided to become a professor during my senior year at Brooklyn
College. When I announced to a counselor whose advice I valued that I
thought I'd like to become a professor (probably a professor of sociology, but I'd consider other specializations), he responded, "Why?"

"Well," I said, "it's a good life. You may not get paid as much as other professionals, but the salaries aren't all that bad, and there are other things that go with being a professor that are terrific: You get to control your time; you don't have to punch a clock; you can work at home if that's what you want to do. It's a high-prestige profession." I continued: "People show you respect. You even get to use a title. And it's a job that helps you stay young. Even as you get older, you're around young people, so you're not likely to lose your enthusiasm and become a routineer." This outpouring went on for several minutes until, suffering mild oxygen deprivation, I paused to catch my breath. My listener interjected, "You certainly have a lot of reasons for your decision. And they all make some sense. But I'm struck by something you haven't said, something you've left out that I would have thought would be your most important reason for wanting to be a professor. You haven't," he said, "mentioned word one about wanting to do the work professors are called upon to do. There's nothing wrong with wanting the perquisites professors have as long as you're enthusiastic about doing the work that earns them. It seems to me," he concluded, "you're mistaking the periphery for the center, the rewards for the work."

The three decades I've spent as a professional academic have convinced me that many of my colleagues mistake the rewards for the work. That this should be so for American professors ought not to be surprising, since the center-periphery confusion is, I believe, characteristic of American work life more generally.[4] Surprising or not, however, this confusion among academics has often diminished their work efforts and rendered professorial accountability little more than a cliché. Excellence is conflated with popularity, and offenses to academic purpose are ignored if recognition threatens personal or institutional rewards. My listener's insistence that I not allow myself to confuse reward with work, that my decision to become an academic be made only after I had considered what would be required of me and only after I embraced those expectations, has led inexorably to the writing of this book.

Throughout my professional life, the center-periphery issue has been inescapable. Confronted before my career actually began, it is the genie that, liberated from the bottle, insinuates itself into its liberator's existence. And as it is with genies, while its presence has been on the whole welcomed, it has also been more than minimally nettlesome. Once you stop mistaking the periphery for the center, your work in-

variably improves and your professional's sense of ethical accountability is strengthened. But since the center and the periphery are so often conflated in American work venues (the academy certainly among them), those who do not do so are likely to find themselves increasingly at odds with their colleagues.

I cannot, in truth, say that my genie has always led me to challenge colleagues on matters deriving from the center-periphery conflation. For many years, I found ways to ignore or otherwise explain away incidents and practices that should have moved me to protest in no uncertain terms. I was ambitious for professional acceptance and thus found ways to avoid the offense to colleagues such protest would invariably have implied. It was enough, I thought, that *I* did not confuse the two, especially since I could convince myself there were more important protests—against the prosecution of an evil Vietnam War, for one, and the failure to ensure the civil rights of all Americans, for another—to engage in. But the genie has been indefatigable, and when I failed to protest unearned rewards or individual as well as institutional reward-protecting inattentiveness, I was unable fully to repress that I had done so. As the years and opportunities to protest passed, the genie burdened my conscience to the point where the prospective ire of colleagues was simply less troubling than the prospect of yet another ethical abdication. And so I began to speak out.

In their important illumination of ethical resistance,[5] Myron and Penina Glazer make it abundantly clear that whistle-blowers must expect almost everything in their work lives to change for the worse once they begin speaking out. Important work assignments are denied them; earned promotions don't come through; they become pariahs, shunned both by those they have offended and those in subordinate positions who have been given to believe that continued fraternization would be tantamount to consorting with the enemy. You might suppose that this characterization would not apply to academic work settings. Colleges and universities, after all, are institutions consecrated to high purpose, and even when they are accused of falling short of that mark, vindictiveness toward accusers seems something professors, in their embrace of academic ideals, would reflexively abhor.

The nastiness my admittedly high-decibel criticism elicited did indeed catch me by surprise. It shouldn't have, but it did. When I first began to raise my voice, I was convinced that academic claims to high purpose, individual as well as institutional, were unfailingly genuine—

and that once my colleagues saw just how the center-periphery confusion had worked its mischief, they would move with dispatch to rectify the situation. Their failure to do so mystified me.

I do not remember when precisely it occurred, but at some point the behavior of my colleagues became less important to me than the unknowns in the American academic system that I assumed rendered such behavior all too usual. What I had first taken to be issues best resolved in the faculty meetings of individual departments now became issues signaling a fault line that ran right through the academy. The rest, as they say, is several years of history, of formal interviews and informal conversations; books, reports, and papers scoured for information (often less available than one would expect); preliminary formulations presented at public meetings;[6] and finally, the preparation of the pages you are about to encounter.[7]

The academy has for me been a crucible—one of the two (the other being my family) forging my person. It therefore gives me no pleasure to call attention to factors I believe render hollow the professoriate's claim of honor. If this book were simply an exposé of the "bad guys," those who willfully exploit the academic system while serving their base motives, I would celebrate its appearance without equivocation. I would take its publication to signal a counterattack, the imminent rout of the villains and the triumph of the "good guys." But this book is less about the bad guys than it is about the good guys who are caught up in a system of self-deception implicating them in the behavior of the very exploiters they supposedly abhor. Thus while I can and do take an author's pride in the completion of a complex and demanding project, I take none of the pleasure authors usually take in the substance of what they have written.

The late American sociologist Charles Page noted in his memoirs that among a group of Young Turks who were his colleagues, I was probably the one most committed to the academy.[8] Whether or not he was correct, I can with confidence assert my commitment to the ideals of academic purpose. Many years ago I did indeed decide that I wanted to do the work that professors are called upon to do. Thus the anger in this book is, I think, the anger experienced by someone whose most cherished ideals have been betrayed by those who promised to stand firm with him. I expected the good guys to join in the defense of the academy's ideals. Some have, but too many have not. I am angry about it, and I would be less than honest if I tried to disguise that anger here.

But I am also sad. H.L. Mencken's epic complaints against virtually every aspect of the human condition spoke of a great sorrow in his recognition of unrealized human possibility. On a much more limited scale, my anger speaks of a sorrow in the recognition of what might be but isn't in American academic life.

Mencken was a brilliant journalist, essayist, and editor. He wasn't, however, a sociologist, and as such he was not inclined to seek or find systemic explanations for our failures. He could describe, he could skewer, and no doubt, when out of the public eye, he could weep, but since he could or would not explain, he was left with a kind of existential hopelessness. Sociologists always have the advantage of hope; for the intellectual heirs of Marx, Emile Durkheim, Max Weber, George Herbert Mead, and later C. Wright Mills, Robert Merton, and (in the instance of this book) Melvin Tumin and his Princeton colleagues, the gods are never crazy. When they act crazy, there are social forces leading them to do so. The fault is never within them; it is, rather, within the modern equivalent of Brutus's stars, social conditions. Identify those conditions, and however difficult the task, the probability for sanity's reclamation is at least greater than zero. I am a sociologist, and so no matter how angry and sad I am about the academy, I am also hopeful that it may yet come close to realizing its ideals. In the pages of this book I attempt to identify the systemic character of its fault and thus to provide a basis for those corrections that hold out the promise of an academy much truer to the ideals its stalwarts espouse than has been the case for quite some time. Although academic reality makes it difficult to be optimistic about reform, my sociologist's credo requires that I (perhaps naïvely) cling to my hopes.

Acknowledgments

Howard Altstein, Bernard Beck, Tim Black, Harvey Choldin, Bob Cook, Thora Dumont, Myron Glazer, Penina Glazer, Joseph Gusfield, John Harney, Rachel Krysa, Ethan Lewis, Hannah Golden Lewis, Harry Lewis, the late Sol Lewis, Sylvia Lewis, Steve Markson, Karen A. Mason, Sabina Merz, JoAnn Miller, John O'Connor, Alice Rossi, Peter Rossi, Michael Shively, Rita Simon, Jon Simpson, Dee Sutton, Gordon Sutton, Martha Taunton—professionals, critics, friends, and family: They are for a variety of reasons implicated in the life of these pages. I am grateful to each.

Michael Lewis
Northampton, Massachusetts

POISONING THE IVY

Chapter 1

An Almanac of Academic Betrayals

The Phenomenology of Denial

This is a dirty book about higher education. No, you don't have to cover it in brown wrapping paper, and you won't have to hide the fact that you've read it from your friends (unless they happen to be professors). But it is about some very dirty things done by people who lay claim to the highest moral and ethical standards. And perhaps more important, it is about a failure of nerve on the part of those who allow such behavior to continue even as they abhor it. In a significant way, it's a book about paradox, about laudable principle too easily prostituted in the service of base motive; about ostensibly progressive reforms that have instead encouraged the debasing of high purpose; about elegance and honor made masks for squalor and humiliation.

A Litany of Woes

Among academic professionals, whining has become endemic. Spend twenty-four hours on any college campus, with any group of professors, and you will be subjected to a litany of complaints that make it appear that these self-proclaimed champions of truth are an endangered species. To hear them tell it, they are a beleaguered band who persist in their heroic calling in spite of conditions that would drive lesser mortals to early sorrow or at the very least a change of career. In their litany of woes they claim to be abused by latter-day philistines who are constantly after them to abandon the disinterested pursuit of truth for a slavish embrace of shortsighted utilitarianism. They are

3

overworked, forced to teach two and sometimes even three courses a semester by administrators who conveniently forget that professors must spend several hours in preparation for every hour in the classroom (not to mention, of course, the additional time needed to counsel students). They are forced to accept this inordinately heavy teaching load in spite of other burdens: After all, are they not expected to maintain the viability of their academic homes by serving on committees dealing with everything from curricular and personnel matters to speaker invitations and student housing? And who else on the campus is charged with the awesome responsibility of scholarly contribution to a body of knowledge in constant need of replenishment? Moreover, they must respond to these demands and burdens without adequate support staff (it is the rare professor, they will tell you, who doesn't have to share the services of a secretary with a minimum of five or six others).

And if that weren't bad enough, they are expected to do all these things in a physical environment that leaves a great deal to be desired: Their offices are too small, the windows are sealed for an air-conditioning system that doesn't live up to expectations, and their health, it seems, is constantly threatened by the chemicals in the carpeting—not quite as bad as a coal mine, a foundry, or a textile mill but only marginally more inviting. All this, however, they might tolerate if only professors received their just financial due. Here they are, men and women who have sacrificed their youth to the rigors of protracted training in their respective disciplines, men and women with years of study behind them, people who have paid their dues in equal measure with other highly trained professionals such as physicians and lawyers, yet compared to what these professionals can command, they will tell you, their salaries are a mere pittance. In sum, the professorial litany of woes portrays a work life where highly talented and trained individuals persist heroically in their tasks ever at odds with those who, insensitive to their value, would have them serve lilliputian ends at an equally diminutive level of compensation.

To sympathetic but unwary listeners, listeners convinced that enlightenment holds the key to human progress and that the higher learning American academics presumably practice is one and the same with this desired state of intellectual grace, the litany's depiction of woe must be cause for considerable alarm. If things are as bad as their professorial informants claim, the cause of enlightened human prog-

ress suffers almost daily injury in the very precincts where they should expect it to be kept free of harm. Moreover, it would take an exercise in Panglossian denial to keep from realizing that this sorry situation is only likely to worsen over time. Heroic though they may be, professors are no more than human; they have their personal hopes to nurture, they have families to support, and there is no reason to believe that notwithstanding their heroism, they have an infinite capacity for resilience in the face of sustained disappointment and abuse. On learning of the troubles afflicting the academic profession, those who want to believe that its selfless minions are our last best hope can only shudder at the prospect that disillusionment will make exiles of the best and the brightest, their places taken by an inferior breed. If such a prospect does not portend the onset of a modern dark age, there can be no faulting those who take it to at least signal the fall of a long winter's night.

Enlightenment's friends should indeed worry about the state of the academy and its future, but not for the reasons given in their informants' incessantly dolorous recitative. The professoriate's list of complaints does not, I am happy to say, accurately describe the conditions of its work life. Professors are not being pressured to abandon disinterested intellectual pursuits: Those so-called philistines are far more likely to interest themselves in what the football coach does than they are to worry about the absence of practical utility in the work of a medievalist or a sociolinguist. They are not overworked: A three-course load implies a likely investment of no more than eighteen hours per week for no more than thirty weeks a year, few students seek professorial counsel on a regular basis, and most academic committees meet no more than once or twice a month. Their access to support services is not inadequate: Department secretaries frequently complain of boredom born of not having enough work. Their physical environment is anything but oppressive and unhealthy: It would be hard, if not impossible, to convince most American workers that the academic workplace is anything to complain about. And if on the face of it they earn less than some professionals, they are nevertheless well paid: Covering all ranks, their average or mean salary is approximately $48,000[1] for no more than a required thirty weeks of essentially unsupervised work in situations where employers make generous health insurance and retirement contributions and where office space, lab space, telephones, and other equipment (not to mention secretarial and professional assistance) are provided cost free. That's the good news.

What's Really Wrong

There is, however, some bad news as well. The higher learning is in fact profoundly troubled, and (irony of ironies) those most responsible for this trouble are those who loudly proclaim their heroic defense of the academy: the professors themselves. Contrary to their self-portrayal, they are not struggling against all odds to hold back the long night threatened in their litany of woes. Some, it sadly must be said, are little more than two-bit princes of the very darkness they claim to abhor, sociopathic manipulators who consciously subvert the academy's permissive traditions as they promote their interests and satisfy their appetites.[2] These rogue professors are frequently joined in their subversion by those who apparently have confused academic life with academic work. Such professors love the academic life—its freedoms, its exclusiveness, and its consequent prestige. They seem to be under the illusion that living the academic life is the same as doing academic work. For these very special people, an occasional stroll with a student down the shaded walks of a campus quadrangle is apparently the equivalent of holding office hours; reading the *New York Times,* as long as it occurs on campus, is scholarship; gossiping with colleagues at a cocktail party is meaningful intellectual exchange; sharing alcoholic beverages with two or more students constitutes the meeting of a seminar; and maintaining an active membership in the faculty club suffices for university service. There's no malevolence in all this, but as any student who has wasted untold hours waiting for professors who fail to show up for appointments or any publisher who has pursued more than one fugitive manuscript for months and sometimes years beyond an agreed-upon deadline can tell you, this confusion between living the life and doing the work is hardly less subversive to academic purpose than is the conduct inspired by more malevolent passions.

To be sure, these subversive elements—the malevolent princelings and their allies, the virtuosi of academic style—probably do not constitute anywhere near a majority of the American professoriate (my research and experience suggest that we are talking about no more than 30 percent of the faculty on any campus[3]), but the damage they do far exceeds what might normally be expected given their numbers. That this is so is in no small measure attributable to a massive abdication of responsibility on the part of the academic majority, those academics who appear to honor the purposes and requirements of their profession.

Scrupulous where their own work is concerned, they are nevertheless complicit in the malfeasance and misfeasance of their wayward colleagues, complicit by virtue of a tolerance for wrongdoing and dereliction, together with a mind-boggling ability to rationalize that tolerance. Hearing evil, they close their ears; seeing evil they shut their eyes. And even those who allow themselves to see and hear, more often than not harbor the evidence of their senses in silence lest they be accused of violating that universal (and indeed perverse) professional injunction—"thou shalt not speak evil of colleagues."

By the time newly minted Ph.D.'s take their first jobs, they are fully aware that academic etiquette requires obliviousness (or feigned obliviousness) to everything their colleagues are doing—everything, that is, except what they choose (usually with hyperbolic zeal) to advertise. Paying uninvited critical attention to collegial effort or its absence is inevitably regarded as unprofessional or a transgression against the most jealously guarded of all professorial protections, academic freedom. Since irrefutable truth is such valued currency in the academy, criticizing one's colleagues in the absence of proof far in excess of even that demanded by juridical standards would most certainly be taken as indicative of just such a transgression. Knowing, for example, that Professor X meets his classes infrequently and irregularly is hardly a sufficient basis upon which to call him to public account; the academic standard of "irrefutable truth" accepts as credible only that evidence of malpractice not subject to exculpable interpretation. Eyewitness accounts from students? (They were there, he wasn't.) Not good enough! (They obviously failed to appreciate Professor X's desire to foster their intellectual self-reliance, and who can criticize him for that?)

Occasionally, despite the professoriate's best efforts to ensure their exclusion,[4] truth-telling deviants do show up on faculties. But their presence rarely if ever makes a difference. They are, after all, deviants, incorrigibles whose refusal to play by the rules of complicity marks their message as symptomatic of their own waywardness. When they insist that the emperor is not only unclothed but also luridly pleasuring himself, the response they are most likely to elicit is disgust at their unabashed voyeurism.

There *is* trouble in academe, but it is hardly the specter summoned up by the professoriate as it attempts to rally support for an extension of its prerogatives and perquisites. It is not trouble imposed by rapacious outsiders whose presumed ignorance and shortsightedness marks

them as implacable foes of truth and reason. It is trouble generated from within the citadel.

The Spirit of Exalted Specialness

In *An American Dilemma,* his landmark study of American race relations, Gunnar Myrdal argued that, paradoxically, it was the egalitarian ideals of the slaveholders that led to the promulgation of the "doctrine of natural inferiority" and consequently the most destructive system of slavery in human history. The slaveholders, because of their egalitarianism, had to justify the departure from their ideals that chattel slavery implied. They did so, Myrdal suggested, by denying that any departure had occurred; arguing that since the Africans were *not quite* human, the moral imperatives of egalitarianism did not apply where they were concerned. This diminution of the Africans' humanity, he reasoned, in turn permitted a repressiveness largely absent in other slave systems.[5] Regardless of the validity of Myrdal's formulation as applied to the specific instance of American slavery, his emphasis upon paradox in human affairs is instructive, particularly as it implicates good in the capacity for evil. Slavery would have been bad enough (it is never less than morally repugnant), but it is, ironically, the good—as represented by the slaveholders' egalitarian creed—that rendered American slavery profoundly evil in its unrivaled repressiveness.

American academic life is today beset by this paradoxical implication of good in evil. Indeed it is this dialectic that renders academic malpractice so troubling. The behaviors that constitute academic malpractice are in themselves surely not laudable, but in many respects they do not differ from what you would expect to find in any precinct of the working world. No matter what the job category, it wouldn't take much investigatory effort to turn up a numerically significant array of self-aggrandizers, exploiters, malingerers, and incompetents. And unless the behavior of such individuals turns out to be grievously and publicly consequential (i.e., when the stockbroker's insider trading scam comes to light, when the contractor's shortcuts result in the collapse of the school's roof), these penny-ante desperadoes and goof-offs within our midst are likely to be left to their own pursuits and indulgences. Moreover, if we leave aside the moral issues involved in what these stalwarts of deceit and default are up to, the costs of their acts appear to be bearable. The work of society does get done in spite of

their malfeasance and misfeasance (less efficiently, no doubt, than would be the case if the deviance in question did not occur), and we seem willing enough to live with a certain amount of what might be called "ordinary wrongdoing." Indeed we take the expectation of such wrongdoing as a mark of sophistication and its absence as an indication of foolish naïveté.

Academic malpractice would not therefore appear to be more than usually troubling. But in this instance appearance does in fact deceive—and in no small measure. Academic malpractice isn't just "ordinary wrongdoing." It can't be, because the very essence of academic purpose intensifies its negative consequences, both moral and functional.

Colleges and universities (whether we are referring to two-year community colleges or to major research universities) aren't, according to their own claims, simply firms that happen to be in the business of providing educational services; and being a professor (according to the professors) isn't just having a job in one of these firms. Academic institutions do not justify their existence on the basis of a fee for service exchange, and professors do not justify themselves as functionaries whose work is necessary to that exchange. It is not mundane purpose that defines the academy's essence but exalted purpose that does so. Some academics (those primarily on the faculties of graduate research universities) lay claim to being discoverers of truth, and all academics consider themselves purveyors of that most scarce commodity. Put another way, the academy defines and justifies itself in terms of its service to something quite extraordinary: "the way things really are" and might become in all conventional as well as esoteric venues of the human experience.[6]

The academy is an institution whose essence is paradox—so much a part of the secular world, a world in which day-to-day life is infused with the values of utilitarian exchange, yet almost sacred in its professed rejection of these values. If the church is God's sacred outpost amidst the doubting, unbelieving multitudes, the academy, according to its apostles, is truth's fortress amidst the multitudes who in short-sighted pursuit of immediate gain neglect its redeeming promise.

It is impossible to ignore this *geist,* or spirit, of exalted specialness on American campuses. It is physically manifest in an architecture intended to elicit awe. Old buildings, having in reality outlived their usefulness, are kept alive as if to proclaim that in the academy, at least, usefulness, such an everyday concern, must give way to something

beyond utility, something so pure that it can resist the ravages of time. New buildings mimic the old or are designed to disguise their temporally specific purposes. There are periodic ceremonies, convocations and commencements, the purpose of which is to confirm the academy's elevated separation from the everyday. Marking the beginning and the end of their own version of a year (which lasts from early September to late May), academics don their gold-tasseled caps, velvet-trimmed robes, and hoods of investiture, and after a procession accompanied by fanfare and flourish, assemble to hear one or more of their number confirm the academy's interlocutory service to truth. With almost no prodding whatsoever, professors can be counted on to characterize what they do as a calling rather than a job. They must, they say, have the protections of tenure (the presumably permanent appointment) because truth, in whose service they passionately toil, invariably antagonizes the utilitarian masses. Without tenure surely some (the more powerful) among these masses would seek, with undoubted success, to deprive them of the opportunity to translate their love of truth into epistles of enlightenment. Because truth and reality can make no accommodation with untruth and illusion, those who champion its cause, they will tell you, must be free in its service, free to seek, find, and communicate its essence without compromise.

It would, of course, be naïve to believe that all academics are sincere in their claims to exalted purpose. The majority, arguably, are, whereas others only make these claims to mask nefarious or dilatory intent. Embraced sincerely or not, however, the ideal of professorial service in truth's cause has a conscious presence for all academics. As such its moral and ethical implications cannot be ignored, not even by those who would cynically use it to cloak their self-serving behavior.

Ordinary wrongdoing, when it occurs in the academy, is thus hardly *ordinary* at all. It represents a grievous departure from those moral and ethical precepts that are to the academy's justifying purpose what the tree's limbs are to its trunk. Truth cannot be served dishonestly; to do so is a contradiction in terms. If it is to be served, it cannot be held hostage to the pursuit of personal gain and advantage. It cannot tolerate incompetence. And it cannot be left to the languid mercies of the lazy and the irresolute.

Where utility and immediate gain are their own justification, some dishonesty and rapacious self-service can be winked at as unsurprising if aberrant extensions of business as usual. But where business as usual

is presumed to be truth's quasi-sacred service, dishonesty and rapacity represent an abandonment of principle, a betrayal of essential purpose. Within limits incompetence and laziness in the mundane world can be shrugged off: human nature, we say; some people just can't cut it. Academic claims, however, don't permit such tolerance. The stakes are presumably too high. Since it is an article of the academics' faith that truth is the most precious resource available to humans, since they assume that in its myriad manifestations it holds the potential for making the world a better place and rescuing our short span from the nasty and the brutish, injuries done to truth by the incompetent and the lazy must be counted as nothing less than sins against the redemptive promise of human progress.

Certainly anyone with a conventional appreciation of learning would not have it otherwise. Without its claim to elevated purpose, the academy would, in their view, be just another service industry, and learning would be reduced to something characterized by marketability. But the academy's claim to almost sacred transcendence and its presumptive abhorrence of behavior that in other settings would be greeted with grudging tolerance ironically create the conditions of Myrdalean paradox, where what is good makes what is bad infinitely worse.

As the academy is a citadel with many chambers (e.g., massive research universities dominated by their professional schools and graduate programs; elite liberal arts institutions; publicly supported four-year colleges; church-related four-year colleges; colleges, usually high priced, committed to avant-garde pedagogy; specialized institutions such as conservatories; privately supported two-year junior colleges; and tax-supported two-year community colleges), this paradox works itself out in a variety of ways. But whatever the specific differences in its situated manifestation, the Myrdalean paradox—species *academicus*—is everywhere characterized by an inexorable and corrosive logic that implicates the professoriate's claim to high purpose in a betrayal of that very same purpose, a betrayal so mindless as to appear wanton.

Extraordinary Claims and Ordinary Pursuits: The Dilemma of Dualism

This logic has its origin in the academy's peculiar status as an institution that rejects the utilitarian standards of the everyday world even as

it is so much a part of that world. Academics may like to believe they are heroically special in their presumed service to truth, but in reality they differ but little from those whose self-conceptions are far less grandiose. They want to get ahead just like the next guy (I've never met a professor who didn't think he or she deserved a bigger salary increase than the one received or one to whom rank was truly meaningless). Like the store managers and optometrists who happen to be their neighbors, they have mortgage payments to make and car loans to retire; they look forward to vacations (longer vacations than most people are able to take); and like everyone else who can afford the search, they are avid in their quest for tax shelters and other loopholes. If the professorial head is presumed to reside atop cumulus-crowned Olympus, other parts of the professorial anatomy are routinely resident in the lowlands of immediate reward and creature comfort.

Those who justify colleges and universities may as a matter of course (and surely quite sincerely) indulge in rhetorical flights of almost otherworldly righteousness, but notwithstanding these awe-inspiring characterizations, the reality of college and university life is far more worldly. Tax-supported universities and colleges are forever engaged in case-making efforts with legislators (hardly a group noted for their idealism) who decide just how much of the public treasury will be expended on higher education, while their privately supported counterparts are similarly engaged in fund-raising efforts with alumni and other potential benefactors. For the less well positioned among truth's fortresses, advertising (sometimes handled by the same firms that push beer and pretzels) is a necessity as they compete for students and their dollars. Presidents and deans accompanied by their entourage of labor lawyers frequently sit across bargaining tables from unionized professors and their lawyers, hammering out contracts that set the terms under which truth's service will be allowed to proceed. There are agreements to be negotiated with funding agencies (frequently government agencies) whose potentially munificent support of large-scale research is intensely coveted. Transactions involving six or seven figures and covering everything from heating oil to mainframe computers or even real estate must be entered into. And on those campuses where, inexplicably, it has been assumed that truth is served best in the circus atmosphere of big-time athletics, there are stadia to be built, refurbished, and maintained; athletes to be recruited, equipped, and coached; as well as telecasts to be contracted for with the likes of

ABC, CBS, NBC, and ESPN (always, to be sure, according to requirements established by that protector of academic purpose, the National Collegiate Athletic Association).

The dualism in truth's citadel portrayed by the juxtaposition of extraordinary claims and ordinary pursuits presents its occupants with a major dilemma. Claims to high purpose simply cannot be sustained in the absence of behavior that realizes these claims. Such behavior, by its elevated nature, is unusual (elevation can only be established *relative* to what *usually* transpires), and those who engage in it cannot, it seems, easily do so without some risk of injury to whatever less elevated or more ordinary interests they may wish to pursue. The ageless lesson of high purpose realized is more often than not the lesson of self-sacrifice and self-denial—or the forswearing of conventionality and its rewards for the pursuit of a magnificent if often cruel obsession.

Modern academics, however, either by choice or by necessity are not likely to relinquish conventional aspirations and activities. Forswearing worldly prizes (and the mundane tactics intended to elicit these prizes) for a single-minded pursuit of truth is, it would appear, an occurrence of unsurpassed rarity on the American campus. Thus the dilemma: How to reconcile the utilitarian compromise implied in conventional life-styles and organizational agendas with the intolerance of such compromise demanded of those who presume (often quite loudly) to serve truth.

While this dilemma permeates the whole of modern academic life, it is never more excruciating than in those instances involving misfeasance or malfeasance. The claim of high purpose, rendering ordinary wrongdoing extraordinary, concomitantly requires those who make such a claim to rectify offenses against it. If truth abhors incompetence, laziness, dishonesty, and self-serving irresponsibility, then those who claim to serve truth are compelled to correct the incompetents in their midst, rouse the lazy from their torpor, and repudiate those who out of dishonesty or simple irresponsibility have betrayed their calling.

Were the academy not subject to the dualism undeniable on all campuses, truth's servants might well meet these demands with a minimum of difficulty. In the first place, without the dualism it is likely that the incidence of behavior requiring rectification would be measurably reduced. Much academic egregiousness is arguably a product of excessive worldliness, and if the academy were principally a community of scholars divorced from the prevailing utilitarianism of everyday life,

such worldliness would almost as a matter of definition be of little or no behavioral consequence. In the second place (and more important), without such dualism academics, having already removed themselves from utility's reign, would be under no pressure to consider the threats posed to mundane pursuits and interests by their vigilance. The absence of this dualism would imply a prior rejection of the conventional, a disavowal of the everyday gains and advantages that might be threatened by too uncompromising a defense of truth against the treachery of those who only pretend fealty to its cause.

But because the dualism exists, dealing with academic misfeasance and malfeasance becomes a task burdened by conflicting interests. Academics imbued with a sense of moral superiority born of their claims to elevated purpose cannot, on the one hand, simply wink at wrongdoing. On the other hand, these academics must entertain the possibility that corrective actions can be taken only at cost to their everyday pursuits and utilitarian interests. Repudiating a colleague for dishonesty or irresponsibility is not as easy as it might seem. Fairness demands that alleged wrongdoers be given due process and therefore an opportunity to defend themselves. Due process requires that a case be made, and in most instances doing so requires an expenditure of effort that might otherwise be invested in the pursuit of personal interest. Moreover, seeking to prove a colleague's wrongdoing is not without risk. Those who press for censure are likely to find themselves the targets of a vigorous and often vicious counterattack, not only by the accused but by his or her allies, as well, as they attempt to discredit the case for repudiation. Even if the attempted repudiation is successful and the wrongdoer is duly censured, there are no guarantees against retaliation. Real or imagined, there is always the threat that one way or another confronting an academic wrongdoer will come back to haunt those who have done so, thereby injuring their everyday interests. What happens if some of the wrongdoer's friends wind up on a personnel committee overseeing the distribution of merit salary increases? What happens if they are in a position to pass on promotions? You never know when one of the wrongdoer's friends will be in a position to review (anonymously, of course) a grant proposal. Because professors do not live in a self-contained community of scholars, because they do not, in reality, forswear the enticements of personal ambition and the utilitarian calculus of gain, these and other similar issues constitute significant obstacles to the behavioral realization of their ethical claims. For most, it would appear, they are insurmountable obstacles.

It is unfortunate that this individual reticence is reinforced by an institutional reticence born of similar utilitarian needs. Academic administrators, whose job it is to act in behalf of their colleges and universities, display minimal enthusiasm for the kind of self-policing implied in the claims to high purpose they regularly make. And little wonder! If case-making requires professors to consume their time and energies in activities that have no personal payoffs, adjudication of these cases (an administrative responsibility) requires deans and other upper-level administrators to use their time and energies in an activity that has nothing to do with the everyday tasks of program management and institutional enhancement.

Truth's service may be the academy's elevated raison d'être, but from the administrator's point of view, efficient attention to routine management and pursuit of worldly gain are equally if not more important. Anything, therefore, that interferes with efforts to maximize efficiency and garner an increased share of the everyday world's lucre, anything that claims time and depletes energies without the promise of commensurate reward for the academic institution, is likely to be perceived as a nuisance at best and a serious imposition at worst. It is safe to say there isn't an academic administrator on the current scene so single-minded in the service to truth that he or she would gladly accept adjudicative responsibility in a case of alleged wrongdoing. No utilitarian gain is likely to accrue to the institution as a result of the exercise of that responsibility, on the contrary there is always a risk of loss arising from the possibility of scandalous public revelation, and love of truth, it seems, is unlikely to move administrators to its valorous defense in the face of such risks.

It might be expected that the solution to the dilemma created by the contradictory coexistence of high purpose and utilitarian interest in the academy could be achieved through compromise. If such were the case, some wrongdoing might be ignored because the costs (both personal and institutional) of dealing with it would be deemed too great relative to the perceived seriousness of the alleged infraction. In other instances an informal mechanism for repudiation, such as isolating the offender, might be employed. This would indicate disapproval without the investment of time and energy required by more formal or officially sanctioned repudiative efforts. These latter efforts would be reserved for those cases and only those cases where the alleged misfeasance or malfeasance was so grievous, the insult to aca-

demic purpose so blatant, that only explicit and definitive repudiation of such wrongdoing could suffice to reassert the unquestioned preeminence of that purpose.[7]

However reasonable such compromise might seem, it is not characteristic of the way academics attempt to resolve the contradictory pulls of high purpose and utilitarian interest when they are faced with wrongdoing in their midst. When an insult to the high purpose of truth's service exists, no matter how minor, it cannot be tolerated without in some way feeling that purpose has been betrayed. The academic's claim to high purpose cannot now and then be set aside as a matter of utilitarian convenience. To consciously do so would be just as consciously to subordinate truth to self-interest, thereby rendering academic claims to high purpose hollow indeed. Academics cannot afford the risk to their self-conceptions, nor the threat to those privileges and immunities that this sense of self allows them to claim—implied in such a course of action. Informal mechanisms of repudiation are only slightly less problematic. If, as suggested, academic claims to an elevated morality in truth's service render *all* instances of academic wrongdoing egregious, there are no instances that require less than explicit and definitive repudiation. A conscious decision to do less than is required by a moral code that does not allow for distinctions between a little dishonesty and a lot, between minor and major irresponsibility, is in effect a conscious *rejection* of that code's superior stringency. It is a decision that can only obliterate the difference that presumably elevates the academic's code above everyday moral expectations. Consciously deciding to do something—but less than is required—is thus hardly different from ignoring perceived wrongdoing and doing nothing at all. It, too, would render academic claims to high purpose hollow, pose a significant threat to the academic's exalted self-conception, and of necessity make it difficult to continue to expect the privileges and immunities implied in that self-conception. Put as simply as possible, for many if not all academics the possibility of reasonable compromise does not exist because their claim to high purpose unequivocally rules it out.

Other than actually meeting the demands implied in the moral stringencies of what might be termed the *academic creed* (an unlikely course given the existence of utilitarian interest in academic venues), there is really only one avenue open to the conflicted professors and their equally conflicted administrative superiors: *self-delusive denial.* By denying the existence of virtually any wrongdoing, by convincing

themselves that obvious academic abuses are simply unorthodox manifestations of acceptable and even admirable academic pursuits, truth's
servants can avoid the necessity of repudiation. They can thus protect
their utilitarian interests while they continue to profess commitment to
the stringencies of their creed—no harm, no foul, and therefore no
need to blow the whistle.

The Shield of Academic Freedom

On the face of it, so widespread an exercise in reality avoidance may
seem farfetched (these are, after all, the same people who are unable to
avoid or deny what they take to be the unsavory reality of compromise). Yet some of the academy's most taken for granted characteristics make it relatively easy to accomplish.[8] Of these, it is probably
academic freedom that figures most prominently. On the sanguine assumption that by and large the professoriate serves the cause of truth
with avid sincerity, it has also been assumed that individual professors
should have the freedom to do so according to the dictates of their own
imaginations, subject only to limitations imposed by the requirements
of their disciplines. The existence of this freedom presumably protects
the academy from incrustation in an orthodoxy that constrains imagination and, even worse, enthrones the specious and unsupportable
as true.

But the great and grand principle of academic freedom is also useful
to those who, out of their need to avoid censuring their mis- and
malfeasant colleagues, would deny the reality of their senses. A commitment to academic freedom makes it easy for those who need to do
so to transform even the best evidence of wrongdoing into nothing
more than an indication of protected innovation or justifiable heterodoxy. For those who would have it that way, such a commitment
allows the dishonest manipulation of a laboratory procedure to be seen
as an acceptable if not laudable exercise of technical imagination; the
failure to meet classes on a regular basis as pedagogically justified; the
appropriation of a graduate student's work as legitimate sponsorship;
and even sexual exploitation as nothing more than an expression of
intense mentoring.

A commitment to academic freedom, moreover, interdicts what
would otherwise be normal curiosity about the work-related behavior
of one's colleagues and so justifies inaction in the name of uncensur-

able obliviousness. Freedom to serve the cause of truth without unwarranted interference is all too often taken to imply an absolute privacy that well-bred academics are at pains to respect. Respecting the privacy of colleagues in the name of academic freedom means you don't have to know what they're up to. (Indeed you *shouldn't* know what they're up to.) And if you don't know it when what they're up to is dishonest or irresponsible there is no need to call yourself to account for failing to repudiate such wrongdoing. Going this route, academics don't even have to deny the evidence of their senses, they simply put themselves in a position where they never have to know what's going on.

The Mystique of Selectiveness

And then there's the mystique of the academic community. Not anyone, you understand, can be admitted into the academy. Because of its specialness, those who are admitted have, it is blithely assumed, survived the rigors of both intellectual and moral apprenticeship. They've been trained and thoroughly socialized. They know the moral requirements of truth's service, and they have learned not to waver in their fealty to its stringencies. Those who have not, do not make it through the seven or eight postgraduate years it usually takes to complete a Ph.D. Having failed the apprenticeship's tests of character and intellect,[9] they've been shunted off into more suitable utilitarian pursuits. Welcomed into the community of academic stalwarts, those who have survived these tests can be trusted not to transgress against its higher morality and not to tolerate those who do. So presumably selective are the community's gatekeepers (from the point of view of many academics it is easier to get into heaven) that surely no one possessing a nefarious capability could elude their vigilance. Professors simply need not worry about in-house wrongdoing: Obviously, it's not likely to occur if all or nearly all the potential wrongdoers have been sent packing.

Critical Resentment

Denial is facilitated, and ironically so, by yet another of the academy's pieties: the time-honored tradition of externally focused critical resentment. If truth is to be served, those who mistake illusion for reality must be made aware of their error. As it was the calling of Plato's philosopher-kings (and what academic does not claim their patri-

mony?) to inveigh against all that shadow mongering in the cave, so it is the professoriate's calling to cry out against illusion peddling in the mundane redoubts of utility. Physicists are compelled to mount truth-inspired campaigns against the deadly illusions spawned by the champions of nuclear energy. Biologists, it seems, have to save the natural environment from the avaricious abuses heaped upon it by industry's unthinking and shortsighted captains. Nutritionists would hardly be true to their calling if they failed to warn us against the false claims of those who purvey high-profit foods of dubious nutritional value. If they are monetarists, economists must cry out against illusory well-being born of deficit spending; if they are left-leaning political economists, they must rail against that false consciousness which ensures labor's loyalty to exploitative capitalism. Sociologists are impelled to rout those commonsense misunderstandings that lead to such ineffective and socially regressive actions as capital punishment, sex role separation, and all sorts of discrimination. Professors in the humanities, of course, feel called upon to redeem the unwashed masses from their ill-considered aesthetic passions. With what they take to be uncommon courage, they wage war against the low culture of television, AM radio, novels by such abusers of the king's English as Judith Krantz and Sidney Sheldon, and music that to their sensitive ears is amplified cacophony.

With so much to do, it is little wonder that the truth-serving professors find it easy to avoid acknowledging the wrongdoing in their midst. The world cries out to be saved from itself, and with so much at stake out there, only the most myopic academics are likely to attend the presumption that there are problems in their own neighborhoods. And that's just the half of it. Crying out against the world's illusions and perversities is likely to antagonize a lot of people who don't share the professoriate's passion for enlightenment. The philosopher-kings, after all, were quite unpopular in the cave of Plato's imagining. Rebuffed and not infrequently ridiculed by those who refuse to understand, the academic truth-tellers forge a knowing, self-protective, in-group solidarity. Others may scorn them; they may be defamed as pointy-headed naysayers, but together they are among friends, allies who, knowing only too well how repugnant truth is to the ignorant masses, can be counted on for support and appreciation. Of course, as any truth-telling sociologist would aver, one by-product of this solidarity of the embattled is an almost infinite capacity to deny wrongdoing on the part of

one's comrades in arms. Being good and brave oneself, pressing on in truth's service in spite of all that abuse emanating from those who care not at all about its redeeming qualities, one can only assume that those who give generously of their support must likewise be good and brave, incapable of any except the purest motivations and most honorable behaviors. Wrongdoing? Oh, maybe a minor peccadillo or two, but nothing requiring censure or repudiation.

The Morally Corrosive Paradox

Each of the characteristics in question—academic freedom, the mystique of selectiveness, and critical resentment—is sufficient to the manufacture of the denial of wrongdoing that gets professors and academic administrators off the hook. When, as is so often the case, they can be invoked simultaneously, those who would thus delude themselves can do so it seems almost blissfully. The academic creed, with its elevated behavioral expectations, can be honored at little or no cost because the good professors, rarely if ever seeing what is there to be seen, can avoid the repudiative actions required by its stringencies. They would, so they tell themselves, act if the situation demanded it, if the high purpose of the academy were really being threatened from within, but seeing no real threat, they can find no reason to do anything at all. Uncalled-for repudiation would in fact be tantamount to McCarthyism, a chilling prospect for those who value unrestricted inquiry in the service of truth.

Professors, like Myrdal's slaveholders (a comparison that will no doubt infuriate many academics), want to be good, but they've discovered that living up to their creed requires the sacrifice of worldly interests and appetites not easily relinquished. The slaveholders, according to Myrdal, resolved their dilemma of conflicting claims by denying the humanity of those they held in thrall. Doing so allowed them to reap the benefits of chattel slavery even as they endorsed, quite sincerely, the American creed of human equality. The tragic legacy of that denial was a system of slavery unrivaled in its physical and psychological brutality and a racist doctrine that even today diminishes us all in so many ways. Professors, it would appear, resolve their dilemma of conflicting claims by denying the existence of censurable behaviors. Persuading themselves that their colleagues are virtually without sin, they relieve themselves of the costly obligation to repudiate those

transgressions which in fact do occur with considerable regularity. Their capacity for denial, in effect, allows them to *be* good without having to make sacrifices likely to be required of those who *do* good.

The legacy of this self-delusion may not have the far-reaching, tragic consequences that Myrdal saw in the slaveholder's denial, but just as that denial demonstrates how good can be implicated in the intensification of evil, so, too, does the academic's well-practiced obliviousness demonstrate that morally corrosive paradox. With its source in the academy's overweening righteousness, the denial of wrongdoing can only increase the incidence of academic malpractice and intensify the corruption of academic purpose. Soon enough do the sociopathic self-aggrandizers learn that they have nothing to fear from their colleagues, that the probability of serious penalty for their egregiousness is close to zero. Whatever their appetites, no one is likely to interfere. The campus, for these predators, has become little more than a well-stocked preserve, and it's open season throughout the academic year. The virtuosi of academic style are no less quick to see that their colleagues will almost never look beyond their tweed jackets, book-lined offices, and portentous rhetoric for the substance of their work. The promotions will come, together with salary increases presumably based on merit, irrespective of laziness and incompetence. All they have to do is look the part. The campus for these performers is a stage, the academic year a 30-week theatrical season during which they are given virtually unlimited freedom to strut their stuff.

The malfeasant and the misfeasant, as noted earlier, of course thrive in other vocational habitats. But it is the academy that, ironically, suits them best. Because in the academy no wrongdoing is ever ordinary, because it therefore requires uncompromising repudiation, because such repudiation is likely to be costly both to individual and institutional interests—almost no wrongdoing *is* wrongdoing. As such, while in principle the penalties for academic malpractice are severe, they are in fact imposed so rarely that their deterrent effect is nonexistent.[10] Thus is the academy's exalted purpose, its presumption to a morality of extraordinary stringency, implicated in the intensification of professorial wrongdoing. In other vocational habitats the predators may rein in their nefariousness out of a fear that they might be caught; the pretenders may occasionally do some work knowing that they can be fired or demoted. But academics of similar predispositions need have no such qualms. The predators can feast illicitly without fear of being

caught, while the pretenders can luxuriate in grand academic style knowing they will almost never be called upon to render an honest account of the way they've been spending their time.[11]

Setting the Record Straight

In recent years a number of books, reports, and articles on the current academic condition have appeared.[12] Some have been intended to stimulate curricular reforms on American campuses, arguing that the neglect of the liberal arts in most existing curriculums is an educational error in need of correction. Their authors (themselves academics) make the expected noises: "Without liberal arts, students don't develop the capacity for critical thought"; "Students are being trained as opposed to educated"; "American society can only suffer if its presumably educated leadership lacks the vision and foresight that only sustained exposure to the liberal arts can bestow." What they avoid saying—and not unexpectedly, given the already noted extent of academic denial—is that no planned curricular reform can transcend the quality of its execution. No matter the elegance of its design, the house will not stand if the carpenter ignores the requirements of that design. The curricular reforms they propose will come to naught if their colleagues willfully misexecute them. The curricular reformers, in my view, have produced a naïve literature that misleads because it overestimates the degree of good faith in the academic community.

The rest of this literature seems to recognize that something has gone awry within the academy, but for the most part it merely codifies the professoriate's litany of woes.[13] We find in these pages a lot of printed worry about the professoriate's loss of real income, about externally imposed conditions that presumably sap the professoriate's vitality and minimize its productivity, about threats to academic freedom, about the need for unionization and other forms of organized response to the presumed assault upon justifiable professional prerogatives. What we don't find—again, not surprisingly—is recognition of a corruption of academic purpose for which academics themselves bear sole responsibility.

The record, I think, needs to be set straight. The American academy cries out for reform, but curricular reform in the absence of behavioral and organizational reform is likely to be an empty exercise. And while something has indeed gone awry, it has little or nothing to do with the professoriate's litany of woes.

I am an academic of more than 30 years' standing; a professor of sociology at a research university. To the best of my knowledge, during my years of academic service, I have been neither malfeasant nor misfeasant. But in the past I have been complicit in the denial of such wrongdoing, and I have thereby contributed to its intensification. This book is my mea culpa, my apology for past complicity, and my attempt to set the record straight. Its pages recount what I have seen, denied, and consequently done little or nothing about. They recount what my peers, many of them valued friends and associates, have chosen to ignore. Because no reader should be burdened with the idiosyncratic discontents of an author, I have gone to some lengths to check on the generalizability of my complaints. I have asked informants in every conceivable academic setting to confirm or reject the accuracy of *my* observations on the basis of *their* experience.[14] They almost invariably set out to convince me that things were not nearly as bad as I was suggesting, only to conclude by the end of our encounters that they were a lot worse than they wanted to admit. My informants as a rule not only confirmed my observations on the nature and extent of academic wrongdoing but in the characteristic protocol of their responses demonstrated the nature and extent of self-delusive denial among even well-meaning academics. Some even articulated the dilemma necessitating such denial. Perhaps it was a professor of biochemistry at a West Coast medical school who put it in the most striking terms. After completing his interview, he invited me to his home for dinner. As we stood on his terrace overlooking a breathtaking expanse of the Pacific coastline, watching the sun lower itself into its oceanic bed, he said in gentle self-mockery, "Now you see why I don't like to think about the things we talked about this afternoon." I did indeed.

Chapter 2

Hear, See, and Speak No Evil
The Facilitation of Denial

It really is a con artist's heaven, the academy. If you qualify for admission, you can work a vast array of scams (including the one in which you don't have to do anything at all) without reasonable fear of detection and punishment. On the contrary, if by some curious set of circumstances, some quirkiness that now and then shows itself, your scam appears to be faltering, you can rest fairly easy in the assurance that some colleagues at least will make every effort to protect it from the types of negative consequence (legal entanglements, fines, loss of compensation, even imprisonment) that failed scams routinely elicit in other venues. And if the academy is the con artist's heaven, it is as well an asylum for those whose lame incompetence would not long be tolerated in less-protected occupational environs. It is thus a place perhaps unrivaled where as long as you possess the right titles (Dr., Professor) you can do very well indeed by doing ill or doing nothing at all.

If the major reason for this license is the self-delusive denial that comes of the professoriate's need to alleviate the tension between its adherence to a morally stringent creed and its utilitarian appetites, there are as well structural characteristics that combine with some of the academy's most revered traditions to facilitate such denial and its permissive consequences. No treatment of professorial exploitation gone unpunished or even unrecognized, of laziness and turpitude rewarded by those who are in effect sworn to do otherwise would be complete without consideration of those characteristics and traditions. Thus, while risking the ire of professors who believe that the inner workings of the academy, like those of the mother church, must be hidden from the barbarians at the gate (you, dear reader), I offer the following.[1]

24

The Democratization of the Academy

A superficial examination of the way colleges and universities are governed will not reveal anything startling. Unless one takes care not to be misled by appearances, it is easy to arrive at the erroneous conclusion that the authority structures of colleges and universities differ but little from those of most complex organizational units. If, for example, a corporation has its board of directors whose task is to set broad policy directions involving such matters as finances, budget, personnel, and corporate initiatives, a college or university has its board of trustees whose members function in a similar manner. If the everyday affairs of the corporation are tended to by a team of professional managers headed by a chief executive officer, the everyday affairs of the college or university would appear to be similarly managed by a president and an assortment of lieutenants—provosts, associate provosts, deans, associate deans, department chairpersons, institute directors, athletic directors, and so on. And finally, if a corporation has a labor force to do those things that will render it viable, so, too, does the college or university: primarily its faculty but including as well librarians, technicians, secretaries, and a variety of tradespeople. The apparent parallel even extends to unionization. Just as some corporate employees are unionized and work under collective bargaining agreements, so, too, are some of those workers (inclusive of faculty) who toil at the tasks crucial to the viability of their academic organizations.[2]

A more careful examination, however, will reveal some profoundly disturbing governance characteristics that have achieved near sacred status in the academy. Perhaps the most significant of these is the democratization, or leveling, of authority. It may appear that academic authority pyramids upward from faculty to department chairs to school deans, to a provost or some equivalent, to the president, and ultimately through the president to the board of trustees, each level having increasing power. But such an appearance is deceptive. On personnel matters in particular, the prerogatives of academic administrators have in practice become so limited that claiming their nonexistence would constitute only a slight exaggeration. Effectively, the real personnel power rests at the bottom of the apparent authority pyramid, with the faculty in their separate departments.[3] In reality, therefore, the pyramid is flattened.

Provosts and deans may determine the number of full-time faculty a

department can hire (presidents rarely bother themselves with such matters); they may determine when hiring can proceed and at what rank, but they do not determine the specialties that will be filled. Moreover, although they interview candidates, only rarely are their opinions taken into serious account when the actual hiring decision is made.

If administrators have little authority over hiring, they have virtually none over the remaining personnel actions. Whether probationary (untenured) professors will be retained is a matter almost always left to their departmental colleagues, except when financial exigencies render the slots they occupy unfunded. In such a circumstance the higher-level administrators may appear to have made a decision, but in fact all they've done is to read the bottom line and relay its message: The money's not there, so you can't rehire Professor X.

Whether professors are to be promoted or, more important, granted tenure in the university seems to involve the decision-making prerogatives of administrators, but in reality their involvement is likely to be nothing more than pro forma. In fact the higher one goes in the apparent authority pyramid the greater are the constraints on administrators—so that all things being equal, the higher their placement the more likely they are to follow lower-level recommendations.

Promotion and tenure deliberations typically begin with departmental consideration of the matter. Most frequently a personnel committee elected by all members of the department (including those who are untenured) deliberates according to guidelines promulgated by the faculty at large (or negotiated in a collective bargaining agreement), votes, and makes its recommendation to the dean as well as some committee usually elected by the school's faculty to "advise" that luminary. Department chairpersons, elected by their colleagues, usually make an independent recommendation. After reviewing the case in question, the dean's committee characteristically makes its recommendation by means of a vote. The dean then forwards a recommendation (together with a report of all actions taken by the candidate's department and the advising committee) to the provost or academic vice president, who forwards the record together with a recommendation to the president, who recommends a final disposition to the board of trustees. In theory, occupants of the next level up are supposed to review the deliberations and actions taken by occupants of the subordinate level and in so doing to make independent recommendations that might reverse the lower-level disposition. Reversal, however, occurs

so infrequently that in reality it is not an issue.[4] The crucial decision is made at the departmental level; the rest is likely to constitute nothing more than legitimation.

About the only time[5] upper-level administrators are likely even to consider reversing a faculty recommendation for tenure or promotion would be when there appears to be a serious split in the personnel committee making the recommendation—let us say two or three negative votes out of a committee of seven. Such an occurrence is, however, unsurpassingly rare. Despite likely differences of approach within a given department, faculty are, as we have seen, notoriously benign in their professional judgments of one another. After all, they have to live together. And there is always the threat of retribution should opposition to the interests of a particular colleague become too vigorous. Unless a department is sundered into unforgiving factions, there usually exists a tacit agreement to support the majority's recommendations with a formally unanimous vote. Thus even when the committee is split, that split will probably not show up because the minority will ordinarily change its vote in conformity with the majority before the action goes to the dean's level.

Faced with a "unanimous" departmental recommendation for promotion or tenure, the dean or the dean's advisory committee is unlikely to do anything except rubber-stamp that recommendation, even if the record doesn't seem to warrant such legitimation. The philosophy in the advisory committee is similar to that in the department's personnel committee: Live and let live. Faculty representatives on the dean's advisory committee understand full well that while today it's another guy's questionable candidate who is up for approval, tomorrow it could well be theirs. The dean, faced not only with an apparently unanimous departmental recommendation but also with similar unanimity from the advisory committee, has little choice but to put an imprimatur on that recommendation. To do otherwise would be to risk accusations of bias, arrogance, and heavy-handed authoritarianism.

By the time the action gets to the provostial and presidential levels, the game is over. Carrying the cumulative weight of apparent strong support from all those who have previously reviewed it, the candidacy in question takes on all the appearances of a juggernaut, and the prudent academic executive (who, by the way, has more "important" things to attend to) isn't likely to do anything except say yes and wave it on its way to the board of trustees.

The trustees, whether of public or private institutions, are more often than not laypersons. In the past such boards often did involve themselves in personnel decisions—for indefensible and usually political reasons. The local Thorstein Veblen was always at risk of losing his appointment for writing or saying things that offended their political sensibilities. With the general discrediting of Senator Joseph McCarthy and his vicious attacks on the academy as well as other institutions during the 1950s, this type of illegitimate interference has come to a deserved end. While left-wing faculty are still quick to cite the threat of trustee intervention, it has all but disappeared on American campuses.[6] No board of trustees is likely to risk the ignominious accusation of McCarthyism by reversing a personnel recommendation of the faculty and the administration unless it is virtually forced to do so. No doubt a faculty member convicted of a felony before the tenure recommendation got to the trustees would be turned away no matter the extent of collegial support, but anything short of such a definitive demonstration of moral turpitude (the conviction would probably require appellate confirmation before the trustees took action) would simply not be enough to move the trustees to reverse a tenure or promotion recommendation. Notwithstanding the frequently articulated fears of the academic left, it happens so rarely that it simply is not an issue.

And then there is the matter of compensation. It is true that at the least prestigious institutions (the community colleges, the open-door state colleges, and schools completely subservient to religious denominations) the power of the purse remains almost totally within the control of upper-level administrators.[7] But in those institutions constituting the academic mainstream (the "better" liberal arts schools, the run-of-the-mill universities, as well as the elite research universities) administrators characteristically share the power of the purse with the faculty. At these institutions administrators may determine what the starting salary for a particular faculty member will be, and because they have access to (so-called) discretionary funds, they may on occasion decide to supplement the salary increase a faculty member might expect, but that's about the extent of their prerogatives in the area of individual compensation. To the extent there is any discretion in determining individual salary increases, that prerogative resides with the faculty—at the department level.

Typically, there are two components to a faculty salary increase in

such institutions. There are, to begin with, cost-of-living adjustments, which are distributed across the board without regard for performance. Where a faculty union exists, such adjustments are likely to be written into collective bargaining agreements. In some public institutions without union contracts, these increases may parallel those given to employees in other agencies, such as the department of public works, the sanitation department, or their like. In some privately endowed institutions without faculty unions, such increases may occur at the discretion of the trustees, who usually feel impelled to offer them as a way of interdicting union efforts to organize the faculty. However it comes about, all faculty from the least to the most productive are likely to get an increment constituting a percent of their previous base salary in response to cost-of-living increases.

The second of the two components—and the one that differentiates most among the salaries of academics, even those holding the same rank in the same university—is euphemistically called merit money. It is also the component most directly controlled by the faculty. In some institutions the merit pool (the amount of money available for such increases) is set up through collective bargaining; in others the size of the pool is established by the trustees on recommendation of the upper-level administration. Once the pool is set, however, and various units (departments, institutes, centers) receive their allocations, decisions on how these moneys will be distributed among individual faculty are left to the faculty themselves.[8]

Most departments of more than just a few members operate with elected personnel committees. As already noted, such committees have an important role to play in tenure and promotion deliberations. However, their most consistently exercised function is the determination of who will get what in the merit pool.[9] In other words, departmental personnel committees are collective Santa Clauses who decide who's been naughty and who's been nice.

This, as one might expect, is a serious matter, and to hear them tell it, professors who serve on these committees make every effort to be fair and responsive to the relative merits of their colleagues' contributions. (It should be pointed out that committee members evaluate each other as well as their colleagues who do not serve on the committee.) Characteristically, professors' merit standings are determined by what they would have others believe is a careful peer evaluation of their contributions in three areas central to their institution's mission: teach-

ing, scholarship, and service. In universities with a major research commitment, scholarship is usually weighted most heavily, followed by teaching and service. In second-rung universities, where the commitment to research is more limited, or at liberal arts colleges, teaching is likely to be weighted most heavily. But how careful these evaluations are is open to serious question. Almost every professor at virtually every institution that engages in an annual review is, it appears, at least minimally meritorious. If merit placements were taken as accurate indicators of the contributions professors make year in and year out, there would indeed be reason to celebrate. They suggest that even the professoriate's weakest scholars are engaged in serious research (a conclusion extensively contradicted by the materials in Chapter 4), that even its weakest teachers foster serious inquiry and learning among their students (a conclusion contradicted by the materials in Chapter 3), and that there is virtually no variation in service contributions (everyone makes them every year). In the academy depicted by personnel committee assessments, there are virtually no screwups; almost no one is a malingerer, and no exploitation takes place. It is about as close to perfection as you can get—so close that if the depiction were taken seriously, it would be hard to explain why despite this near utopian state of affairs so many college graduates are poorly educated and so much of what passes for meritorious scholarship is hardly that at all.[10]

Abdication of Responsibility

You don't have to be consumed with skepticism to see through this charade. Only the most naïve (or those, like the professors themselves, well practiced in denial) would fail to miss the connection between the existence of a structure that endows a group of people with the power to reward one another and their failure to be discriminating in the exercise of that power. Professors do not elect tough personnel committees. Whatever their espousal of high standards, it seems they rarely elect colleagues who can be counted on to uphold them. Instead, they elect their most "compassionate" colleagues, those most likely to be sensitive to their financial needs, those who are not so rigid that they cannot find merit in a colleague's performance, even when it cannot be demonstrated in the expected manner. The most productive among the faculty might see an advantage in the election of a hard-nosed committee, but since they are likely to be in the minority, their views hardly

ever prevail. Their less productive colleagues, seeking to assure continuous incremental growth in their salaries, can be relied upon to present a united electoral front—and that all but rules out the election of an equitably tough committee.

To be fair, it is difficult for those who are elected to make judgments about people they see everyday, people who may be friends as well as colleagues. How do you tell the guy you carpool with that you don't find anything in his work justifying a claim to scholarly merit? How do you tell someone you've known since the trembling times of graduate school that her teaching is so riddled with problems that she's actually injured the department's enterprise? How do you tell a fellow committee member that since he really hasn't lived up to his professional obligations in the past year, his colleagues on the committee have decided not to vote him any merit increment at all? It is difficult, and that's just the problem. For a host of reasons ranging from genuine compassion to personal discomfort and even fear of retribution (you never know when those you judge will be in a position to judge you), sound judgments of merit or its absence cannot be expected where colleagues are given the prerogative of rewarding one another. Such a characteristic has all but mandated the attribution of false merit in the academy as a matter of course.

Potential for Denial

Leveling, or democratization, clearly creates the potential for abuse, leading to personnel decisions that are made without regard for the high performance standards faculty presumably endorse. But even more troubling is the fact that democratization increases the likelihood of denial, with all its pernicious consequences. When the obligation of making tenure and promotion decisions falls to a faculty who must live together, when because of democratization upper-level administrators feel severely constrained in their reviews of such cases, and when because of such democratization trustees are loathe to question tenure and promotion recommendations, denial is likely to be the rule rather than the exception. The faculty who, having to live with one another, cut a deal giving tenure to someone whose record fails even to approach the standards they espouse have placed themselves in precisely the conflict-ridden position that gives rise to truth-bending but tension-reducing justifications that constitute denial: "Well, he doesn't have

many publications, but what he does publish is significant"; "Her teaching methods may be unusual, but who am I to say that they are inappropriate—especially since academic freedom protects her right to experiment in the classroom?"; "Ethical lapse? That's no ethical lapse; that's a brilliant methodological innovation." Confronted as they are with a standard requiring a time-consuming action while they have "more important" things to do on behalf of the university's mission, administrators examining records that don't justify the claims made by personnel committees and department chairs also find themselves in a conflictual position where truth-bending self-justification is likely. "Well, I'm a political scientist and the candidate is a sociologist, so there must be something in his contribution that his knowledgeable colleagues have seen, even if it isn't immediately apparent"; "Oh yes, the complaints about his teaching. Well, there are always complaints. Students will complain if they didn't get the grade they wanted, and for some graduate students it can be a way of getting back at an instructor they think gave them a tough time. It can even be a way of externalizing the source of disappointment in oneself."

And just how do professors who are constantly declaiming on the academy's high standards face themselves after having yet again voted a merit increase for that colleague whose scholarly output amounts to nothing more than another year of unredeemed promises? How do they face themselves after voting to recognize the merit of a colleague who despite a Ph.D. can't seem to distinguish between teaching and seducing? Can those champions of the ethical stringency that presumably distinguishes the academy from the world of shortcuts, the world of caveat emptor, really justify merit increases for colleagues who miss as many classes as possible and who, when they do show up, deliver the same lectures they did five years ago? The democratization endowing faculty members with the power to financially reward their colleagues simply manufactures occasions for experiencing that conflict between ideals and behavior, between the requirement to rise above ordinary morality and structurally elicited failures to do so—which yet again makes denial highly probable. They're not going to fall into the publish-or-perish trap that mistakes publication for serious scholarship. Why it took Vernon Parrington ten years to finish *The Colonial Mind*! And they're not going to penalize someone because of unsubstantiated rumors. That'd be ethically wrong. Of course, if one of the young women came forward. . . . And well, they don't really know about

missing all those classes. Besides, his student course evaluations are about average!

The academic environment is awash in the self-justification that constitutes denial. Given the obligation of serious peer evaluation—on the assumption that their commitment to ethical stringency as well as their certified expertise renders them the most suitable and reliable judges of one another—professors regularly abdicate this responsibility. They do so for ordinary and quite understandable reasons, reasons that in other venues would simply be taken for granted as indicative of unsurprising and not terribly censurable moral imperfection. But the academic creed does not allow for such tolerance. Professors are supposed to rise above the morally ordinary. They are not supposed to take the easy way out. Their claims to a freedom unheard of in the job worlds of most people, their claims to a type of job security that most working people cannot even imagine, their very self-conceptions all depend on the presumably honored expectation of uncompromising moral rectitude. So when they abdicate their responsibility for making careful, performance-based judgments, there's a lot riding on their ability to convince themselves and others that no such lapse has occurred. Academics are case-makers par excellence; it's their stock-in-trade. Thus when democratization puts them in the position of having to act, and when in such a position their very real ethical ordinariness threatens their self-idealization (together with its adjuncts, freedom and tenure), when it threatens to burst forth into troubling conscious recognition, the case-makers, ever protective of themselves, do what they do best. Of course in the process they create an environment that paradoxically makes more ordinary work venues seem ethically superior by comparison. Not only do academics reward each other for work not done, not only do they fail to sanction those among them whose actions are destructive of academic purpose, but they compound these failings by creating what can fairly be called an ozone layer of hypocrisy that engulfs almost everyone who lays claim to a professorial identity.

Ironically, there is probably no work setting so permeated with dishonesty as the academy.[11] Even the majority of professors who go about their tasks with reasonable competence and otherwise commendable integrity, but with the feigned blindness born of a powerful need not to see what is there to be seen, contribute substantially to an environment in which almost anything goes because virtually everything

can be justified. "The emperor is luridly pleasuring himself," you say. And over and over again, they say, "Your voyeurism is abhorrent, and besides, that's not what he's doing. He's measuring his physiological cathexus; see those galvanometers? Or he's giving his students an object lesson in self-expression. If you object to what he's doing, you'd have to object to half of the Old Testament, not to mention Stravinsky's *Le Sacre du printemps.*" Of course if the professoriate did not have the power to make the decisions it does, if the structure of academic authority were hierarchical, if democratization of authority were not a fact of academic life, there would be significantly fewer occasions for this almost mandated denial that gives the lie to the academy's vaunted higher morality.

There seems to be a conundrum at work here. Moral stringency is, almost by definition, difficult to honor in actual behavior. Thus the more often people are called upon to exercise such stringency, the greater the probability that lapses will occur, and justifications, however hypocritical, will have to be invoked. While at first surmise the democratization of academic authority might appear to be unassailable, in conjunction with the moral stringency of the academic creed it is paradoxically problematic in that it multiplies those occasions when academics are called upon to do what in fact is so difficult for them to do. Thus democratization increases the potential for both abdication of responsibility and the self-justifying denial that, in the academy, is its twin. Thus the conundrum: Two goods, high moral/ethical standards and participation of the governed in their governance, each attractive in its own right, combine to create negative consequences. High moral standards and the participation of the governed simply do not go together like the pop lyricist's horse and carriage. A truly hierarchical authority structure in the academy cannot guarantee the exercise of moral stringency, but democratization, it seems, is almost certain to undermine its exercise—and what is worse to create an environment marked by self-justifying denial.

The Disciplines and the Departments

Democratization is closely related to another governance characteristic, the salience of disciplines, that ironically undermines faculty accountability in the academy. A faculty member isn't just a professor; he or she is a professor of *something*—of mathematics, art, English,

Spanish, sociology, physics.[12] To be an academic means that, like the priest who is a Jesuit, Dominican, or Franciscan and the nun who is a Carmelite or a Benedictine, you belong to an order. And just as the church has ceded to its orders certain rights of self-governance, so, too, have the academic orders (or disciplines) been granted such rights, but with a significant difference. The pope's authority transcends the self-governance of the church's orders, and the authority of a university's upper-level administrators presumably does likewise where the disciplines are concerned. In reality, however, the disciplines possess characteristics that limit the exercise of this supposedly transcendent authority, and in their departmental manifestations they constitute fiefdoms that on many counts are a law unto themselves.

Disciplines constitute rather broadly defined areas of inquiry, encompassing their epistemologies, methodologies, substantive theories, results, and interpretations. Most disciplines in today's academic pantheon have accumulated so much material in each of these categories that they are themselves subdivided into loosely connected specialties. On average it requires between seven and eight years of graduate training to be granted recognition as a full-fledged practitioner in a discipline, and even then the newly minted Ph.D. is likely to be considered competent in but one or two of the aforementioned specialties. Disciplines and subspecialties have their own languages, and no outsider, even a highly educated outsider, is likely to feel comfortable or competent in their use. Who except the highly trained physicist would dare to enter into an exchange on the reality of quarks? Who except the mathematician, statistician, or econometrician would be willing and able to entertain the derivation of Baye's conditional probability theorem and its applications to economic decision-making? Would anyone except a sociologist debate ethnomethodology? And what fool would rush in to encounter the literary critics as they define postmodernism in terms of the confusion in the dominant aesthetic techniques constituting modernism and the textual rebellion that is its issue?

The pope's authority transcends and overrides the governance prerogatives of Catholicism's orders because the pontiff is understood to be the supreme interpreter of God's will. When the pope speaks, he speaks as the vicar of Christ, the direct descendent of St. Peter. Whatever is special to the Jesuits or the Franciscans, for example, whatever they take unto themselves, is never presumed to be so special and mysterious that it would prove unfathomable to the vicar of Christ.

Their love and knowledge of God, however divine its inspiration, however true its reading of eschatological purpose, is always less inspired and less true than is the pope's. No member of an order would ever make a claim to religious infallibility, while the doctrine of papal infallibility is a cornerstone of Catholic tradition. But not since Nicholas Murray Butler regularly did so during his lengthy reign at Columbia University (1901–1945) has any college president seriously entertained making a public claim to infallibility.[13] College presidents and those appointed to assist them in the management of universities and colleges are more often than not men and women who can lay claim to knowledgeability in no more than one of the disciplines having a departmental presence on their campuses. Even at that, since they have forsaken research and teaching for administration, the validity of their claims is open to question, often by the administrators themselves. Granting knowledgeability in their own disciplines, presidents, provosts, and deans (upper academic management) are outsiders where the remaining disciplines are concerned. They are virtual strangers to the discipline realities in most of the departments it is presumably their responsibility to oversee. Without a widely accepted doctrine equivalent to that of papal infallibility, they have no basis for asserting decisional superiority over the faculty in matters—particularly personnel matters—that presumably require more than a passing acquaintance with a given discipline. Indeed an upper-level administrator who attempted to do so would be accused of unwarranted and therefore illegitimate interference with departmental prerogatives.[14] If this administrator persisted despite such an accusation, it is likely that a faculty appeal to the trustees would result in an admonishment roughly equivalent to a cease and desist order. A pope may be able to judge the doctrinal acceptability of a Jesuit's contemplations (as, for example, in the case of Pierre Teilhard de Chardin, whose writings on evolution were banned by Pope Pius XII) and even order the excommunication of a Jesuit who persisted in unacceptable doctrine or heresy; a university president would, however, never make a parallel judgment or take a parallel action in the case of a faculty member. The operative assumption is that because they do not possess the competence to address these matters, presidents must delegate their disposition to those who do: the faculty member's departmental colleagues.

It doesn't take a Ph.D. in organizational behavior to understand how, in their departmental manifestations, disciplines are likely to be-

come fiefdoms whose allegiance to the larger institutions of which they are a part, while apparent enough, hovers on the brink of meaninglessness. To the outside world, the professoriate preaches noninterference on the assumption of its special purpose and higher morality rooted in the academic creed. To one another, professors preach noninterference based upon that holy of holies—academic freedom—and, as concerns us here, the assumption that they cannot evaluate each other's professional efforts unless they are fully accredited in the same discipline. Thus it isn't just administrators who are the outsiders, not possessed of the requisite competence to enter into judgments about the way a particular department does or does not honor its obligations; it is as well all professors who, while members of the same faculty, are not practitioners of the same discipline and therefore not members of the department in question. The professor of English may have a nodding acquaintance with the professor of mathematics (at smaller institutions they may even meet now and then for lunch); the professor of engineering may serve on a university-wide committee with the professor of linguistics (e.g., the faculty senate's rules committee), and once or twice a year professors of all stripes may rub robed elbows at a convocation. But as far as issues crucial to their professional standing are concerned, the only colleagues who matter are those who share membership in the same department.[15]

The discipline-based academic department is impenetrable to outsiders, whatever their administrative rank or however distinguished they may be in their own disciplines. Faculty outsiders as a rule will not even consider breaching the discipline-fortified boundaries of departments to which they do not belong. A department's standards are its own business. There might be some "tsk-tsking" about a department known to be particularly lax, but that's about as far as cross-departmental collegial concern is likely to go. Departments have wide latitude in deciding how their assigned resources will be used, and within broad administrative limits they are free to determine their own rules of governance and their own organizational systems. Short of sacrificing a virgin each year in propitiation of a pagan deity, there is very little the members of an academic department cannot do free of the gaze of administrators and of colleagues who pray to other gods.

It should be clear that the importance of the disciplines is causally linked to the democratization of authority in the academy. If it requires a special expertise, gained only after years of study in a specific dis-

cipline, to make informed judgments about the various aspects of academic work, then it would appear to follow that the assessments made by a well-trained faculty should be given primacy in determining the directions of day-to-day decision-making at any college or university. What in fact follows, of course, turns out to be quite problematic, because faculty members caught between the stringencies of their creed and more mundane urgencies don't seem to be up to the evaluative tasks workplace democracy thrusts upon them. Ironically, it is the salience of the disciplines itself that, having placed faculty in a position where their judgments carry considerable weight, also eventuates in a condition nearly guaranteeing the uncritical illegitimacy of so many of those judgments.

The Department Setting

In the existing system the most important faculty judgments are made in the smallest unit of an academic institution's organization, the discipline-anchored department. It is also, as I have indicated, an organizational unit that is a world unto itself, hermetically sealed off from the rest of the college or university by virtue of a discipline-based exclusionary principle. There is no anonymity in this diminutive setting. (Academic departments rarely exceed forty members.) Everyone knows everyone else. And it doesn't take much detective work to figure out where particular faculty members stand on particular issues. Even a secret ballot isn't much help to those who, for whatever reason, would keep their positions private. If a total of fifteen or twenty people vote on something or other, I am likely to know those—let us say the twelve or so—who share my disposition on the issue in question. The remainder, the opposition and the undeclared, would therefore also be known to me. From time to time there may be some slippage, as when somebody who is nominally undeclared winds up voting in support of my position and so makes it difficult (but not impossible) to determine just who the opposition was. But overall, figuring out who has voted for what requires something less than the inductive acuity of Conan Doyle's sleuth. The smaller the department the easier this gets, but few departments are so big as to make such determinations impossible.

The department is a small and intense setting. Decisions matter to those who populate it and who, because of the face-to-face quality of working relationships, cannot make these decisions in isolation of col-

legial scrutiny. The doctrine of academic freedom may be invoked to justify willful blindness with regard to a colleague's work, but it is never used to justify a similar inattentiveness to a position on departmental matters. Do you support Professor X's elevation to tenure? Where do you stand on raising the stipends of graduate assistants? Will you support the candidacy of Professor Y for department chair? Shall we continue to insist that Ph.D. candidates pass two foreign language examinations? Do you support the proposed curriculum reform? In the grand scheme of things, questions like these may count for little; the future of the world clearly does not turn on the positions of one's colleagues regarding such matters. But you'd hardly know that from observing and listening to professors in their natural habitat. A week or two within the confines of a typical academic department would convince anyone that as far as professors are concerned, no questions are more important than these. They buttonhole one another in the halls; they retreat behind pointedly closed office doors to plan strategy; they take undecided "votes" out to lunch—they lobby and, if necessary, even intimidate. Expertise, hard won and time tested, may have something to do with the decisions emerging from academic departments, but only considerable naïveté would lead to the conclusion that it is the single or even the most important determinant of these decisions. Does expertise transcend friendship? Can it, in the small world of the academic department, be exercised free of political constraint? Is the untenured professor free to vote her professional conscience in opposition to those who will later decide whether or not they want her to keep her job? Are we really to conclude that, on balance, professors will doggedly stick to their expert guns even when they know that such principled stubbornness must give offense to people they have to face day after day after day?

The Unlikelihood of Universalistic Judgments

Sociologists have long understood that universalistic judgments— judgments not colored by personal considerations—are unlikely to characterize decision making in groups where face-to-face interactive intensity exists. True, however, to their espousal of inquiry for no sake other than itself, they apparently have found no reason to alert their colleagues in other disciplines to the fact that departmental isolation cannot therefore yield the universalistic exercise of expertise that pre-

sumably justifies such isolation in the first place. Of course it probably wouldn't matter if they did. Academics are not about to give up what they take to be prerogatives of unquestionable legitimacy. Even though intradepartmental politicking goes on right before their eyes, even though they themselves are party to deals that compromise judgments presumably derived from their reading of discipline-inspired precepts, and even though from time to time they are troubled by the outcomes of all the lobbying and leveraging, they can and do explain away every bit of it. To do otherwise would threaten the freedom that the present structure affords. To admit that what goes on within departments falls far short of a universalistic exercise in discipline-based expertise would be to relinquish the only conceivable basis for isolating departmental deliberations from administrators and those colleagues presumably beyond the pale.

So every time a professorial stalwart votes in support of a friend, he or she will find something—anything—to justify that vote in universalistic terms: "The work under way, even if not completed and visible to the naked eye, has the potential for considerable significance"; "In the long run it makes sense to encourage a colleague rather than punish him. If you do the latter, you'll create morale problems that will undermine the department's mission." Every time senior professors lobby their junior colleagues on an issue, they convince themselves that there is nothing untoward about such behavior. Nothing political you understand; just a few colleagues consulting on a matter of consequence to the department. Now how can anyone find fault with that? And of course professors never go along to get along; every consensus is born in the near unanimity the discipline's generalizations inspire among those in the know.

As is the case with the democratization, or leveling, of academic authority, the organizational salience of the academic disciplines (a major source of that democratization) simply creates occasions for a tension-producing clash between ethical demands emanating from the academic creed and utilitarian realities common to human relationships in any workplace, the academy not excepted. As such the organizational importance of the disciplines not only results in an undermining of the very universalism or fairness it presumably exists to serve, but it also contributes to the likelihood of the tension-reducing denial that hypocritically increases permissiveness and makes a bad situation even worse. Do anything or don't do a thing; as long as you do it or don't do

it on campus, chances are no one will ever call you to account. It doesn't take long before young academics harboring nefarious proclivities realize that they have truly lucked out. They've found their way into a work setting where few seem willing or able to distinguish evil from good, where contrary to what one might expect, given all the high-flown rhetoric, scams and genuine work efforts are applauded with equal vigor. And so coexisting with their honorable but often deluded colleagues, they embark upon thirty-five to forty years of scamming, of taking while their colleagues reward them for giving.

Academic Freedom

As important as structural characteristics (democratization and discipline salience) have been in the creation of so perverse an environment, they probably would not have had as much impact were it not for their coexistence with the academy's most sacred belief. Because the cause of truth must be served without compromise, because it can brook no interference from the worldly utilitarians who will take every opportunity to subvert or otherwise interfere with its service, professors believe they must be held harmless for what they write, what they teach, and for that matter nearly everything they do or do not do when they're on duty. This belief in what they call *academic freedom* is accompanied by a reverence rarely found in the secular world. Almost every academic endorses its inviolability on pain of being excluded from the fellowship of his or her peers, and most academics stand vigilant in its defense. A betrayal of academic freedom is tantamount to the heinous crime of Judas Iscariot. Alternatively, its assertion in the face of utility's long odds is celebrated in language usually employed to describe the heroism of a David standing before Goliath, a Socrates defying his accusers, or a Thomas More defending principle despite the foreknowledge that to do so spelled his doom. No principle can compete against academic freedom for the loyalty of the American professoriate. None can elicit such apparent passion, and none possesses its aura of sanctification.

Like so much that is characteristic of the academy, however, this most sanctified of principles turns out to be something other than it appears to be. It is less a protection for truth's conscientious servants against the interference of truth's implacable foes than it is a justification of the academy's self-indulgence, the stuff of delusive denial that

allows the misfeasant and malfeasant to continue on in their merry ways with impunity. Over the years what was once an important but narrow doctrine has been broadened to cover just about every facet of academic work and almost all collegial relationships. As such it has come to provide some professors with a rationale for denying other professors access to their work, while at the same time bestowing legitimacy on the self-imposed blindness of those, the majority, who would rather not see. The principle, so revered by the professoriate, has been broadened by that professoriate into a perversion of its former character, and when invoked in conjunction with democratization and discipline salience, it has become a potent source of the anything-goes irresponsibility that so injures American colleges and universities.

The doctrine of academic freedom emerged in the United States around the turn of the century. By 1915 it had been articulated by a number of academicians, most prominently by those, such as John Dewey, Charles Beard, and Arthur Lovejoy, who were instrumental in the founding of the American Association of University Professors (AAUP). Responding to a growing number of instances—the Ely case at the University of Wisconsin, the Ross case at Stanford, the Nearing case at the University of Pennsylvania, among others—where professors had been penalized for their unpopular views (some with the loss of their appointments), the AAUP set out to ensure that nonacademics did not interfere with a scholar's research or the teaching he did on the basis of that research.

Oversight

The AAUP's position was as clear as it was limited. The academic freedoms it sought to guarantee were the freedoms of inquiry and communication. The villains it sought to protect professors from were nonacademic yahoos or demagogues, politicians and philanthropists who had shown a willingness to pressure university administrators into silencing those whose views they found offensive. Nothing in the AAUP's position could be construed as countenancing a professorial freedom from collegial evaluation and criticism. Indeed in claiming freedom from external interference, the founders of the AAUP were careful to demand an accountability to scholarly and pedagogical standards. This of course meant that no academic could claim immunity from colleagues' justifiable inquisitiveness and no academic could flee

the obligation to be inquisitive by citing the precepts of academic freedom. The AAUP's 1915 Seligman report made it clear that the fledgling organization sought to protect only those scholarly conclusions that were "the fruits of competent . . . patient and sincere inquiry" and that the pedagogical freedoms it sought to protect did not include "taking unfair advantage of the student's immaturity by indoctrinating him with the teacher's own opinions."[16] The existence of standards such as those alluded to in the Seligman report clearly required active professorial oversight of one another's efforts.[17] Far from prohibiting it as a threat to free inquiry and inspired pedagogy, it was championed as the guarantor of these precious academic values. In effect the early protectors of professorial prerogative were telling the powerful unwashed to keep their dirty hands off the academy; they were telling them that because they were unwashed, because they were ignorant, they had no right to impose on truth's service. The quality of efforts made in that service could be judged only by academicians who could be counted on to do so free of unfair preconception. Thus, in its origins, the great and grand principle of academic freedom could never have been used to avoid professional accountability, nor could it have been invoked to justify inattention to what was transpiring in the study, lab, or classroom across the hall.

But, oh, how different it is today. Over the years this protection against unwarranted external interference in truth's service has been transformed into a principle that professors invoke primarily to ward off internal reviews of any consequence. The principle that required vigorous internal oversight as a counterweight to the reign of ignorance threatened by external interference is now the principle that, though nominally allowing for such oversight, is too often interpreted to mean that any professor who is seriously interested in colleagues' efforts is transgressing against the freedoms of those colleagues to inquire and teach as they see fit. Time's passage has tested and transmuted the original meaning of this holy of academic holies. The "red scares" of the 1920s and 1950s reinforced its importance to American professors. In each instance the yahoos were out to get them, and academic freedom became the rallying cry of those in their ranks who had the courage to fight back. During the McCarthyite 1950s,[18] however, an alliance between the yahoos who, emboldened by the senator's sneering attacks, joined his crusade against any hint of political nonconformity in what they took to be America's "little red school-

houses" and opportunistic faculty members who saw some personal advantage in denouncing their nonconforming colleagues contributed significantly to the transformation of academic freedom. Now it wasn't merely the outsiders—the political Neanderthals, the cold warriors, the Visigoths—who posed a serious threat to the unfettered pursuit of truth; it was clear that there were insiders—Ph.D.'s, professors—who when it suited their purposes (whatever they might be) could and would do so as well. There was, in other words, a potentially dangerous fifth column within the academy, and the threat it posed had to be addressed.

There was of course, little that could be done officially. Any attempt to weed out suspected turncoats might itself become a misbegotten crusade that resembled the very activities it was intended to prevent. About the only thing that might protect against such betrayal from within the ranks was an extension of the great and grand principle. True, academic freedom was supposed to immunize faculty from interference by powerful but ignorant *outsiders,* but if these outsiders had agents within the citadel, wasn't it necessary to immunize faculty as well from the potential for harm represented by those quislings? To many academics, it was only logical to extend academic freedom so that truth's service would be protected from ignorant orthodoxy no matter the location of its source. Since the fifth column was by definition the internal manifestation of the external threat, the invocation of academic freedom as a protection against the former was surely consistent with its invocation as a protection against the latter.

This extension of academic freedom did not render accountability to scholarly and pedagogical standards inoperative. The extension was simply intended to ensure that such standards were not subverted by those academics whose agendas were distinctly nonacademic. Professional oversight of one another's work was presumably still the order of the day, so long as it employed standards that were uncontaminated by orthodox prejudices. The only immunity claimed by the extension was a professorial immunity to professionally unwarranted inquisitiveness. And surely only such inquisitiveness was enjoined.

In principle the distinction between warranted and unwarranted oversight was and is clear enough. The former derives from discipline and pedagogical precepts, the latter from presuppositions having nothing to do with either. In practice, however, making such distinctions turned out to be extremely difficult, if not impossible. Was it legitimate

for a department chairperson in the social sciences to inquire into the books being used by his or her colleagues in the courses they taught? Well, it was legitimate if it was done to ensure that students were exposed to competent materials. And of course it was illegitimate if it was done to intimidate unorthodox teachers—Marxists, anarchists, and the like—so that they'd hesitate before designing courses that reflected their points of view. Easy, right? But when the Marxist or anarchist complained of intimidation while the chairperson claimed to be engaging in professionally justified quality control, how was the truth of the matter to be determined? When senior faculty visited the classes of junior faculty, just what were they doing? Helping to improve their younger colleagues' teaching? Ensuring pedagogical accountability? Exerting a form of social control? Spying for the House Un-American Activities Committee, the state legislature, or a group of reactionary trustees?[19] What appeared to be an easy distinction to make turned out not to be so at all. As such, academics quickly abandoned the effort and opted instead for an interpretation of the great and grand principle that shielded almost everything professors did or didn't do from the attentions, however motivated, of their colleagues.

Of course professors still gave lip service to high standards of accountability, but their vigor in behalf of such standards became all but unheard of. Faculty might indeed go through the motions of accountability. They might elect personnel committees and file the required annual reports of activities and accomplishments. Anything more, however, was guaranteed to elicit howls of self-righteous indignation: "Fascist! What are you trying to do—Sovietize teaching? Haven't you heard of academic freedom?"

If there was any lingering discomfort about so broad a reading of what academic freedom rules out, the academic events of the 1960s put an end to it. Student activism on American campuses, stimulated first by the civil rights movement and then by opposition to the Vietnam War, put most of the professoriate on the defensive yet again. Faced with a wide array of challenges—challenges that questioned their rights to accept research support from the U.S. government or from corporations like Dow Chemical that were profiting from the war, challenges that questioned their prerogatives in determining what should be taught and who should be teaching it, challenges that even questioned their rights to bestow grades or otherwise render critical judgments about student performance—faculties from Berkeley to Co-

lumbia, from Wisconsin to Ole Miss, adopted an us-against-them mindset in their dealings with students. Once again they had discovered an unexpected enemy in their midst, an enemy of considerable energy, willing to go to extremes in a struggle to impose its will. Although the majority of students did not involve themselves in such activities, student strikes, sit-ins, and on rare occasions violence terrorized the academic imagination. If the McCarthyism of the 1950s intensified their sense of vulnerability, the student movement of the 1960s pushed American professors to the brink of panic as they confronted what they took to be uncontrolled outrages perpetrated by ignorant infants. Egged on by left-wing faculty malcontents, the students, so the academy thought, were running amok. No professor was exempt. The terrible infants would stop at nothing, and even those faculty sympathetic to their ideals and complaints feared they might find themselves shouted down in their classrooms or locked out of their offices and laboratories.[20]

It should come as no surprise, then, that the "us," the embattled professorial few standing against the "them," the infant hordes trying to impose political tests on scholarship and attempting to destroy the academic traditions of orderly accretion and communication of knowledge, would close ranks in a solidarity that had little or no room for critical attentiveness to one another. Not only would such oversight undermine the professoriate's ability to stand together against what in the view of many was a real threat to the learning upon which civilization itself depended, but questioning what your colleagues were doing or not doing seemed, in this crisis environment, to be little different from what the students were advocating, and as such a violation of the principle of academic freedom.[21]

The Emptiness of Accountability

By the early 1970s academic freedom had become little more than the great and grand legitimator of the inattentiveness that then as now served as an excuse for faculty who did not want to see for fear of having to act. If academic stringencies required faculty responses to perceived misfeasance and malfeasance, responses that would be personally costly, it was better not to see what was going on. But inattentiveness itself could, given the existence of these stringencies, weigh heavily on the academic conscience. What the professoriate needed

and what by the 1970s it had created for itself was a legitimation of inattentiveness, something that rendered mutual ignorance uncensurable, that, on the contrary, made of it a virtue. Professors didn't have to act against their misfeasant and malfeasant colleagues because they didn't know and, in accord with the new precepts of academic freedom, should not have known what these worthies were up to. By the early 1970s about all that was left of the expectation compelling serious faculty oversight of other faculty was its rhetorical invocation. "Accountability? Why should anyone raise that issue? We're an honorable profession. Where else do you find so great an emphasis upon peer review!" Blithely untroubled by what most reasonably intelligent people would see as an inconsistency between such a sentiment and a broad reading of academic freedom, most professors will today espouse both. But of course espousal is one thing and behavior is another. At the behavioral level there is no inconsistency at all; it's only the broad reading of academic freedom that counts. "I didn't know he was doing that, but then I wasn't supposed to be snooping around. It's too bad he got away with it, but like free speech, academic freedom cannot be compromised. Keeping tabs on your colleagues can only have a chilling effect on everyone's freedom of inquiry and everyone's right to search for effective pedagogical approaches. Just as the cost of the First Amendment's protection is the possibility of its abuse (yes, there are pornographers out there), so it is that the cost of academic freedom's protection of creative heterodoxy is the possibility of abuse. But no abuse justifies the abandonment of either principle!"

The twentieth century has seen the professoriate beat a hasty retreat from responsibilities it claims to want but, given their cost, really can't abide. If the early versions of academic freedom emphasized peer accountability, and if discipline salience and democratization created more and more opportunities for its exercise, the broadening of exclusions in the name of academic freedom during the 1950s and 1960s (in conjunction with the structural problems implied in the aforementioned democratization and discipline salience) all but emptied such accountability of any meaning. What is left is the hollowest of rhetorics and a set of superficial procedures that too often amount to nothing more than bureaucratic ritual. To be sure the rhetoric and the ritual have their functions. When on rare occasions outsiders (legislators, parents, alumni, trustees, and other benefactors) worry about whether anyone is minding the academic store, professorial response simply invokes the

rhetoric and points to the procedures. And should any professors feel an attack of conscience coming on, they can reassure themselves by resorting to the rhetoric while examining the six- or seven-page faculty activities report they file annually with their colleagues. But for all the reasons thus far recounted, there really is little approximating serious peer accountability on America's college campuses. And wonder of wonders, the very same doctrine whose original invocation mandated such accountability now serves to legitimate its absence. Academic freedom, which once commanded professors to pay attention to one another, now commands them to avert their eyes in each other's presence.

Tenure

How would you like a job that you won't be fired from no matter what you do or don't do? A job that's yours even if you show up for work less than half the time? A job that will remain yours even if you consistently fail to produce what you've been hired to produce? A job that you can't be laid off from unless your boss proves he or she can no longer afford to employ your entire division? In other words, how would you like a job with even more security than a lifetime appointment to the Supreme Court of the United States? No such thing you say. Nobody, not a Fortune 500 CEO, not a senior partner in a Wall Street law firm, not even an anonymous bureaucrat hidden away in the bowels of the civil service has that kind of job security.

Well, in point of fact, there *is* a job with that kind of security. Not all professors have it, but those who've passed a tenure review, usually in their sixth year of service, possess job security the likes of which is all but unheard of in any other work venue. Tenured professors who come to campus on the two days a week they teach and only on those days are in absolutely no danger of losing their presumably full-time jobs. Similarly, tenured professors who engage in absolutely no scholarship and whose teaching leaves much to be desired are as secure in their jobs as any of their overachieving colleagues. The courts have ruled that in the absence of a collective bargaining agreement that specifically allows administrators to do so, professors in the possession of tenure cannot be laid off unless fiscal problems require the cancellation of an entire academic program. In the words of a country-western song, those same mommas who've been counseled not to allow their

sons (and daughters) to become cowboys (and cowgirls) would do well, it seems, to insist that they become professors.[22]

Tenure is an important structural correlate of academic freedom. By granting them an immunized status, you can, it is assumed, well protect the freedom of professors to serve truth constrained only by their interpretations of what their disciplines require. And that, in short, is precisely what tenure is. Those who receive it are immunized from any and all pressures that might conceivably interfere with their scholarly and pedagogical independence. They don't have to worry about losing their jobs if they offend powerful nonacademic interests in their fealty to truth's cause. No matter how eccentric their views are in the eyes of others, they will not have to back away from them for fear of losing their livelihoods. Unfortunately, tenure, like academic freedom, has also come to protect more than scholarly and pedagogical independence. On today's campuses those who have been awarded tenure are as well immunized against repercussions that might result from either misfeasance (even in the extreme) or the most grievous malfeasance. In other words, those with tenure constitute a class of academic untouchables.

Professors, as we have seen, are not even likely to allow themselves an awareness of their colleagues' wrongdoing. But even when, by a bizarre turn of events, their mechanisms of denial are overwhelmed and they are forced to confront some major fallibilities in their colleagues, it is more than likely they will do nothing about them, particularly if the colleagues in question possess tenure. Taking tenure to be an impenetrable shield, their typical response in such cases is likely to be one of impotent regret: "It's a shame, but what can you do? He has tenure, you know."

Paralleling academic freedom, tenure has gone through a broadening process in the course of the twentieth century. Early in the century its champions construed tenure as a protection against unwarranted external (nonacademic) strong-arming. The AAUP's 1915 report (the Seligman report) made it clear that consistent with its view of academic freedom, the removal of tenured professors because powerful outsiders objected to the scholarly views they professed was unacceptable. By no stretch of the imagination, however, did the report imply an award of tenure should be taken to mean a promise of lifetime employment irrespective of the recipient's ongoing academic performance. In fact, the report directly addressed the matter of removing a

tenured professor. Taking the possibility of removal for granted, viewing it as an unexceptional act that colleges and universities might have to perform from time to time, the report simply set out to define standards and procedures for removal that would be acceptable to the professoriate. Tenured professors might be dismissed, it held, for failure to honor their professional obligations so long as they were presented with explicit statements of particulars and so long as this was the judgment of a committee of peers after affording the accused professors a fair opportunity to rebut the charges brought against them. Removal for cause was not something the AAUP took lightly, but neither did it elevate tenure to a status approaching beatification that insulates those so awarded from all earthly accountability.

The rhetoric of tenure hasn't changed much over the years. Writing in the 1950s, the prominent philosopher and social scientist Robert McIver, reacting to the McCarthyite witch-hunt, claimed as a professorial right "conditions of tenure that will assure . . . against dismissal or professional penalization on grounds *other than* professional incompetence or conduct that in the judgment of . . . colleagues renders [an individual] unfit to be a faculty member."[23] By 1970, after two decades of turmoil on America's campuses, another prominent academic, Robert Nisbet, having fallen victim to the siege mentality so prevalent at that time, bemoaned the "degradation of the academic dogma." Writing in the patrician style of one who was fully convinced of the academy's moral superiority, he defined tenure as "the bond of protection for individuals possessed of knightly honor who [give] faithfully and fully their services to the academic community." Moreover, he continued, "once acquired, tenure [might] not be taken away from the individual for any reason short of flagrant, and fully demonstrated, debasing of [the] academic mission."[24]

Rhetorically, then, tenure has always been viewed as a protection against external, nonacademic pressures and only those pressures. On the face of it, there is little difference between the AAUP's 1915 position and the claims made by academic stalwarts a half century or so later. By the 1970s, however, there was considerable difference in the standard interpretation of "external" and "nonacademic" and therefore considerable difference in the typical professorial understanding of tenure. Because of the fifth-column problem during the 1950s, the meaning of "external" was extended to include virtually everyone external to a given individual, academic or nonacademic, and tenure was

thus taken to mean equal immunization against unwarranted threats that might emanate from within as well as without the academy. Where such threats came from was simply not an issue. Since it was unfortunately true that some faculty, at least, had betrayed their trust and sold out to truth's outsider enemies, the external-internal dichotomy had become a distinction without a difference.

Moreover, as the discussion of academic freedom earlier in this chapter has indicated, difficulties in distinguishing between academically warranted oversight and unwarranted nonacademic interference gave academics the reason they were looking for to avoid such oversight and its action implications. Any oversight was just possibly unwarranted. Who could tell? Maybe legitimate reasons were being invoked as a mask for political savagery directed against the heterodox. Since oversight itself became suspect, tenure became understood as a protection against those actions which oversight might result in. While the rhetoric of professional accountability was retained in association with the concept of tenure, it had become no less hollow than the rhetoric surrounding the principle of academic freedom. For all intents and purposes, few tenured professors would be removed for cause, since there was always the risk of political taint and the danger of a witch-hunt.

As might be expected, the student turmoil of the 1960s did as much to intensify the professoriate's commitment to a broad concept of tenure as it did to intensify its commitment to a broad interpretation of academic freedom. With all those acid-crazed infants running around, demanding their consumers' right to evaluate the services professors were delivering, this was hardly the time to break ranks. Dismissing a tenured professor, even for good cause, would give aid and comfort to those who had of late become the enemy. Doing so might easily be interpreted as caving in to student demands, and in their blood lust the crazed infants would only insist upon more professorial sacrifices. Today it might be someone who had in fact screwed up, but tomorrow it might be someone whose politics they would not abide or even someone whose pedagogical approach they deemed too authoritarian. As the 1960s wore on, it became increasingly rare to find a professor who in fact believed tenure ought to be anything other than a lifetime award of employment irrespective of performance. Then as now, no one would explicitly endorse so absolutist an interpretation, but then as now dismissal of a tenured professor would be understood as an extraordinary occurrence.[25]

That the professoriate has been able to make its understanding of academic freedom and tenure the modus operandi on American campuses may come as a surprise to those who have been misled by its incessant litany of woe. If things are as bad as professors claim, if they truly are an embattled few protecting truth's citadel against insult and injury perpetrated time after time by an apparently inexhaustible supply of philistines and other abominable utilitarians, then how have they been able to create a situation characterized by license to do as they please and job security without rival? Colleges and universities clearly do not exist in a vacuum, and if their environments have been only half as hostile to their purposes as professors have made them out to be, it is difficult indeed to understand how even the narrowest conceptions of academic freedom and tenure, let alone the broader conceptions, could become operating policy. How is it that insensitive trustees and booboisie state legislators (thank you, Henry Mencken!) have not been successful in limiting professorial prerogatives? The answer is quite simple: For the most part, they haven't tried. With notable exceptions (e.g., the red scares of the 1920s and the 1950s), the utilitarians have characteristically kept their hands off American colleges and universities in the twentieth century. Contrary to professorial belief, the barbarians at the gate have been content to mill around outside.

Irrelevance, Complexity, and Specialization

Over time, reasons have changed, but as a rule what has transpired amidst all the ivy has been of less than surpassing interest to nonacademics. Early in this century colleges and universities yet maintained the nineteenth-century aura best described as narrowly elitist. By 1900 the Morrill Act establishing publicly supported land grant universities was but thirty-eight years old.[26] And while education for the professions was becoming increasingly common on American campuses, by no means did it have the presence we are today familiar with. It was not all that unusual for professional practitioners still to have achieved their status through the apprenticeship route. The first graduate program in the United States at Johns Hopkins had only lately been established, in 1881. The total college and university enrollment in 1900 was somewhat short of 110,000,[27] a figure presently exceeded by enrollment at the University of California alone. During the early part of this century, higher education was still the province of the very

few, and its relevance for the "important things" in American life—economic development, technological innovation (were Thomas Edison and Henry Ford college graduates?), the law, and even medicine—was far from established.[28]

The simple truth is that early in this century colleges and universities were not important enough for the barons of industry and commerce or the ubiquitous Babbitts seriously to concern themselves about their day-to-day operations. When there was so much to do, why would any self-respecting entrepreneur, merchant, or farmer cast an eye on the doings of those who spent their days merely theorizing? As for the rest, the ordinary working people, they were too busy just trying to make ends meet—too busy working six of God's seven days—to care much about what was going on "over there at the college." Yes, there were the celebrated cases of interference that led to the founding of the AAUP and the promulgation of the principle of academic freedom together with its corollary, tenure. But important though these cases were, they have been given more weight than they deserve in a revisionist history that does little more than provide a mythic basis for the extraordinary freedoms academics have gained. There is little if any evidence that the persecution of some academics (most of whom were social scientists and thus more likely than their colleagues to be controversial) by trustees and politicians was representative of the on-going relationship between faculties and laypeople in the late nineteenth and early twentieth centuries. Professors who gave public offense to the views of powerful laypeople were unlikely to escape censure and even possible dismissal to be sure, but that in itself cannot be taken as an indicator of continuous interference. A case for such interference can be made only by drawing on evidence of intrusiveness in the absence of controversy. And this has yet to be convincingly done.[29]

If early in this century colleges and universities were not important enough to elicit serious lay attention regarding their daily operations, they have latterly attained so much importance that such attentiveness has somewhat paradoxically become all but impossible. Far from being citadels in opposition to the shortsighted unreason of a world dominated by utilitarianism, colleges and universities have become crucial to that world, so crucial to its purposes that in the absence of unmitigated scandal few outsiders would dare question their operating procedures.

If there is one word that may be invoked to characterize twentieth-century America, it is, without a doubt, *complexity*. Everything or almost everything has become complex and ultrasophisticated. The multiplicity of agencies that have come to constitute a highly bureaucratized government would have been unimaginable in the nineteenth century. The interlacing of corporate entities that dominate the contemporary economy exceeds even the literary nightmares of a Franz Kafka. Almost all transactions have been computerized. You can't have a suit dry-cleaned or place an order for french fries in the absence of microchip technology. Documents can be sent across the country in a matter of minutes; people in one city can hear and see people in another city instantaneously; and sounds unheard by the likes of Bach, Beethoven, and Brahms have become familiar to us all. Staying alive has become one part sophisticated measurement (of your cholesterol level, your triglyceride level, the amount of fiber you ingest, the amount of toxic waste and radiation to which you've been exposed) and one part mind-boggling technological innovation (you can be kept alive for a while at least by machines that can replace your heart, lungs, and kidneys). Raising your children can't be satisfactorily accomplished unless you've been exposed to scientifically established principles of parenting—or so we are forever being told. There is, it seems, a necessary expertise for everything—for making love as well as making war, for planning a holiday as well as planning a corporate take-over—even for baby sitting.

All this sophistication—whether necessary or not—of course presupposes the availability of highly trained people who can create and manage it. This in turn means that advanced education and training have become central to modern American life. Thus colleges and universities, which in 1900 were little more than four-year time-out boxes for the relatively advantaged few, have become critical to virtually everything Americans do and experience. No other institutions are as much involved in the training and certification of those presumably competent to create and manage complexity,[30] and they have thus come to occupy a position of privilege few outsiders believe it prudent to challenge. World War II, the cold war, as well as an ongoing economic competition with Japan and the countries of western Europe have all combined to spur an American investment in complex sophistication, and with that an investment (both financial and psychological) in the correlative importance of colleges and universities. In 1940 there

were no more than 1.4 million students, constituting but 14 percent of their age group enrolled in institutions of higher learning. By 1970 there were 8 million students, constituting nearly 50 percent of their age group. By fall 1991 there were over 14 million students attending colleges and universities.[31] In 1940 only 3,006 Ph.D.'s were awarded nationally. By 1970 the amount had increased tenfold, and it has grown gradually since then, with approximately 43,000 doctorates awarded in 1994 (the last year for which a count was available at the time of this writing). In that same year, universities awarded approximately 75,000 professional degrees requiring a minimum of two post-baccalaureate years of study.[32]

How competent these legions of the educationally certified really are is not the issue here. What is important for the purposes of this discussion is the sheer number of certified and presumably educated adults that American colleges and universities produce every year. As long as complexity continues to be a modern passion, these legions will be regarded as absolutely necessary to our well-being. And unless someone comes up with an alternative to the current practice of relying upon institutions of supposed higher learning to ensure a constant replenishment of the ranks (where's the Wizard of Oz when you need him?) these institutions will continue to enjoy their privileged status.

It's not that colleges and universities have no problems with the outside world. There are, of course, times when recalcitrant legislators refuse to fund state universities in the manner their faculties and administrators deem appropriate. And private institutions occasionally face parallel fund-raising problems. A few have even been forced to close their doors. These problems, however, have little or nothing to do with outside attempts to control or otherwise influence the academy's modus operandi. As long as academic institutions appear (and I must emphasize that appearance may differ considerably from reality) to be meeting the American need for expertise, there will be little motivation for outsiders, however powerful, to tamper with their day-to-day operations. Moreover, when some misguided souls attempt to do just that, the perceived crucial role colleges and universities play ultimately provides them with the leverage they need to defend their turf. Despite some early victories, the McCarthyites did not succeed in establishing a political test for professors after all. While they continue to fulminate publicly over the threat posed by such right-wing pressure groups as Accuracy in Academia, in private few professors take that threat seri-

ously. When a few years ago a powerful New England state legislator sent staff to check on whether faculty at the local land grant university were doing such things as keeping office hours and meeting their classes, the uproar from that faculty and their allies in the business and political communities was so great that the gentleman soon saw the wisdom in backing off.

Despite loud protestations to the contrary, colleges and universities are now very much part of this world. They do not stand apart, and they have arrogated to themselves a near monopoly in the advanced training/certification business. Because of this they've become just too important for outsiders to seriously consider messing with. Once it was functional irrelevance that protected against outside interference. Now ironically, its opposite has the same effect. Certainly there have been incidents of such interference, and certainly some institutions (particularly those sponsored by religious denominations) have always been subject to nonacademic control. But for the most part, mainstream academic institutions have had considerable autonomy during the twentieth century. (Faculty may complain that they don't have enough, but that's beside the point. Do we ever believe we have enough autonomy? Even Caesar complained.) In the enjoyment of that autonomy, they have gradually broadened the meanings of academic freedom and tenure to the point where both have become powerful legitimators of the permissiveness and purposive inattention that have made professorial no-fault zones of our campuses.

A Fine Place for Doing Nothing

And so we have it, the academy: heaven to those con artists in possession of Ph.D.'s and asylum for similarly credentialed incompetents. Democratized (or leveled) academic authority, discipline salience, the broadened meanings given to academic freedom and tenure have all contributed significantly to the creation of an environment where often enough accountability is little more than illusion, where the mean and the lame are free to do as they please because their honorable and competent colleagues have been given enough reasons to see little and do even less.

A system defined by democratization, the disciplines, the norms of academic freedom, and the protection of tenure might work in some idealized world where professors, motivated only by the stringent te-

nets of the academic creed, could be counted upon to do the right thing. But professors do not live and work in such a world. Their motivation is likely to be mixed and conflicting, part devotion to the creed, part devotion to more ordinary pecuniary and self-aggrandizing pursuits. Vigilance, required by the former, is likely to be costly to the latter. And professors seeking to resolve their inner conflicts in a manner that allows them to have their cake and eat it, too, have turned the academy's defining characteristics into the basis for a grotesque permissiveness. Democratization, discipline salience, and tenure virtually prevent the making of hard decisions and the taking of hard actions in the face of misfeasance and malfeasance by one's colleagues, while academic freedom is invoked to justify this abdication as itself an honorable protection against unwarranted impositions of orthodoxy. The result is truly a work setting where anything goes, where good work will no doubt reap rewards, but so will bad work or even no work at all.

Chapter 3

The Seven Pedagogical Sins
Dirty Little Secrets 1

Whatever else they may or may not do, academics are expected to teach.[1] Indeed, from the general public's point of view, colleges and universities are, plain and simple, the schools you go to after you've graduated from high school, and professors are teachers who work at those schools. The defining characteristic of an academic institution is its teaching function. Research and public service may be expected, but a college or university clearly does not exist unless teaching and its correlates (evaluation of student work and degree granting) occur on a regular basis. Without the existence of its pedagogical function, no state-supported institution could make the claim on public moneys it does, and no private institution could raise the funds necessary to its continued existence (there would be no alumni with deep or even shallow pockets).

The Seven Sins of Teaching

Its centrality to academic purpose and viability notwithstanding, teaching in American colleges and universities is in the sorriest condition; it is the academic function most beset by misconduct, most injured by the academy's virtuosic practice of self-delusive denial. While academics can be counted on to indulge in hyperbole when proclaiming their commitment to good teaching, they cannot be counted on to honor that commitment. The circumstances vary from one campus to the next, according to each institution's perception of its mission. But whether we are talking about major research universities, so-called elite liberal arts colleges, or the academy's less prestigious outposts

58

(the state colleges, the open-door private colleges, and the community colleges), teaching is everywhere in serious trouble.[2] And if teaching is in trouble, so is learning, a matter of some consequence to the general well-being of a society dependent on knowledgeability for its economic health, its political responsiveness, and its moral climate.

Consider, if you will, this inventory of characteristic troubles,[3] seven pedagogical sins deadly to the higher learning.

1. *Abandonment:*[4] wherein professors assigned to teach a particular course flee the classroom. Professors desirous of doing so can manage their great escapes by (a) convincing their students, after a few preliminary class meetings, that the subject matter of the course is best mastered through independent inquiry (presumably but of course not really supervised); (b) importuning graduate teaching assistants to teach in their stead (it's easy: most graduate students are flattered at such a request); (c) switching from three one-hour classes per week to one three-hour class per week (usually in the evening) and then actually meeting the class for only a fraction of the prescribed hours; (d) experiencing a series of Job-like misfortunes (e.g., the flu, family emergencies, flat tires, dead batteries) that invariably seem to occur on the days the class is scheduled to meet; and (e) convincing students that the class hour requirement is nothing other than an example of bureaucratic insensitivity to the learning process, which of course cannot and should not proceed according to a fixed schedule.

2. *Harassment and exploitation:* wherein professors, usually male, pressure students, usually female, for sexual favors. Sometimes this pressure can be subtle, as when the professor suggests that sex is just an extension of a close mentoring relationship. Sometimes the pressure is anything except subtle, as when students are told their grades will suffer or they'll be passed over for assistantships unless they submit to the professor's extracurricular demands.[5]

3. *Misrepresentation:* wherein professors, motivated by laziness, do not prepare their courses but rely on materials no longer current or their ability to mimic what teachers do. Since students cannot know beforehand what they are in a class to learn, misrepresentation is the easiest academic con to bring off. All it requires is a convincing professorial style.

4. *Special pleading:* wherein professors, most often in the humanities and social sciences, abuse their pedagogical authority by substitut-

ing propaganda for analysis. Since as a rule academics have total control over what goes on in their classes, they can if they wish structure both readings and lectures in such a way as to cloak mere opinion in the guise of definitively established truth. When this occurs, such disputable apprehensions of reality as "There exists a patriarchal conspiracy to subjugate women"; "Poverty subcultures are responsible for the persistence of economic hardship"; "Generous welfare systems undermine the work ethic"; "Family therapy is superior to individual psychotherapy"; and "Recreational sex signifies liberation from archaic and unnecessary social constraint"—to name but a few—are transformed into indisputable principles, the students' recognition of which is invariably taken to signify their intellectual worthiness.[6]

5. *Default:* wherein professors assume the worst about the abilities of their students and use this assumption to justify teaching practices antithetical to any reasonable conception of the higher learning. Assuming their students read poorly, if at all, professors guilty of default do not require them to read; assuming that they cannot write, they do not require them to write; assuming that they are incapable of grasping complexity, they oversimplify subject matter to the point of intellectual dishonesty.

6. *Proud incompetence:* wherein professors persist in incompetent teaching as though it were a mark of their intellectual superiority. When this occurs, disorganized presentations become indicators of an intellect too powerful to be constrained by the requirements of coherence, exotic syntax can only signify profundity, and solipsism is taken to mean that its practitioner is extraordinarily inspired.

7. *Particularistic assessment:* wherein professors manipulate academic assessment procedures in behalf of selected students. Common examples of this practice include (a) bestowing high grades when they have not been earned (that is, not earned as the result of academic effort); (b) writing letters of recommendation that overstate the abilities of personal favorites; (c) admitting students into programs even when, on the record, they do not qualify for admission (i.e., if you can sink a 15-footer with consistency or pass a football with unusual accuracy, you'll find an academic home somewhere, even if you cannot read or write); (d) creating courses and programs of less than dubious merit for students (usually those who have benefited from the exercise of the third example above) whose entertainment value would be lost if they didn't maintain a minimum grade point average; and (e) manipu-

lating examination committees to ensure the success of those candidates for graduate degrees who have found favor with their mentors on the basis of talents that are neither academic nor, as a rule, publicly demonstrable.

"Unbelievable! How can it be true that these things actually go on? Even if some professors tried this stuff, they'd never get away with it." If my inventory of pedagogical sins has elicited these or similar protestations of disbelief, I wouldn't be surprised. After all, the professoriate has labored (quite successfully, I would say) to create a public image that makes of it a most honorable guild whose imperfections (if indeed there are any) come only of an ethical stringency presumably impractical in the real world. But those who are inclined to such disbelief might wish to reconsider after heeding the following exemplary tales.[7]

Tale 1: How She Got Smart (Particularistic Assessment)

The end of the spring semester is always hectic. There are final exams and term papers to correct. There are reports to write on the fledgling efforts of your graduate assistants. There's the election of the personnel committee for the coming year (the committee that—among other things—decides who will get how much of a raise) and that always turns into a major preoccupation. Indeed, the politicking gets so intense that an unwary visitor might easily mistake the English department for the local Democratic Party, replete with warring factions. Add to this the fact that for some perverse reason Ph.D. comprehensive examinations are scheduled during the last two weeks of the semester (each candidate characteristically produces a typescript of approximately seventy to eighty pages) and you can understand how anyone might become distracted and more than just a little irritable.

The longtime member of the faculty, former chairman of the department and director of its graduate program, was both; and that probably explains his impatience when the young woman, framed in the doorway of his office, stammered her request to see him. She was a graduate student but not one he knew well. Exasperated by what he took to be their penchant for precious nonsense, he had distanced himself from the deconstructionists in the department, and the young woman ever so tentatively occupying the entrance to his academic domicile was doing her major concentration with their local guru. Could she come back

sometime next week when he wouldn't be so pressed for time? When she didn't respond immediately, he filled the silence with a slightly overstated elaboration: He had all these papers to evaluate, and he was already behind, so it really would be better if she could return during the following week. After a few more awkward, nonresponsive moments, the stammering began anew and with an intensity far greater than one might have expected or deemed appropriate, given what to that point had been a rather ordinary encounter. She didn't know if she could come back next week. She meant she could come back, but she didn't know if she'd want to. "Want to" probably wasn't the right way to put it. What she meant was that she didn't know if she would have the courage to come back. Her friend, his assistant, had encouraged her to come and talk with him. He'd told her that if anyone on the faculty could be trusted, he was that person. She'd really like to talk to him now. No, she really *had* to talk to him now.

He wasn't overly fond of the deconstructionist guru. Not only was the professor affronted by what he took to be the solipsistic vacuousness of the man's scholarship—the guru's last published work was an edited collection of essays on the burning issue of textual permission for critical interpretation—but he resented his self-promoting flamboyance (others less hostile saw it as charisma) and suspected him of relationships with female students that, to put it mildly, were not in their best interests. But even a predisposition to hear ill of the guru was insufficient preparation for what his unsolicited informant insisted upon recounting. What she told him was outrageous, so outrageous that he was curiously compelled to take it seriously. If, out of disappointment or jealousy, the young woman had simply given herself up to a spiteful vindictiveness, surely she'd have fabricated a story that, although equally damning, would be easier to swallow: an accusation of sexual exploitation, perhaps, something immediately, albeit unfortunately, recognizable; not something that, as in this instance, tested the listener's capacity to suspend disbelief. At the least that's the way the professor put it to the English department's current chair, when he went to him with the story and sought to enlist his support for a discreet but serious inquiry into the guru's behavior. What the student had recounted to the professor and what he had tried to get the chair to take seriously was a tale of preferential treatment carried to the nth degree.

The young woman who had sought him out shared an apartment with another woman, also a graduate student, who worked closely with

the guru. Not only did she work with him but, according to the professor's informant, they enjoyed a close personal relationship. The roommate had just completed her Ph.D. comprehensives, and her behavior as related to those examinations had, to put it mildly, appeared to be a bit peculiar. Early in the semester she'd manifested all the anxieties and behaviors common to what some graduate students called the "anticipation of annihilation" and others called the "doomsday condition." She'd become obsessed with her preparation for the examinations. Her room took on the appearance of a library fallen into disarray as the result of a librarian's prolonged work stoppage. She went nowhere except to class, her office, or the guru's apartment. Her conversation rarely if ever strayed far from the declamations of Derrida, Lacan, Foucault, and their ilk. She didn't seem to be eating well, and she could not be counted on to do any of the things she normally did to contribute to the apartment's maintenance. All very normal given the circumstances, a condition nearly universal in the biographies of American academics.

About halfway through the semester, however, just when she appeared to be almost paralyzed by her anxieties, things changed rather abruptly. One day she was a total wreck, obsessed by tasks she was certain she could not master; the next or so it seemed she was her old self: optimistic, infinitely more relaxed, sociable, talking about the vacation she and her guru were planning for the summer and the dissertation she would commence upon their return. When asked by her friends about this happy turnabout, she simply maintained she was over the hump, that she'd come to realize the comprehensives really didn't pose the threat they appeared to pose. She maintained this equanimity for the remainder of the semester, right through the two-week take-home examination period and the oral hearing that followed close upon it. And it did indeed appear that her upbeat mood had been justified. She passed.

Then two nights after the orals, she changed yet again, losing her equanimity with the same suddenness that had accompanied its acquisition. She'd gone to a party, a post-comprehensives celebration. There was a lot of drinking, a lot of smoking, and more than just a little snorting. Apollo had given way to Dionysius, and as so often happens in such a circumstance, the privately harbored was publicly expressed. When she spurned the sexual advances of one of her fellow revelers, he became incensed and there was a nasty scene. He began yelling at

her, calling her a bitch and worse. He couldn't offer her the kind of professional advancement the guru had undoubtedly promised, but he'd be happy to set her up in another profession for which she was eminently qualified.

She and her roommate left the party and returned to their apartment. The roommate said all the right things: "Where does he get off? Don't worry, nobody in their right mind would take that slob seriously. The pig just can't stand to see women succeed." All the right things—except in this instance they provided little solace. He knew. How did he know? If he knows, then others must also know. Wasn't she making too much of it? After all, what was there to know—that she was involved with a faculty member? Well, that was hardly a secret. Moreover, everybody at the party was stoned, and they weren't likely to remember what had transpired.

As it turned out, it wasn't what her antagonist knew or what anyone else knew that was so troubling; it was what *she* knew and what, in the early hours of the morning, with her defenses in considerable disrepair, she disgorged. The take-home exam? She hadn't written it. The guru had; every last word. He'd proposed doing that several months earlier, when her anxieties had gotten the best of her. The comprehensives, he'd told her, were an anachronism; they were redundant, presuming to assess what had in fact already been assessed over three years of graduate study. If the results differed markedly from the student's grades, he wouldn't trust them as a predictor of future success. No one asks scholars to take examinations, to write under pressure during an unnaturally delimited period of time. The true measure of scholarly potential is the quality of papers written for course assignments. He'd argued for the abolition of the comprehensives on more than one occasion, but the faculty Neanderthals, the department's old guard who had nothing better to do than to revel in the miseries of their students, wouldn't budge. So he didn't see why she ought to be yet another of their victims. She knew her stuff. He wouldn't bullshit her. He could produce the required essays in a couple of days. It was no big deal. In fact he'd like to do it. It'd be a great joke. The assholes on the examining committee would of course find flaws in the essays, flaws that had to be there because no graduate student would ever write well enough for them. What a put-on! They'd wind up making a show of their idiocy while he, with a straight face, made a show of taking them ever so seriously. She had better things to do with her time than to obsess

over an absolutely meaningless exercise, didn't she? She should be doing the preliminary work on her dissertation, and he was still waiting for her to finish the annotations he needed for the bibliography he was preparing. The rules? Screw the rules. There is, he said, no moral imperative to conform to requirements that are empty and unreasonable, that do nothing but affirm the authority and control of a bunch of old men who hadn't written or said anything worthy of serious attention for years.

He made such good sense. The guru always made such good sense. He had, as she noted on many occasions, this remarkable ability to find the essence of things, to clear away the complicating garbage, the subterfuges employed by the mediocrities whose nature it was to abhor talent and creativity. And so she took him up on his offer. But it must have gotten out. How, she didn't know. He wouldn't have said anything. After all, it was his neck, too; he was as vulnerable as she. Oh, but maybe he did. He really could have. He'd taken such malicious joy in putting one over on his colleagues. He'd gleefully described to her how the examination committee had indeed concluded that the take-home suggested considerable potential even though it was, in places, marred by the simplistic enthusiasms of youth. He thought their pomposity was hysterical. Yes, he could have told someone. He probably found the joke too good to keep to himself. If that were so, he would've told some of his circle about it. And who knows who they told. . . . He really could have done it. Why not? He probably didn't even care if the story got out. After all, he was always talking about how gutless the faculty were; he probably figured they wouldn't do anything even if they knew, and that'd make it even better.

In the days following her confession, she'd remained morose. When her roommate asked whether she'd spoken to the guru about the matter, she testily refused to talk about it. The roommate was herself sorely troubled and conflicted over what she'd been told. On the one hand she felt for her friend. She was concerned about her friend's obvious desperation and what might come of it. On more than one occasion she'd attempted to allay the roommate's anxieties by noting that she hadn't picked up any gossip about the matter; and in a setting where rumor was the stuff of common parlance, if anyone knew anything, surely, she said, that wouldn't be so. On the other hand she was extremely angry. What the guru and her friend had done was so unfair. She'd taken those exams a year previously, and she could remember

all too well the work that went into their preparation and the anxieties that for months had been an excruciating constant in her life. During her tenure as a graduate student, she had seen others go through the same hell. Indeed for some the anxieties had proven too much, leading to their withdrawal from the program. That anyone, on the basis of a personal relationship, should have been able to avoid the unwanted experience everyone else had to endure was just so wrong—nothing short of a fraud that victimized every other graduate student in the department. She was, moreover, angered by her friend's willingness to make her an accomplice in this sordid business. Although her roommate assumed that somehow the story had gotten out, she couldn't be sure; and remorseful over having in her distress revealed too much, she'd exacted a promise of confidentiality from her unwary listener. As it turned out, it was a promise that would not be kept.

Burdened to the limits of her endurance, the woman discussed the matter with the person she was closest to, the English professor's graduate assistant. His first response was that she owed nothing to her roommate and that she ought to report the matter to the department's chair. When she resisted his suggestion, arguing that she didn't want to be responsible for ruining someone's career, he was unsympathetic. If any careers were ruined, he said, it wouldn't be her responsibility; it would be the responsibility of those who had been so cavalier in their disregard of academic ethics. There was another problem, she noted. The guru was the chairman of her dissertation committee. If she went public with what she knew, it could only destroy her working relationship with him. She'd have to find a new adviser, and the only people in the department competent to supervise her dissertation were his closest buddies. Did he really think they'd be sympathetic to her needs after she'd blown the whistle on their friend? Her confidant had to agree that her concern couldn't be easily dismissed. The guru was at the center of the deconstructionist crew, and its members were fiercely loyal to him. She was, her friend could see, in a very difficult position, but he didn't think that she could simply walk away from the mess. First, what had occurred could in no way be justified, and if she did nothing, she would indeed be an accomplice to a serious breach of ethics. Second, he knew her well enough to know that even if she tried, she wouldn't be able to ignore the matter. It'd eat at her.

There seemed to be no easily acceptable solution. Her friend, however, did make one suggestion: He said she ought to go to his professor

with the problem. The professor, he maintained, was a man of integrity, and he certainly knew his way around. Moreover, he could be counted on to be discreet. And so she decided, not without considerable trepidation, to take her friend's recommendation.

Sensitive to the vulnerability and anguish of his informant, the professor suggested a course of action that might ultimately call the guru to account. He would go to the department's chairman with the story, but without revealing its source. He would, further, endorse its face veracity and suggest that since the guru had often been rumored to be professionally irresponsible in his relationships with women graduate students, it was time to look into these rumors. Because his informant was vulnerable to discovery and its possible negative consequences, he would counsel the chair not to confront the guru with the specifics of the incident she had alleged. Rather, he would suggest that the guru be apprised of the chair's intention to look into allegations of his unprofessional behavior more generally, that as chair he had to do so because such allegations were a threat to the department's position in the university and were certainly creating a morale problem within the department itself. According to the professor, the chair could then interview a number of people (including her roommate) known to be in the guru's orbit.

Such a course, he suggested, had the potential for three possible outcomes that in varying degrees held out the hope of calling the guru to account without injuring innocent parties. First, her friend might decide that the personal costs of keeping silent on the alleged incident were just too great and might take the opportunity of the inquiry to unburden herself. If she did, then the chair would have the information he needed, as it were, from the horse's mouth, and he could then seek to discipline the guru without bringing a third party into the matter. Second, the inquiry might turn up other direct allegations. Finally, even if neither of these possibilities became a reality, the guru would, at the very least, know he was vulnerable to exposure and that, said the professor, might be enough to ensure no future repetitions of the kind of behavior she had reported.

And so it was that the professor found himself in the chairman's office recounting what he had heard and trying to persuade him to initiate a discreet inquiry into the guru's behavior. The chairman, noted among his colleagues for his evenhandedness, listened carefully, occasionally interrupting to ask a clarifying question. When the professor

finished, he matter-of-factly observed that if what had been alleged actually did occur, something would have to be done. He could, however, foresee at least two sticky problems. First, there was the issue of due process. He didn't see how he could proceed unless someone who had direct knowledge of this nasty business came forward. After all, if he acted on anonymous hearsay, it would be easy for the guru to accuse him of engaging in a witch-hunt. Then of course there was the not unrelated issue of basic fairness. Didn't their colleague have the right to face his accusers? If in order to protect an accuser from the threat of retribution, he was denied the right to know who that person might be, wasn't that grossly unfair to him? When the professor interjected that he would allow himself to be identified to the guru as his accuser, the chairman rejected the offer. The guru, he said, could be expected to press for an explanation of the accusation. And when he found out that the professor had acted on hearsay, he would certainly accuse him of engaging in a personal vendetta, and that would lend credibility to the witch-hunting charge. No, there was no way around it: Without what might be termed a knowledgeable accusation on the part of someone who was willing to take public responsibility for making that accusation, he didn't see how they could proceed. Why didn't the professor go back to his source and encourage such a course of action? . . . The professor responded that he simply would not feel comfortable doing that. He could not, he said, encourage people to do something that had a good chance of injuring their interests. Graduate students (he had gone so far as to identify his source as a graduate student) are vulnerable because they are so dependent on faculty opinion, and he didn't see how it was right for anyone to counsel reckless disregard for that vulnerability. Could the chairman guarantee there would be no retribution by the guru or his friends? No, he didn't think so. Chances were that at some point the guru and his buddies would exact a price for what they could only regard as betrayal. If the chair wouldn't take formal action along the lines he'd suggested, couldn't he at least proceed informally? Couldn't he shake some trees and see what fell to the ground?

The chairman responded that he'd not been deaf to the rumors about the guru, that he was, for example, well aware of his involvements with women students; so in effect he'd already engaged in an informal inquiry. But, he continued, picking up fruit fallen from the rumor tree accomplished little. What could he do? Go and order him to stop

screwing graduate students? The guru would laugh in his face. He'd probably protest his innocence. But even if he didn't, he could be expected to claim consent, freely given, on the part of his partners. He'd argue that his private life was nobody's business but his own. And at that level he'd have a point. An informal inquiry was really no inquiry at all. In order for him to do anything meaningful about the situation, someone simply had to come forward with a knowledgeable allegation. Unless that occurred, he'd have to treat what had been told him as just one more rumor. He didn't want to lecture him, but he did think that the professor, perhaps because of his personal antipathy toward the guru (an antipathy he could well understand and in fact shared), had lost sight of a couple of important things in this situation. No matter how much the guru deserved collegial censure, to attempt its imposition in violation of due process would be to engage in an ethical breach equal to or even greater than the breach the guru himself was allegedly responsible for. Once you depart from a strict adherence to the principles of due process, you run a serious risk of legitimating irresponsible accusation. Could there, he asked, be anything more chilling to the free pursuit of academic purpose?

And while he was sympathetic to the professor's concern about protecting innocent parties, there was, he thought, an error in carrying that concern to extremes. Certainly there was some risk of retribution. No matter how they tried, they could not guarantee that there would be no cost in coming forward. But, he continued, life, if it is lived responsibly, cannot be lived risk free. If his informant thought the guru guilty of a serious ethical lapse, then he or she had an obligation to come forward, notwithstanding the possible risk. Not to do so would be irresponsible, and it would be wrong to condone such moral timidity, however tacitly.

Amicable though he was, the chairman would not move from his position. The professor agreed to think about encouraging his informant to come forward, but he really didn't feel he could do so. He left the chairman's office experiencing what he would later label a diffuse frustration. He knew the guru was guilty as sin. He also knew that short of a minor miracle, the guru would get away with what he'd done. And in an awful sense no one was to blame: not the young woman whose vulnerability was likely to turn what she had been told into a souring secret; not the chairman, whose position on the matter was certainly understandable (he did, however, resent the fact that the

chairman appeared to be more concerned about his willingness to forgo academic etiquette than he was about the guru's willingness to compromise the department's examination system); and not himself for failing to encourage his informant to accept the risks in making a "knowledgeable accusation."

He would report back to his informant; he had to do that. He hoped that on hearing of the chair's position, she would find the courage to come forward. But despite the chairman's cogent sales pitch, he wouldn't encourage her to do it. He couldn't. It would really be unconscionable for someone who did not share her vulnerability to make such an entreaty. No one was to blame, and that's what was so awful. In dealing with the SOBs of the world, he mused, good folks were at such a disadvantage. If in order to control the indecency of others one had to put one's own decency on hold, decency could only be said to promote indecency. Returning to his office, the professor realized that the guru had probably been aware of that immobilizing paradox for years.

Tale 2: St. Joan, with Tenure (Special Pleading)

The College used to be one of those whose traditions, reaching back to its nineteenth-century founding, made no room for women. It had remained a male redoubt well into the 1970s, but then, either because its trustees were swayed by the arguments of the neofeminists or because the admissions office began noting that a growing proportion of its best candidates were selecting coeducational alternatives, the College freed itself from the past and began admitting women. By 1983 women constituted approximately 35 percent of its student body. The College, not without considerable grumbling from old alums and a small but vocal segment of its faculty, had managed to arrive in the twentieth century albeit just in the nick of time.

Although the trustees thought the admission of women could be accomplished with a minimum of correlative change—some plumbing fixtures would certainly have to be replaced in dormitory bathrooms, a gynecologist would no doubt have to be added to the infirmary's staff, and a few women counselors would have to be appointed in the dean of students' office—they were soon to be disabused of their naïveté. The women who chose the College saw themselves as pioneers whose mission it was to create a learning environment hospitable to their

needs and those of their gender who would follow. They pressed for the appointment of women to the faculty and for the establishment of a major in feminist studies. They demanded that a two-page segment of the campus newspaper be reserved for women's news. And they insisted that the College withdraw its sanction of fraternities because such organizations demeaned women in their exclusion of them.

If they did not succeed completely in pressing their demands, they did elicit some positive response from the administration and trustees. More women were appointed to the faculty, and although it rejected the demand for a feminist studies major, the College did agree to sponsor a nondegree program in feminist studies and even went so far as to appoint a tenured director of that program.

The appointment, carrying the rank of associate professor, went to a woman in her forties who possessed the type of pedigree guaranteed to impress the College's decision makers as well as its increasingly insistent women undergraduates. She had matriculated at one of the Seven Sisters, and had a Ph.D. in philosophy from an Ivy League school noted for both its intellectual excellence and its lack of hospitality to women students. (She knew, it was therefore presumed, what the academic struggle was about.) She'd been teaching at a small liberal arts institution with a reputation for being highly selective. And she had been invited to lecture on many of the most prestigious American campuses. Her choice was nearly unanimous and a source of self-congratulation in almost every precinct of the College.

In the middle of her first year on the faculty, however, self-congratulation turned to chagrin, at least in the dean's office. Soon after the beginning of the second semester, a delegation of three male students made their way to that office to register a complaint. Each had enrolled in Feminist Studies 31, "Explorations in Feminist Ethics," an elective introduced by the new appointee, and each claimed he was made to feel so unwelcome that he had no option except to drop the course. The students were indignant; after all, they (or their parents) weren't paying upward of $26,000 a year only to be denied access to the full range of the College's resources. How, they wanted to know, could the College sanction such unprofessional and discriminatory behavior on the part of a professor? The dean replied that of course the College would never countenance discrimination against anyone. That would not only be a violation of a student's rights, but it would also undermine the institution's mission. He did, however, need more information about

their complaint. What precisely did they mean when they said they were made to feel unwelcome? Were they, for example, actually told by the professor to drop the course? Well no, they responded, not in so many words. But when a professor asks to speak with you after the first meeting of the class, and when she interrogates you on your reasons for taking the course and suggests that you reconsider taking it because, in her experience, men don't do well in courses taught from a feminist perspective, it's hard to avoid the feeling that you're being told to drop the course or run the risk of getting a grade inconsistent with the quality of your work. Without the professor's actually saying so, it seemed clear to them, the students maintained, that she didn't want men in her class; and if that wasn't discriminatory, they didn't know what was!

Not a man to jump to conclusions (and a man whose professional experience during the 1960s had made him wary of student complaints), the dean indicated he would look into the matter, assuring the offended young worthies that the College would guarantee every student's access to courses they were qualified to take. He knew, however, he had to proceed with care. Clearly, if the students' complaint was justified, some action would have to be taken to correct the situation. But the complaint might not be justified. There could have been some misunderstanding. It wouldn't be the first time that students had misread a professorial caution as to their qualifications for a particular area of study. Given the peculiar and some might say highly charged circumstances surrounding the presence of *this* professor on campus, not to mention the selective perspective implied in a course focusing on *feminist* ethics, it was quite possible that the irate young men had been oversensitive and had consequently mistaken a good-faith attempt at guidance for discriminatory intimidation.

Caution, the dean decided, dictated several preliminary steps before any direct inquiry into the matter was made. First, he would check the enrollment in the director's first-semester course, Feminist Studies 10, "Introduction to Feminist Perspectives," to see how many males had been enrolled. If there were none, he would then have the registrar check the drops to see if any male enrollees had left the course. If there were male students who had remained enrolled throughout the semester, he would inquire into the grades they received. Were their grades consistent with the overall distribution for the course, or were they skewed to the lower end of that distribution? Moreover, he would

compare their grades in that course to their grade point averages in the other courses they had taken during the semester. He would as well check the enrollment of the current course to see if there were any males still enrolled, and if there were none, he would check to see if there had been drops by male enrollees other than those who had pressed their complaint upon him. If and only if this preliminary checking indicated the possibility of sex discrimination would he press the matter further by talking with the director of feminist studies.

Within a few short days, the dean had some answers to his queries, answers that compelled him to ask the director to come in for a chat. Although five male students had enrolled in "Introduction to Feminist Perspectives," all had dropped the course during the first week of the semester. There had been one more male enrollee in "Explorations in Feminist Ethics," but he, too, had dropped the course. The pattern, given the small numbers involved, might be accidental, but it was hard to believe that something other than happenstance was not at work in this situation.

The meeting began affably enough, the dean joking about the conflicting pulls and pressures of his job, the director responding that given what he had described, he was probably one of the few men who could truly empathize with the exhaustion every wife and mother experienced at the end of the day. The dean agreed but averred that the rewards of domestic management might be worth the exhaustion, while the rewards of academic management were rarely worth the debilitating nonsense that one had to put up with. The director, clearly intent on getting the last word, noted that she didn't think academic nonsense was in the same league with the domestic brand, especially when you considered that when a woman dealt with dirty linen it was really dirty linen, not merely some metaphoric approximation.

After a little more of this, the dean got down to cases. He had been approached by three male students who complained that she had made them so unwelcome in her feminist ethics course that they felt they had to drop it. He understood that students sometimes misread the cues professors give them but believed he had to look into the matter since the young men were so upset by what they took to be sexist discrimination. No doubt there was an alternative explanation for what they'd experienced, and he needed her input so that he could put the matter to rest before anything got blown out of proportion. He was sure she realized that small misunderstandings had a way of becoming big

problems on college campuses. Higher education, he observed, sometimes went too far in its celebration of imagination and he didn't want
this apparent misunderstanding to become a problem for her personally
or for the feminist studies program.

Fully expecting a denial of the particulars in the students' complaint, the dean, as he would later put it, was "just blown away" by the
director's response. No, the complaining students had not misread her.
She had indeed made it clear that because they were men she thought a
course in feminist ethics was inappropriate for them. Moreover, she
had, in fact, told them that in her experience men do not do well in
courses taught from a feminist perspective. What she hadn't told them
but what she thought ought to be relevant to the dean's concerns as an
educator was that she preferred not to have men in classes where the
content is central to the development of self-understanding among
women. It was an established fact that young women tend to be reticent in coeducational classes, and while nothing could be done about
that unfortunate circumstance in most classes, she was not about to
deprive her women students of the opportunity to freely explore the
nature of their personhood. She understood that she could not bar men
from taking her courses, but it was well within her academic prerogatives to discourage them. It might seem that she was discriminating
against men, but that was not so. A feminist pedagogy mandated the
position she had taken and would continue to take. Abandoning that
position would constitute a betrayal of her pedagogical mission and
would make a sham of the entire concept of feminist studies at the
college.

An experienced dean knows better than to reveal shock or surprise
when a faculty member appears to say or do something outrageous.
Such a revelation usually elicits defensiveness, and that in turn limits
what the professor in question will continue to reveal. The dean was
indeed both shocked and surprised by what he'd just heard: shocked
that the director had in fact engaged in discriminatory behaviors and
surprised that she could apparently ignore the possible consequences
of her candor with him. But the dean was experienced, and so he
reacted to what he had just heard in his best avuncular-neutral manner.
He was, he said, a little confused by what she'd told him. Was she
saying that she thought it alright to discriminate against some of the
College's students in order to benefit other students? Was she saying
that the feminist studies program, ostensibly open to all students, was

in reality only available to approximately 35 percent of the student body? Was he correct in understanding her to mean that feminist pedagogy is inherently gender specific and that any departure from that premise would seriously compromise the feminist studies program?

No, she wasn't condoning discrimination even if it was for a good cause. The male students might believe they had been the victims of discrimination, but the truth was otherwise. Had she excluded them, they might then be justified in their complaint against her. But she hadn't done anything like that. All she'd done was to confront them with a reality. If in the face of this reality, they concluded that continuing in the course would be too risky or too uncomfortable, that was their decision. And having made their decision to withdraw, they were not entitled to shift the responsibility for it to her. The feminist studies program, she continued, was in principle open to all of the College's students; but in principle so were a lot of other programs that in fact limited the enrollment of particular groups of students. Could the dean deny that although the College's astrophysics program was theoretically open to all students, in fact it was principally a male program? Could he deny, moreover, that women were systematically discouraged from availing themselves of instruction in that field? That the skewed demography of majors in astrophysics as well as in engineering programs on other campuses (because of its liberal arts tradition, the College did not have an engineering curriculum) was the result of something other than mere chance?

She realized that by citing such instances of de facto exclusion in support of her position, she might be accused of ethically suspect self-justification. No one could deny that sexism was at the root of the skewed demography but she could, in good conscience, reject the validity of such an attribution. In a perfect world she would never cite such instances; she wouldn't have to. Indeed in a perfect world they wouldn't be sitting here having this discussion because the issues necessitating a program in feminist studies would be nonexistent; women would no longer have to struggle to gain full possession of their lives. In a perfect world this entire exchange would have the character of a non sequitur. But the world wasn't perfect, was it? Women were, after all, still second-class citizens, still only part owners of their lives, unable to avoid manmade rules and manmade obstacles to their personal empowerment. And the virtual exclusion of women from certain fields of study in this imperfect world mandated that they be given

special preference in a field like feminist studies. If that meant some male students were made uncomfortable, uncomfortable enough so they felt they had to withdraw from a course or two, well, that was a small price to pay. The College had an affirmative action policy, didn't it? The premise underlying affirmative action, that privileged groups would in some limited ways have to step aside for those who had previously been excluded for illegitimate reasons, she thought was applicable in this instance. Women needed the preferential treatment they received in the feminist studies program because men had restricted their options. Feminist studies might be conceived of as limited compensation for that restriction. As she saw it, her position was consistent with that of the Supreme Court in the Bakke case, in which the Court held that race and sex could be used as affirmative action criteria but that quotas would be unconstitutional. Well she had used gender as a basis for her pedagogical choices in favor of women, but she had not and would not use it to exclude men entirely.

There might, she continued, even be an important educational gain to those male students who had dropped the course. Although they had clearly missed her purpose—she was not trying to discriminate against them—they had experienced something akin to what women experience all the time. Perhaps because of their feelings, they would in the future be less prone to limit women's options. They now knew a little better the hurt and rage that women experience just because they are women. And yes, he had understood her correctly on the pedagogy of feminist studies. It was, in her view, gender specific. In the imperfect world that made feminist studies necessary to begin with, it had to be.

It was, the dean thought, a brilliantly reasoned but terribly misguided argument. No attempt to deny the students' allegation; instead, an aggressive reinterpretation of the allegation that transformed it from a censurable subversion of academic purpose into an applaudable exercise in principled pedagogy. He couldn't help but admire the director's ability to seize upon the ambiguities inherent in any reality and to recast them as certainties in the service of her interests.

Notwithstanding that admiration, however, what she had done and promised to continue doing was, he believed, clearly misguided. To begin with, no responsible educator could sanction an avowedly particularistic pedagogy. That particularism had sometimes crept into certain academic programs, while, unfortunately undeniable, could not be used to justify explicitly particularistic compensatory responses. The Bakke

analogy was inappropriate. Learning and the pursuit of truth were by definition universalistic and could not be subordinated to any social agenda, even one that an enlightened consensus would applaud. Expanding the affirmative action principle so that it could be used to justify pedagogical particularism would set a dangerous precedent. Who could be taught what would be socially rather than intellectually determined, and legitimating such an approach, as the director was attempting to do, was clearly anathema to the spirit of free and open inquiry that sets the academy apart from other institutions.

The dean, moreover, could not accept the manner in which the director's departure from the norms of universalism had occurred. She had worked a rather profound change in the College's academic policy without so much as a notice of her intention to do so. The ultimate responsibility for academic policy rested with the trustees, who act only after the faculty and administration have recommended a change. Consciously or unconsciously, the director had in effect, engaged in an end run in which the established procedures for policy determination had been rendered inoperative. Even had he been able to support her position, the dean could not support the director's cavalier attitude toward procedure.

Deciding he alone would not be able to convince the director to abandon her position, the dean chose to focus on the procedural issue. If he were able to get the director to go through channels, he assumed she would fail to get faculty and administrative endorsement (not to mention trustee approval) for her brand of particularism. Collegial rejection of her intentions, he reasoned, would make it impossible for her to continue on the course she had set. He was not enamored of the possibility of a full-scale and all too public debate, but he was hopeful that it could be avoided. Before a policy initiative could be brought to the faculty as a whole, the College's bylaws required that it be endorsed by the dean's executive council, made up of department chairs and program directors. The dean was confident that the proposal would receive little if any support in the council, and he reasoned that the director, seeing the handwriting on the wall even before the council voted, would be chastened and withdraw her initiative. Having done so, she could hardly proceed with her intentions unless she were willing to risk losing the goodwill of some important colleagues, goodwill that she had to understand was necessary to the continued viability and growth of a fledgling program like feminist studies.

Without alluding to his own objections, the dean explained the procedural irregularity in the course the director of feminist studies had embarked upon. What she was doing departed from existing College policy and thus needed the approval of the College community. Without such approval he would have no choice but to request that she desist from any future efforts informed by the position she had espoused. He hoped that she would carefully consider the implications of her position and if she continued to find wisdom in it, that she would draft a position paper for consideration by the executive council as a first step toward approval by the College community.

The dean had miscalculated. The brilliance of the director's argument was not accidental, and the acuity at its source was obviously still at work as she listened to his request. She rejected, she said, the implication in his remarks that her position might be ill and insufficiently considered. She had no need to "consider the implications" of her position because she had been doing so for many years. Surely he could not really believe she had only recently embraced a feminist pedagogy, and then only on a whim. When she was hired, she would have thought, her feminist credentials were as apparent as her gender, and those credentials should have meant something to the dean when he assented to her appointment. Her gender alone did not qualify her to direct a feminist studies program. If that were so, the College could and probably should have hired some Playboy bunny. It was her knowledge of and commitment to a feminist perspective that qualified her, and realizing that, the dean should have been able to appreciate the consonance between her pedagogy and her commitment.

Moreover, she would not submit a proposal to the executive council. She did not see any departure from College policy in what she was doing. Her courses were in fact open to any qualified student who wished to take them. If, she reiterated, some students who happened to be men found her approach discomforting, there was nothing she could or would do about that. She could see no reason why she needed College approval for being honest and forthright with her students. No professor could, in good conscience, voluntarily relinquish control over what and how she taught. She certainly would not do so. There was, she reminded the dean, the not so little matter of academic freedom that he seemed willing to ignore and she wondered why. Could it be that he was caught up in his own latent sexism? Would he be so eager to control the teaching efforts of male faculty members? Perhaps

the dean ought to consider the implications of *his* position! She would not, she repeated, submit a proposal, and she would not honor his request that she abandon the feminist pedagogy she was committed to. If the dean wished to persist in his efforts to control her, that was his prerogative. But he should be forewarned that she would publicly resist such efforts with every resource at her command. She was no stranger to controversy; no uppity woman, no avowed feminist would be. Unpleasantness was not something she sought out, but long ago she had come to realize that it went with the territory. Succumbing would be repugnant because it would make her complicit in an attack on both academic freedom and the rights of women to the ownership and expression of their particular perspectives on the world. So if he was spoiling for a fight, she was ready to join the fray. If it came to that, she concluded, she had every confidence that her colleagues would sustain her position.

For the second time during their meeting, the dean experienced shock and surprise at what he was hearing. Caught off guard by the director's impassioned remonstration, he yet again had to draw upon his reservoir of administrative calm. He was not, he said, spoiling for a fight on this matter. Nor could he accept her attribution of latent sexism and academic interference. Despite her admittedly persuasive argument, he was still troubled by the procedural irregularity in what she was doing. As dean of the College, he was obligated to protect the integrity of its procedures and he had offered his suggestion in the spirit of that obligation. He was, he maintained, simply trying to find a way of accommodating her concerns within a legitimate academic framework. Since they had obviously reached an impasse, he would suggest that they recess for a week or so, during which time they could both have the opportunity to find a mutually acceptable resolution to their dilemma. He was, he assured the director, willing to consider any suggestions she might make, so long as they didn't compromise the integrity of the College's procedures. And he hoped that in spite of her strong feelings she would accord him an assumption of good faith when he made his suggestions.

The director agreed to meet the following week but not before she protested the need for such a meeting. As she left, she turned to the dean and fired a parting shot: She felt, she said, that it was important that he be under no illusions. Nothing, but nothing that might in the slightest way compromise her efforts would be acceptable. She would

indeed meet with him any time he wanted to meet with her, but that willingness should not be understood as reflecting a parallel willingness to compromise what was, in truth, uncompromisable.

Knowing that the director's intransigence would not be easily overcome, the dean concluded that he had somehow to convince her that she lacked the necessary support to prevail if she persisted on her confrontational course. To that end he decided to mobilize the director's significant academic others into an opposition he could invoke when next they met. He called in the chairs of all departments that had faculty who participated in the feminist studies program, recounted what had transpired, and asked for their advice, expecting of course that they would see the issue as he did, thus allowing him to convey their opposition to the director.

They did *not* see the issue as he did: Their advice—unanimous, albeit for slightly different reasons—was to drop the matter. The chair of sociology couldn't see why the dean had raised the matter at all. The complaining students, all privileged males, had obviously overreacted to a situation in which their status had been challenged. Echoing the opinion of the director, he said the experience for these students could in the long run prove to be positive. If they learned that being a white, Anglo-Saxon male of means didn't require the world to roll over for them, there was nothing wrong in that. Indeed there was a lot right in that. If, however, the dean acted on their complaint, it would only reinforce their upper-middle-class male egocentricity, a characteristic, the chair of sociology averred, was much to blame for some of the nastier manifestations of contemporary inequity. The chairs of English and psychology were unwilling to go that far in applauding the director's behavior, but they, too, failed to see the issue. She hadn't excluded the complaining students; they had removed themselves. Moreover, the chairs of English and psychology were hard pressed to find any procedural irregularity in what she had done: She hadn't imposed a policy of restricted access, and she wasn't promising to do so in the future. The chair of philosophy, intent, as modern philosophical professionals are, on the pursuit of clarity, suggested a distinction had to be made between form and substance in the matter. He did not doubt that the director had discriminated against the complaining students. Furthermore, he was sure that when the opportunity presented itself she would do so again. They had her own proclamation on that score. In substance, he continued, she had illegitimately limited access

to her courses and in doing so had indeed finessed the College's policies. In form, however, she had neither discriminated nor violated
procedures. For that to have occurred, she would have had to be explicit in imposing a gender requirement, and it did not appear that this
is what she had done or would do in the future. Thus he did not see
how the dean could press ahead with his objections. He was confident
that the faculty would support the director against the dean because in
the absence of a formal violation, they would see only a threat to their
prerogatives in his position. No good end, he argued, would be served
by engaging in what was sure to become a public battle that the dean
could not win. Indeed the futility of such a course could very well turn
out to be counterproductive. Should, as he expected, the director prevail, the College would be on record as supporting particularism, an
embarrassment to be sure. And what was worse, he had no doubt that
the director would use such an outcome as precedent for increased
discrimination against male students. The College community would in
effect have bestowed upon her a license to do just that. He realized that
failure to press ahead would create some problems, but there were, he
thought, remedies available and in any case the resulting problems
would in no way match those that were sure to arise if the dean moved
against the director. Certainly discrimination was a problem, but in this
case it was not likely to affect many students. The feminist studies
curriculum was not now particularly attractive to male students, and
there was little reason to expect that it would become more so. Few
men, he thought, were thus likely to suffer because of what the director
did or didn't do. What to tell the present complainants was also a
problem. The philosophy chair understood that the dean could not
simply ignore them. But he thought the dean could resolve this problem by assuring them of what in principle was true: first, that the
College would guarantee access to courses on a nondiscriminatory
basis. That was, after all, College policy, and the director herself had
assented to it. And second, the dean could honestly claim that he had
made a good-faith effort to see to it that nondiscriminatory access was
honored and that he would continue to do so. As well he should, not
only because it was right to do so but because it would solve a third
problem: how to deal with the director of feminist studies. Having
raised the issue of her behavior, the dean could not simply drop the
matter. That would send the wrong signal: The director could take it to
mean the dean had been convinced by her argument and was willing to

allow her to continue. Since she was in practice doing something objectionable, she ought not be given occasion for such an interpretation. Thus the chair of philosophy proposed the dean go ahead with his scheduled meeting and continue to make clear his obligation to ensure the integrity of college policy without committing himself to any specific course of action. Doing this would constitute an ongoing good-faith effort to protect student rights while at the same time avoiding a costly and no doubt futile confrontation. Although the philosophy chair was not sanguine about it, the director might eventually get the message. But even if she didn't, he had every reason to believe she would at least have to proceed with a caution born of her sensitivity to the dean's continuing attentiveness. The ideal of the harmonious world, observed the chair of philosophy, stood upon the unity of form and substance—an aesthetic, as it were, of the Platonic potential in reality; but it would be a serious error to mistake the ideal for actuality. The world was not harmonious; form and substance were infrequently unified—and then only in the rarefied precinct of high art. In an inharmonious world one had to be very clear as to the form/substance disjuncture—and recognizing it for what it is, he concluded, one had to be content with the avoidance of total chaos.

Uneasy though he was about it, the dean—whose first responsibility it was, after all, to protect the College's educational mission to the fullest extent possible—decided that he had no choice except to follow the advice proffered by the chair of philosophy. If he could not muster any opposition from the director's academic peers, playing hardball on this issue would likely lead to a nasty public confrontation. And even were he to prevail in such a confrontation, the College would be the loser. Adverse publicity as well as charges and countercharges of discrimination, violations of academic freedom, and sexism could only harm the reputation of the institution. He did have to keep his priorities straight. But he could only wonder at the ease with which Ph.D.'s transformed the unacceptable into the acceptable and always, it seemed, in the name of truth and high purpose.

Tale 3: The Confidence Man (Abandonment and Harassment)

Apparently, he knew a good thing when he saw it. Where else could you pull down a guaranteed $50K per year for so small an investment of time and effort? Where else could you be assured of a constant and,

thankfully, always changing coterie of adoring females ever at the ready to demonstrate their appreciation for your being? And where else could you surround yourself with a host of suckers whose vanity and smug self-importance could so easily be played for your own purposes? True, there were few if any opportunities for the really big score, but then again the cumulation of small and moderate scores in an environment that is virtually risk free shouldn't be denigrated. The ability to find such a hospitable preserve obviously indicated more than ordinary shrewdness. In the long run he would probably cash in to a greater extent than the vast majority of con artists. And while most of them had constantly to elude discovery and consequent penalty, free of that possibility he had only to use his guile in the pursuit of pleasure's almost infinite variety.

At least that's the way a self-identified former friend and colleague (he'd left the academy because of an accumulation of grievances) characterized the approach to higher education taken by the professor of economics. (Con artists, even the best of them, have a way of making former friends. Since they are characterologically incapable of genuine friendship, sooner or later they wind up treating those they call friends like the rest of the suckers. Some eventually catch on and relinquish, curiously, often with regret, the mark's dunce-cap.) The former friend understood that by so identifying himself, he ran the risk of not being taken seriously. He did, after all, have an ax to grind, and in his experience that often led people to assume he was being less than objective. (He'd always thought it strange how we are so quick to assume objective validity when absolutely nothing is at stake—wasn't there a potential for bias in that?—and how we are equally quick to discount the truth value of anything said by someone who openly proclaims that he or she is talking about something that personally matters. Such a predisposition, it seemed, implied nothing less than a nightmarishly bizarre epistemology in which only the inconsequential can be true.) But he wanted to be fair, so he could not hide his personal distaste for the professor of economics. Since he'd been asked to give his reasons for leaving the academy, a complete account had to include this story, which he believed demonstrated the academy's indefensible practiced obliviousness to the indecency in its midst.

The professor of economics had joined the faculty of the university (one of those large, urban-based institutions known more for its professional schools than for its undergraduate programs) as a tenured asso-

ciate professor several years before, as his former friend observed, "the excrement hit the cooling system." He carried with him a reputation for being difficult, but he had been recommended by a number of former colleagues who had written of his perceptiveness and potential for sustained contributions to the literature of economic decision making. To that point his actual contribution was nothing much to speak of (one paper published in a respectable journal, two others in second-rate journals, a coauthored chapter in a book, and a few reviews), but he had the right pedigree (a Ph.D. from a major department), and the strong testimonials to his potential convinced the economics faculty to enlist him in their pursuit of excellence (or at least national visibility). In truth he was difficult. His former friend would observe that in hindsight this appeared to be a tactical choice. As he saw it, by being difficult the professor of economics accomplished two goals: First, since academics naïvely associate the enfant terrible with brilliance, the professor of economics embraced that persona because he believed the suckers would think him brilliant; second, by being difficult he intimidated his colleagues into an extraordinary permissiveness where he was concerned. He complained loudly and often about everything, from the view his office afforded to the quality of computer facilities and the limited intellects of the department's graduate students. He constantly criticized both the direction of the department and the direction of the discipline. In department meetings he used a well-honed talent for invective to savage anyone who took issue with his positions. And he rarely spared any student his ridicule. He was, in short, the antithesis of the live-and-let-live gentleman professor on a faculty where that was the norm.

But if he was difficult, he was also by turns charming and attentive. He could be counted on to listen patiently as a senior colleague offered up endless accounts of the way it used to be. He ingratiated himself with his most prominent colleague through a deft combination of personal flattery and the type of professional criticism that always communicates the critic's awareness that what he is criticizing is nevertheless of transcendent importance. His former friend was won over by avowals of a shared commitment to high standards and shared distress over the academy's ethical lapses. A colleague whose psychic appetite for praise was nothing short of voracious routinely got it. Several graduate students, most of them women, were made to feel special indeed.

During the first two years of his tenure, there were some intimations of trouble. His annual reports of activities and accomplishments continued to show potential for scholarly contribution but offered no demonstration of its realization. He seemed to miss more classes than was the norm for his colleagues. Several graduate students complained that he did not return written work within a reasonable period of time and that when he finally did so, his comments were limited to a few uninstructive criticisms. There were rumors that he drank early and excessively. Most of the faculty ignored such intimations, however, and those who took notice simply interpreted them as indicators of his complexity. Over the next three years, nothing much changed. He did add a few lines to his curriculum vitae, and he signed a contract to produce a book-length, systematic review of the decision-making literature. But he still missed an inordinate number of classes, some graduate students continued to complain, and the rumors about his excessive drinking persisted. During his sixth year on the faculty, he asked to be promoted to full professor. Some members of the department's tenure and promotion committee (comprised of all those who held the rank of professor) went on record during a preliminary discussion as opposing his request. They cited the skimpiness of his CV and what they called his uncollegial demeanor. His record, they argued, simply did not warrant a promotion to full professor. Their opposition, however, dissolved in the face of strong pleas by four other members of the committee—the four he had gone out of his way to cultivate. They reminded the committee that some of those sitting around the table had been promoted to full professor with vitaes little different from the candidate's, and it wasn't fair to impose higher standards than had traditionally been employed. Moreover, it was always wise to promote people with potential a little ahead of schedule. Such a course constituted a vote of confidence and was likely to encourage the full realization of that potential. A denial would serve no purpose except perhaps to embitter an already tenured member of the department. And embitterment, as they all knew, was negatively correlated with productivity. The charge of uncollegial demeanor was without foundation. It was refreshing to have someone around whose standards were high enough to confront issues head-on. True, the candidate's personality rubbed some colleagues the wrong way, but it would be setting a terrible precedent to deny promotion simply because of a personality conflict. Surely they could appreciate how unjust that would be.

Their argument was as persuasive as it was wrong. Within a year of his ascension, the professor of economics had managed to prove his supporters incorrect at every turn.

A conversational fragment started it all, something overheard in passing, its very incompleteness both intriguing and disturbing to the listener, the professor's onetime friend. "Micro is a real gut. My professor is so disorganized. She just talks about anything that comes into her head. She's already postponed the first hourly twice because we haven't covered what we're supposed to." Microeconomics, a required course for all majors, was supposed to be taught by the professor of economics, so why had this student referred to the instructor as "she"? Perhaps, thought the professor's colleague, he had misheard, or perhaps the student was referring to the teaching assistant. The former was possible, but the latter, he quickly concluded, was not: Microeconomics did have an assistant assigned to it, but only for grading purposes; it had no discussion sections and therefore no assistant would be doing any sustained classroom instruction. And though he might indeed have misheard, he really didn't think so. He was sure he'd heard the pronoun *she* as characterizing the student's instructor at least twice. It bothered him, but not enough to do any immediate checking. It was one of those things that gives you pause, something you intend to check into but in the round of more immediately consequential concerns you put on the back burner.

And there it would probably have remained except for a luncheon comment made a few days later by the professor of economics himself. In the course of a conversation focusing on the need to review the department's undergraduate curriculum, he observed that something had to be done about microeconomics. It probably should run for two semesters, he said, instead of the current single semester. There was just too much material to cover, particularly when you took into account that the students are poorly prepared. During the current semester he had in fact been forced to postpone the first hourly exam because he found it necessary to go over things that the students were not getting the first time around. Their quantitative skills were so poor that unless they were spoon-fed, they wouldn't have a clue as to what was going on. His teaching assistant complained almost from the start of the semester that she could not teach according to the schedule he had outlined in the syllabus.

Remembering the overheard fragment, the professor's friend

quickly made a connection between it and what he was now hearing. What did he mean by saying his assistant couldn't teach according to the schedule? Wasn't he teaching microeconomics? Well, yes, of course he was, but hadn't he told him about his new teaching technique that integrated graduate and undergraduate instruction—delegated teaching? He thought he had. In any case he had come up with a way of killing two pedagogical birds with one stone, thereby maximizing his teaching output per unit of teaching input. And by increasing his teaching efficiency, he thus conserved time for his research. He hadn't discussed delegated teaching with him? God, he was sure he had. He couldn't believe he hadn't done so. It was, if he said so himself, such a good idea. You couldn't do it with every undergraduate course, but with a little planning you could do it often enough to save yourself an appreciable amount of time. It was simply a matter of finding the parallels between your graduate and undergraduate teaching responsibilities. Your TAs either had to have done graduate work in the substantive area of your undergraduate course or wanted to do so. You then designed the course as though you yourself were going to deliver the lectures, instructed the TA how to do so, and allowed that person to proceed under your supervision. Depending on how much confidence you had in the TA, you either made up the exams or commissioned the TA to do it. Since graduate students were eager for teaching experience—they somehow thought that by casting their pearls before the swine they achieved a grandeur otherwise denied them—it wasn't difficult to find assistants who were willing to take on the additional responsibility. And it really wasn't exploitive because the situation involved a reasonable exchange: You got in effect released time, and they got psychic income, real teaching experience, not to mention anywhere between three and six graduate credits that you could offer through the independent study mechanism.

But what, the professor's colleague asked, of the undergraduates? Didn't they have a right to be instructed by the faculty member assigned to teach the course in question, the faculty member whose name is in the course schedule? And what about quality control? There had to be a qualitative difference between instruction offered by a knowledgeable, experienced faculty member whose qualifications had been thoroughly reviewed and that offered by some green kid who just happened to be available.

The professor of economics didn't miss a beat. Rationales are the

stock-in-trade of the confidence man. For any scam to work, the mark has to be put in a position where he is willing to ignore transgressions against common sense, where he is willing to abandon sensible doubt and caution. Rationales, seemingly reasonable justifications for what ordinarily would appear to be unacceptable—fabrications, whose use of the familiar disarms the mark—are thus crucial. Expounded with what appears to be the utmost sincerity (some say the best practitioners of the con come themselves to believe in what they are declaiming), they are the confidence man's most significant tool—the hallmark, it may even be argued, of his nefarious creativity.

The undergraduates certainly had a right to be taught by the instructor listed in the schedule. And as far as he was concerned, delegated teaching did not conflict with that right. He designed the course and supervised the execution of that design. Design and supervision were far more important than delivery. He was as central to the course as is the architect to the construction of a building, the playwright to the production of a play. Nobody complains because the architect doesn't drive in nails or install plumbing fixtures, because the playwright doesn't read the lines. Or closer to home, does anyone believe that an economist who authors a monograph has done everything from collecting the data to typing the manuscript? Of course not. Assistants and other subordinates have carried out the tasks of execution. And no one feels cheated because of that. Delegation, he continued, is a fact of modern life, a function of its complexity. It is nearly universal—nearly only because there are still some activities yet to be rationalized, activities made sacred by long and unexamined tradition.

University teaching, he thought, was still in the nineteenth century and still hostage to an assumption that experience had thoroughly discredited. Any undergraduate knows that the possession of a Ph.D. doesn't make you effective in the classroom, and yet the academy clings to the assumption that it does. On the contrary, an argument could be made that a Ph.D., and especially one possessed for a number of years, was likely to get in the way of classroom effectiveness. The disjuncture between what possessors of Ph.D.'s do, that is, what they do as scholars, and what they are supposed to teach undergraduates was at the heart of the matter. Why, he asked rhetorically, should we expect mature scholars whose enthusiasms are at the cutting edge of their disciplines to be equally enthusiastic about communicating routine, low-level materials that they mastered fifteen or twenty years

ago? It doesn't make much sense. Graduate students, however, have yet to confront that disjuncture and the pedagogical ennui it is bound to generate. They are only too eager to be in the classroom. Their energy levels are high, and since they're in the process of mastering what they're being called upon to teach, they don't find it beneath them. If anything, he concluded, delegated teaching was likely immeasurably to improve the quality of undergraduate instruction because it wed the expertise and experience of the professor to the energy and enthusiasm of the graduate student. He'd tried it now in three courses, and he'd compared student evaluations with those he'd received when teaching those same courses in the traditional manner. As high as his ratings were when he taught traditionally, they were, he said, consistently higher when he delegated classroom duties.

For a time, the rationale had its desired effect. The professor's friend, while not himself willing to embrace delegated teaching, was able to put his questions aside, reassured by the argument he had heard. He had to agree that the possession of a Ph.D. was no guarantee of classroom effectiveness, and if he was a bit uneasy about the professor's willingness to absent himself from the classroom, he was confident that this willingness represented a good-faith attempt at pedagogical innovation. He could hardly think otherwise, since they had spent so many hours discussing and not infrequently condemning the slipshod instruction that was all too prevalent in the department. Certainly, the professor of economics would not knowingly abandon his commitment to pedagogical excellence.

Soon enough, however, the effect began to wear off. There were just too many things that were troubling to the assumption of good faith. For example, no other faculty member seemed aware of the professor's innovation. If, as he claimed, it was such a good idea, why had he not brought it to the attention of his colleagues? The professor of economics was anything but modest and could thus have been expected to do no less than trumpet his discovery. But he had done nothing of the sort. There was also his failure to honor promises he had made to show his friend the current syllabus for microeconomics and to invite him to sit in on a class meeting. When reminded of the former, he apologized for his inadvertence ("You know how disorganized I can get"); when reminded of the latter, he invoked his concern for the feelings of the classroom instructor, who he thought would be ill at ease in the presence of a faculty visitor ("I'll schedule it when she's worked through

her classroom problems"). There was his increasing penchant for local invisibility. Not only had he absented himself from the classroom, but his appearances on campus had become so few and far between you would have thought he was on sabbatical. And finally there was a disturbing rumor to the effect that the professor of economics had put his research for the decision-making monograph on hold and was instead pursuing a highly profitable albeit time-consuming consulting venture.

The graduate student doing the classroom teaching in microeconomics was not unknown to the professor's friend. She had taken his graduate course on regulatory policy and had served as a grader in one of his undergraduate courses. When he could no longer ward off his discomfort at the possibility of bad faith, he decided to have a talk with the young woman. As a member of the department's graduate studies committee, he told her, he was interested in the extent to which teaching assistantships provided opportunities for professional development. He knew she was assisting in microeconomics and wondered if she had any thoughts on the matter that she could share with him.

As it turned out, she did have some thoughts on the usefulness of teaching assistantships. They were not, she believed, helpful at all in developing professional skills, unless of course you found yourself in the unusual situation where you got to do a lot of teaching. With all due respect, she hadn't learned much about teaching when she was his grader, but her present assignment in micro was something else. She'd been left on her own to do the course as she saw fit because the professor of economics was involved in the completion of some work and because he thought—correctly, as she saw it—that she needed to experience a degree of professional independence. He'd called it delegated teaching, although in truth there wasn't much delegation, since she was free to do as she pleased as long as she kept him informed about the course. He'd likened it to the apprenticeships served by those who aspired to the mastery of an art or a craft during the Renaissance. It was truly wonderful, she continued, how he could draw on his vast knowledge, how, for example, his command of history enriched his originality so that he saw possibilities others missed. In this instance he'd been able to transform a time problem he had into an opportunity for her because he was aware of a model that had worked so well in the past. In any case, she thought, the only way you learn to teach is to teach, and she was grateful for this opportunity. It hadn't been easy;

she'd made her share of mistakes. She'd tried to teach too much in too short a period of time, for example, and that led to a minor embarrassment because she had to postpone some scheduled exams. And she found she sometimes went into too much detail about things beginning students could not see the importance of. But it certainly was a wonderful learning experience, and one no other TA afforded.

The talk was nothing if not disquieting. The marked discrepancies between the professor's version of delegated teaching and the teaching assistant's version were not conducive to a continuing assumption of good faith. Intending to credit the professor of economics for his creative adaptability, the teaching assistant had instead (unbeknownst to her) intensified doubts about his veracity and his purposes. Whereas the professor of economics claimed to have designed the course in question, the teaching assistant suggested otherwise. Whereas he claimed to be supervising the efforts of the teaching assistant, she made it clear there was no supervision at all. The requirement that he be kept abreast of what was transpiring in the course seemed no more than a ploy to ensure that he had enough information so that, if challenged, he could lay persuasive claim to the supervisory role. He may have called it delegated teaching, but as the assistant naïvely testified, there was no delegation. The avowal of a good faith pedagogical purpose seemed, more and more, nothing other than an exercise in blowing smoke.

The confidence artist, contrary to popular belief, does not merely manipulate a mark's weaknesses in working a scam but also manipulates the mark's strengths, knowing that self-assuredness can obliterate doubt and render the mark complicit in his own victimization. It's somewhat analogous to what happens in football when an excellent pass rusher is allowed, by the offensive line, to penetrate the backfield only to have a running back (who had lined up in a passing formation) take the ball around the rush and through the hole that's been vacated. The pass rusher has been had, his strength used against him. By suckering him into abandoning all caution and doing what he does best, the offense creates an opportunity that would otherwise not be theirs. In football the scam is immediately apparent. In everyday life the scam can be hidden for a time—although not, it seems, forever. At some point the mark is going to discover this victimization and see that his strength has been used to make him vulnerable. Of the two discoveries, the latter is by far the more infuriating because it is by far the more

threatening. Given the right circumstances, anyone can be victimized by anyone else. The awareness, however, that you have been enticed, as it were, into creating your own victimization and that you've done so not out of weakness but out of strength is devastating. You can no longer fully trust what you had to that point trusted most completely in yourself, and no other realization is likely to be more shattering.

So it should not be surprising that when the professor's friend concluded that he had been conned, his reaction was, as he put it, "one of overpowering rage." Sophisticated though he thought himself to be, he hadn't been able to see through all those protestations of high pedagogical purpose. He hadn't recognized that he'd been set up, that the good professor had applauded his commitment to professionalism not out of genuine sympathy for his views but only so that he in turn would champion the professor's cause within the department's councils. The presumed passion for pedagogical excellence was nothing more than a sham, but not seeing it as such, he had been among those largely responsible for the professor's advancement within the department, an advancement that had already proven costly and was likely to continue to do so.

What followed this denouement, the professor's former friend would later freely admit, was a function of his anger and the desire for retribution that accompanied it. His first impulse was simply to confront the professor. He'd let him know just how he felt and warn him against continuing. He checked that impulse when he realized he would probably accomplish very little by pursuing such a course. The professor of economics, he concluded, would not be easily cowed. He'd probably claim to have been misunderstood and continue on his merry way, albeit with a bit less abandon for the time being. Assuming that the delegated teaching caper was not an isolated incident—those intimations of trouble he had earlier dismissed now seemed worthy of serious attention—he decided to try to build a case against the professor that would lead to some disciplinary action on the part of the university.

And build a case he did, with, as he saw it, unsurpassing ease. Delegated teaching was just one of several ploys the professor of economics used to avoid his classroom responsibilities. Graduate students who had enrolled in his seminars reported that he met with them for the first few weeks of the semester and then, to foster their intellectual independence, sent them off to write their seminar papers. Teaching

assistants in his "nondelegated" undergraduate courses described the professor's practice of scheduling a midsemester moratorium on class meetings, usually two weeks in the spring semester surrounding the break, during which students were told they would have the opportunity to test their scholarly maturity by working independently on their term projects. When, moreover, the moratorium was not in effect, the professor characteristically taught but two of the three hours per week his classes were supposed to meet. The third hour, almost always on Fridays, was dropped in lieu of what he termed a scheduled preparation period, again, he claimed, to encourage scholarly independence.

That all this had apparently occurred over an extended period of time was, according to the professor's former friend, amazing. But what was even more amazing was that many students, both graduate and undergraduate, seemed to see nothing wrong in it. To the best of his knowledge, none had complained, and while he had no trouble eliciting descriptions of the professor's practiced avoidance, he had considerable difficulty eliciting any student condemnation of it. Some bought his independence rationale in its entirety and even praised him for it; others simply had no opinion, taking the rationale and the accompanying behavior as professorial prerogatives protected by the norms of academic freedom.

One student complaint, however, did surface, and according to the professor's former friend its seriousness was of such magnitude that any lingering reservations he might have had about his feelings toward this self-proclaimed paragon of academic virtue were burned away in the intense heat of his indignation. He'd approached the department's chair with his concerns about what he took to be the professor's pedagogical malfeasance. Because the chairman's commitment to the university characterized him as a local in the best sense of that term, he believed he would be incensed by the professor's apparent rip-off of his students and would be disposed to take some disciplinary action. He hadn't proceeded far into his account when the usually laconic chair abruptly interrupted. If he was coming to complain about their esteemed colleague, he could save his breath, especially if he wanted some action taken. He'd already tried to have him disciplined, and over a matter far more serious than missing a few classes. He'd failed, and he wasn't about to waste his energy on the SOB yet again, particularly since the complaint was coming from someone who in the past had been ardent in his behalf—and who consequently had to bear a full

measure of responsibility for his continuing and lamentable presence on the faculty. Surely he could recall a certain female graduate student who had been the good professor's teaching assistant a couple of years ago? Had he seen her around lately? No, he hadn't. And the reason? She had dropped out of the graduate program. She'd dropped out not because she couldn't do the work—she'd sailed through her master's in fifteen months—and not because she'd decided to pursue another career but because their esteemed colleague was so persistent in his desire to bed her that she could no longer tolerate even being in the same building with him. The poor woman had come close to suffering a breakdown by the time she withdrew from the program. She tells him to keep his hands off her and to keep his fly zipped up, so he decides to make her life miserable; it was as simple as that. He'd threatened her with a negative evaluation of her TA work if she didn't sleep with him, claiming there was going to be a cutback in the number of stipends available for graduate students and that whether or not she got one would depend largely on his evaluation. When that didn't achieve the results he wanted, he began bad-mouthing her to other graduate students: She was an instrumental bitch who was screwing her way through the graduate program, nobody else got over the master's hurdle so quickly and easily. He felt sorry for her husband, he said. One of these days she'd probably give him a dose or something worse. And then he started to call her at home in the evening. He'd keep her on the phone interminably, using a variety of pretexts. He was driving her crazy. She went to his office to ask him to stop, and what did the son of a bitch do? He made another pass at her. She threatened to tell his wife, and he laughed in her face, claiming that she'd never believe her: He'd already explained to his wife that there was an unstable student who apparently had become obsessed with him, that he'd been trying to help her to little avail, that it was one of those problems that occasionally arises when you teach. Before she left he told her that she really had no choice except to come across, that is, if she wanted to survive in the graduate program. Well, to save her sanity she decided that she didn't want to survive in the program. She withdrew, but not before she'd told her story. The chairman had asked her to stay, promising to do something about the professor's behavior. Her mind was made up, she said, and coming to him with the story was the end of it as far as she was concerned.

Why had he believed her story? Why hadn't he just written it off as

the rantings of a neurotic who wanted out but couldn't take responsibility for her decision, some woman with a minor grievance against the good professor who had blown the situation all out of proportion? Well, for starters there was nothing in her record to indicate any ambivalence about graduate training. Moreover, during her tenure in the graduate program she seemed to be the very model of stability—steady, poised, and hardworking. But he had, he said, an even better reason for believing her. Their wonderful colleague had, in fact, confirmed her tale of woe. When he'd confronted him with the woman's story, the good professor denied nothing except that he had bad-mouthed her. He tearfully recounted how, after what he took to be some sexually provocative behavior on her part, he'd made a pass to which she objected—but not, he said, so strenuously that he took it to signal an absolute no; how, on a couple of occasions when he'd had too much to drink, he'd been emboldened to try again, with the same results; how, after coming to suspect that his own wife might be cheating, his judgment had become distorted enough so that, again when in his cups, he'd made those phone calls. He was truly sorry, but this had been a bad time for him. He had, he said, been working hard to get control over his life. He hoped, from the bottom of his heart, that the chairman could convince the young woman to return to the program. He had his word there would be no repetition of his regrettable behavior.

It was, the chairman observed, a pretty convincing performance. Listening to this sorrowing tale of the professor's fall from grace, he'd almost been won over. After all, no decent human being kicks a man when he's down. But then he remembered the desperation of the professor's victim. Innocent of any wrongdoing, she'd paid a terrible price for an association she had not even initiated. It was the department that had assigned her to work for the professor, exposing her to this madness. He concluded that as chairman he thus had a responsibility to initiate disciplinary proceedings against the professor. Besides, he was, he said, convinced that despite the professor's promise not to repeat his behavior, the past was the best predictor of the future, and in light of this any failure to respond would certainly encourage new transgressions with other students.

He did try to have the professor disciplined but failed to accomplish anything. The university's ombudsman (the official designated to deal with student grievances) told him that since the student in question had not lodged a complaint with his office he had no grounds for involving

himself in the matter, serious though it might be. The dean of the graduate school was no more helpful. It was, he agreed, an unfortunate situation, but who really knew what the truth was? It was a mistake, he argued, to overreact. The professor had been under duress, and the woman, without even realizing it, may well have been sexually provocative. It wouldn't be the first time something like that had occurred. The professor had admitted to bad judgment and that spoke well for him. He could have denied the entire business, as it came down to his word against hers. He was sure that since the chairman had confronted him, the professor would be chastened; in his experience such a confrontation was usually enough to prevent any reoccurrence of this type of problem. Instead of attempting to discipline the professor, he thought the chairman could make more productive use of his energies by attempting to get the student to renew her graduate studies. Given the circumstances, the graduate school would make it easy for her to reenter the university. So he'd tried. Having failed, he was pretty bitter about the entire matter and had absolutely no inclination to go after their wonderful colleague again. It would simply be a waste of time and energy to do so.

The professor's former friend argued that there was now a more complete case, that the professor's abdication of teaching responsibilities together with the young woman's complaint constituted a record that no administrator could ignore, that if they didn't press the matter—knowing what they knew—they would be complicit in any further difficulties that contrary to the dean's opinion were indeed likely to arise. The chairman, however, was resolute in his determination not to pursue the matter any further. He was not, he said, going to tilt at windmills. He felt he had lived up to his responsibility by doing what he'd already done. He was not going to play Quixote; there were simply more important things to do.

For several years running, the professor's former friend had found himself increasingly disenchanted with the academy. He had wearied of the pretentiousness that seemed to infuse everything academic; department meetings that invariably turned out to be forums for professorial self-advertisement; doctoral examinations at which exchanges between the candidate and members of the examining committee would have overtaxed the satiric imaginations of Kingsley Amis, Evelyn Waugh, and Nathanael West, taken together; convocations at which the rhetoric was always as flowery as it was substantively banal;

(how often, he mused, would young people be told their future was before them, that they had a right to dream and, wonder of wonders, to even ask questions . . .); empty claims to institutional excellence made with alacrity and by a kind of tacit agreement, it seemed, never challenged (he marveled at how many different top-twenty lists there were—at least one for each college and university in the United States). But more than anything else, he maintained, his increasing disenchantment was the function of a recognition that the academy rarely delivered the goods it claimed to deliver—and that this disparity between claim and behavior seemed to trouble very few academics. He knew of too many cases, undoubtedly less severe than that of the professor of economics, where teaching was in one way or another subverted by those whose responsibility it was to teach. He knew of too many cases where potential as opposed to achievement was sufficient to the making of a scholarly reputation. (He himself had erred in this manner with regard to the professor of economics.) He knew, moreover, that nothing or next to nothing was being done about these problems.

Disenchantment had not, however, lessened his commitment to the ideals of his profession. If anything, he observed, it probably intensified that commitment. Reflecting back on the period preceding his decision to leave the academy for a full-time position as chief of research for the state's public utilities commission, it seemed as though he'd experienced something much akin to the power surge that precedes an electrical blackout. He'd been sorely distressed by the chairman's story and his unwillingness to take further action against their colleague. He'd told the chairman that he was going to proceed with or without his support, and he did just that. He drafted a memorandum on the professor's behavior for the university's provost. When he received no response, he called the provost, who politely but firmly maintained that there was nothing he could do about the matter unless the department, through its chair, initiated formal disciplinary proceedings. He was, he said, constrained in such matters to abide by the collective bargaining agreement that existed between the university and the faculty's union.

Taking the provost's words to heart, he campaigned among his colleagues in the hope that he could get them to vote the start of those proceedings the chairman was loathe to undertake. To his dismay (although not really to his surprise) he got little support. Some worried

about the threat to academic freedom they saw in any action based upon a criticism of a colleague's teaching performance. It would open a Pandora's box, they implied. Even if it could be proven that their colleague was malfeasant, the action would, they believed, set a precedent that the administration might invoke any time it decided to move against an unorthodox faculty member. Sometimes, he was told, you have to swallow, you have to overlook certain things because to do otherwise could jeopardize those fragile understandings that require overzealous administrators to hold their natural proclivities in check. And who was to say their colleague's classroom absences were evidence of malfeasance? He'd made no effort to conceal what he was doing, and he could claim that he was effective simply by pointing to his student-generated course evaluations, which were consistently average or above. Others reacted with alarm at his willingness to give any credence to the young woman's complaint. Hadn't he heard about her? She's the one with a reputation for sleeping around. The woman obviously had a serious problem. How did he or the chairman know that she hadn't been provocative; that she hadn't offered herself to their colleague in return for academic favors; that she hadn't gone off the deep end when their colleague, undoubtedly vulnerable to her seductiveness, backed away at the conditions she attached to her offer? Protestations to the effect that there was no evidence of such an instrumental offer's ever having been made, that, moreover, the characterization of the woman as a promiscuous sexual predator had no foundation except in the rumors spread by their wonderful colleague, were to no avail. Those who were intent upon defending the professor, and in particular those who had shared an earlier enthusiasm for the professor's promotion, simply refused to doubt the essential innocence of their embattled colleague. In their eyes he was the victim, the target of a vicious slander perpetrated by a vindictive woman. Lending support to her accusation was tantamount to a betrayal of the norms of collegiality and, worse, the academic's commitment to truthfulness and fair play.

The chairman was, he sadly had to admit, right. Pursuing this matter *was* a waste of time, a fool's errand, an exercise in futility. With, it seemed, every avenue of redress closed to him, he ceased his efforts, experiencing an overwhelming sense of defeat. When the job with the public utilities commission became available, he took it. By that time, he claimed, he had no alternative. He was really quite desperate. His

disenchantment was as profound as it was complete. Staying on was no longer an option if he valued his self-respect.

He did have one final encounter with the professor of economics, however. Several days before leaving to take up his duties with the commission, he was visited in his office by the professor. The professor hoped there were no hard feelings. He certainly had only the greatest respect for his former friend, even if his misguided attack had hurt him deeply. Struggling to keep himself under control, he asked the professor of economics to leave. He simply had nothing to say to him. The professor turned as if to go but then turned back; and with what his former friend took to be a smile that could only have been inspired by unstinting and unadulterated malevolence, he delivered himself of one final observation calculated, it seemed, to claim his victory in no uncertain terms. His former friend was naïve to a fault, he said. Justice and fairness were empty concepts, at odds with life's realities. Of necessity one had to tolerate that or else succumb to the utopian's disease, the confusion of *ought* and *is*. There are no utopias, he said, not even within the academy. A man of learning and experience should have known that.

Subversion and Denial

Tales from the dark side? Grotesque cartoons? Hardly. The details may vary, but academics of more than a few years' standing would, if they were being honest with themselves, recognize the similarity between these stories and their own experiences. And readers lacking intimate knowledge of the academy's inner sanctum should attend to the following. In *The Lecherous Professor* Billie Wright Dziech and Linda Weiner estimate that no less than 30 percent of women students are harassed or sexually exploited by at least one faculty member during their undergraduate years. If you use a broad definition of sexual harassment (something I would be wary of doing), the estimate can reach as high as 70 percent of all women students.[8] After Charles Sykes's muckraking book, it would be quite incautious for anyone to assume the insignificance of professorial flight from the classroom.[9] While the preponderance of documented faculty cheating focuses on academic scientists (for example, the material William Broad and Nicholas Wade brought to light in their controversial but interesting book, *Betrayers of the Truth*[10]), there is no reason to believe they are more

prone to be dishonest than are their colleagues in the humanities and professional schools. Thus I believe that such evidence establishes a prima facie case for the significance of dishonesty in the academy, whether by scientists or others, whether in their research or in activities associated with their teaching. Of course special pleading may not always take the form it does in the case I have presented; in my experience it is likely to be more subtle, and students are unlikely to protest, if only because they are unaware of the manipulation they are being subjected to. Nevertheless, the toll exacted by the substitution of ideology for independent analysis is attracting increasing attention.[11] The cases presented in this chapter are tales of the ordinary—exemplary, to be sure, but only because they graphically illustrate the two sadly characteristic aspects of those pedagogical sins troubling higher education: *subversion,* sometimes willful, sometimes simply mindless, and *denial,* sometimes well meaning, sometimes instrumentally manipulative, always delusive, and ultimately the more serious of the two, resulting as it does in the complicit inaction that often renders misdeeds worse in their consequences than would otherwise have been so.

That faculty cheating amounting to fraud occurs is itself no small matter. But that such cheating (which exploits students and colleagues alike) can go unpunished even when it ceases to be a secret constitutes the type of irresponsible abdication that results in an environment that too often encourages the realization of nefarious intent. That particularistic exclusion and special pleading occur is indeed repugnant to the creed of open inquiry, to the academy's unequivocal endorsement of universalism. But the fact that such behaviors can be and are explained away by professors who have an obligation to resist their occurrence sends a message of encouragement to those of their colleagues poised to launch yet other subversive efforts. Do what you will, they are in effect told; we have neither the will nor the intelligence to stop you. The fact of sexual harassment on the American campus is itself certainly ugly, but that ugliness is increased manifold by the ease with which faculty are likely to fault the victims instead of those—their colleagues—who victimize. Quick to criticize the judicial system for putting sexual assault victims on trial when they lodge criminal complaints, many academics, it seems, have blinded themselves to their propensities for doing precisely the same thing. And just as the threat of public humiliation reduces the number of complaints the courts actually get to adjudicate, so, too, does the threat of an ordeal by rumor

silence many of those who have legitimate harassment complaints that academic institutions should act on. Denial, it would appear, too often transforms academic freedom into academic license to cheat, distort with impunity, exploit, and when it suits a professor's purposes, harass and intimidate. Denial, moreover, transforms the norms of collegiality into a protective shield for the mis- and malfeasant, a shield so impenetrable as to rival any Star Wars fantasy fully and perfectly realized.

Permissive Obliviousness: Misrepresentation, Default, Proud Incompetence

The three exemplary tales I've chosen to present at this juncture do not, of course, attend to all seven of the pedagogical sins I have alluded to. Misrepresentation, default, and proud incompetence have only been noted in passing if at all. They are the less dramatic but no less subversive of the sins, and no less subject to the denial that increases their potential for injury. If anything, they are the sins most likely to occur, because denying their existence is so easy that deterrent intervention, which depends upon the confrontation of conscience with an awareness of wrongdoing, is extremely improbable, indeed perhaps next to impossible. If the truth be told, it is rare for professors to know what their colleagues are doing in their classes, and it is unusual for professors to be eager for their colleagues to know what they are doing in their classes. Academic freedom, the holiest of the professoriate's protective doctrines, is almost everywhere perversely invoked to create environments characterized by permissive obliviousness, as professors turn a blind eye to the pedagogical misfeasance of their colleagues. Course syllabi are rarely exchanged. Rarer still is any regular pattern of classroom cross-visiting. Whatever is "known" about a colleague's teaching is usually based upon uninformed student opinion, either in the form of gossip or as the result of access to course evaluations that at best do little else than assess an instructor's popularity.[12]

Permissive obliviousness is, in effect, ready-made denial, automatic denial. Indeed it may even be said to constitute a metadenial rendering specific denials unnecessary. The perversion of academic freedom, in which paying serious attention to the teaching efforts of one's colleagues becomes defined as unwarranted interference, allows professors to lay righteous claim to ignorance. Not only are they oblivious to what transpires in their colleagues' classes, they believe they *ought* to

be. If in cases involving the more dramatic of the seven sins (abandonment, harassment and exploitation, special pleading, and particularism) denial requires some effort, some imaginative attention to the reality in need of denial, no such effort is required in instances involving the less dramatic sins. A blanket denial is built into the academic system, and being party to that system means that you are likely to use it.

Permissive obliviousness can, of course, do nothing except encourage those pedagogical derelictions associated with misrepresentation, default, and proud incompetence. Few faculty, for example, will do anything about the outdated lectures of a colleague because they are not likely to think it appropriate to inquire into the substance of those lectures. With each passing year such lectures can only become more and more antiquated and increasingly misrepresent the state of the art being addressed. The contempt for students built into course syllabi that require little more than regular attendance for the award of a passing grade will go unmarked even by those who would abhor and condemn such contempt in principle. Those who harbor it, absent any pointed criticism, are thus free to delude themselves into mistaking their course "requirements" for a sympathetic response to the plight of underprepared students. Those for whom conventional syntax proves too constraining will be encouraged to bemuse students with their unconventional incoherence. So what if the students don't get the message? With no colleagues to criticize, professors can continue their obfuscatory pedagogy secure in the belief that one shouldn't really expect the students to get it. Only the most brilliant student should be expected to follow the intricacies and complexities of what is being taught, they believe, and, Lord knows, in this age of open educational access there are just too few of those around in most classrooms.

It is, I believe, safe to say that the metadenial anchored in permissive obliviousness renders misrepresentation, default, and proud incompetence the most routine of pedagogical indulgences. Routine . . . but costly.

The Cost of Sustained Miseducation

There is probably no accurate way to calculate the costs of sustained miseducation, but surely there is every reason to believe they must be enormous. To appreciate *how* enormous, one need only contemplate the following: Thousands of students are each year graduated by our

colleges and universities despite seriously flawed educational experiences. Thousands of students are each year certified to the rest of us (and to themselves) as knowledgeable, when through no fault of their own they have learned precious little.[13] Their resulting incompetence and speciously authoritative ignorance can only have undesirable consequences of considerable magnitude. In any instance where they are called upon to use what they have presumably learned, they will likely have too little to draw upon. Minimally, this results in lost time and the need to go back to basics for people who should have mastered them, both likely to drive up the costs of goods and services in the U.S. economy and render U.S. firms disadvantaged in their competition with more efficient producers such as the Japanese and the Germans. Maximally, trained incapacity can lead to failures with tragic consequences (i.e., the flawed building design that results in a collapse and loss of life) as well as other destructive conditions that competence would conceivably have avoided.

In any instance where citizenship requires *informed* participation in debates likely to shape the American future, such participation would seem to be out of the question for ill-prepared college graduates. It would, of course, be foolish to argue that the problems plaguing American society would be solved if citizens were truly informed, but it is reasonable to suggest that uninformed participation in the debates on issues such as environmental protection, education, and distributive justice makes no positive contribution to their solution; indeed it may even hinder the search for effective solutions. Uninformed college graduates, believing that they are informed (they have every reason to believe they *know* something; they have diplomas issued by learned professors who have taught them and examined them) are among the most likely of rigid true believers. They "know" what needs to be done, having learned it in the hallowed halls of alma mater—and if what they "know" is outmoded or oversimplified, if it is nonresponsive to the problem at hand, their persistence in invoking the lessons taught by their derelict professors can only impede the search for appropriately responsive solutions. If the costs of misrepresentation, default, and proud incompetence cannot be precisely calculated, it is thus nevertheless impossible to believe they are negligible. There are just too many people who become the often unwitting victims of these pedagogical sins, too many people who, without intending to do so, consequently visit the sins of their teachers on those they live with, work with, and serve.

Together, the seven pedagogical sins and the well-practiced denial that at the very least tolerates their sustained existence are seriously and deleteriously consequential both for the academy and the society that succors it.[14] Students, many of whom incur financial obligations that will last for years so that they can pay for their educations, are victimized directly. Unsuspecting as they are, their interests are so easily sacrificed. Some are the victims of fraud and intimidation in an environment where they have been led to believe such worldly evils would never be tolerated. Many more simply do not get full value for their money.[15] The rest of us, former students and nonstudents, are no less injured even if our victimization is one step removed from its ultimate source. We are injured by the incompetence and ignorance that is the product of miseducation. We are injured by the failures that drive up costs and by the ignorant arrogance of those who like Scarecrow have petitioned the Wizard (read the professoriate) for a brain (read an education) only to be granted a diploma in its stead. We are therefore injured by soluble problems that remain unsolved for want of the informed intelligence so necessary to their solution.

Pedagogical malpractice as manifested in the seven sins is not merely a parochial issue of little or no consequence to those who do not enjoy the privileges and perquisites of academic life. It has a pernicious ripple effect. All too often unnoticed, it is a problem whose manifold and variegated presence subverts both the academic creed and the general struggle to render life more livable in American society. It is thus no mean betrayal either to indulge in such malpractice or to countenance it in the silence of denial—no mean betrayal, but one all too common to the academic scene.

Chapter 4

The Bad Joke of Scholarship
Dirty Little Secrets 2

If teaching is *the* defining characteristic of academic institutions, scholarship—or at least its presumption—enjoys a nearly equivalent status. What distinguishes the academic from other teachers (let's say high school teachers) is the assumption that the academic is both creator *and* purveyor of knowledge, whereas other teachers are merely purveyors. Academics are presumably trained to discover and create; their most characteristic credential, the Ph.D., does not in fact establish their bona fides as purveyors, but rather as individuals who have demonstrated a capacity for independent discovery or, in the more interpretive disciplines, its analogue, uniquely illumining argumentation. Whereas teachers at other levels are in one way or another licensed to teach, no such license exists for those who constitute the faculties of postsecondary-level institutions. In the august precincts of the academy, knowing *what* to teach is assumed to be more important than knowing *how* to teach it. And knowing what to teach is presumably a function of those scholarly competencies the possession of which is attested to (at least in theory) by the earned title "doctor of philosophy."[1]

The Demands of Scholarship

The assumed importance of scholarship on American campuses has at least two implications significant in determining the nature of academic work and academic governance. The requirement that professors be discoverers and interpreters as well as purveyors of the truth is at the heart of the academy's workload assumptions. Whereas the typical teacher at the secondary level will spend five hours a day, five days

105

a week in the classroom, it is the rare professor who spends more than four hours a day, three days per week meeting classes, and such a "full" schedule is unlikely in all but the least distinguished institutions. In the typical liberal arts college, the teaching load is nine hours per week; in universities heavily invested in graduate and professional education the typical load is no more than six hours.[2] Even if one were to give credence to the professoriate's usually dubious claim that hours of preparation are additionally necessary, the time professors typically allocate to teaching would hardly add up to a full-time job as defined by the forty-hour workweek.

The professoriate's justification for so light a teaching load is as simple as it is predictable. Teaching, professors are at pains to explain, is but one part of their job. They are expected to and, they claim, do in fact devote the preponderance of their remaining working hours to the development of new knowledge. They teach so little, they explain, because of their commitment to the truth that is yet to be mined. If they were to teach full time, they would have little or no time for the creative excavation that is as much a part (or even the greater part) of their calling.[3]

Of course time is not the only necessary precondition for effective scholarship. There is something even more basic: freedom. If scholars lack the freedom to seek the truth limited only by what they can imagine and the analytic power of their disciplines, the cause of enlightenment must suffer. Extraneous constraints of any stripe (political, economic, religious, etc.) can only distort what passes for the scholar's truth, rendering it by degrees untrue and misleading. Given the presumed centrality of scholarship to the professorial role, it is not surprising therefore that the academy has been zealous in guarding against even the slightest hint of unwarranted interference. Nothing arouses a faculty more than a perceived threat to its inquisitional prerogatives. Even an unsubstantiated rumor of such a threat can be counted on to transform what is normally a collection of Clark Kent lookalikes into a squadron of rhetorical Supermen. They may not be able to leap tall buildings at a single bound, but when they sense a challenge to their scholarly independence their heroic verbal flights are nearly as breathtaking. It is safe to say there is no other profession where the individual freedoms of its practitioners are considered as important. The academy is probably the only professional venue where so much of what passes for work goes unsupervised and, moreover, where any

attempt at supervision, however benign, would be viewed with suspicious alarm.[4]

In theory this freedom does not imply an absence of accountability. Professors are quick to point out that if their scholarly efforts justifiably abhor supervision, they must with some regularity submit the products of those efforts to a jury of their peers. They will call attention to the fact that much research requires financial support and that in order to receive such support one has to submit detailed proposals that are picked over by expert panels instructed to recommend funding for only those projects of the highest quality. They will insist that scholars gain an informed audience for their work when and only when other professionals acting as editors or manuscript reviewers find sufficient merit in it to recommend publication. And publication, they will aver, does not guarantee that a scholar's work will find acceptance. Once published, it has to withstand the public scrutiny of the book review or, if it has been published in a journal, the public scrutiny of a critical communication. If in its preliminary form the research is presented at a professional meeting, a national or regional convention, it is hardly likely that it will escape criticism from the floor. And finally, they will claim, there is no way to hide your work if you want to thrive in the academy. Academic tenure and promotion, they will tell you, depends to a considerable degree on the success an individual achieves as a scholar. Failure to demonstrate that success by seeking and receiving grants as well as by publication is likely to mean a concomitant failure to make tenure and to advance steadily from assistant to full professor.[5] So if scholars within the academy proceed without supervision, that freedom—the absence of which can imply unwarranted interference—should not be mistaken for license. Academic scholars, they will claim, pay for their freedom and pay dearly by making themselves publicly accountable to their peers on a regular basis.

The presumption that academics are almost everywhere seriously engaged in scholarship is thus a major determinant of the quality of academic life. Take away that presumption and it is impossible to justify the light teaching loads. Take it away and the freedoms accompanying professorial status lose their rationale. Without the essentially unchallenged belief that professors are all but universally engaged in creative discovery, it is likely they would be required to do more teaching and that day-to-day supervision would be a fact of their work lives.

The Realities of Scholarship

But are academics almost universally involved in good-faith scholarly efforts? Do they as a rule use the many nonteaching hours of their workweeks in serious pursuit of truth's elusive variety?[6] Do they really justify their freedom from daily supervision by producing work that is almost always available for serious criticism by their peers, criticism which itself can be understood to serve the cause of enlightenment? There are no definitive answers to these questions, but existing materials suggest that the realities of academic scholarship are something other than the claims typically made by American professors. In some instances the claims appear to be hyperbolic; in others they seem to be out-and-out falsehoods.

Even those commentators who champion the cause of the professoriate (e.g., those who believe professors are overworked, underpaid, and steadfast in their commitment to the truth) produce materials that belie the actual centrality of scholarship as an academic activity. Using professorial self-reports, one study has estimated that on average university professors devote a bit more than fifteen hours per week to research, while their colleagues at four-year undergraduate institutions are hard pressed to devote an average of five hours per week to their pursuit of truth.[7] This same study indicated that among university professors only those in the natural sciences exceed the aggregate of fifteen-plus hours and that for the remainder of those included in the report,[8] scholarship on average occupies approximately ten hours per week, hardly a figure that suggests a professoriate bent on carrying out the demanding tasks of inquiry—and this in institutions, universities, that lay particular claim to a heavy investment in scholarship. Another monograph reports that 68 percent of all faculty (inclusive of those who teach at two-year colleges) spend nine hours or less per week on research. Moreover, even at those elite universities where as a matter of policy research takes precedence over teaching, fully 40 percent of faculty spend nine or less hours per week on such endeavors. Corresponding percentages for other institutional classifications, as should be expected, indicate that whatever else they are doing, a large number of self-proclaimed scholars are involved in systematic inquiry but minimally if at all. At nonelite Ph.D.-granting institutions, 55 percent spend nine hours or less on research; at so-called comprehensive colleges and universities (e.g., institutions that do not grant Ph.D.'s but

have some graduate or professional programs) the corresponding figure is 79 percent; and at liberal arts colleges as many as 90 percent of
the faculty apparently spend nine hours or less per week on research.[9]

This same monograph reports another set of statistics that should
trouble even the most ardent apologists for the American academy.
Fifty-seven percent of faculty members at liberal arts colleges are reported as not having published within two years of the time they were
interviewed.[10] In other words, nearly three-fifths of those who claim
the mantle of scholar at liberal arts colleges, who justify their freedom
from everyday supervision at these institutions by invoking the pretty
rhetoric of scholarly accountability, had not published word one for
two years prior to their participation in the study. We don't know what
percentage of those who had not published had tried to and were not up
to the task (it would hardly be comforting if that percentage were
high), but as most academic disciplines are awash in publication outlets, it's hard to believe that a large proportion of these folks had
simply failed in their efforts to get into print. The proliferation of
outlets has been such that, as one journal editor put it:

> There seems to be no study too fragmented, no hypothesis too trivial, no
> literature citation too biased . . . no design too warped, no methodology
> too bungled, no presentation of results too inaccurate, too obscure and
> too contradictory, no analysis too self-serving, no argument too circular,
> no conclusion too trifling or too unjustified and no grammar and syntax
> too offensive for a paper [not] to end up in print.[11]

No, it's not that the liberal arts professors tried and failed. The much
more reasonable conclusion is that they simply did not try. (Certainly it
is a conclusion consistent with the report indicating 90 percent of liberal
arts faculty spend nine hours or less per week engaged in research!)

The picture is not quite so bleak at other types of institutions: 46
percent of faculty at comprehensive colleges and universities had not
published, 32 percent had not done so at nonelite Ph.D.-granting universities, and 18 percent had not done so at elite research universities.[12] But the picture still suggests that large numbers of faculty at
these institutions regularly fail to submit their work to a jury of their
peers.

It is impossible to put a good face on statistics such as these. They
describe a reality at considerable odds with the claims academics use

to justify their very light teaching loads as well as their freedom from everyday supervision. And when we consider how these statistics have been produced, it is more than plausible to conclude that what they purport to describe underestimates the departure of academic reality from what surely must be self-serving academic claims. Ultimately, all such statistics are based on self-reports by members of the professoriate. Even when investigators use official activity reports (e.g., reports of activities mandated by academic administrators), those reports are prepared by individual professors who may not be required to document assertions of their workloads or achievements. It is only natural to expect that academics, influenced by the claims of their profession, will overestimate the time they spend in truth's service.[13] Thus the findings alluded to above probably reflect this inflationary tendency. Of course if this is so, it's fair to conclude that academics in each of the designated categories are spending even less time on scholarly pursuits than their reports would seem to indicate, and, as compared to the profession's claims, that wasn't much to begin with.[14]

These statistics also suggest that for a large number of academics the rationale that frees them from everyday supervision has a mythopoetic quality. It is true that scholarship will not thrive in a work environment where scholars feel they are constantly being watched, in an environment where they feel they are not free to follow the dictates of their disciplined imaginations. But if we are to take these statistics seriously, there are many academics whose claims to freedom from immediate supervision are unfounded and therefore illegitimate. They simply are not putting enough time into scholarly endeavors to warrant such freedom. Moreover, if the statistics on publication are any indication, the justification for the freedom that stands on the assumption of scholarly accountability to their peers would seem to have considerably less merit than academics would have us believe. If large numbers of professors are not bothering to submit their work for this type of peer review, such accountability can hardly be said to exist in lieu of everyday supervision.[15]

The Appearance of Scholarly Activity

These statistics, inflated as they are, don't begin to tell the whole story. One need only consider a number of standard academic practices to find the validity in this assertion.

The Spurious Syllogism

Academics as a rule are quite fond of asserting the seamlessness of their lives. If they can be believed, one thing that renders their profession so challenging is that it cannot be temporally segregated from the rest of their activities. Whereas other people can leave their work at the office, the store, or the factory, academics are unable to do so. Their profession requires a constant refinement of consciousness. They are, so they say, never really off duty. They don't work an eight-hour day; there is no day shift, night shift, or swing shift. Thinking is at the core of their profession, and it's not something they can stop doing as they cross over their domestic thresholds.[16]

In effect many academics are likely to invoke the following syllogism as they convince themselves they are at work even in circumstances that would not ordinarily be recognized as work related:

Premise 1: Academics are human beings.
Premise 2: Thinking is ongoing during periods of human wakefulness or consciousness.
Premise 3: Thinking is a professionalized skill among academics, a function of their trained capacity for refined consciousness.

Thus the conclusion:

When human academics think, as they must do during periods of wakefulness, they are exercising a professional skill—in other words, when they are awake, they are working.

Thus many academics recast even the most mundane activities as scholarly work, and when asked how much time they devote to scholarship, they can be expected to include the time spent on those activities.[17] While this practice crosses all disciplines, it is particularly prominent in the humanities and social sciences. After all, the stuff of these disciplines is frequently the stuff of everyday life made truth as it is filtered through the refined consciousness of the trained observer. Others may simply be whiling away the hours watching television, but many professors in the humanities and social sciences are assimilating popular tastes and culture as they sit transfixed by *Home Improvement, NYPD Blue, ER,* and *Frasier.* For ordinary mortals, the *New York*

Times is a pretty good newspaper to read with their morning coffee; for many of the academy's humanists and social scientists it's a reference work the reading of which is professionally mandated. Football isn't merely football for these Ph.D.'s but rather a metaphoric transformation of the militaristic aggression whose dominance in American life cries out for observation and critical assessment. And ever since the late Erving Goffman[18] revealed the social truth that exists just below the surface of ordinary behaviors such as riding in elevators and playing twenty-one in Las Vegas, everyday sociability has presented a new challenge to the observational capacities of his colleagues. The Thursday night poker game has become a research project, and boarding an escalator has become the occasion for more than a few field experiments. These activities may from time to time yield scholarly products, but for the most part those who engage in them appear to be no more productive than the ordinary Joes and Janes who are just watching TV, who are just reading the *Times,* who are just playing cards—and who are just avoiding the exertions of climbing stairs. If these activities are indeed occasions for scholarly activity, the scholarship involved appears to be of the elusive genre, the type that leads to the publication statistics cited above.

Double-Dipping

Without so much as a second thought, a great many academics engage in the highly questionable practice of claiming credit for scholarship to which their contribution has been no more than minimal. There are two subroutines involved in this practice. The first is double-dipping, whereby faculty members append their names to student-authored publications when those publications have evolved out of teaching interactions with the students. Professors double-dip by claiming both teaching and research credit for precisely the same activity. In reality the only legitimate claim is pedagogical. Their classes or seminars may have stimulated the students' thinking and they may have reacted to several drafts of the students' work, but in such instances they have neither engaged in the study the publication reports on nor have they written any of the text that finds its way into print. They feel justified in appending their names (and thereby taking credit for work they have not done) merely because they have in one way or another been connected with the work in question, and among academics authorship by

association has become the rule rather than the exception. That student authors rarely resist the acquisitiveness of their mentors should hardly be surprising; they are, after all, dependent financially and professionally on the opinion faculty have of them. And given the widespread nature of this practice, they really have little basis on which to question it.

Backscratching

The second subroutine is something quite akin to the backscratching that is so much a part of the political scene (a venue academics frequently regard with sneering disdain). Academic backscratching simply involves crediting a colleague with coauthorship even though that individual's contribution to the work in question is difficult to locate or specify. For the most part, there has in fact been a contribution, but it usually is of the kind that should warrant an acknowledgment as opposed to a credited coauthorship—a consultation that helped clear up a technical problem, perhaps, or a critical reading of an early draft, or assistance in finding resources to support the research. The reasons motivating this tendentious award of credit are several. In some instances it is done in the hope that the recipient of such largess will recognize the quid pro quo for what it is and return the favor in precisely the same manner (something that is indeed likely to occur). In other instances the recipient is a powerful colleague whose favor the gift giver is seeking to curry. In other instances still (particularly in the physical sciences) there exist unwritten rules about crediting research administrators with coauthorship if any work has been done in a program or laboratory under their overall supervision (even if that supervision is many levels removed from the research in question). And there are even those instances where author's credit is awarded because not to do so would be to invite hassles with the colleagues whose overweening self-importance leads them to assume that they make a significant contribution to everything and anything in which they might have the slightest interest (those who bestow coauthor's credit in such cases are trying to scratch their own backs in the perhaps vain attempt to eradicate an annoying itch).

The net result of both double-dipping and backscratching is the appearance of scholarly activity on the part of many professors when in fact no such activity has taken place. It is not, for example, an exaggeration to suggest that many of those who report they have pub-

lished during a specified period, while technically correct, are being quite misleading. Surely they've received credit for publishing, but if we take that to mean they've invested hours of effort in the creation of scholarly products that have survived the critical scrutiny of their peers, we would be seriously mistaken.[19]

Reincarnating the Word

There are professors who, without intending to do so, make the best case for reincarnation I have yet seen. The papers they do in fact write invariably appear to have more than a mere solitary published existence. Such papers seem to live on and on, published over and over and over again. Well, they're not really the same: The titles differ somewhat, the order of authorship is likely to change a bit, and careful (very careful) textual comparison reveals some rearrangement of paragraphs as well as some variation in the use of articles and prepositions. But aside from these minuscule differences the paper remains the same from one published appearance to the next.

In theory the editors of scholarly publications are supposed to guard against this practice. When a paper is published in a journal, an annual, or a collection, the editors of that publication have presumably warranted its originality—presumably, but all too often not really. If, for example, only the publication's editor has reviewed the paper (as is frequently the case with annuals and collections), there is a good chance that, not being a specialist in the subfield the manuscript is supposed to be addressing, he or she will be unaware of any previous published versions. Sending the paper out for review by experts in the subfield reduces the risk of such lack of awareness but not to the degree that might be assumed. There are experts and then there are "experts." Under pressure from their subscribers, journals have since the 1980s democratized their review procedures. Whereas in the past reviewing was undertaken by a relatively small and select group of associate editors appointed for their scholarly reputations in particular areas of inquiry, today reviewing is characteristically undertaken by self-designated "experts" whose reputations exist only in their imaginations. Since many colleges and universities accept manuscript review as a bonafide scholarly activity justifying merit increases in salary, so-called elitist review procedures have given way to the will of the professors, and they've willed that any card-carrying Ph.D. in a

particular discipline who announces (usually on preprinted forms provided by the journals) that she or he is an expert in a certain subfield
has a right to review manuscripts in that subfield. As can be easily
imagined, one of the overlooked implications of democracy's spread in
the scholar's workplace is the problem of quality control. With little
up-to-date knowledge of the subfields they claim to have mastered,
some manuscript reviewers are unlikely to recognize a but slightly
altered iteration of something already in print. Their recommendation
for publication is thus no warrant of originality.[20]

Of course the less selective the journal the less likely is its editorial
staff even to have qualms about the originality issue. Thus a group of
authors whose paper has been rejected because it merely repeats an
earlier report can simply continue to submit it, as it were down the line,
until it finds a home. There are professors for whom publication is
purely instrumental: more lines on a vitae equal a larger salary increase
as well as more rapid advancement, and there are institutions where all
that counts is the number of lines on a vitae. It is hardly surprising
therefore that authors of reincarnated papers are not chastened by rejection; given their motivation and their environment, they will proceed until they find those "expert" reviewers who don't know or don't
care if the paper they are looking at has had more lives than the
proverbial feline nine.

Reincarnating papers is surely among the more minor of academic transgressions. If it is the only sin a professor indulges in, it
is hardly likely that the judgment upon him would be sufficient to
stoke the fires of Dante's imagined retributive furnace. Minor though
it may be, however, its not uncharacteristic existence on the academic scene (together with the other practices under consideration
in these pages) does suggest that claims about the centrality of scholarship to the professoriate's professional existence are at best hyperbolic. That the academy is clearly willing to tolerate (and perhaps
even encourage) such a practice suggests yet again that the statistics
on professorial involvement in scholarship, not cheering to begin with,
overestimate that involvement. Publication during a two-year period
may indeed mean that you've actually been up to something new, but it
may mean that you've been emulating Count Basie in *One More Time*.
You have to wonder whether those who report spending a good portion
of their workweek engaged in scholarly pursuits are in fact doing so. It
could be, of course, that they are simply rearranging paragraphs on

their computers as they seek a home for yet another version of their
golden oldie.

Turning Research Tricks

There is one practice engaged in primarily by academics on the faculties of graduate research universities and professional schools that is
sadly analogous to the way the world's oldest "professionals" work.
Hookers never give it away free; and they never really get turned on by
what they're doing. They "trick," that is, they act as though they enjoy
doing whatever the john wants (if they have any preferences of their
own, they never express them during working hours), but what they
are really after is the money the john is offering for services rendered.
There are professors who, like hookers, never give it away free and
never get turned on by what they're doing. Like the practitioners of the
world's oldest profession their real passion is for presidential pictures
etched in silver-green. They, too, are willing to do anything the john
(in academic parlance, the funding source) wants as long as the price is
right. And if it is, they will feign moves necessary to convince the
"john" of their enthusiasm for the services they're being paid to render.
    Turning research tricks occurs for two not terribly surprising rea-
sons. First, there are some universities where, protestations to the contrary
notwithstanding, the yellow brick road to tenure and promotion—the
surest route—is really a tollway. Faculty at such institutions are not so
much encouraged to publish as they are to develop funding proposals.[21] Publication, it is assumed, is the natural final stage of a research
project. It will take care of itself. What is of greater concern to those
who manage such institutions is finding moneys to do research in the
first place, dollars that will pay for equipment, support graduate research assistants and secretaries, keep the toner flowing and the supply
cabinets stuffed with all manner of office goodies. At such institutions
the pressure to bring in the bucks can be intense indeed; and while
faculty do undertake legitimate fund-raising activities (e.g., generating
proposals consistent with the scholar's discipline-informed curiosity),
there is the ever present temptation to turn a research trick or two. This
is especially so because there really are a lot of funding sources out
there whose agents, in a manner of speaking, cruise the academy offering handsome rewards to professors who are willing to do the things
they want them to do. The Tobacco Institute lusts after those scholars

who can discredit (objectively, of course) existing research on the health hazards of smoking. The drug companies look for hustling bio-chemists who can find all manner of life-enhancing qualities in their elixirs. The U.S. government is ready to keep any physicist, mathema-tician, or engineer ready to come across for the military establishment. Organized labor is desperately seeking economists who can fake an economic orgasm any time some politician proposes protectionist trade legislation. Even the Japanese look for economists who are willing to do the same thing for free trade proposals that apply to every market save their own.

Second, there are situations where administrators actively encourage tricking as a means to reduce salary inequities. Medical school deans, for example, frequently do so (they of course would deny that they are doing so) in an attempt to bridge the salary gap between the M.D.'s and the Ph.D.'s on their faculties. In order to make academic medicine attractive to highly skilled practitioners, universities have to pay sala-ries that can compete with what physicians would likely earn in private practice. M.D.'s, however, are not the only professionals on a medical school faculty. There are as well Ph.D. biochemists, physiologists, anthropologists, psychologists, and even sociologists. The basic alter-native labor market for these professionals exists in other sectors of the academy: four-year colleges, graduate research departments, and so on. While academic salaries are reasonably munificent (on the whole they exceed the American median by many thousands of dollars), they are not as munificent as the annual incomes of physicians in private practice. It is not surprising, therefore, that the salaries medical schools offer to these Ph.D.'s are likewise less attractive than those they offer to the M.D.'s. They pay what amounts to the going rate for medical specialists (usually a bit less, but there are other inducements, such as time and facilities for the treatment of private patients) and the going rate for Ph.D.'s. Since these rates differ and since the M.D.'s would be advantaged by this differential in the big wide world beyond the medi-cal school, they are also advantaged within its organizational environs.

If the Ph.D.'s in question looked to their professional peers in other academic settings, they would likely be no more than minimally and conventionally discontented by their level of compensation. But since, as might be expected, they tend to use the salaries of their physician colleagues as the standard for reasonable and just compensation, their discontent can likewise be expected to intensify unless some remedy is

found. The remedy medical school deans have hit upon bears a superficial resemblance to the perks offered the M.D.'s. The physicians are allowed to use the school's facilities for their private patients, so it would seem only fair that the Ph.D. researchers on the faculty be allowed to use those same facilities in their consulting work. The deans actually encourage such work because in their view the Ph.D.'s will be less concerned about their base salaries if they can close the gap between what they earn and what their M.D. colleagues earn, especially when they are abetted by purposive inadvertence (the winks and nods of their administrative superiors).

Universities, as a rule, have regulations intended to protect against professorial abuses of consultative prerogatives. Most universities specify a maximum number of hours that may be spent on consulting activities, and most universities try, in principle, to ensure that consulting work does not in any way compromise the academy's mission of service to the truth free of utilitarian considerations. Rules are one thing; rules effectively enforced are quite another. And while in the example cited here every medical school dean would *endorse* the university's rules on faculty consulting, those who would *enforce* these rules are much fewer indeed. The medical school Ph.D.'s are characteristically given free rein to consult to the extent they see fit (as are professors of business and engineering, for similar reasons), and questions are rarely if ever asked about the nature of that consultation, about the ends it is intended to serve. So for those intent on lining their pockets with silver and gold, the sophisticated laboratory facilities the university provides on the assumption that they will be used to discover the biochemical, genetic, and physiological causes of human affliction are easily put to use in the service of some drug company's search for a greater profit margin. (Drug companies frequently farm out research activities to academic consultants because they need only pay for the consultants' time, since the consultants already have access to excellent laboratory facilities. This, moreover, frees their own research staffs to pursue other activities. In this way do universities actually underwrite some of private enterprise's development costs.)

Research tricking is inherently dishonest and thus an affront to what scholarship is supposed to be. While it would be erroneous to claim that tricking is the academic order of the day, it is, I would maintain, present in sufficient measure to be considered more than a merely peripheral problem. It's not just a few miscreant hustlers betraying the

trust of their colleagues; it's a substantial cadre of hustlers who view their tricks as standard practice, and it's an even larger cadre of academic witnesses who look on and yet refuse to see, lest they be required to act in defense of academic purpose.[22]

Tricking, moreover, is not just an affront to scholarship; it is as well an agency of academic betrayal, the Trojan horse that allows truth's utilitarian enemies access to the academy's inner sanctum. Even as academicians wring their hands in public worry about the threat posed to disinterested inquiry by the interests of mundane utility, there are many who for no reason other than personal profit continue to invite those very interests into their laboratories and offices, who, out of a desire for personal aggrandizement, allow anyone willing to pay the freight to dictate research priorities and creative agendas.

While their colleagues look on but refuse to see, the academy's whores have made a commodity of truth. Thus what at first blush appears to be scholarship and what would be reported as such in studies like those noted above (those who turn research tricks do spend time on activities easily mistaken for genuine research, and frequently their "johns" would be disappointed if they did not publish) turns out to be its antithesis—and more than that: a set of activities whose corrupting implications reach well beyond the hustlers themselves to those whose silence encourages their continuation.[23]

The Realities: A Reprise

The closer one looks, the more it appears that there are two quite different groups of academics justifying their light teaching loads and their freedom from everyday supervision by claiming a serious and sustained involvement in scholarship: those for whom the claim is reasonably valid and those for whom it is not. The former probably constitute a majority,[24] but the latter, it is clear, constitute a significant minority. That so many academics avoid the rigors of scholarship or otherwise engage in activities that bear only a superficial resemblance to those rigors, that their professionally scrupulous but self-deluding colleagues, denying the evidence of their own experience, tolerate (and even reward) this retreat from responsible behavior can only mean that the professoriate has (as was the case with teaching) yet again compromised itself. The facts strongly suggest a work environment where,

contrary to their impassioned espousals of scholarly involvement and accountability, professors have done little to secure the characteristic reality of either.

Of course this opens up some serious questions about the professoriate's light teaching load and freedom from everyday supervision. As we have seen, American professors justify their light teaching assignments by claiming scholarly involvement and their freedom from everyday supervision by claiming the necessity of creative freedom for scholars whose work will ultimately be subject to the accountability imposed by stringent peer review. If there is considerably less scholarly involvement and accountability than the professoriate would have us believe, these justifications are hard to take seriously. And as such, increased teaching loads and more than nominal supervision would seem to be warranted. But more of this later.

Four Instructive Cases

Those professors still attending these pages will surely have recognized this chapter's realities. But as was the case with the previous chapter's broadside on teaching, I recognize and fully appreciate that much of what I have written will most probably be greeted with disbelief (real disbelief, as opposed to the howls of feigned disbelief that can be expected from wounded academics) by those readers who do not have intimate and sustained contact with the academy. It's one thing to encounter laziness, cupidity, and self-serving apologetics in those of life's venues that are unabashedly utilitarian, you kind of expect many among those whose gain-loss calculus is explicitly defined by self-interest to manifest such less than desirable characteristics. But professors? Deep-thinking men and women whose passion for the truth is so powerful that in its pursuit they have been known to miss meals, go without sleep, and otherwise ignore worldly urgencies? That these ostensibly self-sacrificing, impractically honest stalwarts may not be so stalwart after all is a bit difficult to accept. They may be unrealistic—they're fond of recommending things that would only make sense in a perfect world—sometimes even a bit pretentious—all that fancy talk and so little straightforward action. But lazy and blatantly self-serving? Such characteristics are just not part of the professoriate's popular image.[25]

But whether or not popular imagery allows for it, professors are as

capable as anyone of avoiding work, as capable as anyone of putting personal gain or comfort before all else, as the following cases amply illustrate.[26]

Case 1: In Pursuit of Excellence

April may be a cruel month for poets and disappointed lovers, but not, apparently, for political scientists. April, you see, is merit month, the time when the elected personnel committee evaluates accomplishments of the past academic year and recommends merit increases based upon that evaluation. Of course, given the distributional nature of accomplishment (and particularly scholarly accomplishment, which these academics are supposed to weigh heavily), you would think that at least some of the political scientists might indeed join the poets and lovers in their melancholy, that rueful sense of a year's missed opportunities. None of the political scientists, however, suffers such regret. Instead, because their colleagues on the personnel committee possess an uncanny ability to find merit in anything and everything, the worst feeling they are likely to experience is disappointment over the *amount* of merit money the committee has seen fit to bestow. In their benign if Orwellian world, everyone, it seems, is meritorious, albeit some more so than others.

From time to time there *are* difficult cases that test the creative capacities of committee members. Down deep, however, even the most slothful and negligent political scientists know that their monetary fate is in good hands. As social scientists, they know that the best predictor of future behavior is past practice, and when it comes to merit increases that turns out to be reassuring indeed.

It certainly must be reassuring to the tenured political theorist who for nearly a decade has not published anything save an occasional book review. Every April his colleagues on the committee conclude that during the previous academic year he has engaged in serious scholarly efforts. For ten years, the theorist has received merit increases averaging $400 per year. His department chairman is quick to point out that this increase falls below the median for the department, which reflects the theorist's limited scholarly output. Surely other of his colleagues have done better, but the theorist hasn't done all that badly, especially when you consider there's more to these increases than meets the eye. Merit money, you see, becomes part of its recipient's base salary, and when, as is required by an existing collective bargaining agreement,

the theorist receives his bargaining unit increase, that percentage is calculated on a base salary inclusive of the merit increase. The $4,000 awarded to the theorist for his presumably meritorious service over the past decade has thus had a multiplier effect on his salary. Simply put, the presumption of merit has meant considerably more than the $4,000 directly attributable to it; it has meant that $4,000, plus the extra dollars resulting from the difference between a percentage of a base salary without the additional $400 per year and a percentage of a base salary with the additional $400 per year.

In his annual reviews of the theorist, the chairman has for several years emphasized the potential for significance of his work in progress. The theorist is supposed to be at work on a monograph examining the role of state subsidies in reducing economic risks and the role of the state in establishing economic agendas. No one, however, has seen a single page of the manuscript he is supposedly preparing, and the only public presentation the political theorist has made on the topic was a lunch colloquium delivered when he was presumably beginning his research. But the chairman is not at all dismayed by the undocumented progress the theorist's colleagues have been rewarding with sustained regularity. He knows the work will be completed (although he is hard pressed to predict just when that will occur) because in conversation the theorist has revealed himself to be very well informed on state subventions. It would, so the chairman avers, be highly unlikely for someone to go to all the trouble of a literature search and review if he wasn't going to eventually produce a scholarly product.

That no manuscript has been made available for review was initially troubling, but the chairman has come around to accepting the theorist's explanation for his apparent secretiveness. He's not trying to hide anything (e.g., his lack of real progress); it's just that he has this perfectionist streak that prevents him from showing his work to anyone until he is satisfied with it. The chairman would not be so retentive, but he takes pains to point out that the theorist, in his perfectionist pursuit of excellence, has indeed sacrificed. Were he willing to show the manuscript to his colleagues on the personnel committee, they would no doubt be willing to vote him a merit increase commensurate with his progress. As it stands, without the evidence of a manuscript, their merit awards, while crediting the theorist's claims to scholarship, have placed him below the median for the department as a whole.

That the theorist has never complained about this is, for the chair-

man, another mark of his sincerity. An academic hustler, he reasons, would not be willing to accept a financial penalty because he would not really be striving for excellence. He'd be fuming over the fact that his colleagues wouldn't just take his word for what he's doing. The theorist, however, seriously committed to his work and his work style, is comfortable, so the chairman says, with reduced merit moneys in the present because he knows that when completed his scholarship will bring him the rewards he deserves. The chairman does not, however, speculate as to whether the theorist's commitment would be strong enough to foster the same equanimity if his colleagues withheld *any* merit award until his claimed project was made palpable. Below the department's median or not, thousands of dollars given on a promise that may never be redeemed would appear to buy a lot of equanimity, principled or otherwise. But the chairman won't speculate along such lines because that would not be fair to the theorist. After all, no one has come up with compelling evidence that he's not pursuing excellence.

Case 2: The Leisure Arts

Allan Bloom no doubt approves: Introducing late adolescents to the eternal verities is at the heart of this small, highly select liberal arts college's pedagogical mission. Its faculty looks backward to the classics, the great books of the ages, so that they can prepare their youthful students to wrestle with the timeless dilemmas that will confront them in the future. Exactly what Professor Bloom has recommended. So busy are they with eternal verities and timeless dilemmas that the faculty cannot often be bothered, it seems, with the situationally specific and quite mundane requirements of preparing scholarly manuscripts for publication. Few publish with any regularity, but what might ordinarily be taken for failure to honor a professional obligation is apparently not viewed as such in the college's expectedly book-lined offices.

The director of the program in language and logic, for example, makes it clear that she views publication as irrelevant at best and a considerable distraction at worst. It may be otherwise at more conventional institutions, she argues, but at a classically oriented college it would be an error to conflate publication with scholarship. Contemplating the core issues of human existence is as demanding a scholarly task as can be imagined. You don't, she avers, take on such issues as

the evolution of human reason, the ethical consequences of memory, or the survival of faith in a secular world without making a considerable scholarly investment. But that, she continues, doesn't mean you'll publish on these matters or that you should even consider publishing on them. She wouldn't necessarily feel that way about professors at large state universities or even at the state colleges. Their mission, after all, usually has little to do with the classics. But when you concern yourself with the big questions, when you confront the greatest minds in human history wrestling with these questions, you gain the proper perspective on your own contributions. The classics speak for themselves. What is there to say to the world after the giants have spoken? Teach their wisdom, apprehend their struggle—use all of your scholarly powers to aid your students as they stand awestruck before the likes of Plato, Augustine, Aquinas, Hobbes, Locke, Rousseau, Marx, Darwin, Nietzsche, James, Freud, and the rest—but don't add to the distracting clutter of treatises laying false claim to their philosophical patrimony. Unless you honestly believe that your understandings approximate the standard set by such masters, she concludes, truth is best served by sticking to your lathe, which in this instance is classroom teaching.

And toiling in the long shadow cast by the immortals is seemingly not the only source of the humility that protects against rash and unnecessary forays into print by this faculty. According to the faculty's senior humanities professor, the college's students themselves inspire a selfless modesty that his colleagues rarely overcome, and then only when they have experienced an epiphany of insight so powerful that it virtually overwhelms any and all intellectual reserve.

Many academics have, he asserts, an inflated view of their intellectual prowess, and not surprisingly such a view is correlated with the sense that they ought to find their way into print as often as possible. According to the senior professor, this tendency toward self-inflation is a function of both past experience and present circumstance. People who become academics were pretty smart students who in graduate school were associated with mentors themselves suffering from an overweening and unrealistic sense of importance. The soon-to-be-professors, smart to begin with, come to believe that since their very important mentors have chosen to smile upon them, they likewise must have what it takes to be important. For most, this belief is reinforced when they assume their teaching positions, because they are in fact so much more sophisticated and

informed than those they teach. In his avuncular manner, the senior humanities professor is at pains to point out that it is ever so easy to mistake such sophistication for considerable wisdom and thereby to conclude that failing to allow the widest possible audience access to it would be selfish indeed.

That understandable but really quite regrettable error in judgment is, he suggests, less likely to occur among his colleagues because while their past experience as students doesn't differ from faculty at most institutions, their present experience with students is much different. The students they teach may be less sophisticated and less well informed than their professors, but not by a whole lot. They have been recruited from among the best and the brightest of America's high school seniors, kids whose SATs are so high as to be gaudy, kids who are Merit Scholar finalists and the like. And while they have much to learn, they don't for a moment allow their teachers the illusion of wisdom allowed by less gifted students in other institutions. At a school like this, the senior professor maintains, it is simply quite difficult for faculty to inflate their importance; there are always those kids, those eighteen- and nineteen-year-olds who by their own extraordinary gifts remind you that however smart you might be, you've got a lot of company. In such a situation, says the professor, faculty become quite realistic about themselves and so avoid the publication hubris.

They *are* scholars, however, he insists. They have to be, or given the piranhalike intellects possessed by their students, they'd be eaten alive in class. Some people, he is sure, won't be able to appreciate the arduous demands of an appointment at a college such as his. People who think of work in terms of hours spent in a place doing something will not understand that contemplation is work and that it is work few people are capable of. It's amazing, observes the senior professor, but even some academics don't seem capable of appreciating the fact that contemplative scholarship does not have to be copyrighted to be valuable. A friend teaching at another institution, a nuclear physicist, an experimentalist, recently betrayed his inability to understand when, in complaining about something or other related to his own work, he bemoaned his choice not to work in the "leisure arts." He was kidding, of course, but according to the senior humanities professor his comments revealed a profound misunderstanding on the part of someone you'd expect to know better. According to the professor, his school is about nothing less than the life of the mind, and that requires ongoing

creative thought by faculty members, which means that you are almost always working. If, he concludes, you take the mean annual salary of the faculty and divide by the number of hours they actually give to the labors of the mind, the hourly rate would be appallingly low. "Leisure arts" indeed.

Case 3: Life at the Institute

There was a time in the not too distant past when many police officers in a major U.S. city were implicated in a highly organized bribery scam. According to informants, it worked this way: Payoffs were collected on a regular basis from licit and illicit businesses within a given police precinct. The take was then divided up among officers in the precinct according to rank and seniority. On payday each officer received a paycheck plus a little extra cash representing a share of the precinct's payoff take. (In many precincts the take was simply referred to as petty cash.) Because most officers didn't have to do anything for the extra money and because they believed they were underpaid, it was easy for them to pocket the cash with no questions asked. As soon as they accepted their first extra payment, they were implicated in the scam. Since they ran the risk of being dismissed from the force and even facing criminal corruption charges, the acceptance of that first extra payment virtually ensured their silence even if at some future point they thought better of continuing to accept the graft. Any officers who refused to go along with the system were quickly labeled badasses and found themselves, as they say, pounding a beat in Canarsie.

The system, by virtue of its inclusiveness, was thus relatively safe. By giving a stake in its undisturbed continuation to as many officers as possible, those who controlled the payoffs did indeed pay a price for the benefits they received, but it was small compared to their share and well worth it since by being inclusive they in effect made grafting so commonplace that few insiders did anything other than take it for granted along with a host of other not so nice practices that are part of big-city policing.

To anyone familiar with life at the Institute, this story of a highly organized scam should be nothing short of disquieting in its familiarity. To begin with, Institute staff, like the police in the narrative, have been engaged in activities that are contrary to their ostensible purpose. Like the police, whose solicitation of graft contradicted their sworn

oath to uphold and enforce the law, the psychologists and computer scientists constituting a preponderance of the Institute's staff have regularly engaged in activities that subvert its proclaimed purpose of open, disinterested inquiry into human perception and information processing. Some, funded by one or another of the armed forces, are busily engaged in projects spoken of in protective generalities if they are spoken of at all. Asked about their work, they may respond by telling you that it is too preliminary to report on, or they may launch into a jargon-filled discourse that when boiled down to its essentials says only that they are studying human perception and information processing. Others work on contracts let by the personnel departments of some large corporations. These contracts cover test development ranging from those intended to assess leadership potential to others presumably for use in determining vulnerability to substance abuse problems. The rights to these tests are owned by the corporations paying for the Institute's work. Thus what looks like research that meets the standards implied in the academic creed is really quite something else. Developing tests for profit-making businesses while relinquishing control over one's work to those businesses hardly qualifies as free and open pursuit of truth for its own sake.

Everybody (or almost everybody) at the Institute seems to be in on what looks very much like a scam (or, in the earlier parlance of this chapter, a research trick). So widespread is participation that the scam is taken as a commonplace not easily distinguishable from research that would in fact pass muster if judged against the ideals the Institute academics, however wayward, invoke at every opportunity. Nobody at the Institute seems the slightest bit troubled by what they and their colleagues have been up to. And little wonder.

While their colleagues who are not members of the Institute have to fund their summer activities by soliciting grants on a competitive basis, Institute members are virtually guaranteed summer support. Ongoing projects yield enough surplus revenues to cover a research associate's summer salary and ancillary activities even if he or she happens to be between funded projects. While the overall university ratio of faculty to secretaries is something in the vicinity of five to one, the comparable ratio at the Institute is two to one. Institute members have easy access to state-of-the-art computer hardware and software regularly upgraded out of surplus revenues, whereas other faculty have to make do with store-bought PCs purchased with either grant funds or their

own dollars. No expensive Pentium processors for them; if they need the kind of speed and power available with a Pentium processor they have to purchase time on the university's crowded mainframe. Members are never without competent research assistants; the Institute's largess is one of the first things incoming graduate students hear about, and many of the best gravitate to those faculty who, because they are in the Institute, can assure them of ongoing financial support. And a research associate who wants to do a bit of traveling doesn't have to think twice about it because of financial constraints. As long as the travel in question appears to be work related, the Institute will, within reason, pick up the tab. Other faculty may get travel money from the university, but the amount is rarely worth the bureaucratic hassles a request for funds is likely to elicit. We should therefore hardly expect those who have been thriving while engaging in activities that bear a superficial resemblance to the pursuit of truth to see the scam for what it is—or even to be alert to its possibility. The Institute specializes in organized research tricking developed to a point where the hustlers hustle themselves along with virtually everyone else. It's the rare professor who would be the envy of a big-city cop, but the cops who ran the scam alluded to in these pages would no doubt admire these professors, seeing in them, as they would, kindred spirits.

Case 4: Her First Time

For a serious academic, the first time you see your words in print ranks right up there with the other memorable firsts in life. It's terribly exciting, and even though modesty dictates feigned denial of ego gratification, it's hard not to feel something roughly akin to afterglow. Of course it's not always that way for everyone. Sometimes it's a bit disappointing, and for more than just a few it may even be accompanied by some pain—the kind of pain nobody in the business likes to talk about.

That's exactly how the graduate student in history experienced it: excitement but some disappointment and more than a little pain. There it was, her first published paper: twenty-eight pages of peer-reviewed, typeset, margin-rectified journal article challenging the sociologically inspired shibboleth about the inability of male slaves to protect female slaves from overseer rape. She ought to have felt very happy, but because of what had happened she couldn't quite get the feeling. She

had done the research as part of her preliminary work for a dissertation on the daily routines of South Carolina plantations in the two decades preceding the firing on Fort Sumter. Having presented the results in the dissertation development seminar to the admiring comments of her student colleagues, she was also encouraged by her adviser to prepare a paper on the subject for publication. She finished the paper at the end of June, when her adviser was away. Rather than wait for his return in September, she decided to submit the paper to one of the leading journals, assuming it would not be accepted but that the feedback she could expect to receive would, in conjunction with the comments her adviser was sure to make on his return, prove useful in revising it for serious submission to another journal. To her surprise and delight, in late August she received a letter from the journal's editor indicating the enthusiasm for the paper he and its reviewers shared. If she agreed to make a few minor revisions, he would be happy to publish the paper. The revisions, he wrote, were more stylistic than substantive, and upon receipt of a revised manuscript he would make the final publication decision without sending it out for further review. Energized by her unexpected success, she made the requested changes and returned the manuscript almost by the next mail. The editor in turn quickly wrote back with his now not surprising decision to publish the piece.

As the fall semester approached, she sought out her adviser to tell him of her good fortune and to thank him for suggesting that she prepare the paper (something, by the way, she had done in writing on the cover sheet). He wasn't in his office, so she left him a note briefly describing what had occurred. On checking her mailbox later that day, she'd found a note from her adviser that, without offering any congratulations, rather tersely summoned her to his office.

What transpired in his office was, she recalled, painfully embarrassing. He was indeed pleased about the publication, but at the same time he was, he said, quite disturbed that she could proceed as far as she had on their paper without so much as a phone call to consult with him. He was not, he continued, accustomed to having his name on a paper he hadn't actually read. True, since she had made a presentation in the seminar, he was well aware of her argument. That was why he had encouraged her in the first place. But she should have been more considerate of his reputation. It would have been a major embarrassment to him had she made one of those graduate student errors that, had he read the paper, would have been corrected. Sending the paper in

with his name on it indicated their joint responsibility for its contents. Had she made such an error, he would look like an incompetent in the eyes of the editor and the reviewers, who by the way could be counted on to circulate their negative opinion of him. History, after all, was a bitchy business.

As he spoke, she felt as though she'd been struck by a cat-o'-nine-tails: no change in position will allow you to retreat from the pain; the hurt will simply follow the rearranged contours of your body. It had never dawned on her that her adviser would expect to be listed as a coauthor of the piece. After all, he hadn't done any of the research, nor was her work part of a larger project that might arguably be attributed to him. True, he had suggested that she write the paper, and, yes, the work had been developed under his thesis supervision, but that hardly seemed to justify a claim to coauthorship. So there she was, being lectured to by an irate professor who no doubt would be even more irate if he found out that she hadn't done what he assumed she had.

Her first impulse was to try to hide what now seemed to be a serious faux pas. She could call the editor and ask that the professor's name be added to the title page. It would be a bit awkward, but she could always say she wanted to share credit with a man who had taught her so much. In the meantime she would redo the title page before giving the professor a copy of the paper. But rearranging the contours couldn't work. Her adviser would surely want to see the editorial comments, and in lavishing his praise on her work, the editor made it clear that he had no more than one author in mind. And what if the editor refused to add the professor's name? While that was unlikely, there might be some reason for such a refusal that she was not aware of. If that happened, then her adviser would not only find out that she hadn't designated him as coauthor at the outset, but he would also become aware of the fact that she had tried to con him into believing she had.

She really had no choice, she quickly and painfully concluded, except to tell him the truth and to plead ignorance of the appropriate etiquette. He seemed understanding, particularly when she admitted how embarrassed she was. Well, maybe it was his fault; he probably should have made certain that she understood the nature of scholarly authorship. So many students, he reflected, had this romantic notion of authorship, of the tortured thinker driven by a thirst for truth and self-expression. It came, he thought, from the soulful artist conception that is so much a part of popular fiction. Of course scholarship was

something else. He was of the opinion that scholars had to learn to accept that they are engaged in a collective enterprise. Well, in any case there was no damage done because she could call the editor and explain that after considering the contributions he'd made, she thought it only fair that her professor's name be added as a coauthor.

So there it was: her first published paper, coauthored as her adviser had requested. The entire incident was discomforting and not the least because she could not really convince herself that she had honorably acquiesced. Looking at the article before her, she couldn't help but think that something had been taken from her and only because she wasn't strong enough to resist.

The Occurrence of Fraud

It is really quite bizarre. The presumptively brightest, in a virtuosic exercise of denial, behave so stupidly that they cannot or will not distinguish the procrastination and laziness in their midst from energetic eagerness and hard work. The self-declared champions of truth and equity cannot or will not distinguish between prevarication and straight talk, honorable purpose and willful abandonment of that purpose, exploitation and helpfulness. Denial is so much a part of the academic's world, apparently so necessary to resolve the conflict between the stringent requirements of the academic creed and the utilitarian calculus motivating the everyday behaviors of most professors, that time and again prominent academics are moved to defend the indefensible by shameless resort to its powers of distortion.

There is nothing more abhorrent to the academic creed than the willful assault on truth that occurs when a researcher falsifies results or procedures. Fraud, unacceptable even in the utilitarian redoubts of business and industry, is supposed to be anathema in the academy, where truth's service presumably replaces money and power as the only acceptable raison d'être. And so it is, in principle. Individual academics employ their not so paltry rhetorical resources in affirmations of scholarly honesty and condemnations of its obverse. The professional associations representing disciplines constituting the current academic firmament all have codes of ethics that condemn dishonest scholarship in no uncertain terms. But when an actual case of fraud comes to the attention of the academic community, the affirmations and condemnations in principle seem to count for very little. When, for

example, John Darsee admitted fraud in his cardiology research at Harvard, the university's report to the National Institutes of Health (NIH), the agency funding the work in question, concluded that none of the published results generated by Darsee's project was fraudulent. An NIH-appointed panel of experts with no connection to Harvard, however, concluded that almost all of Darsee's published work was fraudulent.[27]

When the National Institute of Mental Health (NIMH) after considerable prodding requested that the University of Pittsburgh investigate accusations of research fraud in the work of Stephen Breuning, who was evaluating drug treatment protocols for retarded children with behavior disorders, the university did so but only superficially. Breuning was allowed to resign without a finding of fault and was thus allowed to continue his career. After an examination by its own staff, NIMH concluded that virtually all of Breuning's work was fabricated. Breuning eventually pleaded guilty to research fraud in federal court, but not before his former employer, the University of Pittsburgh, had made it possible for him to continue disseminating false and potentially harmful research reports on the effectiveness of drug therapy.[28]

These are not isolated cases: It was not so long ago that the inspector general of the U.S. Department of Health and Human Services concluded that most universities did not have procedures for dealing with research fraud, and the congressional committee receiving his testimony concluded, "Even those university policies that have been developed are not always followed, resulting in investigations that are *not* timely."[29]

Leading science journals have characteristically closed their pages to papers exposing fraudulent research. For example, without the support of any significant evidence, the editor of *Science,* a major journal published by the American Association for the Advancement of Science, has proclaimed that 99.9999 percent of scientific reports are fraud free.[30] This same journal recently refused to publish the work of Judith P. Swazey and her colleagues, whose survey results offer a serious challenge to its editor's Panglossian position. And God help you if you're a whistle-blower. If, like Heidi Weissmann, you accuse the chief of your division at Albert Einstein College of Medicine of plagiarism and copyright infringement, expect to be locked out of your office and laboratory as well as to lose your faculty appointment, notwithstanding a court decision in your favor. Expect this to happen to

you even as your former colleague, now branded a plagiarist by the courts, receives a promotion.[31] Like Robert Sprague, whose testimony before a House committee forced the hand of NIMH in the Breuning case, expect threats of legal action, not to mention unprecedented cuts in the research funding provided you by some of those your whistle-blowing has embarrassed.[32]

In light of experiences such as these, it's hardly any wonder a study carried out by June Tangney found that less than 50 percent of faculty suspecting fraud in the research of their colleagues did anything to verify their suspicions.[33] Nor is it surprising that Swazey and her colleagues found that while many faculty claimed to endorse an obligation to report research misconduct, they were reluctant to confront it.[34] In both studies the message expressed with undeniable clarity is that since corrective action can be personally costly, it is simply better not to know whether or not your colleagues are proceeding honestly in the execution of their research efforts.

The Power of Denial

Few things in the world are as powerful as academic denial. It has a feel-good, narcotic effect. There is little, it seems, dishonest or injurious enough to move those practiced in the art of self-deception even momentarily to accept the evidence of their senses and act accordingly. Indeed some cases suggest the existence of a causal dynamic between egregiousness and academic denial. The more serious the offense, the greater the potential for injury, the more vigorous it seems is the denial on the part of those who, according to their creed, should be mobilizing against the offense in question. And when you think about it, such a dynamic makes considerable albeit perverse sense. The more serious the offense, the more compelling the demand for action on the part of those sworn to uphold the moral stringencies of the academic creed. But as we have seen, such action is likely to be costly to everyday ambitions and pursuits. The tension between what academics are supposed to do and what they see as in their own best interests is therefore greatest when the observed malfeasance is seriously consequential. Thus the perverse dynamic: the greater the harm or potential for harm the greater the need to deny the existence of the foul so that no action will be required and no guilt will be experienced for failure to have honored the endorsed stringencies.

Unbelievable? Can't happen? There are offenses too serious to be ignored? Well, perhaps. But then what explains such patently outrageous behavior as occurred in the following instance? A number of years ago the national association of sociologists committed to achieving social justice through increasing knowledge of social problems, the Society for the Study of Social Problems (SSSP), bestowed its highest award (the C. Wright Mills Award) on a published study of anonymous homosexual encounters. In itself this would not have been surprising, given the association's purpose. A closer look, however, reveals that this association gave its award to a sociologist, Laud Humphries, who had exploited the very people his study was supposed to help. The SSSP did so even though its membership was aware of uncontroverted allegations of such behavior on the part of the study's author. Furthermore, unless scatological significance is taken for sociological significance and prurience for profundity, the SSSP honored a study that did not make much of a contribution to the understanding of those social issues surrounding homosexual behavior.

Humphries, posing as a "watch queen" (a lookout), made contact with numerous men who engaged in anonymous oral sex in park rest rooms. His observations of the interactions in these public bathrooms constituted one part of his award-winning study (which also earned him a Ph.D. at Washington University).[35] Observations of fellatio, however detailed and jargonized, do not a publishable monograph or even a Ph.D. dissertation make. And so, demonstrating his excellent sociological training and with the encouragement of his faculty mentor, the author decided to collect data on some of the usual "suspects" (read background variables), family and work. But how to accomplish so daunting a task? After all he was disguising his identity and his purpose in order to be in a position that would allow him to record the realities of bathroom orgasm. The men he was observing had no idea they were making a contribution to knowledge, and they certainly had no intention of doing so. To tell them that he wasn't, after all, seeking cheap thrills but the facts about impersonal homosexual encounters would probably result in responses unlikely to yield data on family and work. Demonstrating considerable patience, as well as intrepid qualities not usually associated with academics, Humphries hit on a scheme that would allow him to collect the data he needed. In order to locate the men who visited the bathrooms for sex, he would secretly jot down their license plate numbers and with the connivance of motor vehicle

authorities identify those plates. To avoid recognition by the men he had traced in this way, he would wait a year or so before contacting them and even change his physical appearance. When he met with them, he would tell them he was doing interviews for an ongoing health survey. All this he did, and all this passed muster with his Ph.D. committee, which agreed that no offense to the academic creed had occurred because the purpose of this dissembling was to elicit social scientific truth. And all this was known to the members of SSSP when it honored Humphries and the study. Now, this inspires a riddle you might have trouble with, unless you're an academic social scientist.

Question: When is lying and misrepresentation not dishonest, or (put another way) when is lying and misrepresentation not lying and misrepresentation?

Answer: Apparently, when social scientific truth is at stake.

The ideals of the academic creed cannot countenance the dishonesty in what Humphries did. They cannot abide the exploitative abuse that was part and parcel of the study's execution. Therefore the author's Ph.D. committee should not have allowed such behavior, but it did. The author's university should have refused to award the Ph.D., but it did not. An association of academics claiming principled opposition to any and all forms of human exploitation should have censured the author, his mentors, and his university, but not only did it fail to do so, it actually legitimated the author's efforts by bestowing its most prestigious award upon him.

At each level the tensions between ethical demands and self-interest were considerable, and the denial at each level increased the pressure to deny at the next level. The advisers should not have allowed the dissembling to occur. But stopping it might have required abandoning the entire study. So it doesn't have to be stopped, because while an outsider might see it as unethical behavior, those in the know recognize such behavior as methodologically required in truth's service and thus, contrary to appearances, not unethical.[36] The Washington University administration should not have awarded the Ph.D., but adopting such a course would have been messy indeed. It would have meant a possible lawsuit. It would have meant having to censure not only the graduate student author but his adviser, other members of his committee, and others on the faculty who endorsed the study's procedures.

But as stewards of the academic creed, the university administrators could not justify inaction if there was actual malfeasance. So there was no malfeasance, just scientifically justifiable innovation: no foul, thus no need to call a penalty. SSSP, were it true to its purpose, should have gone on record in opposition to the exploitative methods employed in the study's execution; it should have censured Washington University for rewarding such abuse of unwitting research subjects. But taking such actions would have embroiled the organization in a time-consuming, energy-sapping controversy. It would have meant attacking not only the study but the ethical and methodological judgments of colleagues. It would have placed SSSP in the uncomfortable position of taking an academic institution to task for failing to require the honorable exercise of truth's service. Surely such a posture would have rendered the association vulnerable to an accusation claiming violations of academic freedom. Moreover, any SSSP action would likely have been seized upon both by those who'd keep a tight rein on universities and those who had made it patently clear that they considered the social sciences a threat to American morality.

Clearly organizational self-interest weighed in heavily against any condemnation of the study. But there was also SSSP's purpose, its commitment to the honorable pursuit of truth in the name of social justice. Failure to take any required action would itself be censurable in light of that purpose—unless, of course, no action was required. And what better way for the association's leadership to convince itself and the rank and file that no action was required than to characterize the study as path-breaking and innovative, as brave and bold, as a landmark in the understanding of homosexuality and therefore as a contribution to social justice through social inquiry. Thus was the prurient made profound, the intellectually commonplace (the study uses only the most conventional of sociological elements: interaction, family, work) recast as brilliantly insightful, while these transformations in turn put to rest any lingering concerns about ethics. Condemn the ethical lapses in this study? Censure the faculty who had at least tacitly encouraged dishonesty and exploitation? Criticize a great university for not honoring its oversight obligations? What on earth for? If any irregularities did occur in the course of the study's execution, surely they were more than justified by its genius in behalf of an oppressed and closeted minority. The author wasn't exploiting the men he deceived; he was helping them. Far from being a bad guy, he's a good

guy, a hero of sorts, because he was willing to go ahead with his path-breaking research even though he must have known that those objecting to its subject matter would be after his scalp. His mentors don't deserve censure; if anything they deserve praise for standing behind their courageous protégé. The same, of course, should be said for the university that awarded the author his degree. A lot of places would have backed off from the project for fear of a public uproar and bad publicity. On the whole the university behaved admirably.[37]

Perhaps there are offenses to their creed serious enough to overcome the professorial proclivity to see no evil in anything done by other professors, but the foregoing material strongly suggests they must be limiting cases or otherwise exceptions that prove the rule of self-imposed obliviousness. I'm pretty sure (but not absolutely) that violence as part of a research design could not be explained away as scientifically justified, and I doubt that child pornographers with Ph.D.'s could convince their colleagues that those films and photographs are absolutely necessary to their studies of human sexuality. (I doubt it—but who knows.) Any offense short of instances like these is likely—for the reasons I have noted—to be transformed into its opposite, a praiseworthy exercise in truth's service. Unless what occurred in the case I've just described is dismissed as aberrant and idiosyncratic (and there is little reason to do so, involving as it did what amounts to a representative sample of the social science professoriate), there is no choice except to conclude, as I have, that even the most egregious examples of scholarly malfeasance will likely escape censure precisely because of their egregiousness.

The Importance of the Problem

Okay, so the claims professors make about their scholarly involvements are overblown. And, yes, even extreme cases of malfeasance in the course of a study's execution are likely to be denied by those who would be called upon to intervene if they owned up to what was really going on. That's a shame. They really ought to be less hypocritical. But when you consider all the social, political, moral, and ethical problems requiring our attention, isn't it a bit much to ask that we add bad faith in the study and the laboratory to the list? After all, professors don't constitute a very large group, so even if they are willing to tolerate incompetence and bad faith in their midst, the harm they do is

not likely to have widespread effects. No doubt we ought to be concerned, but not with the same intensity that we reserve for such scourges as poverty, racial violence, narcotics abuse, AIDS, and the degradation of the environment. Next to these, that some professors don't do what they say they're doing and others do what they ought not be doing while their colleagues cheer them on (or at least maintain a discreet silence) pales so as to appear barely significant.

In point of fact such an appearance is more than a little deceiving. Just as it was with their failure to honor teaching obligations (see Chapter 3), the failure of many professors to discharge scholarly obligations in good faith and with the requisite competence has direct and indirect consequences that are both quite far-reaching and costly. In a society as dependent upon expertise and creativity for its economic and social well-being as this one is, such professorial failure cannot be dismissed as a parochial matter, important only to those who work within the academy's environs. It is a problem likely to touch us all in one way or another. Indeed it is a problem that cannot help but reduce our collective effectiveness as we attempt to overcome the more obvious evils in American life. Consider, if you will, the following.

Undermining Creativity

By tolerating and even rewarding unproductive scholars, universities and colleges undermine that creativity which, minimally, might better illumine our lives and, maximally, might contribute solutions to our most wrenching problems. The chummy permissiveness that characterizes too many American campuses can only result in an underutilization of talent, as many academics find that they can lead comfortable professional lives without working hard.[38] It is just too much to expect ordinary human beings to maximize their productivity when virtually everyone is rewarded regardless of productivity and when the rewards differ but little between the most and the least productive individuals.[39] And while there is no assurance that the stick of greater accountability would necessarily lead to major creative breakthroughs, we can be sure that the precious self-congratulation that presently exists in its stead impedes such breakthroughs by rendering them largely irrelevant to rank and emolument.

Furthermore, by granting tenure to those who don't produce—or those whose products pervert the meaning of creative scholarship—

colleges and universities reduce the number of opportunities available to those who would in fact do what they are expected to do. A professor who is granted tenure at the age of thirty-five can occupy a faculty slot (FTE, or full-time equivalent, in academic lingo) for as much as thirty-five years or more. The number of FTEs is not infinitely expandable on a given campus or throughout the academy as a whole. Indeed at this writing it is shrinking. Thus the large number of academics who do little or nothing effectively creates a long-term diversion of resources that might otherwise be used to hire reasonably productive scholars. While it is probably true that the most gifted and productive of scholars will find professional homes nevertheless, there is that substratum of young scholars (not stars or potential stars, just well-trained and hardworking men and women) for whom permanent employment can only mean bussing tables or driving a bus, even as their tenured elders are rewarded for the exertions of "thinking big thoughts." Each of the aforementioned, reward unjustified by effort or results and exclusion by virtue of the unearned tenure awarded to others, leads to underutilization of available talent, and such underutilization undermines the exercise of creativity so necessary to the maximization of human serviceability amidst the complexities of life in our times.

The Effect on Educational Costs

A four-year undergraduate education costs somewhere in the neighborhood of $100,000, inclusive of tuition, books, room, and board. At state-supported schools about one-half of that cost is borne by the taxpayers, leaving individual students or their parents responsible for a still considerable $45,000–$50,000. At privately endowed institutions, the full tariff less scholarship assistance must be borne by students or their families. Law school tuition (just tuition: books, room, and board are not included) can run about $60,000 for three years. Medical school tuition is even higher: approximately $70,000 over a four-year period. All such costs are the responsibility of the students in these programs or their families. If a family tries to put several children through college and professional school, the cost soon becomes astronomical. And although there are various low-interest loan programs available to students, at some point such loans have to be repaid. It is thus not uncommon for recent college graduates to be facing as much

as $25,000 in debt, and the figure can be much higher for those who go on to professional school.

The financial burden of higher education is thus extraordinary, and as many observers have noted, the existence of this circumstance is likely to have some untoward consequences. It has, for example, been argued that the high cost of medical education is ultimately passed on to patients by physicians who must repay their loans, and together with other factors such as high malpractice premiums, this pass-on drives up the cost of medical care. The cost of legal education, it has been suggested, is such that facing the debt burden they do, many law school graduates who might have opted for lower-paying public service careers choose high-paying corporate practices instead. The injury to the commonweal in such a choice is obvious. At the undergraduate level the cost burden can have similar implications by affecting the students' choice of major. If you or your family is faced with thousands of dollars in educational debts, there is the not so subtle pressure to choose a major that is linked to the more remunerative employment opportunities, irrespective of your noneconomic predispositions and the social value of that choice. The precise value of the commonweal's losses in such choice is impossible to calculate, in part, of course, because assigning monetary values to what can fairly be called a misdirection of talent would only underestimate the loss. Suffice it to say that the potential for loss is considerable, involving as it does a reduction in the availability of problem-solving talents.

It would be foolishly incorrect to attribute the soaring cost of higher education,[40] with its attendant negative implications, solely to the waste that comes of less than adequate scholarly productivity and the academy's willingness to reward it. It would, however, be foolishly naïve not to consider the contributory relationship of such waste to the cost spiral.

When faculty members are promoted, their salaries go up. When many of them are promoted even though they have not produced much of anything, their salaries go up without justification. When, as we have seen, faculty are the recipients of merit increases for doing little more than reading newspapers, watching television, and thinking big thoughts, those increases are unjustified. And, when those "merit" increases are factored into the total base pay on which cost-of-living increments are calculated, at least a part of *those* gains is unjustified. It is one thing to confront a cost factor when it is justified by performance and quite another when it is not. Too often those who pay the

tariff for higher education, shelling out ever larger sums and going into inordinate debt to do so, are paying for false claims and unredeemed promises. Plain and simple, the professoriate's penchant for taking care of itself is likely to be unfair and hurtful. In this instance it constitutes the unwarranted expropriation of other people's money and makes an unwarranted contribution to those pressures that result in a socially costly misdirection of talent.

And that isn't all. As noted earlier in this chapter, teaching loads are light, in part because it is assumed that faculty need time to engage in their scholarly pursuits. The norm of light teaching loads is, of necessity, related to increased costs per course. It's simple: If an academic unit is going to offer fifty courses per semester and the expected teaching load per individual is five courses per semester, the unit will have to employ ten full-time faculty. Since the expected teaching load, in reality, is likely to be three courses per semester, the number of full-time professors required to teach the same number of courses will in fact be just about seventeen. If, moreover, the teaching load is two courses per individual for each semester (as it is in most research-oriented universities), the unit will have to employ twenty-five full-time faculty to teach the same fifty courses per semester.[41] It would be considerably less expensive to pay the salaries of ten professors than to pay the salaries of seventeen or twenty-five.

If the rationale for light teaching loads were supportable by reference to what professors actually do, the resulting increased costs per unit of instruction—costs that must be passed on to students, their families, or taxpayers—would have to be accepted, however painful that might be. But the professoriate's proclaimed rationale for light teaching loads is more than just a tad suspect. Taken together, the statistics and the standard practices referred to earlier in this chapter strongly suggest that there are large numbers of professors for whom the rationale is inapplicable. They simply do not engage in the scholarship that justifies their light teaching loads. In each such instance, then, the contribution to higher instructional costs made by the light teaching load is unwarranted and constitutes a waste factor that must be regarded as unfair. The cost per instructional unit (or course) could be considerably reduced if all those faculty members who don't really do the research they claim to do were required to increase their teaching loads by even a single course per semester, and some could justifiably be required to add two courses per semester.

The Intrusion of the Cash Nexus

Before drawing this contemplation of negative consequences to a close, I must make special mention of research tricking. While they make much of their devotion to a higher morality in truth's service, academics, I have argued, either typically ignore or actively encourage the intrusion of the cash nexus into their world. Research tricking means selling your intelligence and your skills to the highest bidder. It means, therefore, that research agendas will be determined by the ability to pay, over and above considerations of contribution to the common good. Those who trick and those who allow tricking to occur contribute to an environment in which the dollar sign sets priorities. And where tricking is an established practice, contributions to human well-being must, protestations to the contrary notwithstanding, suffer. The biochemist who sells his skills to the Department of the Army for one of its pet biological weapons projects is not only depriving his fellow citizens of research efforts that might benefit them in their struggle with disease and pain, but he is as well creating something that, when used, is supposed to inflict disease and pain on others. The engineer who has hopped aboard the armament express might otherwise put her expertise to use in solving the mass transit problems that threaten to strangle our metropolitan areas. The psychologist whose studies of persuasion serve only the interests of the advertising firms that have commissioned them might otherwise be providing teachers with some guidance on how best to teach recalcitrant learners. Tricking has the sorry consequence of drawing academic talent into the creation of those things that can only injure and away from those things that might conceivably help in our struggle to avoid injury. It is thus hardly a parochial matter.

The Need for Correction

It is true that other problems are more immediate in their devastation, but the academic malpractice that is born of mis- and malfeasance, their denial, and therefore their unwarranted tolerance in the academy has an importance that we can ignore only at considerable peril. Such malpractice must sooner or later hurt us all by rendering higher education costlier than it needs to be and diminishing the professoriate's capacity for making contributions to the solution of those problems

that do in fact steal pieces of our lives. When academics are guilty of scholarly malpractice or when they tolerate and reward such malpractice, they are little better than those they profess to oppose with all the strength at their disposal: the utilitarian hucksters who subvert the dreams and aspirations of their fellows while pursuing a rapacious self-interest.

If the past few pages betray an urgency that appears unseemly to some, I would plead the occasion by suggesting that time is not on the side of the angels where scholarly malpractice is concerned. Nor is it, for that matter, where pedagogical malpractice is concerned. If the situation is not soon made better, it will soon get worse. Every time scholarly malpractice occurs and denial makes a mockery of academic accountability, the probabilities of repetition are increased. Scholars who go unpunished for their mis- or malfeasance are more likely to commit offenses a second time than they were the first time, more likely a third time than the second, more likely a fourth time than the third. The offense is least likely to occur when the virginal perpetrators, not actually knowing that they will not be called to account, hesitate. But once experience confirms what they had only sensed before, hesitation becomes less and less probable. Every time, moreover, a faculty enters into the conspiracy of silence that is denial, it becomes more apt to do so again. Collective acts of accountability somewhere down the line would call into question earlier inaction in the same or similar circumstances. Thus while the early conspiracies are entered into to avoid the conflict between utilitarian self-interest and the stringencies of the academic creed, later conspiracies are likely to be entered into for that reason and for the additional reason of denying past denials. As faculties become increasingly habituated to denial, the academic environment becomes more and more permissive, the sins of mis-and malfeasance more likely, and in turn the need to deny more and more intense in a spiral of betrayal where hurtful consequences will only intensify as well. Time will not heal. On the contrary, time's passing can only cumulate the offenses and thereby intensify the injury.

Chapter 5

The Spurious Shield of Specialness

The Need for Reform

I want the academy to change. I want an end to its pretentiousness, its laziness, its license, and its wastefulness. I want an end to the permissiveness that comes of the remarkable capacity for delusion and denial possessed by so many academics. I want an end to the injury that all this visits upon students and others who have naïvely placed their faith in the professoriate's self-proclaimed honorable intentions. There are in our daily lives problems of considerable magnitude that need the attention of well-educated men and women, but our institutions of higher learning appear to be more committed to the growth of faculty comforts and perquisites than they are to ensuring that their students have the opportunity to become well educated. Many of these problems cry out for research that academics might do but don't simply because, contrary to what they would have nonacademics believe, professors do not have to engage in research to survive or even to thrive.

I want the academy to change because if it is allowed to continue as it is presently constituted, things can only get worse. Without change in the short run, our colleges and universities will cumulatively become little more than another massive drain on our scarce resources, a sector characterized by financial insatiability while the realization of its ostensible purpose is just an illusion. Unless there is change in the academy, we will awaken one day to a depletion of ideas and expertise so considerable that the continued viability of our way of life will have been cast into doubt.[1] After thirty-plus years within the belly of the beast,

144

I can only conclude that it is out of control and bent on a course that is frighteningly consequential.

The Problem of Corroboration

I have some ideas about what needs to be done to reform the academy, and I will develop them in concluding this contemplation of higher learning's troubled condition. Before doing so, however, I would like to turn my attention to one more issue. Because colleges and universities are so important to the way we live, lay readers in particular may well require considerable certainty about widespread academic malpractice and its toleration before they commit themselves to any course of action intended to reform those institutions. In other words, before they start fixing the academy, they will want to be sure it's broken. If I were such a reader, I would not be prepared to act solely on the basis of the first four chapters of this book. I'd be upset by what I had read and I'd be prepared to act if I had some independent corroboration of what these chapters purport to indicate, but without such corroboration I'd be cautious indeed about pressing for change. I would take the contents of these pages to constitute an indictment, but there is considerable difference between an indictment and a verdict. Before enlisting in the cause of academic reform, I would need a verdict of guilty as charged.

The problem of corroboration is a thorny one, since the pertinent facts are not readily available. Delusion and denial, central to the thrust of the indictment, do not leave a clear statistical trail. If delusion and denial do characterize the academic environment as charged, in their very nature they would operate to transform evidence of wrongdoing into something else. Merit money would never be awarded to faculty who were without merit because colleagues would manage to find or fabricate some reason to pronounce them meritorious. In the presence of delusion and denial, failure to teach will be explained away as at worst a flawed but good-faith search for a more effective pedagogy; sexual harassment will too often be given the *Rashomon* treatment, lending credence to the assertion that the truth of the matter cannot be ascertained; and ethical lapses in the execution of research will often enough be recast as brave and bold methodological innovations. What's worse, given the need for delusion and denial, we can expect that most wrongdoing will never even be consciously apprehended

because it simply will not be seen by those academics who have used the principle of academic freedom to render themselves honorably (so they believe) and blissfully blind. The stringencies of the academic creed mean that seeing would require costly interventions, and thus using the broadest interpretation of academic freedom as their justification, academics do not see because looking is presumably forbidden.

So in these last pages I am faced with a dilemma. On the one hand, my experience and the inquiries I've undertaken have convinced me that serious malpractice exists in the academy and that far-reaching reform is urgently required. In pursuit of that end, I am prepared to ask my readers to do whatever is necessary to bring about changes such as those I propose later in this chapter. On the other hand, I know that if I were a reader who came to these pages without years of intimate familiarity with the academy, I would be wary of responding to any clarion call for fear of unnecessarily disrupting an institution so important to the way we live. It's frustrating. I know something to be so. I know it to be hurtful in the present, and I am convinced of its potential for escalating damage in the future. I thus feel compelled to cry out in warning and appeal for support of an undertaking whose goal is an academic future not foretold in present academic practice. And yet I know that even if my warning is taken seriously, my appeal for action will not be as compelling as I would like it to be. I have simply not unearthed enough evidence independent of my experiences and those of my informants (however well placed) to convince even people who have carefully followed my argument that the true bill indictment it constitutes should be treated as a verdict.

The Next Step

Were I to follow the traditional intellectual etiquette in this situation, I would back off. I would write something to the effect that proof of my assertions and arguments is really not required since all I have been trying to do is to raise some important issues. Having done that, I would continue, I can rest content in the belief that what I have written will cause others to include the problem of academic malpractice in their ongoing discourses. My proposals for reform, I would conclude, are thus to be understood as no more than hypotheticals like everything that has come before them in these pages, set down to stimulate discussion.

But if I were to invoke such a disclaimer, I would be dishonest. I have not written this book as an exercise in consciousness-raising. And I will not be satisfied to have stimulated cocktail-hour conversation, no matter how animated. I have written these pages because I believe there is trouble in our academic paradise—enough trouble to warrant a mobilization in behalf of its extensive reform. And thus if I am unable to sound a compelling call to arms, I will have failed to accomplish what I set out to accomplish. The dilemma I have alluded to is consequently something more than a literary conceit, and my purpose requires that I try to find some way of transcending its frustrations.

To do so I will need the active cooperation of those who, having read the first four chapters of this book, agree that they constitute a true bill. I will need their willingness to embrace the literal meaning of *indictment* and to *act* accordingly. Although an indictment does not require the action a guilty verdict would, it is not the case that it requires no action at all. An indictment constitutes a finding of reasonable cause for an assertion of wrongdoing that, if proven, would call for remedial action. While of itself an indictment cannot mandate remediation, it can and does mandate further weighing of the charges in pursuit of a verdict that might quite possibly require it. It is in the spirit of this meaning that I appeal to those who have found these pages disquieting. If you believe that I have rendered a true bill on the serious matter of academic malpractice, then as a next step weigh the charges it contains and deliver yourselves of a verdict.

I am aware that this appeal may appear to be puzzling. After all, it seems to ask that those who respond accomplish a task I have argued may be next to impossible. But I really have something else in mind. I am not appealing for a coordinated investigation intended to weigh the reality of academic malpractice as a general phenomenon. Granted, I have made my charges at that level, and I am certain enough of them to call for an equally general overhaul of the academic system. But given the limitations imposed by the difference between an indictment and a verdict, a difference implying the need for factual corroboration that will at best be difficult to achieve, it makes sense to embrace a strategically more modest course—at least at the outset. My appeal is thus not for an investigation of academic malpractice in general but for an inquiry into the *possibility* of such malpractice at those specific colleges and universities to which my readers are in some way connected.

Virtually everyone has some connection—some consequential con-

nection—with at least one college or university. Some of us are alumni, or we are currently enrolled as students. Others of us are parents called upon to pay thousands of dollars in tuition and fees. And if we are not alumni, students, or parents, we are taxpayers whose obligation it is to underwrite public higher education. My appeal to those who believe that I have established a prima facie case for the reality of widespread malpractice is simply this: Use your consequential connection with at least one college or university to move its academic guardians to respond to the charges of malpractice contained in these pages.

Colleges and universities recognize the need for good public relations. Almost all have offices of public affairs; some even retain big-time lobbyists to protect their interests in the halls of power. There isn't an institution of higher learning that doesn't employ several full-time staff whose job it is to keep alumni happy. Those who administer colleges and universities are acutely aware of the fact that the well-being of their institutions depends upon external support. (This awareness is particularly acute when, as is now the case, colleges and universities are faced with serious fiscal problems.) They really don't need their Ph.D.'s to understand that there is no such thing as a self-sufficient, self-contained college or university. Up to this point these administrators have been free to set their own agendas when dealing with their institutions' publics. The profusion of glossy alumni magazines; the artistically lithographed annual reports to parents, students, and alumni; the fact sheets released to legislators all suggest that faculty have been hard at their tasks of teaching and scholarship. The message delivered by these publications is this: We have been doing an excellent job of educating those who come to us for that purpose, and we have been faithfully serving truth through the application of scholarly ingenuity. So alumni, parents, students, fellow citizens, please continue to support us.

Recognizing that there does exist among academic managers some sensitivity about institutional image, those who have questions about malpractice should now ask them of these managers in no uncertain terms. They must insist upon responsiveness to an agenda not determined by the university's vice president for public affairs but rather by themselves—alumni, students, parents, and friends of the university whose continued support is deemed consequential to its well-being.

There are questions that can and should be asked and once asked,

answered. If no answers are forthcoming, or if the answers are not responsive, that in itself should be taken into account when weighing the accuracy of the charges contained in the true bill. I am convinced that the asking of these questions as they pertain to specific institutions of higher learning will yield enough evidence of trouble to validate this book's indictment, at least so far as those institutions are concerned. If concrete questions focusing on teaching loads and scholarly productivity are asked and answered with appropriate documentation, I am convinced they will yield a picture that casts considerable doubt on the justice of light teaching assignments. If concrete questions about the relation between professorial effectiveness (e.g., scholarly productivity and teaching skill) and merit compensation are asked and answered, again with appropriate documentation, I am convinced that the presumed direct correlation between demonstrated excellence and reward will receive less support than would be expected. If asked about it, spokespersons for many of these institutions will not be able to document effective disciplinary responses to willful professorial malfeasance. Nor will they be able to demonstrate how their institutions have moved to reduce the incidence of professorial misfeasance. Some spokespersons will doubtless refuse to respond to such queries, politely suggesting that because of the widely accepted norms of academic freedom, they represent an inappropriate intrusion. Some, I am sure, will cite academic freedom as the reason for their institutions' justifiable inattentiveness to behaviors that, they admit, might turn out to be examples of academic malpractice. Of course, if contrary to my expectations such queries elicit responses that cast doubt upon the indictment brought in these pages, if the schools can document the legitimacy of their teaching loads, the direct correlation between the professional effectiveness of their faculty members and the extent to which they are rewarded, the characteristic existence of effective disciplinary procedures as well as measures routinely taken to reduce the incidence of misfeasance—if all of this can be documented, there will be nothing further to do (except perhaps deposit this volume in the nearest recycling bin). But if my expectations are indeed borne out, what was simply an indictment will have become a guilty verdict applicable to many of those schools to which the questions have been directed. Remediation will then have been mandated.

The following set of questions might fairly be posed in an attempt to weigh the validity of the indictment at specific institutions:

A Protocol of Interrogatories

1. During the past five years, what has been the faculty's characteristic teaching load? How many courses per semester has each professor taught? On average, how many contact hours (hours in the classroom) does this course load represent?
2. Over the past five years, what has been the average ratio of courses taught more than twice by a faculty member to total courses taught by that faculty member?
3. During the past five years, what percent of the faculty has published at least one authored monograph or book? What percent has published at least one edited book?
4. During the past five years, what percent of the faculty has averaged the publication of at least one paper every year? What percent has averaged the publication of at least one paper every other year?
5. During the past five years, what percent of the faculty has failed to publish either a book (authored or edited) or a paper? (Book reviews should not be counted as published papers since they are not subject to editorial decision making.)
6. Does the institution have any rules requiring documentation of publication claims? If so, what are they?
7. Of those faculty who have published nothing during the past five years, what percent have received salary increases presumably attributed to meritorious performance? Were these salary increases justified by reference to meritorious performance in teaching and/or public service? If so, what documentation was required pursuant to these justifications?
8. What was the mean percent merit increase for those identified in question seven above? What was the mean percent merit increase for those faculty who have published no books and less than one paper every other year during the relevant five-year period?
9. Does the institution have explicit procedures for adjudicating charges of professorial misconduct? If it does, what are they and how often have these procedures been used during the past decade? If the institution does not have such procedures, why is this so?

10. During the past decade what would the institution's president or provost (acting as its chief academic officer) identify as the most serious case of professional misconduct to have occurred? What was the institution's disposition of this case?

I know how easy it is to dismiss this appeal as a kind of literary gimmick. It does have that hortatory ring that thoughtful readers will no doubt associate with stump speeches delivered by politicians who really don't expect to be taken all that seriously. "Does he really think laypeople who already have many demands placed on their time and energy will engage academicians in so serious an inquiry and even confront them with insistent petitions for reform? And does he really believe that pressure brought to bear by outsiders can successfully elicit change, assuming such change is necessary?" Please be assured that however hortatory my appeal may sound, it is nevertheless meant to be taken quite seriously. The stakes are too high for anything else. Yes, I do expect busy people to take on the burdens implied by the actions in question. Again, the stakes are too high for these burdens to be shirked. And while external pressure for the reform of a particular college or university may indeed be insufficient to bring about its accomplishment, exerting such pressure is nevertheless the only tactic with a realistic probability of success. The priesthood, it has been said, never reforms itself. Well, academicians are nothing if they are not secular priests whose very traditions blind them to the existence of conditions in their midst requiring reform. If the preponderance of academicians could be depended upon to correct what needs to be corrected in their work venues, the circumstances informing the first four chapters of this book would not exist. Since experience and inquiry have convinced me they do, I can only conclude that the matter of academic reform is far too serious to be left to professors and administrators. (Even those struggling to reform their institutions will need the help of outsiders.) However long the odds, academic reform and the revitalization of our institutions of higher learning will occur only if and when academics can no longer manipulate their significant lay publics or otherwise take them for granted. So, far from being a gimmick, my appeal constitutes a last best hope. Please weigh the charges contained in the indictment as they apply to a college or university of your choosing, and if you find that institution guilty as charged, enlist in the struggle for its reformation.

The Presumption of Specialness

During the course of the twentieth century, American academics have sold the public at large as well as themselves on a characterization of colleges and universities that makes of them special institutions, special in their presumed service to humanity's laudable pursuit of truth's variety and special in their presumed responsiveness to a creed whose moral and ethical requirements are far more stringent than those governing social intercourse in the more numerous redoubts of worldly utilitarianism. Throughout this book I have argued, on the contrary, that the only thing rendering most colleges and universities special is their appalling willingness to tolerate and even encourage behaviors that in less "special" work settings would incur the wrath of superiors as well as fellow workers and would therefore result in disciplinary responses acceptable to both labor and management. Moreover, I have attributed this latter specialness (hardly admirable by any stretch of the imagination) to the distortions of reality inherent in the bill of goods constituting the former.

It should come as no surprise, then, that my recommendations for academic reform are inspired by the following premise:

> Eschewing the timeworn and counterproductive assumptions of specialness, institutions of higher learning should be treated as ordinary work settings, and faculty, however demanding their assigned tasks, as ordinary workers.

Since in my view the academicians' claim to specialness has resulted in an epidemic of misfeasance and malfeasance, that claim must be abandoned if the epidemic is to be brought under control. Once the presumption of specialness has been cast aside, colleges and universities will be free to negotiate with their employees, their faculties, just as General Electric, United Airlines, Columbia Presbyterian Hospital, the New York City Police Department, and social service agencies across the country do with theirs. Such negotiations, over work rules, salaries, productivity, and most important, the issue of accountability, can constitute occasions for candor, something I think the illusion of specialness has kept in short supply on American campuses. And out of these negotiations we might hope to see our colleges and universities become what too often they now are not: places where a fair day's work can be expected in return for a fair day's pay.

I can hear the howls of outrage, those self-righteously indignant arias delivered by professors who find such a suggestion unthinkable, an insult that in the past would have called for satisfaction on a field of honor. "Whatever can he mean by proposing that there ought to be some similarity between the way General Electric is run and the way our institutions of higher learning are run?" "How in the world can he suggest that professors be considered employees of the university? They *are* the universities." "I suppose next he'll propose a profit-making university that raises capital by selling shares on the stock exchange!" "Truth is not a commodity and scholars are not workers. Inspiration and insight are not subject to work rules!" "If you abandon the academy's specialness, you will have to abandon academic freedom, and truth's service will then fall under the oppressive control of the yahoos and know-nothings!"

The misfeasant and malfeasant, of course, will yelp the loudest, since they rightly view any change as a threat to the permissiveness that makes the academy so attractive to them. But even well-meaning professors, including the few who would agree that the accusations leveled in these pages are by and large valid, can be expected to raise their voices in angry defense of the academy's specialness, so habituated are they to that seductive assumption. While the former don't deserve to be taken seriously, and while it probably won't do much good to address the anxieties of the latter (were I to assume otherwise, there would be no need to appeal for pressure on behalf of change from "outsiders"), those anxieties simply have no basis in reality.

Abandoning the assumption of specialness does not of necessity mean throwing in your lot with those whose only measure of success is black ink on the bottom line. Nonprofit institutions like hospitals and social service agencies, institutions arguably no less critical than colleges and universities to the public's well-being, operate with fairly ordinary organizational assumptions. Their functions, curing and caring, remove them from those orbits where greed and pecuniary competition hold sway; nevertheless, management and labor in these institutions characteristically negotiate situationally specific work rules, compensation levels, as well as accountability procedures.

Abandoning the assumption of specialness does not mean giving up academic freedom, although it will no doubt result in a far narrower construction of its meaning. What we will probably witness, and what is to be devoutly hoped for, is a return to the original meaning of academic freedom, where the freedom to teach and write is defined by

the dictates of one's discipline and only by these dictates, but where consequently professors take seriously their professionally mandated oversight obligations. Abandoning the assumption of specialness does not even necessitate the abandonment of tenure. It would remain on the academic scene, but as in the case of academic freedom, it would revert to something near its original meaning. Like civil servants who have passed their probationary periods, tenured professors would indeed be subject to dismissal—but only for some work-related cause. Put as directly as possible, the end of academic specialness means nothing other than the end of the academic self-conceptions and practices typically implicated in the delusive permissiveness that fosters professorial malpractice. If professors continue to defend the special status quo, that's their prerogative. But those campaigning for academic reform should not allow them to do so under the banner of a just cause. Theirs is little more than a defense of ease and comfort unjustified by anything commonly associated with the academic mission.

The abandonment of academic specialness must begin with some clear-eyed consideration of two interrelated questions. First, what are the requirements of the social contract between institutions of higher learning and their significant publics—in other words, what is the real quid pro quo that trades function for support? Second, what are the interests that really motivate the work of academics?

The Academic Mission

If you want to know the answer to the first question, stay away from commencements and other such convocations. On these occasions academics, done up in the medieval regalia of their orders (aka disciplines), assert the heroic and thus misleading version of their mission. In a manner so solemn as to conjure up a mood of priestly reverence, they voice pieties that probably have never had much basis in fact—and that most certainly do not now. To hear them tell it, their mission is first and foremost to serve truth and by doing so, society, albeit indirectly. By unraveling cosmic riddles, cracking nuclear and genetic codes, and demystifying social relations; by making the unconscious conscious; by unveiling the deep structure of human syntax and casting healing beams of light upon the dark, hurting places of the soul; by doing all this in full view of the young, academics, we are told, serve society and all humankind. Such service frequently goes

unappreciated, but professors are committed to rendering it, and it is the only service academics offer in return for the beneficence of their significant publics. There is no greater good, they proclaim, than the truth; thus those who serve truth serve the cause of human well-being. Philosopher-kings, they deserve (but do not always get) such support as befits their princely stature.

In reality the social contract between institutions of higher learning and their publics assumes that academics will perform functions far more mundane and directly responsive to socially determined agendas. As I have noted earlier (in Chapter 2), the complexity of modern living has led to the valuing of colleges and universities on the assumption that they are the institutions that can be relied upon to train those who are necessary to the management of that complexity. Moreover, because the existence of such complexity has spawned an unremitting need for sophisticated inventiveness, colleges and universities have also become valued because of their presumed commitment to stimulate and nurture such creativity.

The last thing in the world that academics want to own up to is the fact that they are engaged in a fairly down-to-earth exchange based on their presumed ability to deliver on a promise to train those who will manage the complexities of our lives and to create or discover sophisticated solutions to the problems fostered by such complexity. But that is precisely what they are engaged in. Notwithstanding the commencement rhetoric and regalia, which together communicate an almost unworldly specialness, academics are engaged in activities that are both worldly and quite ordinary. The reform of our colleges and universities must therefore begin with those activities. Their requirements must guide any and all proposals intended to replace the present milieu of irresponsible permissiveness with one of reasonable accountability.

Professorial Motives

If heroic representations of collective academic purpose bear scant relation to reality, so, too, do accompanying heroic representations of the motives that drive individual academics. Professors, as we have seen, are prone to present themselves as selfless seekers and purveyors of truth's variety, as people whose passion for truth is so great that in its service they are willing to sacrifice those rewards which their intelligence and training would bring in other venues. To hear them—particularly when

outsiders are within earshot—it would be difficult to find any other professionals whose motivation equals theirs in its purity. Practicing physicians? Attorneys? Just look at the money they pull down. College professors have known from the day they began their years of arduous training (seven or eight to the physician's five or six and the attorney's three) that their incomes would never be commensurate with what other professionals routinely expect. And yet they went ahead with these years of study and continue to follow their dreams in relative penury even as their friends in the other professions accumulate considerable wealth.

No doubt there are some professors whose motives conform to such a characterization, but the vast majority, even those who do their work competently and honor the expectations of their profession, have been motivated in considerable measure by their appreciation of the fact that a faculty appointment is a good gig. Surely the readers of this book do not have to be reminded that many professors are paid full-time salaries for what is in effect part-time work. Even those who honor all their obligations to the colleges and universities employing them have between three and four months of free time each academic year (not to mention the one year in seven given to a partially paid sabbatical). Any obligations undertaken during such periods are almost invariably accompanied by extra salary. And readers ought by now to be well aware that academics' comings and goings during the school year are largely their own business. I sometimes think professors must be an extraordinarily healthy bunch, judging from the fact of their under-used sick leave. Of course, in reality, they get sick about as often as anyone else, but although they're as likely as anyone else—and perhaps more so— to rest and recuperate, they rarely if ever use their sick leave; they simply don't have to. Let us not forget, moreover, the fringe benefits that really ought to be figured into an academic's typical compensation package. Most institutions will not go as far as the business school at one of our elite universities, where faculty are given expense accounts of $10,000 per annum above salary; but no faculty at any college or university has to pay rent on an office, none has to ante up for secretarial assistance, many find personal computers in their offices delivered gratis by their employers, all have the right to order library materials at their employer's expense,[2] and subject to budget considerations, all faculty can make claims on travel moneys typically provided to underwrite work-related journeys. Finally, despite some ambivalence toward

them by the general public, professors enjoy considerable popular prestige. Studies of occupational prestige consistently rank them right up near the top, slightly below physicians but above such highly rated occupations as architects, corporate managers, and artists. All in all, a very good gig—very good indeed.

Now there is nothing wrong with choosing a profession in large measure because working conditions are excellent and compensation levels are at least very good. There's no reason why, given a real interest in both the substance and methods of professorial performance, academic aspirants shouldn't choose to join the profession because the jobs its members hold are, comparably speaking, very good jobs. Such motivation is not (or should not be) suspect; it is not unethical. But it is also not heroic, and consequently it is not particularly special. Whatever their heroic self-conceptions, academics are little different from anyone else who works for a living. They want to be well compensated; they want opportunities to get ahead; they want respect for what they do, safe and reasonably comfortable surroundings, paid vacations, good health insurance, and a liberal retirement plan. None of these desires is censurable; but none is particularly applaudable either. They are simply what you'd expect from any working adult.

Academics nonetheless have claimed heroic motivation since it enhances their work-related freedoms. Because, however, the claim for most is patently false, it has only resulted in taking unjustified liberties by some, while the rest, responding to the conflict between claim and reality, neither hear nor see what their wayward colleagues are doing. Thus those seeking to reduce the incidence of mis- and malfeasant professional conduct would do well to campaign for reforms anchored in the ordinary realities of academic motives as opposed to the hyperbolic heroism whose invocation seems only to deprive so many professors of their senses.

Reform, in sum, must be based on an awareness that no matter how heroic their claims, colleges and universities fulfill ordinary functions, even as they employ people whose job motivations would hardly qualify them for seats at King Arthur's table.

Reform 1: Performance Contracting

The first reform I recommend is the adoption of individualized performance contracting as the basic personnel mechanism governing the

employment and tenure of faculty members. In principle a performance contract constitutes an agreement entered into by employer and employee that specifies a compensation-for-services-rendered exchange in force for a given period of time. In academic practice these agreements would cover such matters as:

1. the relative emphasis given to teaching or research by individual faculty members
2. the nature of a faculty member's service obligation
3. compensation levels for the duration of the contract inclusive of any salary increases and their timing
4. procedures for performance evaluation and contract renewal or renegotiation.[3]

Individual performance contracting has at least two advantages over the present system, which is both vague and rooted in the heroic and therefore inaccurate conceptions of institutional function and faculty motivation. To begin with, performance contracting allows for flexibility in meeting the college or university's functional requirements. As noted, the two main functions are *educative,* or the training of individuals competent to manage complexity, and *creative,* or the stimulation and nurture of imaginative responses to the problems presented by such complexity. Different institutions, however, are characterized by the different priorities they give to one function or the other. Some, like the major research universities, weight the latter more heavily than the former. Some tend toward a mix that is more or less equal. Some, like the state colleges, emphasize the former to the virtual exclusion of the latter. Moreover, within a given institution some units or departments may favor one function over the other. In technical universities, for example, the engineering and science departments are likely to give the two functions equal weight, whereas the social science and humanities departments are likely to emphasize the educative function over the creative function. Instead of proceeding with the currently established fiction that all faculty are both teachers and researchers who consequently need light teaching loads so that they may serve their scholarly interests, performance contracting allows institutions to enter into a variety of agreements with individual faculty, recognizing that not all institutions place an equal premium on scholarship and neither do individual faculty. Contracting would allow col-

leges and universities to up the teaching loads of faculty who are not expected to do much research during the period the agreement is in force. Conversely, it would allow them to reduce teaching loads for researchers when circumstances warrant such a reduction. In the former instance it would be a matter of record that the faculty members in question are being compensated for competent execution of their teaching responsibilities. In the latter instance the record would indicate that the faculty in question are being compensated for competent research.

If we consider the waste and cost problems that now occur because of unwarranted light teaching loads, the adoption of individualized performance contracting appears to hold out the promise of a significant change for the better. Where now faculty teach as few as four courses a year because they "need" time for research they are not in fact engaged in, these same faculty could be induced or, if necessary, required to teach as many as ten courses per academic year. In institutions where research is not a high priority, increases in individual teaching loads can reduce average class size (thus creating a potentially more effective learning environment) and reduce the size of the faculty. The latter could be expected to lower the costs of instruction, which would undoubtedly constitute a brake on those runaway financial circumstances that now threaten to put a college education out of reach for so many Americans. Even at those institutions where research is a top priority, faculty members who are less involved in research than their colleagues could be expected to increase their teaching, both improving learning environments and lowering instructional costs.

There are those who will no doubt object to performance contracting for increased teaching on the premise that it will create an increased presence of the least competent in the classroom, which, if it occurred, would certainly be regrettable. I believe, however, that the objection is groundless. First, it is based upon an academic piety with little more than rhetorical standing: that only accomplished scholars at the postsecondary level can be effective classroom teachers. But as best as we can tell, some of the most effective classroom teaching is done by graduate students (who, by definition, are not accomplished scholars). Second, performance contracting can bestow new respect upon the instructional function among academics, thus creating incentives to teach, even on the part of the most gifted. Although teaching is

supposed to be the coequal of scholarship on the present academic scene, in reality it takes a backseat to scholarship as a component of academic self-conception and professional identity. As a rule, academics receive no systematic pedagogical training (as graduate students, they do a lot of teaching, but little attention is given to their preparation and supervision), and institutional reputations depend more upon scholarship than they do upon teaching. While almost every academic, even those at institutions where research is not a priority, professes to be working on a project that promises a major scholarly breakthrough, you are not likely to hear similar devotional paeans to their pedagogy. Individualized performance contracting would render teaching more than a mere adjunct to scholarship. It would indicate in no uncertain terms that teaching is a career line consistent with the importance of the academy's educational function, that for some, at least, effective teaching can constitute the sole requirement for professional advancement. It would indicate clearly and unequivocally that salary increases and named chairs await productive teachers as well as productive scholars. Once it is no longer a mere add-on, college and university teaching would not attract only those who cannot do otherwise. Individualized performance contracting can transform teaching itself into a first choice for academics who presently hide their pedagogical proclivities as though they are just a bit shameful. Performance contracting is the best hope for the emancipation of closet pedagogues and as such holds out the promise of enhancing the ability of colleges and universities to execute one of the two functions their publics require of them.

If a major goal of reform is increased academic accountability, then the second advantage of individualized performance contracting is that it would require faculty work efforts to be evaluated and could specify how such evaluations would be used in future contract negotiations. No one who has read the earlier chapters of this book can be comfortable with current evaluative practice (if it may even be called that) on American campuses. Theoretically, there is an annual peer review of collegial efforts based largely on self-reports. In reality these reviews are superficial at best, finding merit (albeit in varying degrees) in virtually everything every faculty member claims to have done or to be doing. The current system is permissive in the extreme, creating the illusion of accountability even as it rewards people for doing ill or doing nothing at all.

Individualized performance contracting, however, can result in an evaluative system that, if imperfect, would nevertheless represent a considerable improvement on the present. If, for example, a contract specifies teaching as the primary service to be rendered, it would also specify how, when, and by whom the employee's teaching performance will be evaluated. If, alternatively, research or a combination of research and teaching constitutes the primary service(s) rendered during its duration, the contract would specify an evaluative mechanism intended to be responsive to whichever specification is emphasized. Instead of assuming that evaluation will occur as a matter of course and will focus upon both research and teaching in roughly equal measure (as in the present illusory system), performance contracting would set up an enforceable requirement while tailoring the contractually mandated evaluation to what in fact a given professor has been hired to do. Moreover, beyond the specifics of each case, writing both evaluative method and emphasis into negotiated contracts will draw attention to accountability issues. Increased awareness of and attention to these issues would, in my view, constitute the best insurance we can have against the superficiality that presently makes a sham of so much academic evaluation.

Oh yes—the critics are stirring again: "C'mon now. Earlier you argued that tenure could remain part of the academic system. How can that be so if performance contracting is adopted?" "See, it's just like we said. You're recommending the destruction of academic freedom. Performance contracting is a pretext for the micromanagement of academic work, and that's got to be the death of academic freedom." "What's more, if there are problems with the present evaluative system, its hard to see how performance contracting really represents a new departure. Nothing guarantees that individually contracted evaluations will be superior to those which now apply across the board to all faculty. Since the same people will be doing these evaluations, what makes you think they will be more responsible than they are now?"

Contrary to what the critics might argue, tenure and performance contracting can coexist quite comfortably. After a faculty member has been awarded tenure, that person's performance contracts can continue to be the bases for establishing levels of compensation and accountability requirements. Where, however, failure to perform up to established standards during a single contract period could conceivably and might likely lead to a decision not to reappoint a nontenured faculty

member, that would not be the case for those enjoying tenure. For such faculty, failure to perform up to the explicit standards contained in the performance contract would be used to adjust compensation levels downward during the period of the next contract. (Dare I say it? This is somewhat like the situation for professional athletes.) If the failure to perform persisted over several contracts, a record of sustained mis- or malfeasance would have been established and that record could be used as cause for dismissal. Remember, in its original form tenure did not rule out dismissal for cause. If a nonprobationary employee (a tenured professor) has, by the record of his or her past performance, earned a greater margin of tolerance than a probationary employee (a nontenured professor), dismissal would occur only when that margin had been exceeded over several contract periods. In the recent past, faculty have rarely moved to dismiss a tenured colleague, in part on the assumption that nonprofessional motives and reasons might underlie such an action (see Chapter 2). By specifying the professionally based standards of behavior a tenured faculty member is expected to meet, performance contracting would certainly reduce the possibility of such unfairness. It would protect the job security of tenure while making it possible to establish cause in dismissal proceedings if in fact such cause existed.

Any assertion that performance contracting would represent an attack on academic freedom is as groundless as the assertion that it would mean the end of tenure. Its adoption would certainly narrow the meaning of that principle. It would make it difficult for faculty to argue that academic freedom mandates the oblivious permissiveness now found on our campuses. Since that permissiveness should be a major target of reform efforts, the threat of its demise is hardly a legitimate basis for criticism of performance contracting (or any other proposal). The specification of performance expectations, as well as the when, how, and by whom of evaluation, would actually reinvigorate academic freedom. Such specification would clearly rule out nonprofessional infringements on faculty members' freedoms of inquiry and pedagogical expression even as it established what faculty members were professionally accountable for—and therefore what their peers might freely attend to and criticize in their work. The specification at the heart of individualized performance contracting would, in my view, return academic freedom to its original meaning. It would protect academic work from nefariously motivated interference while at the same

time making professors responsible to one another for the quality of their professional contributions.

Reform 2: Evaluation and Accountability

Does performance contracting really imply a new departure in evaluation and consequently in accountability? Can we expect those who presently do such an inadequate job of evaluating the work of their colleagues to do an acceptable job were performance contracting to become the basic personnel management mechanism? I would be less than honest if I claimed that I could with considerable confidence answer in the affirmative. I *believe,* however, that performance contracting can lead to a new departure in the evaluation process because I believe there is an approach to evaluation that, if written into the contracts, would maximize the likelihood of effectiveness.

Faculty evaluation needs to be demystified. Instead of the sanctimoniousness that presently surrounds the process, it needs to be approached as a routine activity. Instead of seeing it as a process to assess and reward excellence in truth's service, we ought to view it as a process to monitor compliance with specific performance expectations that are contractually mandated.

Under the existing system faculty receive salary increases based on the vague presumption of their meritoriousness.[4] They've been meritorious in their scholarship, meritorious in their teaching, and meritorious in their service, so let's raise their salaries because such merit speaks of their excellence in truth's cause. No one, however, is quite able to specify the indicators of such merit. It's just some kind of excellence. You really can't operationalize it. You can't reduce it to a matter of A versus non-A, B versus non-B. You simply cannot subject it to precise measurement the way a sales manager might in reviewing the performance of a sales force. It is this vagueness, this deep-breathing puffery that celebrates imprecision as the hallmark of academic value, that of course allows those doing faculty evaluations to reward their colleagues indiscriminately. Anything and everything can be judged at least a little meritorious since no clear standards are being invoked.

And there is some reasonableness, of course, to the assertion that excellence in truth's service cannot be precisely defined and measured. Short of the great paradigmatic breakthroughs and discoveries in science,[5] what is deemed important, it seems, is always arguable. In the

humanities and social sciences, there don't seem to be any such break-throughs at all; there are merely claims and counterclaims. Ask what constitutes pedagogical excellence and you will elicit a variety of responses, making it virtually impossible to invoke a standard of excellence most of us would be comfortable with. Is excellent teaching provocative, profound, entertaining, and disturbing? Is it a matter of technical proficiency? Must it change the way students think? Can it be appreciated in the short run or, parallel to the wisdom of Pericles's funeral oration, must it be contemplated in the perspective of the long run? But if it is reasonable to assert the imprecision of excellence in truth's service, it is not reasonable to champion that imprecision in the process used to evaluate faculty work efforts. The record, I believe, is clear; doing so results in misfeasance and malfeasance not merely tolerated but rewarded. If assessing academic excellence must ever be imprecise, it is, I submit, a foolish and mischievous errand. If we really cannot precisely and fairly measure it, then notwithstanding the obvious appeal (since we want an excellent higher education system, we ought to evaluate its pursuit as manifest in the efforts of individual professors), academic excellence ought to be abandoned as the characterizing purpose of faculty evaluations.

Instead of asking after the meritoriousness of a faculty member's service, we ought to ask a much simpler question: Has the faculty member provided the service he or she has agreed to provide by signing an individual performance contract? If that contract specifies the teaching of x number of courses during, let us say, a three-year period, have those courses been competently taught? If it specifies the completion of a book manuscript during that period of service, has the manuscript been completed? If it specifies the publication of x number of journal articles, have they been accepted for publication?

These and similar questions pegged to an agreement the faculty member has entered into are eminently answerable, the answers allowing for considerable precision and ample documentation. The evaluators would not, for example, be asked to assess the pedagogical brilliance of their colleague's teaching, merely its competence. Evaluators would review syllabi with an eye to whether or not course materials were up-to-date and whether or not they promised reasonable coverage of subject matter—and to assess the appropriateness of student exercises and grading. Evaluators could judge pedagogical execution and coherence in unannounced visits to classes.[6] Student

questionnaires could develop information on the faculty member's class attendance and availability for course-related consultation. The evaluators would not be asked to determine the importance of a scholarly contribution but simply whether the contribution has been made as promised. A book manuscript and letters of acceptance from journals can be submitted as proof of the honored contractual commitment. And deciding whether someone has achieved funding of a grant proposal should not require heavy-duty critical contemplation.

Ultimately, what recommends this—shall we call it minimalist?—approach to evaluation is its fairness to the parties involved. Faculty would know at the outset what tasks will be subject to evaluation, as well as the methods and standards that will be employed in its execution. Because all of this would be written into the agreements they sign, any attempt to change the process surreptitiously would constitute a breach of contract on the part of the employing institution. Alternatively the colleges and universities using this method would be protected against those judgmental vagaries that now result in what can only be viewed as an epidemic of meretricious (or false) merit, a condition that, in its wastefulness, drives up the cost of higher education. By reducing the role of unspecifiable evaluator judgment, the minimalist method would reduce the opportunities colleagues have to reward each other for work not done or done poorly. Indeed a contractually specified minimalist review, wed inextricably to the services-rendered-for-compensation exchange, requires less evaluation than it does performance monitoring and certification that the terms of the exchange have been met. While there are situations in which evaluative judgment will no doubt play some role—most probably those where the teaching function is at issue—such judgment will pale in comparison to nonjudgmental monitoring and certification. All that faculty would be asked to do is to follow the methods specified in Professor A's contract to certify that Professor A, having promised to do x, has or has not delivered on that promise.

There are, of course, those who'll see in minimalist evaluation the abandonment of high standards, a disavowal of excellence when its pursuit is more critical than ever. Such a view could not be further from the truth. There is nothing in a proposal tying faculty evaluation to the terms of a performance contract that counsels the abandonment of high standards and the pursuit of excellence. The proposal does indeed plead for the abandonment of a foolish errand, the short-run

evaluation of presumably meritorious performance based upon un-specifiable criteria, but that does not imply a concomitant legitimation of mediocrity. Teaching excellence should of course be the goal of every professor who sets foot in a classroom, but whether or to what extent it has been achieved is a matter that probably only the long-run assessments of former students (e.g., their appreciation of the teacher's role in their work and, more important, in their lives) can speak to, and these cannot be made available for annual reviews. Scholarly excellence must of necessity be the ideal every genuine academic aspires to, but the significance of scholarly contributions as well must await judgment that assesses their long-term impacts. Pursue excellence, by all means, but don't for a moment succumb to the delusion that such pursuit is amenable to evaluation in the here and now. And if it is not, how dangerous to behave as though it were. Succumbing to such a delusion has meant and will continue to mean rewarding the incompetent as well as the competent, those who willfully fail to honor their professional obligations as well as those who are responsible in their discharge, because imprecision allows an almost universal claim to merit. In other words it has meant and will continue to mean the perpetuation of an "anything goes" atmosphere on our campuses. Those who profess to be concerned that minimalist evaluation must imply the abandonment of high standards would better serve higher education by coming to grips with the fact that despite all the high-flown rhetoric to the contrary it is the present system that too often makes a costly mockery of high standards in the academy.

If anything, minimalist evaluation will invigorate the academic pursuit of excellence. It will serve to establish an acceptable functional minimum where presently none exists. It will work against the continuation of the anything-goes milieu and so will influence many faculty to do more than they are presently required to do. While it cannot ensure excellence in teaching and scholarship, it will certainly make the abandonment of its pursuit costly to those who are so inclined.

There are some who will no doubt see creeping bureaucratization in the procedure I am recommending. After all, people will have to keep track of what they've accomplished, and they'll have to document their claims to success. Doesn't that mean a wasteful siphoning of energy better used in executing one's pedagogical and scholarly tasks? Moreover, isn't all this documentation going to increase the paperwork of those who must do the evaluations? And isn't that going to result in

negative selection, where those most qualified to act as evaluators will refuse to do so in order have sufficient time for their own work? Such worries are insubstantial. Since the performance contract will specify what needs to be kept track of and documented, it should require minimal effort to do so. How much energy, over and above that ordinarily expended in developing a syllabus, does it require to set copies aside for the evaluators? How much energy does it require to set aside copies of completed papers or to photocopy letters indicating that these papers have been accepted for publication? As far as all that paperwork is concerned, it's hard to see why that would be a problem. The evaluators would probably use precoded forms to indicate the disposition of their certification. If anything, the evaluators' workload would probably be reduced. Long meetings in which invidious merit distinctions are arrived at in the absence of any firm criteria would, for example, become all but unnecessary. Furthermore, since professors would be subject to evaluation only during the last year of their contracts and since the starting dates of these contracts would be staggered, every faculty member would not be evaluated every year. Common sense seems to indicate that the annual workload of the evaluators would thereby be reduced in comparison to what (in theory at least) it presently is.

Reform 3: Imposition of Hierarchy

Individualized performance contracting would clearly go a long way toward establishing ordinary work expectations for faculty. There are, however, two other reforms that must as well be supported, because their adoption is crucial to successful performance contracting. The purpose of performance contracting—establishing the expectation of an honest day's work for an honest day's pay—can easily be undermined if the agreements themselves turn out to be nothing more than sweetheart deals. If the terms of performance contracts are vague and if the mandated evaluative process reflects this imprecision, little will be gained from their adoption. The permissive atmosphere on our campuses will remain even as faculties give the appearance of getting serious about the provision-of-service-for-compensation exchange.

Unfortunately, as long as leveling, or democratization (see Chapter 2), remains a fact of academic life, there is a good chance performance contracts will indeed be sweetheart deals. Leveling, you will remem-

ber, has weakened the authority of academic managers and concomitantly strengthened the hand of the faculty on personnel matters in particular. Since on the whole faculty have an abiding interest in maximizing their freedoms (or alternatively, minimizing their accountability), there is little reason to expect that if leveling persists and faculty thereby have a disproportionate influence over what goes into performance contracts, these contracts will be drafted in such a way as to constitute a marked improvement over the present. If, for example, department chairs and personnel committees, all elected by faculty, are designated to represent the employer side (the college or the university) in negotiations with employees (their departmental colleagues), it is difficult to imagine resultant contracts that truly reflect interests other than those of the faculty. In effect the faculty would be negotiating with itself, and all the reasons presently working against accountability (e.g., freedom for them is actually freedom for me, constraints placed upon them must also be placed upon me; too much awareness of the of the other guy's biography—his impending divorce, the problems she's having with her daughter, and so on; it's really hard to be tough on your next-door neighbor) are likely to work against the development of a contractually specified fair exchange.

Unless there is at least a semblance of hierarchical authority on personnel matters, the probability that performance contracting will make a real difference must be quite small. The trend toward democratization needs to be reversed in a manner responsive to the realities of self-interest, realities that if left unchecked (as they now appear to be) can only minimize the extent to which faculty are held accountable for their work efforts. Put as simply as possible, those who would support the adoption of a system of performance contracting must also support the establishment of a clear distinction between faculty and academic management. For performance contracting to work, faculty cannot be allowed to negotiate with themselves; they must negotiate with the "bosses": provosts, deans, or their designates.

Of course those of us recommending this will immediately become the targets of virulent professorial attacks. We will doubtless be painted as know-nothing enemies of higher education whose only interest is to wrest control from those who presently stand tall as the protectors of intellectual heterodoxy and pedagogical innovation. We will be cast as Visigoths intent upon imposing the darkest of academic dark ages or, at the very least, where faculties have fallen in love with

the idea if not the tactics of unionization, as union busters on a par with the Frank Lorenzos and Carl Icahns of the world. I'd suggest a bold response to these attacks. If excoriated for wanting to wrest control, plead guilty but don't allow the claims of faculty heroism to go unchallenged. It is not heroic to stand tall in defense of mis- and malfeasance; they aren't indicators of heterodoxy and innovation. When condemned for championing a future darkness against the presumptive light of the present, turn the condemnation on its head. There is no light, no openness in a system that makes teaching a secretive exercise; an activity to be hidden from one's colleagues, with their complicity, of course. There is no openness in a system that insistently protects the right to commit all manner of scholarly indecencies and claim immunity from critical accountability. If you are accused of being a union buster, remind your accusers that bargaining requires two parties, and have the impertinence to suggest that if they really want a union, they ought to take the opportunity your proposal affords to clearly identify themselves as workers.

Surely the case for increasing hierarchical authority in the academy confounds our modern liberal sensibility that holds equal distribution of anything (including authority) to be better and therefore more desirable than unequal distribution. The abandonment of democratic leveling will thus be no easy reform to institute. Besides vituperative rhetorical response, reformers can expect to be confronted with job actions (work stoppages, strikes, etc.) and a growth of faculty unions, as academics struggle to protect a most precious prerogative—control born of a power balance that over time has tipped decisively in their favor.

Some may rue such a turn of events, seeing in it a serious threat to the existing academic order. I do not. In the first place the demise of the present academic order, with its protections of the mean and the lame, is not something I would mourn. On the contrary it would doubtless constitute an important first step toward the reconstitution of an academic system fairer and more productive by far than the system being abandoned. Second, there is a dialectical quality to such actions, should they occur, that must move personnel matters in the very direction endorsed by those who support academic reform. As professors move collectively to protect their personal prerogatives; as they unionize, stop work, and man the picket lines, they will ironically define themselves as workers in relation to the bosses, the academic manag-

ers. In itself this would reestablish the principle of hierarchical authority even as the precise characteristics of that hierarchy were being negotiated. Like it or not, it seems that if reformers push for the reestablishment of true hierarchical authority, professors must eventually accept it as a fact of their work lives. If they acquiesce in a spirit of cooperation, well and good; if they resist, as I expect many will, their very resistance must establish an us-them, workers-bosses distinction that is basic to hierarchical work organization.

When all is said and done, we must support a return to hierarchy. Failure to prevail would put the potential gains of performance contracting at serious risk. Such jeopardy suggests the dismal likelihood of apparent as opposed to real reform and, of course, the continuation of academic business as usual, a grim prospect for anyone who recognizes the importance of higher education.

Reform 4: Licensing Professors

Earlier in these pages I made a connection between leveling and the central role of the disciplines in academic organization (see Chapter 2). These have, in fact, occurred conjointly, and discipline salience, a principle implying only those with appointments in the same departments are competent to pass judgment on each other's work, has provided a strong rationale for tipping the balance of authority in the faculty's direction. As things stand, it is unthinkable that a dean who might be a physicist would claim the ability to evaluate the work of a sociologist and vice versa. Absent such a claim it is, for the most part, only departmental colleagues who can judge, thus bestowing upon the faculty more power than they are likely to use and more responsibility (their rhetoric to the contrary notwithstanding) than they are likely to accept. Reformers would therefore do well to take the measure of discipline salience and make every effort to reduce its impact on the academic scene.

How to go about this, however, is not easy to specify. In a very real sense discipline salience is as much a state of mind as an organizing principle; probably more so. Every faculty member has identified with his or her discipline at least since entering graduate school (maybe even since choosing an undergraduate major). Professors are not trained to be professors but rather to be sociologists, physicists, philosophers, historians, biologists, engineers, economists, and so on. They

take no courses in what might be called the crafts of the professorial role (e.g., academic advising, syllabus preparation, lecturing, grading, committee participation, grant preparation, supervision of research assistants, and while not crafts themselves, pedagogical and scholarly ethics), and they sit for no examinations to earn certification in these crafts. By the time they are first appointed, they have almost invariably come to define being an academic in terms of whatever discipline they have earned their graduate degrees in. They share in a collective identity, professor, and they endorse a presumably transcendent set of expectations, the academic creed. But the identity and the creed both are likely to be suffused in a conception of what it means to be a sociologist, a physicist, a philosopher, or whatever. For the vast majority of those who remain in the academy, the passage of time does little or nothing to undermine such parochialism. When they sit on multi-departmental committees, they sit as representatives of their departments, and while the desirability of interdisciplinary collaboration can be added to the academy's long list of pieties, like most pieties it is more often spoken of than successfully realized. In over thirty years of active participation in the academy, I've yet to meet a professor whose academic identity hasn't been anchored in one discipline or another. Ask after an academic's profession and you will never be told that he or she is a professor but rather that he or she is a professor of physics, English, psychology, or mathematics.

While it is difficult enough to change an organizational principle, changing a collectively held state of mind would seem to be even more difficult. Indeed it would appear that such a state of mind might only be changed if the conditions producing it were themselves changed. Yet in one of those demonic tricks reality so frequently plays, the conditions in question can be changed only if the state of mind did not exist. As long as discipline salience is an organizational principle on our campuses, graduate students will be molded into clones of mentors who heartily endorse it. Moreover, when they are appointed as assistant professors, their professional futures may depend in considerable measure upon a willingness to identify with their disciplines.[7] Thus by the time they themselves ascend to positions of influence, they can hardly be expected to do anything except continue a process that reproduces discipline salience in the hearts and minds of academics no less than in the organizational characteristics of the institutions employing them. The condition in need of reform begets a mindset that if un-

changed must beget that very condition that begets the mindset that begets the condition—and on and on and on in a process seemingly immune to any corrective intervention.

If left to the academics themselves, this behavioral tautology must certainly persist. There is, however, an alternative course, and while its proposal will no doubt once again move academicians to expressions of outrage, it would do no more than bring professors into line with physicians and attorneys. I propose that reformers seek state licensing of professors *as professors*. Should such a move be successful, it would virtually ensure that graduate schools devote time and effort to instruction in the professorial (as opposed to the sociological, biological, historical, etc.) crafts. This, of course, would improve the execution of professorial tasks and move apprentice academics to reflect on their professorial as opposed to their discipline-centered identities. Embarking on their own instructional careers, new Ph.D.'s would likely do so with an awareness of as well as a loyalty to both their disciplines and their profession. Moreover, because those who teach in universities are likely to be asked to participate in the *professorial* preparation of succeeding generations of graduate students, it is highly probable that "being a professor" will become a permanent component of their mindset. No longer will they simply be called upon to teach biology, history, English, or philosophy; they will also be called upon to teach professorial practice. In doing so they will, to a certain extent at least, have to think of themselves as professors plain and simple, not as professors of x.

Attorneys, no matter their specialties (corporate, criminal, entertainment, or public interest law) must pass a bar examination testing their general competency before a state will admit them into practice. While physicians are usually examined in their specialties, they are as well examined for their general competence as physicians before a state will license their practice. A law degree and a medical degree may each certify the successful completion of a course of study, but in themselves they are insufficient to permit those who hold them to practice upon a necessarily unwary public. States, it is assumed, have an abiding interest in the legal and medical welfare of their citizens and as such can regulate professional access to them. Curiously, such an interest is not assumed to apply to the advanced education of these same citizens (primary and secondary school teachers are, of course, licensed). Hoisting the banner of academic freedom, the professoriate

has rendered licensure as applied to themselves all but unthinkable. Merely mention the possibility and you will be attacked for inviting both political and bureaucratic interference in higher learning. Those very same people who wouldn't dream of being attended by an unlicensed physician, who would use an early failure to pass the bar as a basis for excluding someone from government service,[8] have come to believe that the practice of advanced education can and should be left unregulated. To be consistent, of course, these same defenders of professorial prerogative should be no less concerned with political and bureaucratic interference in the practice of law and medicine. That they are not is doubtless a tribute to the ability of so many professors to persuade themselves of anything.

In reality, licensing examinations for the professoriate would be prepared by professors, just as lawyers and physicians prepare their professions' licensing examinations. Thus while there is some risk of professionally unwarranted interference, it is no more likely for professors than it is for lawyers and physicians. The examinations would focus on professorial craft, those skills necessary to the successful execution of the professorial role irrespective of specialty. They would, moreover, be administered regularly, and newly appointed professors could be given provisional licenses allowing them a year of service before having to present themselves for examination. All in all, it could be a relatively simple procedure parallel to that used by the other learned professions.[9]

If the professoriate does indeed constitute a profession (an honorable profession, according to its practitioners), there ought to be no difficulty in generating licensing examinations, the fairness and appropriateness of which are beyond serious question. If this cannot be accomplished, then all the rights and perquisites that come to professors because the public honors their professional claims may well be nothing other than ill-gotten gains, the fruits of fraudulent claims expertly advanced by very persuasive people. I believe, however, that such examinations can be devised, and that in convincing state governments to commission them, reformers will have found a way to break into the tautology presently ensuring the problematic existence of discipline salience as both state of mind and organizational principle on American campuses. The examinations will change the conditions of professorial preparation, which in turn will open academics to their cross-discipline professorial identities, which in turn will have positive

consequences for professional accountability. It will make it possible for the dean who is the physicist to tell the sociologists that while he is unable to judge the sociological substance of their work, he can indeed tell whether or not they have honored their professorial obligations. This would reestablish the legitimacy of managerial authority in the academy, put teeth into minimalist evaluations, and in so doing increase the probability that individualized performance contracting will constitute a significant reform of the excessively permissive academic milieu. Should this come to pass, colleges and universities may yet become workplaces where honest, competent efforts exerted in reasonably sufficient measure will justify the relative munificence of professorial salaries.

The Abandonment of Specialness

Candor requires that those who would support the changes outlined in these pages (as well as similar proposals of their own devising) confess without caveat their willingness to blame, at least in large part, the faculties of our colleges and universities for the increasingly sorry state of higher education. Would that it were not so, but the experience and research informing the first four chapters of this book make it abundantly clear to me that faculty malpractice and a truly remarkable professorial capacity for denying even the strongest evidence of its occurrence are dominating facts of everyday academic life. They undermine the ability of colleges and universities to realize the functions their publics expect of them. They are significantly implicated in the inflationary spiral that threatens to put higher education beyond the reach of all save the most affluent. (The spiral has already driven so many students into major debt—at graduation they receive a diploma together with notice of their first loan payment—that self-serving avarice may be their only salvation. Hardly what we would hope for from educated men and women!) And they have made hypocrisy so very usual on campus, as almost all professors—the good and the competent, the mendacious and the incompetent—conspire to keep their dirty little secrets from coming to light. In 1919 when Thorstein Veblen published *The Higher Learning in America,* he identified bankers, industrialists, and their lackeys, the college presidents, as those responsible for learning's lilliputian scale and the corruption of its purpose. Were Veblen alive today, he doubtless would shudder to admit that

whatever the external threat to the vitality and effectiveness of higher education, the internal threat is more than its equal. Like Walt Kelly's Pogo, on alert in that steamy rain forest—the Okeefenokee swamp—those now vigilant in behalf of the higher learning must sadly report that "we has seen the enemy and they is us."

Reformers must prevail upon the academy to abandon its claim of elevated specialness. The claim and the irresponsible autonomy it implies are the villains in the piece. Because of the near impossibility of translating the academic creed's idealized stringencies into enforceable standards, because doing so would be much too costly to the real-world aspirations of both individual faculty and the institutions they serve, the profession of such specialness simply renders professors blind, deaf, and dumb when there is so much that if seen or heard would require them to roar their condemnation.

Academic specialness and in particular the autonomy that has been its issue have not, moreover, had the predicted effect of encouraging innovation or heterodox courage. The assumption has been that if colleges and universities were constituted as free zones where even professors propounding the most outrageous ideas could be made immune from the retribution of those they had outraged, members of the professoriate would be encouraged to take chances and to allow their imaginations the freest rein. In such an environment some of their ideas at least, ideas that in more constraining environments might never have been expressed or perhaps even conceived could be expected to have positive implications for all sorts of real-life valuables, from life-saving medical technologies to foreign policy initiatives to an enriched poetry.

This theory, when one reflects upon it, is quite tenuous to say the least. It argues that protectiveness and security elicit acts of courage and expressions of creativity. The history of ideas, of science, of the arts, not to mention any account of political or moral courage, strongly suggests the opposite. Galileo possessed no tenure, nor did Newton (except perhaps as a tax collector), and Einstein's scientific revolution was imagined by a man who made his living investigating patent claims. Karl Marx never served on a university faculty and was constantly in jeopardy of being expelled by government authorities (as he was in fact on more than one occasion) because of his ideas and his activities. Sigmund Freud could count on nothing except the fees he received from his patients and the assistance offered by some of the

wealthier members of his inner circle. Michelangelo had to depend upon the popes; Mozart upon the princes; Liszt upon smitten women; Gershwin, O'Neill, and Williams upon money-grubbing producers and critics whose considerable influence was matched only by their considerable ignorance. Arguably the most important American literary journalist and editor of the twentieth century, H.L. Mencken, wouldn't have been caught dead on a faculty. (Burn down the universities and hang the professors, he railed, albeit with tongue in cheek.) What intellectually and politically secure zone stimulated Camus's contemplations of human meaning and the morality of political refusal? What protections did Pasternak, Brecht, de Beauvoir, and so recently Václav Havel have?

Surely some professors do and have done some good. Surely professors have made contributions. There is nothing, however, to suggest that the most important of these were made because of the protection and security afforded by academic autonomy. On the contrary there is reason to argue that such "safety" significantly reduces the probability of courage and creativity on the academic scene. To begin with, there is the matter of selection. Brave men and women do not crave safety; those whose reservoirs of fortitude are depleted do, however. The safety afforded by academic autonomy is thus not likely to constitute an attraction for the courageous among us, but its allure is likely to prove irresistible to the timid. As such we should expect the latter to congregate on our campuses while the former disperse themselves over a range of less secure venues. Unless one is willing to embrace the highly dubious proposition that sustained fraternization of the timid with the timid will, contrary to all good sense, transform those so engaged into paragons of courage, it is hard to see how the safety provided by academic autonomy can have its presumed effect. That there are courageous professors is of course true, but their presence has doubtless been motivated by factors other than the safety inherent in the academic environment.

As far as innovation and creativity are concerned, it is difficult indeed to envision how the security of an autonomous faculty would stimulate their occurrence. First, there is an inverse correlation between timidity and imagination. Thus the attractiveness for the timid of the safe academy virtually ensures a dearth of imagination on our campuses and consequently net deficits in the creative accounts of our colleges and universities. Second, because the safe academy tolerates

and even rewards professorial sloth, too many faculty find no reason to exercise what imagination they do possess (except perhaps to conjure up mythologies of the work they are presumably but not really doing). Envisioning how it is that a work setting where doing nothing at all is rewarded can stimulate innovation (it does, after all, require effort to be creative) necessitates a degree and type of imagination only those capable of pushing counterintuition to absurd limits can possess.

The bottom line on our colleges and universities is this: In their presumed specialness they accord too much safety to their faculties. They have extended faculty protections beyond reason and in doing so have ironically slighted those the faculty are supposed to serve. Students are characteristically less well taught than they need and deserve to be. And we are all deprived of scholarship's highest potential for doing good; for maximizing the human serviceability of our social, economic, and political arrangements; for making the only lives we can live less perplexing, more coherent, and ultimately more harmonious.

The specialness of the academy begs to be abandoned. Of course there are risks in doing so. But it is those very risks, the risks inherent in creating academic institutions sensitive to the ordinariness of both their purposes and their participants, that I suspect will revitalize our colleges and universities. Presumptive specialness has not brought and cannot bring the courageous or the inventive to our campuses in sufficient measure. Accepting and perhaps even celebrating the ordinary on these campuses may. The nation's students do not need to be taught by those who claim to be mandarins. They simply need to be taught by people who recognize that they have contracted to do an important job and are proceeding in good faith to do it. Nor can we wait on promises of scholarly deliverance made by pretenders whose rhetoric leaves them breathless and us so intimidated that we dare not ask when the redemption of these promises might be expected. We need simply to be served by scholars who recognize the distinction between word and deed, who recognize that they are no less obliged to deliver on their promises than is any other worker having entered into a compensation-for-services-rendered agreement. We do not need the heroic but unenforceable proclamations of moral stringency so common to academic convocations. We need everyday ethical standards and contractually negotiated procedures for guaranteeing that

they are enforced. Those who believe colleges and universities should constitute special free zones, who believe professors should be held harmless, have got it wrong. The freedom has become license, the harmlessness harmful. Whatever the potential risks in moving toward the ordinary, they are far outstripped by the dangers ironically inherent in the special safety that now characterizes the academy. Those dangers have been realized.

Appendix

A Single Standard, Please

Poisoning the Ivy has been heterogeneously crafted. The information constituting its substantive core was developed from both systematic and unsystematic sources. Among the former were previously published materials (books, reports, and articles) as well as accounts offered in interviews with strategically located academics, each with more than twenty years of experience. Among the latter were my own experiences and observations; newspaper accounts that I have latched onto somewhat opportunistically; phone calls to the offices of the American Association of University Professors, the American Council on Education, the *Chronicle of Higher Education,* and others in less than completely fruitful attempts to get up-to-date national estimates of academic malpractice together with the incidence of professionally mandated disciplinary response; and anecdotes that came my way once word of my project got out. Some of this information was part of the public record; some of it was not and was passed on to me only after I promised anonymity to my source and some disguise of the institution at which the reported events occurred.

Were I claiming the mantle of social science, this is the point at which I would invoke the presumed sophistication of my analytic method. I would claim considerable competence for the likes of my measures and statistics, my observational protocols, my semistructured interview schedule, my coding system, and my inferential framework. What I have written does not, however, rely upon the sophistication of presumably impersonal methods to advance its truth claims. It relies instead on whatever personal sophistication I have been able to draw upon in making the argument I'd like my readers to consider. In effect

it relies upon years of academic experience and the inferential resources I have accumulated over the course of a lifetime. Ultimately,
the truth claims of *Poisoning the Ivy* come down to how good my
judgment has been. The better my judgment the greater the likelihood
that I have accurately broken the code that protects academic reality
from serious critical scrutiny.

Instead of relying upon scientifically endorsed rules and methods, I
have allowed myself the hubris of relying upon my own intelligence
and imagination. From the point of view of those who are too easily
enamored of science, this is risky business. In a very real sense they
feel a powerful need to be protected from the exercise of imagination.
While they recognize or at least pay lip service to the causal connection between imagination and enlightenment, they shudder at its potential for distorting abandon. The free exercise of imagination may
indeed bring us closer than we have ever been to an accurate apprehen-
sion of our social environment, but, they believe, only in a minority of
instances. Untethered imagination, they protest, is far more likely to
promote inaccuracy because, unchecked by scientifically established
rules and methods, it is little more than an expression of investment, of
what for a variety of reasons we *want* to be real as opposed to what
reality is in fact, For those enamored of science, imagination (by definition idiosyncratic) and the judgments it implies must be subordinate
to a discipline's rules (by definition collectively established) and the
methods that are its issue.

Pretty risky if I may say so. Certainly no less risky than my reliance
upon inferential resources accumulated over many years and the personal judgments I have made in their use. Risky because contrary to
the facile social scientific cant (or any scientific cant, for that matter)
now so much in vogue, the rules and methods presumably invoked to
protect us from bad analytic judgments are themselves inseparable
from judgment issues. In other words, there is really little if anything
automatic about the application of scientific rules and the use of scientific methods. Individual social scientists are always in the position of
having to decide which scientific rules and methods are apposite to
their inquiry, and this is nearly always a matter of interpretation. Text-
book procedures more often than not must be modified to meet the
exigencies of real-world inquiries, and whatever guidelines there are
for doing so usually leave much to be desired. Although their idealized
reconstructions of what they did frequently lead the unwary to con-

clude otherwise,[1] social scientists are no less likely to avoid the challenges and pitfalls inherent in idiosyncratic judgment calls than are those of us who prefer unscientific (so called) pathways to truth.

Social scientists love to enthuse about their hard data (the facts, just the facts!), dismissing by comparison work where such data appear to be less prominent. But careful examination of the procedures employed in the collection and assemblage of such data suggests they are softened considerably by judgments no less idiosyncratic than those made when social science is not being invoked. Consider the following: At one point in *Poisoning the Ivy,* I estimated that the proportion of faculty actively engaged in malpractice hovers around 30 percent on any given campus. The estimate clearly constituted a judgment I made based upon my interviews with informants, my perusal of published and unpublished accounts, my largely frustrating experience in trying to elicit systematic data on incidence, as well as my years of academic experience. I freely admit that the estimate, because it is judgmental, is soft, subject to significant fluctuation from one campus to the next. Surely I would like to be able to be more precise, but after exhausting every effort to achieve greater precision, I've concluded that at present it is unattainable.

For some issues, imprecision can be crippling. In my judgment the precise proportion of a faculty constituted by its resident malefactors was, however, not crucial to my argument. What was crucial is the deleterious impact of their behaviors and the degree to which that impact is fostered by the inattentiveness of their generally more applaudable colleagues. As long as the soft character of my estimate was clear and as long as my recommendations did not advertise themselves as implications of more precise estimates, I felt I might justifiably proceed with my argument.

In this circumstance reader skepticism is appropriate, and I have in fact invited its active expression as the engine that will drive further inquiries into the precise extent of academic malpractice and disciplinary response (see Chapter 5). Those eager, however, to dismiss what I have done by juxtaposing it against the presumably nonjudgmental alternative that social scientists pursue might want to hesitate just long enough to consider the judgment issues that Peter H. Rossi has identified in the efforts of social scientists to estimate the extent of homelessness in the United States. Rossi, one of sociology's most prominent methodologists, has made it clear that there is nothing auto-

matic, routine, or judgment-free about these efforts. Definitional variation from one study to the next understandably effects numerical estimates: The more restrictive the definition the smaller the national estimate.[2]

Identifications of homeless people irrespective of the definition being used are likely to be problematic. Social scientists using their own best judgments have adopted different methods to identify and "count" the homeless, often enough inaccurately. Rossi writes of an influential study prepared by researchers for the federal Department of Housing and Urban Development. He notes:

> The first HUD approach uses unevaluated estimates that simply "happen" to exist. The second approach is somewhat better in that local estimates were solicited in a systematic way, but there was no systematic assessment of the "expert opinions" used.
>
> The third approach simply restricts the opinions solicited to a single type of source, shelter operators, whose guesses about the total number of homeless people in their cities may be better than anyone else's but are still of unknown accuracy.
>
> . . . [The] fourth approach makes the simplifying assumption that the ratio of street homeless to shelter homeless is uniform across cities and across seasons.[3]

Precision? Nowhere to be found. Elimination of idiosyncratic judgments? Not according to Rossi's account. If I may be so bold, whatever the differences between the approach to estimation taken by those social scientists who prepared the HUD report and the approach I have taken in this book, they simply are not visible to the naked eye. That doesn't purchase additional respect for my "unscientific" approach, but it should chasten those who would dismiss it by invoking a comparison that is presumably—but not really—unflattering.

Social scientists would have us believe that the numbers, percents, tables, graphs, and equations that festoon the pages they produce constitute representations of *discovered* reality when, on the contrary, they are representations of *constructed* reality. Hidden beneath a cool, disinterested reportorial style are the realities of idiosyncratic judgments implicated in purported discoveries, thus rendering them at least in part the creations of those who claim them as findings. Arrays of raw survey data, for one example, represent wording decisions made by item writers, decisions on the treatment of missing data made by researchers on a case-by-case basis, coding decisions, and finally item

responses. Three of the four components constituting such arrays are matters of judgment, often enough idiosyncratically expressed. Indications of statistical significance, for another example, regarded as absolutely crucial to hypothesis testing are often as not the products of individual research judgments. In principle significance levels are supposed to be predetermined, usually at the .01 or .05 levels. If a researcher predetermines the acceptable standard to be .01, then results that do not meet this standard should in fact be considered statistically insignificant or too prone to occur by chance. But this is not the way social scientists have in fact proceeded. Instead of predetermining a specific standard for statistical significance, they have generally tested their hypotheses and if their results are not significant at .01, they then assess significance at .05 or even .10. Today, with the advent of advanced statistical software, computers automatically calculate significance values, allowing the researcher to judge after the fact whether perceived differences are too likely to have occurred by chance. Whether or not abandoning predetermined significance standards for ex post facto specification can be justified is a matter of some debate. However, their can be no debating the fact that ex post facto decisions regarding statistical significance are matters of judgment and as such are subject to idiosyncratic variation.

One of the techniques I used in preparing this book was case construction. Instead of merely reporting cases, I took the liberty of dramatizing several of them. I chose to do so because I concluded that my reader's understanding of the malpractice involved and the inattentiveness that allowed it to thrive would best be served by their near experience of the incidents in question. None of the cases is fiction, but I crafted each to draw readers into the action and its consequences. My intention in these pages was to rouse my readers, to render them indignant, and ultimately to move them to take those actions that will return the academy to a more responsible course. This, I believe, cannot be accomplished if cognition is divorced from emotion. Consequently, I wanted readers to share in the anger I have experienced at the academy's tolerance of wrongdoing within its midst. In my view only such strong emotion is likely to overcome the live-and-let-live entropy that is any wrongdoer's best protection.

Nothing in this book is likely to prove more controversial. There are doubtless readers who found these constructions unacceptable, fearing that their truth value was compromised by my dramaturgical approach.

There assuredly were others who resented what they took to be my effort to manipulate their emotions. Other than to specify, as I have in these pages, my purpose in doing what I have done, there's little else I can do to assuage the critical anxieties of such readers. Clearly, if they are unpersuaded by this specification, they will be unpersuaded by the substance of the dramatized cases, and I doubt that this book will move them to the reform efforts I should like it to stimulate. This is a risk I gladly assume because I believe that dramatization, with all its attendant problems, communicates an urgency appropriate to the issues this book assays.

I have no quarrel with those who after careful consideration find the case construction method troubling. They are entitled to their doubts and their criticisms. Those, however, who dismiss my approach by comparing it to the presumably judgment-free discoveries of social science are another matter. Their dismissive condescension is groundless because the science they invoke as their comparative standard is itself replete with constructions in which the researcher's judgment is implicated, often enough to a considerable fault.

In a brilliant traversal of social measurement issues, Otis Dudley Duncan puts to rest any social scientific claims to a serviceable theory of measurement.[4] Since no such theory is available, social scientists characteristically construct measures in the absence of conceptually reliable guidelines. At best, the measures social scientists typically employ are thoughtful but nevertheless ad hoc (and thus judgmentally idiosyncratic). Too often they are not even very thoughtful.

At the conclusion of his book, Duncan, identified with some of the best contemporary social scientific research, cannot resist harpooning the papier-maché Leviathan held in such awe by his more (much more, I would say) credulous colleagues: "Coupled with downright incompetence in statistics . . . we often find the syndrome that I have come to call *statisticism:* the notion that computing is synonymous with doing research . . . the delusion that decomposing the covariations of some arbitrary and haphazardly assembled collection of variables can somehow justify . . . a 'causal model.' "[5] And later he comments, "In a chemistry laboratory one learns to be a little cautious about 'combining' substances. But, so far as I know, the somewhat analogous 'combining' of information has not been widely recognized to have a property analogous to blowing up in the experimenter's face. That it could happen, though, seems evident . . .[6] [I do not] believe that index construction is . . . measurement. . . . Even so, we may continue to rely

heavily on composite indices for a merely pragmatic reason to achieve data reduction, data reduction at a terrible cost . . . , on account of the conceptual ambiguity that is (almost) inescapable."[7]

In citing Duncan's stinging qualms about social measurement, I do not intend to dismiss as valueless the work of social scientists. I do, however, want to stress once again that it is a major mistake to dichotomize inquisitional strategies, placing the so-called scientific strategies on the preferred side because their methodological sophistication promotes objective *discovery,* while relegating nonscientific strategies to the maligned other side, where the absence of such sophistication is assumed to promote mere *opinion.* Even allowing for some exaggeration on his part, Duncan makes it clear that social scientists characteristically construct their measures idiosyncratically, more often than not in the absence of the much-heralded methodological sophistication they presumably possess. No one can come away from reading Duncan confident in the belief that while the rest of us construct our subjectively flawed versions of social reality, social scientists, employing the rigorously tested tools of their disciplines, discover the reality there to be discovered. If Duncan is to be taken seriously, there is less difference than meets the eye between the case constructions in *Poisoning the Ivy* on the one hand and the so-called hard data measures and indices that social scientists revel in on the other. The currencies of their symbolic expression may differ—for the former, words; for the latter, numbers, equations, tables, charts, and graphs—but ultimately the substance of each is to a considerable degree constructed and to that same degree the truth value of both is a matter of fallible idiosyncratic judgment.

Come to think of it, there is one major difference after all, a difference that should give pause to those who so easily suspend disbelief whenever the discovery ethos of science is invoked. Case constructions such as those I employ in this book are not likely to be mistaken for anything other than the versions of the truth that they are in fact. The style of their expression is hardly ever misleading. The measures and indices social scientists employ are, however, quite likely to mislead. Too often, as numbers, equations, charts, and graphs are wont to do, they communicate a false claim to objective discovery, a truth value not actually achieved. If nothing else, this suggests that the numerical symbolic currency so beloved of social scientists can be dangerous in the false sense of assurance or certainty it promotes among the unwary. Readers of this book are unlikely to act until they persuade themselves

that its argument has the validity its author claims. Readers of a book on the same subject invoking the discovery ethos of social science and its quantitative symbolization may not be so cautious, even though the actual constructed nature of its truths would seem to warrant no less caution.

I am a sociologist who makes no claim to being a social scientist. I hope I have successfully applied my sociological imagination to the critical enterprise that is this book. I have submitted this work to anyone willing to engage its contents. I hoped to persuade, and in so doing I hoped to create an appetite for academic reform not satisfied by half-measures or insubstantial rhetoric. I do not fear any skepticism readers may have brought to the contents of these pages. I only appeal for a fair opportunity to overcome that skepticism, an opportunity denied when works such as this are dismissed or otherwise condescended to because they do not meet standards of inquiry and discovery that supposedly characterize social science (or for that matter probably any other science). In the final analysis neither science nor criticism can be any better than the idiosyncratic judgments made in their service by scientists and critics. If readers of *Poisoning the Ivy* embrace this position, they will have afforded me a fair opportunity to overcome whatever skepticism they have brought to its pages. In such a circumstance, I like my chances.

Writing this book from within the academy has reminded me of what it was like during the 1950s to root, with every bit of passion I could muster, for the New York Giants while virtually everyone around me did the same for their archrivals, the Brooklyn Dodgers. Being a Giants fan in Brooklyn meant that while you and your friends loved the same game, you could never share in the joys they took from that game, and even if you were accepted as one of the guys, you always had to explain the madness of your allegiance to that team from Manhattan, though no explanation would ever really suffice. About all I can say at this point is that in offering these contemplations, I have been trying to explain. I hope in doing so I haven't overintellectualized. The greatest ball player I ever had the privilege of seeing in action was the Giants' Willie Mays. Once asked some arcane question about the game he played so brilliantly, he responded by dismissing the query with the observation that he thought baseball was a simple game. "When they pitch it," he said, "I hit it. When they hit it," he continued, "I catch it." After all is said and done, criticism, and in particular my criticism of the academy, like Mays's game, is pretty much as it appears to be. Thanks, Willie.

Notes

Preface

1. Some of these latter schools (e.g., Bronx Science, Music and Art; Performing Arts; Stuyvesant; and Brooklyn Tech) had competitive admissions policies that limited access to those whose talents were demonstrable.

2. These institutions still exist as part of the City University of New York (CUNY), but they are no longer tuition free.

3. Although the vast majority of these people were not real property owners, they nevertheless paid property taxes. It would have been a foolish landlord who did not include this tax when establishing a rent.

4. Modern labor economics emphasizes exogenous reward in analyses of work incentives and disincentives. Sociologists considering the nature of occupational stratification have, with a few notable exceptions, emphasized the motivating force of external reward. The ingrained nature of this center-periphery confusion is, I think, best exemplified by the ease with which critics of a single-payer or government health care system suggest that although such a system would maximize patient access, it would drive away those best suited to become physicians because the financial rewards they might accrue would be deemed insufficient. The critics pay virtually no attention to the intrinsic challenges of the healer's art.

5. Myron Glazer and Penina Glazer, *The Whistleblowers* (New York: Basic Books, 1989).

6. Such presentations characteristically met with a bimodal response. Younger, less established academics, many of them graduate students, were generally sympathetic. Older, more established academics were frequently critical to the point of outrage. There are, of course, several interpretations of this pattern. I prefer the one suggesting exposure of a raw nerve among the latter. My presentation on what I call the seven pedagogical sins (see Chapter 3 of this book) so incensed one prominent academic at an annual meeting of the Eastern Sociological Society that during the discussion segment he could barely keep his emotions in check. After the session, its organizer told me of her chagrined surprise at the professor's behavior. I replied that I was not at all surprised since he had committed at least eight of the seven pedagogical sins I had discussed.

7. A discussion of this book's method can be found in the Appendix.

8. Charles H. Page, *Fifty Years in the Sociological Enterprise: A Lucky Journey* (Amherst: University of Massachusetts Press, 1982).

Chapter 1. An Almanac of Academic Betrayals

1. National Educational Association, *The 1996 Almanac of Higher Education* (Washington, DC: National Education Association, 1996).

2. See, for example, Billie Wright Dziech and Linda Weiner, *The Lecherous Professor: Sexual Harassment on Campus,* 2nd edition (Urbana: University of Illinois Press, 1990). For a statement reflecting the academy's ambivalence on the issue of harassment, see Lloyd D. Elgart and Lillian Schanfield, "Sexual Harassment of Students," *Thought and Action: The NEA Higher Education Journal* 7, 1 (Spring 1991): 21–42.

3. See the Appendix for a discussion of the difficulties in trying to develop a more precise estimate.

4. These efforts include

    1. sustained exposure of academic aspirants to the norms of obliviousness and silence while they make their way through graduate school

    2. frequent testing (again, during graduate school) of the degree to which these norms have been internalized; although not standardized, these tests usually focus on such current academic practices as
  - *phantom authorship*—whereby faculty append their names to papers they haven't written
  - *Napoleonic self-proclamation of genius*—whereby faculty pronounce their genius to graduate students and await the correct appreciative response
  - *pedagogical invisibility*—whereby faculty find ways not to teach and expect graduate students to ignore or otherwise accept the legitimacy of their absence
  - *manipulative mentoring*—whereby faculty (usually male) require graduate students (usually female) to accept as legitimate their presumption that classrooms and bedrooms are interchangeable

    3. Letters of reference that warn of a job candidate's "prickliness," "irascibility," "headstrong qualities," and other tendencies, indicating that, however talented, the subject of the letter "does not work and play well with others."

5. See Gunnar Myrdal, *An American Dilemma* (New York: Harper and Row, 1944).

6. David Reisman, a distinguished analyst of the American academy, long ago noted the historical roots of this claim to august purpose. Writing of the founding of colleges in the nineteenth century, he commented: "There remained in the idea of a college a certain visionary element, whether religious or secularized, which linked education with more than training for professional success—linked it with the promise of a nobler, less demeaning life." See *Constraint and Variety in American Education* (New York: Doubleday Anchor, 1958), 26.

7. Such matters as the following would no doubt have to be formally addressed: appropriation of funds for private purposes unrelated to the academic functions for which they were intended, willful falsification of research results,

physical abuse of students, falsification of academic records, and so on.

8. The characteristics discussed in this chapter are, I believe, most prominent in the phenomenology of academic denial. They are, however, not the only characteristics that significantly contribute to the ease with which academics refuse to see the wrongdoing of their colleagues. In Chapter 2 I discuss the academy's organizational characteristics and revered if perversely distorted traditions.

9. Tests presumably quite different from those described earlier in these pages (see note 4).

10. So rarely, in fact, that when they are imposed it is likely to be a media event. Two recent cases, one at a state college in Indiana and the other at perhaps the most prestigious American university, Harvard, attracted widespread coverage in the print and electronic media. In the first case a tenured professor fired for misfeasance and nonfeasance lost a suit to get his job back. In the second a prominent tenured professor was forced to resign because of extensive sexual misconduct with female students and junior faculty.

11. One important indicator of the denial that results in an academic environment bereft of accountability (an environment in which therefore almost everything is permitted) is the failure to generate statistical accounts of existing malpractice. My inquiries to the American Association of University Professors, the Carnegie Foundation for the Advancement of Teaching, the *Chronicle of Higher Education*, and the Higher Education Research Institute at UCLA in 1991–1992 yielded but one unfortunate conclusion: No publicly available statistics exist detailing the extent of professorial misconduct in American colleges and universities. While some might argue the failure to generate these statistics means that the problem of professorial misconduct is negligible, I believe the failure to do so strongly suggests the denial I discuss here.

12. See Allan Bloom, *The Closing of the American Mind: How Higher Education Has Failed Democracy and Impoverished the Souls of Today's Students* (New York: Simon and Schuster, 1987); Ernest L. Boyer, *College: The Undergraduate Experience in America* (New York: Harper and Row, 1987); Ernest L. Boyer, *The Condition of the Professoriate: Attitudes and Trends* (Lawrenceville, NJ: Princeton University Press, 1989); E.D. Hirsch Jr., *Cultural Literacy: What Every American Needs to Know* (Boston: Houghton Mifflin, 1987); Martin Anderson, *Imposters in the Temple* (New York: Simon and Schuster, 1992); Russell Jacoby, *The Last Intellectuals: American Culture in the Age of Academe* (New York: Basic Books, 1987); Roger Kimball, *Tenured Radicals: How Politics Has Corrupted Our Higher Education* (New York: Harper and Row, 1990); Alexander W. Astin, William S. Korn, and Eric L. Dey, *The American College Teacher: National Norms for the 1989–90 HERI Faculty Survey* (Los Angeles: Higher Education Research Institute, UCLA, 1991); Howard R. Bowen and Jack H. Schuster, *American Professors: A National Resource Imperiled* (New York: Oxford University Press, 1986); Martin J. Finkelstein, *The American Academic Profession: A Synthesis of Social Scientific Inquiry Since World War II* (Columbus: Ohio State University Press, 1984).

13. An exception is the book by Charles Sykes (a journalist), which does attempt to hold academics accountable for their misbehavior. See Charles Sykes, *Profscam: Professors and the Demise of Higher Education* (Washington, DC: Regnery Gateway, 1988).

14. I developed much of the case material presented in the following chapters in this manner.

Chapter 2. Hear, See, and Speak No Evil

1. Some readers will doubtless argue that my negative characterization of the academy is overgeneralized. I would be the first to assert that not all academics are mis- or malfeasant and that not every academic is delusively tolerant of those who are. There are indeed many exceptions to the picture I offer. But as far as I am concerned, they are just that: exceptions. The absence of good statistics on academic malpractice makes it difficult to come to a definitive conclusion about its incidence. No characterization of the academy, positive or negative, therefore has a calculable probability of being accurate. Consequently, those who would portray the academy more positively than I must themselves confront the uncertainty of their own views. From a methodological perspective, I cannot—strictly speaking—claim to know the extent of academic malpractice and the degree of its tolerance. It would appear that no one can. I can, however, indicate what I *believe* to be characteristic while I develop my reasons for that belief (others are of course entitled to do the same). I believe my negative characterization of academic reality is accurate, and this book contains my reasons for arriving at such an admittedly burdensome conclusion.

2. For examples of the conventional or mainstream literature on academic management and organization, see John W. Creswell, David Wheeler, Alan Seagren, Nancy Egly, and Kirk Beyer, *The Academic Chairperson's Handbook* (Lincoln: University of Nebraska Press, 1990); Ann H.L. Sontz, *The American College President* (Westport, CT: Greenwood Press, 1991); Paul S. Westmeyer, *Principles of Governance and Administration in Higher Education* (Springfield, IL: Thomas Publishers, 1990).

3. In most colleges and universities, professorial appointments are made in departments even if certain individuals spend the preponderance of their time in research institutes.

4. It once was. See the sections on academic tenure in this chapter.

5. Other than those instances when the institution has decided to limit tenure for financial reasons.

6. During the Vietnam War, an outspoken left-wing professor recommended for tenure at a prestigious liberal arts college went to its president with his concern that the conservative trustees might reject the recommendation. He was reassured by the president, who was reported to have remarked that unless he was "caught buggering a sheep in the middle of the campus," there would be no risk to his tenure from the trustees.

7. Some of these institutions have unionized faculty, and this control is thus somewhat limited by collective bargaining. See National Education Association, *The 1996 Almanac of Higher Education* (Washington, DC: National Education Association, 1996).

8. Faculty unions apparently make a difference as regards overall salaries. In 1995 faculty in bargaining units earned $8,300 more on average than did faculty at institutions without collective bargaining agreements. See ibid.

9. So important is this function that even in those years when merit moneys are not allocated to the departments, personnel committees insist upon going through their "reviews"—just in case the moneys become available. I leave it to the reader to decide what this demonstrates.

10. See Allan Bloom, *The Closing of the American Mind: How Higher Education Has Failed Democracy and Impoverished the Souls of Today's Students* (New York: Simon and Schuster, 1987). Also Russell Jacoby, *The Last Intellectuals: American Culture in the Age of Academe* (New York: Basic Books, 1987).

11. It is not that other work settings are free of dishonesty; it is just that, contrary to expectation, faculty motives in combination with the academy's revered traditions and its characteristic structure yield the inherently dishonest permissive obliviousness that in my view is peculiar to colleges and universities.

12. The importance of discipline distinctions among the professoriate is documented in reports that ostensibly focus on academics as a single, undifferentiated group. See, for example, the Carnegie Foundation for the Advancement of Teaching, *Scholarship Reconsidered: Priorities of the Professoriate, 1990* (Lawrenceville, NJ: Princeton University Press, 1990). See also Tony Becher, *Academic Tribes and Territories: Intellectual Enquiry and the Culture of Disciplines* (Bristol, PA: Society for Research into Higher Education, Open University Press, 1989), for a British view of disciplines in the UK as well as the United States.

13. It's possible that Robert Maynard Hutchins, who served as president of the University of Chicago from 1929 to 1951, did so. There is every reason to suspect that in the privacy of his study, Hutchins believed himself to be infallible, and he sometimes behaved in public as though he were convinced of it. On the contemporary scene, John Silber, recently president of Boston University, has certainly behaved in a manner Butler would have approved of. But even this worthy has stopped short of an outright claim to infallibility. If these figures are in fact exceptions, they are exceptions that prove the rule.

14. This would in fact occur even were the administrator a practitioner of the discipline in question. The principle of noninterference is likely to be stronger when the administrator is not a practitioner, but it is generally accepted across the board.

15. Historically, as soon as scholarship became central to academic purpose and professional self-conception, discipline boundaries became important to the concept of academic freedom. See Richard Hofstadter and Walter Metzger, *The Development of Academic Freedom in the United States* (New York: Columbia University Press, 1955).

16. As cited in Ellen W. Shrecker, *No Ivory Tower: McCarthyism and the University* (New York: Oxford University Press, 1986).

17. Whether such oversight was likely to occur is another issue. For reasons developed earlier in this chapter, I think these early stalwarts were unduly optimistic about its likelihood.

18. See Shrecker, *No Ivory Tower*. For another treatment of Joseph McCarthy's assault upon American academics, see Robert Nisbet, *The Degradation of the Academic Dogma: The University in America, 1945–1970* (New York: Basic Books, 1971).

19. The difficulty in making such distinctions was brought home to me during the period I served on the American Sociological Association's Committee on

Freedom of Research and Teaching. For those interested in the character of academic freedom in the United States, an examination of that association's post-1950 archives, would, I believe, prove instructive.

20. See Michael Miles, *The Radical Probe: The Logic of Student Rebellion* (New York: Atheneum, 1971). Also see Gerald Grant and David Reisman, *The Perpetual Dream: Reform and Experiment in the American College* (Chicago: University of Chicago Press, 1978).

21. The faculty counterattack upon student activists was led by such prominent academics as the philosopher Sidney Hook, who founded an organization called the Centers for Rational Alternatives, and the semanticist S.I. Hayakawa, whose aggressive response to student activism at San Francisco State University while serving as acting president vaulted him into the U.S. Senate.

22. For a handy and brief discussion of the concept of academic tenure, see Joseph A. Simecca, *Education and Society* (New York: Holt, Rinehart and Winston, 1980), chapter 2.

23. Robert M. McIver, *Academic Freedom in Our Time* (New York: Columbia University Press, 1955), 238 (emphasis mine).

24. Nisbet, *The Degradation of the Academic Dogma,* 63.

25. I could find no actual count of such dismissals (see Chapter 1). However, the following may be used in support of this assertion. In June 1988 the *Chronicle of Higher Education* reported the attempted dismissal of a tenured professor at Rutgers, noting that this was the first such action in thirty-five years. Now, either Rutgers professors are as honorable and competent as they claim to be, or there's been a surfeit of denial at that institution. I'd bet on the latter.

Consider also the following quotation from a study favorable to the professoriate:

> The problem is that the procedures for ridding the profession of misfits are so arduous and so embarrassing that few administrators are willing to take the time of themselves and of the faculty to prosecute the cases. . . . Moreover faculty persons as members of review committees have been notoriously reluctant to assume their full responsibility for self policing and high levels of professionalism and ethics.

Howard R. Bowen and Jack H. Schuster, *American Professors: A National Resource Imperiled* (New York: Oxford University Press, 1986), 243.

26. The Morrill Act of 1862 ceded federal lands to the states in return for their willingness to establish universities on these lands. Since public moneys and public properties were being used, it was assumed that these institutions would be easily accessible to the citizenry and committed to a distinctively practical education. Today the term *land grant institution* is most popularly associated with state universities in the Midwest. In fact, however, state universities in other regions as well characteristically originated as a result of the Morrill Act.

27. The total population of the United States in 1900 was just short of 76 million.

28. Simecca, *Education and Society.*

29. As fond as I am of Veblen's *Higher Learning in America,* it is too reflective of Veblen's personal situation to be taken as a descriptive account of everyday intrusiveness. It should be read as his warning rather than his report. See

Thorstein Veblen, *The Higher Learning in America* (New Brunswick: Transaction Publishers, 1993; original publication 1918).

30. Colleges and universities also serve as settings for the creation of such complexity, albeit without the dominance displayed in their training and certifying missions.

31. U.S. Department of Education, National Center for Education Statistics, *Digest of Education Statistics 1991* (Washington, DC: National Center for Education Statistics, 1991). Through such programs as the GI Bill, National Defense Scholarships, and various guaranteed low-cost loan programs, the federal government is largely responsible for the prevailing notion that financial circumstance should not bar qualified students from pursuing higher education.

32. *The Chronicle of Higher Education Almanac,* 43, no. 1 (September 2, 1996): 22.

Chapter 3. The Seven Pedagogical Sins

1. There are occasional exceptions to this general rule, as in the case of the distinguished professor who is hired to grace a campus with his or her prestige or as in the case of so-called research professors and associates who pursue their vocation in institutes with no teaching mission even though they are housed on university campuses.

2. An indication of this trouble can be found in the following, published in 1993: "At the very least," writes Milton Greenberg, former provost of American University, "we should *begin* to view our college or university employment as . . . full-time . . . and insist upon rigorous and thorough peer judgment of all professional work, be it teaching, research or service." *Begin* to view? In 1993? And if academics need to be exhorted to insist upon rigorous and thorough reviews, what conclusion can we draw except that such reviews are characteristically absent? And if such reviews do not generally exist, is it not the case that we would have to out-Pangloss Pangloss in order to conclude that college and university teaching, absent a system of real as opposed to claimed accountability, can be in good shape? See Milton Greenberg, "Accounting for Faculty Members' Time," *Chronicle of Higher Education,* October 20, 1993, A68 (emphasis mine).

3. For the most part, there are no trustworthy statistics on the extent to which these troubles exist (see Chapter 1), as academic denial rules out the accurate collection of such statistics. But a majority of my informants recognized each of the inventoried troubles as more than minimally present in their own academic environments.

4. Although academics do not sanction abandonment, there exist faculty policies that allow professors to escape their teaching obligations in a more or less "legitimate" manner. See Charles Sykes, *Profscam: Professors and the Demise of Higher Education* (Washington, DC: Regnery Gateway, 1988).

5. See Billie Wright Dziech and Linda Weiner, *The Lecherous Professor: Sexual Harassment on Campus,* 2nd edition (Urbana: University of Illinois Press, 1990).

6. Special pleading has a long if undistinguished history among academics, not simply in the United States but in western Europe as well. The great German

social scientist Max Weber took aim at this phenomenon in his classic essay "Science as a Vocation," originally presented as a lecture in 1918. See Hans Gerth and C. Wright Mills, eds., *From Max Weber* (New York: Oxford University Press, 1946). For a treatment of this problem on the contemporary scene, see Roger Kimball, *Tenured Radicals: How Politics Has Corrupted Our Higher Education* (New York: Harper and Row, 1990).

7. A note on my method of presentation: The stories you are about to encounter (as well as those presented in the following chapter) are based on informant accounts. Consistent with the time-honored tradition in my discipline of promising anonymity and confidentiality in exchange for candid revelation, I have disguised actual venues. I have as well employed a technique frequently used by practitioners of the "new journalism" (e.g., Tom Wolfe, Bob Woodward, and others) wherein events are not merely reported but are reconstructed so that the reader can enter into rather than just read about what has transpired. This seems to be the best way to communicate the traumas inherent in academic malpractice. See "A Single Standard, Please," the methodological afterword to this volume, for a more extended treatment of my case construction method.

8. See Dziech and Weiner, *The Lecherous Professor.* Also see Michele A. Paludi, ed., *Ivory Power: Sexual Harassment on Campus* (Albany: State University of New York Press, 1990).

9. See Sykes, *Profscam.*

10. See William Broad and Nicholas Wade, *Betrayers of the Truth* (New York: Simon and Schuster, 1982).

11. Although marred by an antileft bias, Kimball's book *Tenured Radicals* needs to be taken seriously on this matter. See also Daphne Patai and Noretta Koertge, *Professing Feminism: Cautionary Tales from the Strange World of Women's Studies* (New York: Basic Books, 1994).

12. Some institutions, those liberal arts colleges that sell themselves to prospective students as schools where teaching excellence is the number-one priority, are more likely than others to open teaching to collegial scrutiny. Few of my informants, however, including those at liberal arts colleges, felt they had any systematic knowledge of their colleagues' pedagogical efforts.

13. For the last decade or so, I have been teaching a required general education course at the University of Massachusetts. This assignment has given me access to a wide range of undergraduates at this reasonably representative state university. During this period I have taken the opportunity to quiz these sophomores, juniors, and seniors on matters you might fairly expect educated men and women to know. While it cannot be taken as proof of miseducation, the following constitutes a list—in no particular order—of things my students don't seem to know much about: the Enlightenment; the French Revolution; how the U.S. electoral college works; the Austro-Hungarian Empire; Emile Zola and the persecution of Alfred Dreyfus; the doctrine of separate but equal; Benito Mussolini (identified by one brave student as an Italian opera singer); the difference between deductive and inductive inference; the Nuremburg laws; the difference between mean and median; *Brown vs. the Board of Education of Topeka, Kansas;* the First and Fifth Amendments to the U.S. Constitution; the Dred Scott decision; chance; the Manhattan Project, J. Robert Oppenheimer, and Edward Teller; what *unconstitutional* means; Margaret Sanger; the Raj; the Cultural Revolution, graduated in-

come tax. Limited space prohibits my continuing the list, but I think readers will get the point.

14. When considering the issue of academic malpractice in any and all of its manifestations, we should not overlook the fact that the American academy is extremely privileged in comparison with its counterparts throughout the world. On any scale—compensation, freedom from nonacademic interference, availability of promotions, and the provision of support—the American academy would rank near or at the top. Underlying this advantaged position is the realization that the complexities of modern life create an ongoing demand for well-educated individuals. It is assumed that members of a robust and well-treated academy will in return take their educative responsibilities seriously. Thus when some members of the academy fail to do so while their colleagues ignore the fact of that failure, there is an abrogation of the tacitly assumed reciprocal arrangement, an abrogation, as it were, of a contract no less significant for being unwritten.

15. Occasionally a particularly egregious case of a student's not getting the education he or she paid for finds its way into the media. For the most part, such victimization goes unrecognized and therefore unreported.

Chapter 4. The Bad Joke of Scholarship

1. Over the years there has been some criticism of the academy's neglect of the how. Indeed during the 1960s and 1970s the American academy began to give some lip service to the importance of how. Teaching improvement programs did in fact begin to spring up on college and university campuses. Participation in such programs was not, however, mandatory for faculty members, and while they still exist and administrators find them useful for public relations, little is known about their efficacy. Suffice it to say the increased emphasis on the how has nowhere supplanted the dominance of the what in college and university teaching. The Ph.D. (or some roughly equivalent degree) still stands supreme as the credential that best qualifies an individual for appointment to a faculty, and it remains something other than a teaching degree.

2. In my years of service on the faculties of two such universities, I have never been called upon to teach more than two courses a semester. A course typically meets three hours per week. A recent study reports that 61 percent of all public university faculty and 72 percent of all private university faculty teach less than nine hours per week. The same study reports that 78 percent of all faculty at four-year institutions (colleges and universities) teach twelve or less hours per week. See Alexander W. Astin, William S. Korn, and Eric L. Dey, *The American College Teacher: National Norms for the 1989–90 HERI Faculty Survey* (Los Angeles: Higher Education Research Institute, UCLA, 1991).

3. See Charles Sykes, *Profscam: Professors and the Demise of Higher Education* (Washington, DC: Regnery Gateway, 1988, especially pp. 33–67. See also Ernest L. Boyer, *The Condition of the Professoriate: Attitudes and Trends* (Lawrenceville, NJ: Princeton University Press, 1989).

4. See "Newest Threats to Academic Freedom May Come from Faculty Members, Scholars Tell AAUP," *Chronicle of Higher Education* October 28, 1987, A15–A16.

5. See Boyer, *The Condition of the Professoriate.*

6. Scholarship is not the only nonteaching activity professors are expected to engage in. They are also expected to devote some time to service to their department, the university, or the community at large. Service, however, is rarely expected to occupy a preponderance of the professor's nonteaching work time. For example, Astin and his colleagues found that 94 percent of all faculty at four-year institutions spent eight or less hours per week in committee work and meetings. See Astin et al., *The American College Teacher,* Table 1, p. 40. In my experience it is rare for a professor to spend more than three hours per week on committee work.

7. Howard R. Bowen and Jack H. Schuster, *American Professors: A National Resource Imperiled* (New York: Oxford University Press, 1986), 73. Nothing has occurred to suggest major changes since this study's publication.

8. These are as follows: math/statistics faculty, computer science faculty, engineering faculty, psychology faculty, and the social science faculty grouped together. Inexplicably, Bowen and Schuster include no material on faculty in the humanities.

9. Martin J. Finklestein, *The American Academic Profession: A Synthesis of Social Scientific Inquiry Since World War II* (Columbus: Ohio State University Press, 1984), 88. Astin et al. have generated results that are consistent with those of Finklestein as follows: 40 percent of faculty at public universities, 35 percent of faculty at private universities, and 80 percent of faculty at four-year colleges report spending eight or less hours per week on research. See Astin et al., *The American College Teacher,* Table 2, p. 41.

10. Astin et al. have also produced a result consistent with Finklestein on this point as follows: 52 percent of faculty at four-year colleges report not publishing or having anything *accepted* for publication (a more generous standard) for two years prior to their study. See Astin et al., *The American College Teacher,* Table 5, p. 42.

11. Drummond Rennie, senior contributing editor of the *Journal of the American Medical Association,* as quoted in an AP dispatch July 21, 1988.

12. As reported in Finklestein, *The American Academic Profession,* 89.

13. For examples of why this is so, see *The Appearance of Scholarly Activity* in this chapter.

14. For a university administrator's candid observations on this matter, see Milton Greenberg, "Accounting for Faculty Members' Time," *Chronicle of Higher Education,* October 20, 1993, A68.

15. There no doubt will be those who claim that local (same faculty) peer review of scholarship can and does exist. Thus they can be expected to argue that the statistics on publication constitute an insensitive measure of scholarly accountability. (Boyer found that 74 percent of faculty at four-year institutions endorsed a view that argues against publication as the primary evidence of scholarly activity; see Boyer, *The Condition of the Professoriate.* While I do not endorse the ontological significance of those statistics, I think it is clear that whatever their limitations, they are better indicators of accountability than are unverifiable assertions. Are we really to believe that colleagues who share the same corridors, colleagues who lunch with one another, play racquetball with one another, borrow books from one another, know about each other's family problems will constitute a jury whose only concern is the quality and quantity of each other's work? There may be more scholarship going on than these statistics indi-

cate, and indeed there may be more accountability, but arguments such as the one alluded to here are, to say the least, hardly persuasive on the matter.

16. American folklore, in fact, supports the professoriate in this self-conception. Absent-minded professors forget to do the mundane things they're supposed to do not because they've simply forgotten to do them but because they're preoccupied with the problems of general relativity, information theory, the uncertainty principle, conditional probability, emergent properties, the latest Oxfordian challenge to Shakespeare's authorship, or the deconstruction of *The Scarlet Letter,* while those not professionally called to truth's service are focusing on picking up the laundry, making the mortgage payment, and basting the leg of lamb. And academics themselves push this folkloric conception for all it's worth. A favorite apocryphal story in academic circles involves the late Norbert Weiner, acclaimed as the father of cybernetics. As the story goes, Weiner, leaving his MIT office one day, head filled with equations and theorems, couldn't remember where he lived. Knowing that Norbert Weiner was something of a celebrity in the MIT-Harvard orbit, he reasoned that students might know the location of the Weiner residence. He thus approached a young man and inquired as to the location of the Weiner homestead, whereupon the young man is said to have responded, "It's okay, Dad. I'll take you home."

17. This supports the assertion above that self-reports are likely to overestimate the time professors spend on scholarship.

18. Erving Goffman was a sociologist who served on the faculties of the University of California—Berkeley, the University of Chicago, and the University of Pennsylvania. He was also elected president of the American Sociological Association just prior to his death in 1982.

19. For a discussion of inappropriate authorship claims, see Judith P. Swazey, Melissa Anderson, and Karen Seashore Louis, "Ethical Problems in Academic Research," *American Scientist* 81, 6 (November–December 1993): 542–553.

20. For discussions of and confessions regarding academic editing, see Rita Simon and James Fyfe, eds., *Editors as Gatekeepers* (Lanham, MD: Rowman and Littlefield, 1994).

21. Astin et al. note that nearly 60 percent of all faculty identify raising moneys as an institutional priority. See Astin et al., *The American College Teacher,* p. 24.

22. Devastating documentation of this observation can be found in House Committee on Government Operations, *Are Scientific Misconduct and Conflicts of Interest Hazardous to Our Health?* 101st Cong., 2nd sess., 1990, H. Rept. 101, 688.

23. See Robert Nisbet, *The Degradation of the Academic Dogma: The University in America, 1945–1970* (New York: Basic Books, 1971), for a discussion of the development of this Trojan horse phenomenon, especially chapter 5, "The Higher Capitalism."

24. This classification of course leaves aside the issue of quality. Since quality is often a matter of point of view and since speaking to quality in general would require an expertise in fields that I do not possess, I must regretfully refrain from commenting on this question—regretfully, because I believe that too much of what passes for scholarship is trivial, pretentious, and dull.

25. It is, I think, interesting to note that negatives in the popular image of professors actually protect the lazy and self-serving among them. If professors are

unrealistic or pretentious, it stands to reason they are less likely than others to engage in down-to-earth sin. Sin implies a worldliness that a lack of realism and a surfeit of pretense do not.

26. Case materials are based upon interviews with informants noted in Chapter 1 as well as my own observations.

27. See *Are Scientific Misconduct and Conflicts of Interest Hazardous to Our Health?* 688.

28. Ibid.

29. Ibid., p. 59 (emphasis mine).

30. See Daniel E. Koshland, "Fraud in Science," *Science* 235, January 9, 1987, p. 141.

31. See the unsigned article titled "Plagiarist Gets Promoted, Victim Is Out of Her Job," *Science and Government Report* 20, 8 (May 1, 1990): 1–7.

32. See *Are Scientific Misconduct and Conflicts of Interest Hazardous to Our Health?* 688.

33. Ibid.

34. See Swazey et al., "Ethical Problems in Academic Research."

35. The study was published as Laud Humphries, *Tearoom Trade* (Chicago: Aldine, 1970).

36. A number of social scientists were forthright in their criticism of Humphries's ethical lapse. In later editions of *Tearoom Trade,* Humphries expressed regret at the use of methods he had earlier believed to be justified and indicated that he would no longer advocate the use of such methods. For a critical statement that influenced Humphries to reconsider, see Myron Glazer, *The Research Adventure* (New York: Random House, 1972), 107–116. For Humphries's response, see Laud Humphries, *Tearoom Trade,* enlarged edition ("with a Retrospect on Ethical Issues") (Chicago: Aldine, 1975).

37. For a recent homage to Humphries (who died several years ago) that blithely continues to support his personal originality, see Glenn A. Goodwin, Irving Louis Horowitz, and Peter M. Nardi, "Laud Humphries: A Pioneer in the Practice of Social Science," *Sociological Inquiry* 61, no. 2 (Spring 1991): 139–147.

38. See Greenberg, "Accounting for Faculty Members' Time."

39. A recent in-house study of the compensation system at the University of Massachusetts indicates that seniority (as opposed to scholarly productivity) is the best predictor of salary.

40. According to the College Board, between 1980 and 1988 the cost of a four-year baccalaureate increased approximately 34 percent (after inflation) at a public institution and approximately 45 percent at a private institution.

41. If, as is the case in some institutions, there are limits on class size, the fifty courses may necessitate multiple sections, thus requiring ever more faculty if teaching loads are to be kept at their expected levels.

Chapter 5. The Spurious Shield of Specialness

1. Remember we live in a time characterized by the creation and management of complexity. Moreover, there are few if any indications that the future portends an intended return to simplicity.

2. The ease with which this occurs fluctuates as operating budgets expand and contract.

3. For the sake of simplification, this discussion does not refer to temporary faculty appointments. Where temporary appointments are made, performance contracts would be similar except for renewal or renegotiation procedures.

4. They may also receive cost-of-living increases that are not determined on a merit basis.

5. Even these may not be immediately and indisputably recognized. The work of Copernicus and Galileo was thought to be apostasy and nothing else. The work of Freud is yet regarded by many as little more than fraudulent.

6. A multiplicity of such visits over the contract period by different evaluators would guard against biased observation and reporting.

7. While there are few things that will buy trouble for an academic, one of them is sure to be insufficient loyalty to one's discipline.

8. Certain presidential appointments have been held up in the U.S. Senate when opponents have used such early failures as grounds for withholding consent even though the attorneys in question later passed their bar examinations and were admitted into practice.

9. To the objection that professors are not likely to practice in the states where they went to graduate school and may thus be unprepared for these examinations there are four counters. First, the same can be said for lawyers and to a lesser extent for physicians, yet they somehow manage. Second, the yearlong grace period should provide ample opportunity for preparation. Third, it is conceivable that a nationwide examination procedure could be devised. Fourth, states could enter into reciprocal agreements so that someone who had passed the examination in one state would be automatically licensed in the state of her or his first or new appointment.

Appendix. A Single Standard, Please

1. Abraham Kaplan, a very useful philosopher of science, wrote of the distinction between the messy realities of scientific inquiry and the characteristic idealization of that endeavor offered up after the fact by those who engage in it. He labeled the former "logic in use" and the latter "reconstructed logic." See Abraham Kaplan, *The Conduct of Inquiry* (San Francisco: Chandler, 1964). For a confession substantiating Kaplan's distinction, see James Watson, *The Double Helix* (New York: Mentor Books, New American Library, 1968).

2. This discussion takes as its major resource Peter H. Rossi, *Down and Out in America: The Origin of Homelessness* (Chicago: University of Chicago Press, 1989), 45–81.

3. Ibid., 69.

4. See Otis Dudley Duncan, *Notes on Social Measurement: Historical and Critical* (New York: Russell Sage Foundation, 1984).

5. Ibid., 226.

6. Ibid., 227.

7. Ibid., 229.

Bibliography

Anderson, Martin. *Imposters in the Temple.* New York: Simon and Schuster, 1992.

Aronowitz, Stanley. *Science as Power: Discourse and Ideology in Modern Society.* Minneapolis: University of Minnesota Press, 1988.

Astin, Alexander W.; Korn, William S.; and Dey, Eric L. *The American College Teacher: National Norms for the 1989–90 HERI Faculty Survey.* Los Angeles: Higher Education Research Institute, UCLA, March 1991.

Atlas, James. "When Fact Is Treated as Fiction." *New York Times,* July 24, 1994, p. 5 of "News of the Week in Review—Ideas and Trends."

Becher, Tony. *Academic Tribes and Territories: Intellectual Enquiry and the Culture of Disciplines.* Bristol, PA: Society for Research into Higher Education, Open University Press, 1989.

Bloom, Allan. *The Closing of the American Mind: How Higher Education Has Failed Democracy and Impoverished the Souls of Today's Students.* New York: Simon and Schuster, 1987.

Bowen, Howard R., and Schuster, Jack H. *American Professors: A National Resource Imperiled.* New York: Oxford University Press, 1986.

Boyer, Ernest L. *College: The Undergraduate Experience in America.* New York: Harper and Row, 1987.

———. *The Condition of the Professoriate: Attitudes and Trends.* Lawrenceville, NJ: Princeton University Press, 1989.

Broad, William, and Wade, Nicholas. *Betrayers of the Truth.* New York: Simon and Schuster, 1982.

Carnegie Foundation for the Advancement of Teaching. *Scholarship Reconsidered: Priorities of the Professoriate, 1990.* Lawrenceville, NJ: Princeton University Press, 1990.

The Chronicle of Higher Education Almanac 3, no. 1 (September 2, 1996): 2.

Creswell, John W.; Wheeler, David; Seagren, Alan; Egly, Nancy; and Beyer, Kirk. *The Academic Chairperson's Handbook.* Lincoln: University of Nebraska Press, 1990.

Duncan, Otis Dudley. *Notes on Social Measurement: Historical and Critical.* New York: Russell Sage Foundation, 1984.

Dziech, Billie Wright, and Weiner, Linda. *The Lecherous Professor: Sexual Harassment on Campus.* 2nd edition. Urbana: University of Illinois Press, 1990.

Elgart, Lloyd D., and Schanfield, Lillian. "Sexual Harassment of Students." *Thought and Action* 7, 1 (Spring 1991): 21–42.

Finklestein, Martin J. *The American Academic Profession: A Synthesis of Social Scientific Inquiry Since World War II.* Columbus: Ohio State University Press, 1984.

Foucault, Michel. *Power/Knowledge: Selected Interviews and Other Writings, 1972–1977.* New York: Pantheon, 1980.

Gerth, Hans, and Mills, C. Wright, eds. *From Max Weber.* New York: Oxford University Press, 1946.

Glazer, Myron. *The Research Adventure.* New York: Random House, 1972.

Glazer, Myron, and Glazer, Penina. *The Whistleblowers.* New York: Basic Books, 1989.

Goodwin, Glenn A.; Horowitz, Irving Louis; and Nardi, Peter M. "Laud Humphries: A Pioneer in the Practice of Social Science." *Sociological Inquiry* 61, no. 2 (Spring 1991): 139–147.

Gouldner, Alvin. *The Coming Crisis of Western Sociology.* New York: Basic Books, 1970.

Grant, Gerald, and Reisman, David. *The Perpetual Dream: Reform and Experiment in the American College.* Chicago: University of Chicago Press, 1978.

Greenberg, Milton. "Accounting for Faculty Members' Time." *Chronicle of Higher Education* October 20, 1993, A68.

Hirsch, E.D. Jr. *Cultural Literacy: What Every American Needs to Know.* Boston: Houghton Mifflin, 1987.

Hofstadter, Richard, and Metzger, Walter. *The Development of Academic Freedom in the United States.* New York: Columbia University Press, 1955.

Humphries, Laud. *Tearoom Trade.* Chicago: Aldine, 1970.

———. *Tearoom Trade.* Enlarged edition. Chicago: Aldine, 1975.

Jacoby, Russell. *The Last Intellectuals: American Culture in the Age of Academe.* New York: Basic Books, 1987.

Kaplan, Abraham. *The Conduct of Inquiry.* San Francisco: Chandler, 1964.

Kimball, Roger. *Tenured Radicals: How Politics Has Corrupted Our Higher Education.* New York: Harper and Row, 1990.

Koshland, Daniel E. "Fraud in Science," *Science* 235, January 9, 1987, 141.

Lieberson, Stanley. "Einstein, Renoir and Greeley: Evidence in Sociology." *American Sociological Review* 57, 1 (February 1992): 1–15.

McIver, Robert M. *Academic Freedom in Our Time.* New York: Columbia University Press, 1955.

Miles, Michael. *The Radical Probe: The Logic of Student Rebellion.* New York: Atheneum, 1971.

Mills, C. Wright. *The Sociological Imagination.* New York: Oxford University Press, 1959.

Myrdal, Gunnar. *Value in Social Theory.* New York: Harper and Brothers, 1958.

———. *An American Dilemma.* New York: Harper and Row, 1944.

National Education Association. *The Almanac of Higher Education: 1992.* Washington, DC: National Education Association, 1992.

———. *The 1996 Almanac of Higher Education.* Washington, DC: National Education Association, 1996.

———. "Newest Threats to Academic Freedom May Come from Faculty Members, Scholars Tell AAUP." *Chronicle of Higher Education* October 28, 1987, A15–A16.

Nisbet, Robert. *The Degradation of the Academic Dogma: The University in America, 1945–1970.* New York: Basic Books, 1971.

Page, Charles H. *Fifty Years in the Sociological Enterprise: A Lucky Journey.* Amherst: University of Massachusetts Press, 1982.

Paludi, Michele A., ed., *Ivory Power: Sexual Harassment on Campus.* Albany: State University of New York Press, 1990.

Patai, Daphne, and Koertge, Noretta. *Professing Feminism: Cautionary Tales from the Strange World of Women's Studies.* New York: Basic Books, 1994.

———. "Plagiarist Gets Promoted, Victim Is Out of Her Job." *Science and Government Report* 20, 8 (May 1, 1990): 1–17.

Reisman, David. *Constraint and Variety in American Education.* New York: Doubleday Anchor, 1958.

Rossi, Peter H. *Down and Out in America: The Origin of Homelessness.* Chicago: University of Chicago Press, 1989.

Schrecker, Ellen W. *No Ivory Tower: McCarthyism and the University.* New York: Oxford University Press, 1986.

Simecca, Joseph A. *Education and Society.* New York: Holt, Rinehart and Winston, 1980.

Simon, Rita, and Fyfe, James, eds. *Editors as Gatekeepers.* (Lanham, MD: Rowman and Littlefield, 1994.

Sontz, Ann H.L. *The American College President.* Westport, CT: Greenwood Press, 1991.

Swazey, Judith P.; Anderson, Melissa; and Louis, Karen Seashore. "Ethical Problems in Academic Research." *American Scientist* 81, 6 (November–December 1993): 542–553.

Sykes, Charles. *Profscam: Professors and the Demise of Higher Education.* Washington, DC: Regnery Gateway, 1988.

U.S. Department of Education, National Center for Education Statistics. *Completions in Institutions of Higher Education, 1988–1989.* Washington, DC: National Center for Education Statistics, 1989.

———. *Digest of Education Statistics 1991.* Washington, DC: National Center for Education Statistics, 1991.

U.S. House Committee on Government Operations. U.S. House of Representatives. *Are Scientific Misconduct and Conflicts of Interest Hazardous to Our Health?* 101st Cong., 2nd sess., H. Rep. 101.

Veblen, Thorstein. *The Higher Learning in America.* New Brunswick: Transaction Publishers, 1993; original publication 1918.

Watson, James. *The Double Helix.* New York: Mentor Books, New American Library, 1968.

Westmeyer, Paul S. *Principles of Governance and Administration in Higher Education.* Springfield, IL: Thomas Publishers, 1990.

Wolfe, Tom. *The New Journalism.* New York: Harper and Row, 1973.

Index

About the Author

Michael Lewis is professor of Sociology at the University of Massachusetts/Amherst. He has authored or edited seven books, numerous papers and book chapters, as well as pieces appearing in major American newspapers.

DATE DUE